THE BIG SUR, MONTEREY BAY & GOLD COAST WINE COUNTRY BOOK

A COMPLETE GUIDE

3RD EDITION

THE BIG SUR, MONTEREY BAY & GOLD COAST WINE COUNTRY BOOK

Buz Bezore
&
Christina Waters, PhD

The Countryman Press
Woodstock, Vermont

We welcome your comments and suggestions. Please contact Great Destinations Guide Editor, The Countryman Press, P.O. Box 748, Woodstock, Vermont 05091, or e-mail countrymanpress@wwnorton.com.

ISBN 1-58157-074-0
ISSN data has been applied for.

Maps by Mapping Specialists Ltd., © The Countryman Press
Book design by Bodenweber Design
Text composition by Kristin Sperber
Cover photograph by Ron Niebrugge
Interior photographs by the authors unless otherwise indicated

Published by The Countryman Press, P.O. Box 748, Woodstock, Vermont 05091

Distributed by W. W. Norton & Company, Inc., 500 Fifth Avenue, New York, NY 10110

Printed in the United States of America

10 9 8 7 6 5 4 3 2 1

To our mothers,
Norma Starnes Cilia *and* Marie Waters,
who taught us to care and to see and
to love the California landscape.

Contents

Acknowledgments

We were lucky enough to be able to draw on a wealth of expert regional informants whose suggestions, insights and generous contributions allowed us to present readers with a comprehensive taste of the splendid and varied Central Coast.

As they have always done in past projects we've shared, award-winning photographers George Sakkestad, Randy Tunnell, Robert Scheer and Shmuel Thaler infuse these pages with the atmospheric images of the Central Coast landscape and sense of place.

Everywhere we traveled throughout the length of this stretch of California, we met experts on history, local color, restaurants, recreation, attractions and wines who were generous with their accumulated wisdom.

The careful reading by historian Ross Eric Gibson lent expert credibility to the research intensive History section. Seasoned wine and food writers Jeanne Howard (Monterey and Carmel) and Christopher Weir (San Luis Obispo and the Santa Ynez Valley) contributed to the wine sections for those two areas of the Central Coast. And nods of appreciation to Kelly Luker and Tai Moses who added polish and perfection to the writing on some pages.

Throughout the writing of this book, we were inspired by the accomplishments of a great interweaving of cultures—the Chumash and Ohlone, the Spanish and Yankee immigrants, the 20th-century adventurers and new-millennium entrepreneurs—all of whom at one time or another called the Central Coast home and all of whom make us who live here today what we are.

Buz Bezore and Christina Waters
Santa Cruz, California

INTRODUCTION

In the 25 years that we have lived and worked together on the Central Coast, we've never taken for granted the sheer beauty of the place that we call home. How clever of our great-great-grandparents to have settled in what amounts to one of the natural treasures of the country. We've been fortunate to have our professional lives segue smoothly with our personal interests. In creating countless weekend getaway pieces for a variety of regional publications, we've combed the area, enjoying unforgettable accommodations, sampling cuisine that continues to set trends and soaking up ambiance that attracts visitors from all over the world.

From our house, we can walk to the beach in under three minutes and can thread through coastal bluffs and ancient oak groves by the simple act of driving to work. The walk from the parking lot to the office affords astonishing views of the shimmering Monterey Bay in the distance through a frame of towering redwoods. It would be impossible to take all of this for granted. Besides, we're there gawking at the hypnotic waves right along with visitors from New York, Italy and Australia. Fine fall weather sends us out beachcombing or wine tasting at some of our favorite microwineries.

Not a day goes by that we aren't firmly impressed by the fact that we happen to live in a place that other people covet as a destination. That's another reason why vacations often find us exploring some new nook or cranny of the Central Coast instead of getting on a plane to somewhere else. We already live in one of the most desirable parts of the world. And while we're convinced that it will take a lifetime to explore it all and to savor its richness, we've already begun tasting the best of the region. Frankly, we don't mind sharing it one bit. After all, we can hardly blame visitors smart enough to make our slice of paradise their next vacation spot.

Buz Bezore and Christina Waters
Santa Cruz, California

The Way This Book Works

This book is divided into seven chapters. There are three geographically based chapters covering the following regions: the Santa Cruz coast; Monterey Bay, Carmel and Big Sur; and San Luis Obispo and the Santa Ynez Valley. Each has its own introduction, orienting the reader to the unique personality of the region. The remaining four chapters, History, Transportation, Wineries and Information, are thematic and concern all three regions.

Travelers driving along the Central Coast can turn to the regional chapter that they're interested in and can look over where they may want to stay, dine, shop or simply enjoy whatever activity would enrich their visit in towns coming up on their trip.

Some entries include specific information (Web site, e-mail, telephone numbers, addresses, business hours, etc.), which is organized for quick and easy reference in blocks at the top of each entry. All information was rechecked as close to publication date as possible, but since these details can change unexpectedly, it's a good idea to call ahead.

In our travels up and down the Central Coast, we sometimes encounter lodgings, restaurants or cultural sites that transcend the everyday. These establishments usually combine character, charm and idiosyncratic flair, in varying proportions, that place them in a category all their own. We think of them as "pearls of the Pacific," and we have marked each one with a star in a circle next to its name in the text.

Do not pass these places by. They're worth a stop or even a detour, and in the case of lodgings and restaurants, they're worth every penny charged. The experiences they provide will be cherished for years to come.

Lodging Prices

Within each regional chapter, lodging prices are noted in information blocks and are based on a per-room, double-occupancy charge. The cost range runs from the least expensive off-season room to the most expensive suite available during the busy summer months.

The price range below includes the cost of a single dinner that includes an entrée, appetizer or dessert, and glass of wine or beer. Tax and gratuities are not included.

Inexpensive	Up to $15
Moderate	$15 to $30
Expensive	$30 to $50
Very Expensive	$50 or more

Credit Cards are abbreviated as follows:

AE: American Express	MC: MasterCard
D: Discover	V: Visa

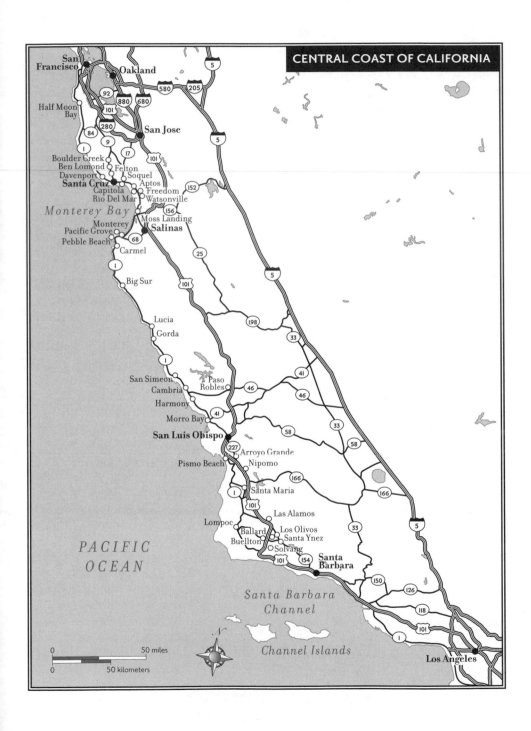

CENTRAL COAST OF CALIFORNIA

San Francisco
Oakland
580
205
92
880 680
Half Moon Bay
101
San Jose
84
280
5
1
9
Boulder Creek
17
Ben Lomond
Felton
101
Davenport
Soquel
152
Santa Cruz
Aptos
Capitola
Freedom
Rio Del Mar
Watsonville
Monterey Bay
156
Monterey
Moss Landing
Pacific Grove
Salinas
Pebble Beach
68
Carmel
25
1
5
Big Sur
101
Lucia
198
Gorda
33
41
San Simeon
Paso Robles
46
Cambria
46
Harmony
41
Morro Bay
58
33
San Luis Obispo
58
227
Arroyo Grande
Pismo Beach
Nipomo
166
1
Santa Maria
166
101
Las Alamos
Lompoc
33
5
Ballard
Los Olivos
Buellton
Santa Ynez
Solvang
Santa Barbara
101
154
PACIFIC OCEAN
150
126
Santa Barbara Channel
118
101
1
Channel Islands
Los Angeles

0   50 miles
0   50 kilometers

HISTORY

Of Blue & Golden Dreams

Erupting and pushing the length of California, the coastal mountain range forced its way through Golden State soil over 100 million years ago when two great continental land-masses collided, a red-hot and contentious meeting that marked the birth of the infamous San Andreas Fault. The slow-grinding dance of the Pacific and North American tectonic plates pushed the northern ranges up to a height of 5,000 feet and moved the edge of the land 100 miles westward. Once upon a time—a mere 150 million years ago—the coast of California called eastern Nevada home.

Fourteen million years ago, volcanic activity formed the archipelago of the Channel Islands 11 to 40 miles off the Santa Barbara coast. One trace of former molten activity still on dramatic display in the San Luis Obispo area is Morro Rock, a volcanic plug landmark that juts suddenly out of surrounding smooth sand beach.

At Point Conception, halfway between Pismo Beach and Santa Barbara, the northwest shoreline of California takes an abrupt 90-degree turn, creating south-facing beaches—and highly prized surfing conditions—through the entire stretch of Santa Barbara County. As late as five million years ago, the geologically adolescent mountains of the Santa Lucia

The Central Coast lifestyle is passionately devoted to active (and not-so-active) outdoor pursuits. Shmuel Thaler

Golden hills, like these near Cambria, parallel the sea throughout the southern portion of the Central Coast.
Visnius

Ranges began lifting up out of the shoreline behind Santa Barbara, and natural deposits of tar—whose Chumash Indian word, *pismo*, christens a beach and some of its most famous shellfish—still ooze from the oil-rich ocean floor off the Central Coast.

Erosion of strata from millions of years ago carved the labyrinthine tide pools of the northern Santa Cruz and Monterey coastlines, and the action of wind on sand has produced acres of softly shifting sand dunes along the southern stretches of San Luis Obispo. The combined effect of glaciers formed during the last ice age and the resulting lowering sea level—a process reversed as the glaciers melted—gently flooded channels carved into the land, forming estuaries and fingers of wetlands throughout the region.

The influence of a persistent high-pressure system lying offshore has resulted in the felicitous dry summers and mild, wet winters that give the Central Coast a Mediterranean climate unique in the continental United States. The persistent summertime fog, which both moistens and cools, is responsible in large part for the year-round growing season and abundant harvests, and over the last 50-plus years, the Central Coast's limestone soil and microclimates helped launched a boom in fine winemaking.

NATURAL HISTORY

Natural harbors and sheltered coves teeming with marine wildlife dominate a coastline still young in geological terms, while offshore, the ocean conspires with a strong high-pressure system to create the Central Coast's distinctive Mediterranean climate. Winter days tend to be wet and mild (although in sheltered canyons, nights are chilly enough for a roaring fire and down jacket), and summers remain blissfully tolerable thanks to the daily blanket of fog. Locals never mind the thick, gray mornings, knowing that the fog usually burns off by noon.

The summer fog brings other rewards besides relief from the sort of heat that sears valleys just 10 miles inland from the coast. It nurtures lush ferns and lofty redwoods that starve in drier, warmer climes. In response to the climate, highly specialized ecological niches—tide pools, estuaries, chaparral, oak woods, redwood forests—flourish today in all of their rich diversity.

The northern Central Coast is a showcase for forests of towering redwoods, the *Sequoia sempervirens* first noted by early Spanish explorers, who called the trees *palo colorado*, which the English later translated literally as "red wood." Reaching heights of up to 325 feet and living to a great age—some 2,000-year-old specimens have been identified—the astonishing evergreens, whose tough wood is remarkably fire-resistant, attracted ax-wielding hordes of 19th-century loggers, who often posed for early cameras on stumps large enough to accommodate a team of horses and wagon. But many redwoods withstood the onslaught, and today great stands still stretch down to the sea.

The heart of the Central Coast preserves its ranch land sprawl of chaparral grasslands dotted by enormous Spanish oaks, a zone above and beyond the fog line where wild lilac

Whole Lotta Shakin' Goin' On

The formidable San Andreas Fault runs halfway up the California coast, from the Gulf of California in the south to just off San Francisco's Golden Gate Bridge in the north. This capricious terror has been responsible for earthshaking mischief ranging from the nerve-racking to the deadly during the last century. The shiftings and bucklings of neighboring continental plates that produce this volatile seismic activity have been responsible for the 1906 earthquake, which hurled the cultural outpost of San Francisco into international headlines, as well as the 7.1 (on the Richter scale) Loma Prieta quake that rearranged private and public fortunes, as well as buildings and bridges, along the northern stretches of the Central Coast in 1989.

While countless adjacent fault lines create seismic disturbances, none has acted with more dramatic impact than the San Andreas, a tension-racked gash where the earth's crustal plates drift and snag uneasily. The Pacific plate sidles northward past the larger North American side at the rate of 2 inches per year. When the stress of this enormous and largely invisible encounter builds up sufficiently, the effect creates ruptures, many as mild as ocean tides. Some, however, create temblors of unforgettable impact.

These fault-line upsurges invariably wrench landscapes apart, not to mention gas lines and water mains, and prove especially devastating to areas lying upon sandy soils, where a liquefaction effect magnifies the violence of the shift. When a major quake occurs, ensuing shock waves ("aftershocks" to anyone still standing) often serve as deadly collaborators, exponentially enlarging the initial damage. The miracle is that the Central Coast has preserved as much of its architectural heritage as it has. Unfortunately, many of its oldest settlements, including almost all of the earliest mission complexes, retain only pieces of their original structure, with the rest painstakingly re-created in the lulls following episodes of seismic destruction. Shaken, but not stirred, Central Coast residents periodically rebuild, invariably accepting earthquakes as a small price to pay for living in what many consider the most beautiful spot on earth.

Back from the brink of extinction, elephant seals get up close and personal with each other at their Año Nuevo breeding grounds. Shmuel Thaler

and manzanita bloom in the summer heat. By August, the high grassy hillsides are dried to the color of gold. Seen the entire length of the Pacific Coast Highway, the yellow hillsides of late summer remain one of the most indelible visual impressions of the Golden State.

However, these same hills and neighboring agricultural fields in very early spring assault the eye with acres of chartreuse wild mustard, a plant once prized by industrious Chinese immigrants who pressed it into multipurpose oil. The state flower, the brilliant orange California poppy, grows abundantly along every roadside, often in the company of broad swaths of Kool-Aid–smelling purple lupine.

In the dappled woodland sunlight of 1,000-foot elevations, solid oaks coexist with the graceful madrone, whose thin red bark peels off in tightly rolled curls to expose flesh-colored limbs. In the heat of the afternoon, the heady scent of bay fills the upper canopy, while low to the ground grows the pungent *yerba buena*—the "good herb" prized by Native Americans and latter-day tea drinkers alike. Western gray squirrels, raccoons, opossums and skunks share the harvests of acorns and native berries with woodpeckers, while over-head soaring hawks survey the entire scene.

Although the grizzly bear disappeared from California early in the 20th century, mountain lions, wild boar and black bear still roam protected niches of the coastal mountains. With little to disturb their solitude, gray fox, mule deer and coyotes flourish in the brush-lands of steep coastal canyons.

Winter ushers in the annual migration of millions of monarch butterflies, which drape their favorite coastal groves of eucalyptus trees with a living fabric of fluorescent yellow wings. Winter also announces the yearly return of gray and humpback whales, an event that brings legions of nature lovers within easy viewing distance of some of the planet's largest mammals. The barnacle-encrusted cetaceans join sea lions, dolphins, salmon, shellfish and bonito in the region's teeming marine sanctuaries.

Vast expanses of sandy beach invariably give way all along the coast to spectacular tide pools and jagged cliffs carved over the millennia by wind and wave. The rocky outcroppings of Año Nuevo and Point Lobos provide safe harbor for the delicate ecology of tide pools and their resident hermit crabs, anemones, starfish and sand dollars. Majestic underwater kelp forests stretch tendrils up onto the rocks and sand, while unusual seaweeds make tide pooling an exotic adventure.

Sharing these harsh and secluded areas are prides of elephant seal, astonishing creatures growing up to 16 feet in length and 3 tons in weight. At Año Nuevo State Reserve, the sea lions literally take over every inch of rock each winter to mate, give birth to their pups and bellow over territory. Sea otters, cruising for their favorite shellfish foods, frolic along the rich tides of the Central Coast. One of the best places to observe the antics of these playful virtuoso swimmers is along the Monterey coast and its deep underwater canyon, now protected as a National Marine Sanctuary.

Where the Central Coast's many small rivers meander to the sea, wetland estuaries provide ecologically sensitive habitats for a plethora of diverse sea life, including oysters, shrimp and crabs, all of which feed on the nutrient-rich blend of salt and fresh water. These shellfish, in turn, attract amazing throngs of harbor seals, sea otters and scores of fish and bird species. At Elkhorn Slough, where the Salinas River meets Monterey Bay near the village of Moss Landing, bird-watchers often think that they've reached the Promised Land. Here tens of thousands of shearwater gulls, white egrets, blue herons and migratory ducks and geese gather, feed and nest. Needless to say, the fishing here is excellent.

Thanks to a chain of rigorously maintained state parks and beaches, the Central Coast tempts nature-loving visitors with ample opportunities for wilderness hiking, beachcombing and wildlife observing in accessible, protected environmental preserves.

SOCIAL HISTORY

Paradise Lost: The Native Californians

At the time Hernando Cortez began his New World expeditions in the 16th century, the Central Coast was home to hundreds of thousands of Native Americans, the largest tribes being the Ohlone in the north and the Chumash in the south. These nomadic hunter-gatherer peoples had arrived in the region at least 5,000 to 8,000 years earlier. The temperate climate, ample fresh water and abundance of edible plants, wild game and marine life allowed these peaceful native Californians to exist in harmony with their environment. But, their uncomplicated, Edenic social structure, as well as lack of agriculture, made them no match for the Europeans who invaded their lands in the 17th century.

From San Francisco Bay south to San Luis Obispo, the Ohlone dwelled in temporary villages of dome-shaped, tule-thatched huts, invariably clustered close to springs and rivers along the coast. The villages of these great basket makers included burial grounds and men-only ceremonial sweat lodges. From the sea, the Ohlone gathered abalone and oysters, whose shells piled up over the years into giant middens, some of which persist to this day.

From the forests, which they managed through controlled burning techniques, the Ohlone gleaned the berries and pine nuts that formed staples of their diet. Blanching acorns to remove toxins, they ground them into an all-purpose meal that provided a year-round supply of starch. The region's huge herds of buffalo, together with quail, deer, elk and bear, augmented their simple, yet diverse, diet.

South of San Luis Obispo, the Chumash had evolved a more complex culture, one involving active trade links with the tribes of the Channel Islands. Here also the sea provided a wealth of fresh produce—bonito and sardines caught by net, salmon speared by stick, even the occasional whale taken by harpoon. These native peoples, who so skillfully employed the natural elements of their environment, were in turn to provide the raw material for an abrupt religious and territorial conquest that transformed the face of the western frontier forever.

Men with a Mission: The Spanish Conquest

Thanks to overblown reports of potential riches and the discovery of fabulous natural harbors in the area by explorer Juan Rodriguez Cabrillo, Spain laid claim to the entire coast of California in 1542. Once claimed, the land remained largely unexplored for the next 50 years, during which Spanish galleons laden with trade sailed near the Central Coast on lucrative voyages between colonies in Mexico and Manila.

The need for a convenient port on the California coast prompted new exploration in Alta (upper) California. The search was on for a spot that could be used by Spain's ships to lie over and restock much-needed supplies halfway through the arduous intercontinental trading voyages. Basque mariner Sebastian Vizcaino set out on such a venture in 1602 and discovered Monterey Bay in the process. Naming it for the viceroy of Mexico, Vizcaino described Monterey in such wildly exaggerated terms that it took several encounters before those who followed could recognize it.

When King Charles III took the Spanish throne in 1759, he was determined to pump more muscle into Spanish New World enterprises (both economic and religious) and ordered an expansion of the mission system already present in Baja (lower) California. Taking up the quest was the Spanish governor of Baja California, Gaspar de Portola. In 1769, he led the "Sacred Expedition" to Alta California, accompanied by the *padre presidente* of the Franciscan missionary effort, the indefatigable Padre Junipero Serra.

When the mountains of gold that they pursued evaporated to fantasy, the colonial powers of New Spain re-envisioned El Dorado in the form of land and potential Christian souls in the people who lived upon it. Joining forces, the military and the Franciscan clergy set out together to found missions and spread the word of Christ, to cultivate the fertile land and to erect military forts, *presidios*, which headquartered the soldiers accompanying the monks and served to protect the newly won territory. Their successes inspired hopeful civilian colonists from Mexico, who followed and built settlements, *pueblos*, in the shadows of the missions.

Bringing with them herds of cattle, which would form the backbone of thriving beef, leather and tallow (for soap and candles) industries for over a century, Serra and Portola began their conversion of territory and native peoples in San Diego in 1769. With Serra remaining in San Diego to found the first Californian mission, Portola continued overland (the first European to do so) through San Luis Obispo and Monterey, whose bay, of course, he failed to recognize, turning around within sight of San Francisco Bay. On a second trip a year later, Portola finally extracted the reality of the Monterey Bay from Vizcaino's hyperbole and developed a presidio there.

Painting of the original Santa Cruz Mission. Covello & Covello

Mission sites were chosen for their proximity to fresh water, prime grazing and agricultural acreage, as well as for the pliant native populations, which would serve as a rapidly Christianized workforce for the padres. Like their adjacent presidios, mission complexes were organized around a central quadrangle. Constructed of the abundant adobe provided by native clay soils, they were further protected from the elements by a plaster coating of lime.

As the missions prospered and grew, long open-air galleries of graceful arches connected the padres' living quarters and offices with the main chapel. Deeply shaded cloisters and 3-foot-thick walls—some elaborately decorated with stenciling and murals created with native dyes and pigments—kept mission interiors cool during the hottest summers. Trained by imported stonemasons and wood carvers, many of the missions' Christianized flock (called neophytes) became competent artisans whose handiwork still adorns original altars and pulpits.

Within the walls, native peoples accustomed to roaming freely along the coast for their simple livelihoods were now corralled like wayward cattle. Their lives strictly regimented by the padres' work schedules, the neophytes provided the labor that made the missions self-sufficient. Beyond the mission walls were stables and corrals, mills, orchards, vineyards and limekilns.

In time, these clusters of missions, presidios and the growing number of Indian huts erected within their protection became the first prominent cities of contemporary California. Some of the finest jewels in this necklace of Catholic missions still remain on the Central Coast today, mute witnesses to the swift and irreversible elimination of native populations who succumbed to European diseases and mistreatment while forced to work the missions' agricultural and ranch holdings.

There must have been a few peaceful moments among natives and newcomers, since accounts of colonists comment on the comeliness of Chumash women, not a few of whom married Spanish soldiers. But there was also much resistance. In 1776 the mission at San Luis Obispo was destroyed by fire, thanks to a flaming arrow shot by a nonpacified native into the original thatched tule reed roof. (After that, the red tiles we associate with Spanish California became the missions' roofing of choice.) In 1812, dissident converts murdered the presiding padre at Mission Santa Cruz, an event echoed during the final years of the missionary period by a series of Chumash uprisings in the area of Santa Barbara and Santa Ynez.

Between 1769 and 1823, Serra and his successor, Fermin Francisco de Lasuen, established 21 missions, spaced at roughly the length of a day's ride along the California coast. Presidios were established in San Diego (1769), Monterey (1770), San Francisco (1776) and Santa Barbara (1782). When the missions were secularized after Mexico won independence from Spain in 1833, the resident *Californios* of Hispanic heritage converted the Franciscan lands into land-grant *ranchos*.

By this time, the missions were in decline, their native life force dramatically depleted by diseases against which the Indians had no natural immunity. At this point, the Indians who had not already succumbed to syphilis, smallpox and multiple epidemics of measles were cut adrift to return to what remained of their original culture.

Considering the Central Coast's past with the benefit of hindsight, it's compelling to wonder what the landscape might have been like had the Spanish never set foot among the abundant wildlife, pristine landscapes and nomadic cultures of coastal California. The padres and soldiers brought with them agriculture, orchards, vineyards, irrigation techniques, the waterwheel, horses, cattle and written language. They also brought about the demise of many societies, wiping entire peoples from existence. In the pages of the missions' history, the shape of the present Central Coast was indelibly written.

Requiem for the Rancho and Birth of the Bear Republic

Once Mexico successfully won its independence from Spain in 1821, vast holdings once belonging to the Catholic Church were divided into generous land grants. These were deeded to the loyal *Californio* citizens or sold at rock-bottom prices to the highest, and most adventurous, bidder. The name of the game was ranching. Family fortunes were made and sustained by herds of cattle whose hides were tanned—by another booming local industry—and sent by ship to destinations around the world. Some of the ranchos subsequently became the core of the Central Coast's richest territory, surviving today as huge ranches, private farms, golf courses and state-owned natural parklands.

With the Spanish monopoly on trading irrevocably broken, new American entrepreneurs came to seek their fortunes. Many ended up staying and marrying into *Californio* families. From England and New England, Virginia and France, Canada and Kentucky, the middle part of the 19th century saw an influx of whalers, tanners, dairy farmers, merchants, fur traders, loggers—all redefining the term "Yankee ingenuity" as they tangled with the unlimited possibilities of an almost virgin coast.

Attracted to the huge herds (called "pods") of California gray whale that migrated between Arctic waters and Baja California spawning grounds, whalers began plying Pacific waters in the very early 1800s. By the mid-1840s, the Central Coast boasted profitable whaling stations at Davenport, Moss Landing, Point Lobos and San Simeon. During this time, eyewitness reports recalled the sidewalks of Monterey being literally paved with the bleached white vertebrae of the giant sea mammals. Taken in such great numbers for their valuable oil, the gray whale was approaching extinction by the beginning of the 20th century.

The early 19th century was also a colorful period of Mexican hospitality, of famous weeklong fiestas and rodeos at the cattle-wealthy *Californios'* lavish *casas*. The money-fueled mood was punctuated by the brisk mercantile development and sea trading economy of the American and European newcomers. This is the era eloquently evoked in Richard Henry Dana's *Two Years Before the Mast*, where Dana re-created his sailing voyages and visits to the Monterey home of his cousin, Charles Dana, a leading coastal citizen.

Even as dissatisfaction with Mexican rule intensified in the 1830s, American settlers were busy building gristmills, tanneries and dairies. In the 1840s, John C. Frémont—pathfinder, military engineer and future U.S. senator—explored Central California on a mission from the U.S. government, whose alertness to the Far West was rapidly increasing. With the help of Frémont's men, and aided by the underground efforts of wealthy Yankee merchants like Monterey's Thomas Larkin, a peaceful coup occurred in 1846 at the Sonoma headquarters of Mexican General Mariano Vallejo. There, a makeshift flag bearing the emblem of the territory's mighty grizzly bear proclaimed the end of the Mexican era.

The Bear Republic (itself an unofficial and very short-lived affair) marked the swan song of the die-hard *Californios*. With the Spanish era long gone and Mexican domination now out of the way, California looked like a wealthy ripe plum ready for picking by Russia, England and France, each of which had taken preliminary stabs at California settlement and exploration in past centuries.

However inevitable it seemed that America would officially claim the former Spanish colony as its own, it was a single patriotic gesture—the raising of the American flag over the Custom House of Monterey by resolute U.S. Navy Commodore John D. Sloat in 1846—that announced California as a de facto member of the Union. Presiding over the capital of Alta California and the most important harbor of the land, the Custom House had seen the flags of Spain (1770–1821), Mexico (1822–1846) and now the United States fly over its tile roofs.

Anticipating statehood, delegates from all over the state convened in Monterey in 1849 for a constitutional convention. In 1850, the sun officially set on Old California one day and raised again the next on the new State of California.

Golden Opportunities: The Rush Was On

The discovery of gold near Sacramento in 1848 attracted a rush of Americans, Europeans and Chinese eager to get rich quick in the gold fields of the Sierra Nevada foothills. Raising the temperature of migration, gold fever helped trigger a tidal wave of adventurers to the Central Coast, where a wealth of virgin timber spewed forth an avalanche of sawmills, wharves and logging settlements, expanded further still by an overnight shipping industry. Sawmills sprang up on every bluff, and ships laden with lumber sailed up and down the coast, a coast increasingly dotted with schools, churches, courthouses, Victorian cottages and mansions. Though the mines and streams quickly ceased to "pan out"—the expression itself is another legacy of the 49ers—the youthful new population of Americans stayed on to become the business and political leaders of the late 19th and early 20th centuries.

Tanbark oak, a key ingredient in the tanning of hides, fueled another industry fed by the wealth of cattle growing fat on huge land-grant ranchos. More than one man made a fortune in limestone—a prime ingredient in the latest building material, cement. Isaac Davis and Albion P. Jordan, who constructed the state's first limekiln in Santa Cruz, also built their own fleet of ships and bought a wharf to handle their brisk international trade

Quong Chong was a leading Chinese merchant (and proud father) in turn-of-the-century Santa Cruz. Special Collections, UCSC

in lime. Eventually, Davis hooked up with Henry Cowell in 1864 and, along with two other firms, produced half the lime used in California. Cowell's name is remembered today in enormous groves of old growth redwoods in Henry Cowell Redwoods State Park and in the ranch that became the campus of the University of California at Santa Cruz in 1965.

The story of the Central Coast's accelerating fishing industry is also a saga of cultural competition. Chinese immigrants, who came to mine gold and build the growing network of railroads after statehood, stayed to establish the first fishing industry in a succession of highly lucrative villages hugging the coast. They established highly visible and (by Yankee standards) exotic enclaves in the state's larger cities as well. Well over 100,000 Chinese had taken up residence in the state—including large settlements in Santa Cruz, Watsonville and Monterey—by the mid-1870s. But by 1890, following an unfortunate period of vigilante activity against the industrious Asian immigrants, who were willing to work for well below the going wages, the Chinese domination of the maritime wealth was eclipsed by Italians, Portuguese and Japanese.

Captains of Industry and the Pursuit of Pleasure

Americans of European ancestry soon put the stamp of Victorian architecture on the growing towns along the coast. Prosperity was being fed by a plethora of industries, and fortunes boomed in the new communications networks—shipping and the railroad. Crocker, Stanford, Huntington and Hopkins were some industrial gamblers who gave their names to banks, hotels, universities and highways up and down the coast. Once the Golden Spike was laid in Utah in 1869, linking railroads across the continent, settlers rushed to the West from all over the country. Writers like Charles Nordhoff wrote such glowing accounts of the natural wonders of the Golden State in popular books and magazines that California was literally put on the map overnight.

Travel up and down the Central Coast was an arduous undertaking in the years following California's statehood. Impossible or nonexistent roadways and the rugged terrain of the coastal mountains kept townships relatively isolated, and most travel involved lengthy sea journeys. In 1861, a stagecoach line began carrying mail and passengers three times a week from Los Angeles to San Francisco, with a stop in San Luis Obispo. Once the system had been "refined," the journey, including four relays of horses, could be made in just under four days. Each year, new towns were added to the stage lines, which were met in 1873 by the Southern Pacific Railroad as far south as Salinas. It took 20 more years for the relative safety and comfort of rail travel to extend down the Central Coast as far as San Luis Obispo.

When Santa Maria and Santa Barbara were finally linked to San Francisco by rail in 1901, a growing Central Coast bourgeoisie busily populated the coastline with seaside resorts. The enduring reputation of the balmy California coast as a seaside resort par excellence was firmly entrenched and the great retreats of the coast thronged with Victorians enamored of salt air vacations, eager to loosen their corsets with a bit of sea bathing.

With the birth of the Hollywood movie industry, even Santa Cruz became—for a short, sweet while—an open-air movie set for a glut of celluloid Westerns, romances and cliffhangers that filled nation's nickelodeons. Sycamore Springs, Tassajara and other coastal hot springs suddenly enjoyed new cachet, as tourists who couldn't get to Baden Baden or Evian could now sample the therapeutic waters, in pools and open-air tubs, along the Central Coast.

In 1906, entrepreneur Fred Swanton concocted a fabulous Brighton-style resort casino, dance palace and amusement park at the water's edge in Santa Cruz. A major attraction for legions of tourists from its opening day, the Boardwalk thrives today as the last example of its kind on the California Coast. The turn of the 20th century saw the germination of efforts to preserve the region's breathtaking natural resources, with the first coastal parklands—Big Basin Redwoods in Santa Cruz—purchased with the help of the Sempervirens Club in 1902.

In 1890, a few plucky capitalists formed the Union Oil Company in Ventura County south of Santa Barbara. Oil was discovered the next year underneath downtown Los Angeles in such quantity that derricks went up everywhere and barrels of crude flowed to destinations all over the country. A lot of this fossil fuel, plus the petroleum being refined from oil fields just off the Santa Barbara coast, soon ignited the Central Coast's love affair with the automobile. Fine weather and unlimited cheap gasoline helped spark a mania to drive that prompted highway construction taxes and, ultimately, produced the infamous freeways of southern California. Eager to get everywhere in a hurry, Californians demanded more and better roads, the culmination of which was unarguably the Pacific Coast Highway.

Out of the Dust, Into the Future

The rise of the glitzy Hollywood movie, which painted California as a land of romantic opportunity, coupled with the crushing grip of the Depression, lured yet another wave of eager immigrants to the temperate climes of the Central Coast during the 1930s. They came from America's drought-stricken dust bowl to add their energy and urgency to the creative melting pot. They were the Okies, Arkies and other heartland refugees who fled foreclosed farms to pick the lettuce, work the sardine factories of John Steinbeck's *Cannery Row* and fuel the gritty drama of his *Grapes of Wrath*. But times were tough in California, too. By 1935, almost one-fifth of the state's population was on the dole. But unlike the harsh Midwest, the climate was mild and, if a body were to go hungry, paradise was a good place in which to do it.

Steinbeck's *Cannery Row* vividly recalls the boisterous, down-at-the-heels scene at Monterey's waterfront during the Depression. Where once huge canneries had processed a billion pounds of sardines each year, only the shuffling sounds of the unemployed were heard. Sardines disappeared from Monterey Bay for good 10 years later, and today Cannery Row functions only as a colorful reminder of days gone by.

In 1906, the legendary Fred Swanton built his pleasure dome in Santa Cruz to attract San Franciscans with leisure time and open wallets. Covello & Covello

During the 1920s and '30s, Works Progress Administration work teams left their mark on the land in the form of many gravity-defying feats of engineering (both roads and bridges) that eased access to the natural scenery of the region. Dynamite, nerves of steel and fiscal desperation helped sculpt the steep sides of the coastal ranges into the thrilling vistas of Highway 1, which runs, with a few minor detours inland, the entire 1,100-mile coastline of California. Along the tortuous roadway, the occasional breathtaking bridge— like the archetypal Bixby Creek Bridge curving hundreds of feet above a canyon crevasse— reminds us of how much access to the Central Coast depended on backbreaking effort combined with architectural poetry.

Those who came and hung in during the lean times were rewarded by the full employment of World War II, which brought military bases, steel mills and the aeronautics industry to eager workers. The opening of the University of California at Santa Barbara just after the war piqued the fortunes of that community, as did the coming of University of California– Santa Cruz to that tiny resort in the mid-'60s.

The postwar period witnessed an increase of private building and public ownership along the Central Coast. Enormous military bases built for coastal defense scooped up prime beachfront real estate. These installations lured defense industries to the region and sculpted the growth of entire towns full of families and businesses dependent upon the military presence. A state park system that was to become a showcase for the rest of the nation burgeoned to protect huge expanses of native flora and fauna.

Artists, Dreamers and the Age of Aquarius

In the years between the two world wars, the scenery and seclusion of the Central Coast acted with the force of a siren song on literary bohemians, free thinkers and metaphysical cults. Isadora Duncan, Henry Miller, Robinson Jeffers, Jack London, Robert Louis Stevenson, Emil White and Mark Twain all immortalized the liberated lifestyles and meditative splendor of the region's secluded canyons, natural springs and coffeehouses.

If San Francisco was the spiritual headquarters of the Beat Generation, then Big Sur was its vacation hideaway. When quintessential bad boy Jack Kerouac went *On the Road*, he did it along the coast roads linking San Francisco with Big Sur, where he stopped for a breather in the mountain cabin owned by poet Lawrence Ferlinghetti and penned the book that spawned a generation of rebels without a cause. At Carmel, photographers Ansel Adams and Edward Weston captured the haunting marriage of earth, sky and sea, creating indelible black-and-white images that still define the California coastal magic a full 50 years later.

Hidden and out of the way, the rugged coast formed a logical sanctuary for those marching to a different drummer. Theosophists, led by the Russian expatriate Madame Blavatsky, Zen Buddhists and naturalists came, stayed, set up salons and meditative retreats and preached the good life far from the status quo of staid and traditional America.

The free-loving, arts-and-crafty "Dunites" set up camp during the 1930s in eclectic beach shanties on the dunes west of San Luis Obispo. There they foreshadowed the next generation of hippies, doing their own thing outside the strictures—and comforts—of indoor toilets and Big Brother's watchful eye. Only middle age and its need for creature comforts forced them to put on their clothes, pack up and leave the spacious beaches to the sheltering sky, wispy dunes and seabirds.

During the 1960s, consciousnesses expanded up and down the western seaboard and the Central Coast became a nursery for the emerging human potential movement. As the counterculture entered the New Age, the Central Coast led the way with its consciousness-raising centers at Esalen, Tassajara and Big Sur. The hippies' experimentation with mind-altering drugs gradually gave way to attitude adjustments of nonchemical varieties. After being found, the "inner child" needed to be fed—organically. The leading edge of the natural foods and organic gardening movement emerged here, and doing one's own thing was further institutionalized when the University of California opened its innovative campus in Santa Cruz.

Before they cut their hair and moved on (though quite a few never did), the hippies had infused every inch of the Central Coast with their attitude of tolerance. It was a logical fit, since people had been "doing their own thing" in the relative inaccessibility of the rugged coastal mountains since the beginning.

The hills and canyons of Big Sur, San Luis Obispo and the Santa Ynez Valley were—and still are—alive with the truly laid-back and self-sufficient, all seeking an alternative approach to life in Eden. Up and down the coast, the footprints in the sand remain more likely to be made by thong sandals than anything resembling a leather oxford, and the bewitching landscape and maverick heritage that attracted pathfinders a century before continue to exert their voluptuous pull.

The New Coast Guardians

With consciousness raising inevitably came political correctness and, by the 1970s, the Central Coast boasted what appeared to be an entire population of environmental activists.

Beaches, increasingly snapped up by the state for management and protection, were kept clean with a vengeance. Litterers became outcasts and recycling an unwritten law. Acknowledging its spiritual alliance with those early environmental preservationists of the Sempervirens Club, whose zeal and fundraising began the purchase of private lands for public ownership, the Sierra Club helped raise awareness in California of the state's priceless natural heritage and helped broker deals to place pristine lands in the public trust.

With the rise of offshore oil drilling along the southern reaches of the Central Coast, environmental protection legislation aggressively signaled concern for the region's natural treasures. The infamous Santa Barbara oil spill of 1969 focused worldwide attention on that city and catalyzed local activists to scrutinize the precarious balance of natural elements and man-made technologies.

The state formed the Coastal Commission in 1976 to serve as a watchdog of unchecked development and to maintain and protect the unique biosystems of the coastline. National wildlife sanctuaries were designated to protect rare wildlife habitats along the coast and in the sea, the latest and largest being the Monterey Bay National Marine Sanctuary. Famed for setting precedent in environmental issues, the Central Coast stands firm in its opposition to nuclear energy, going so far as to—in the case of Santa Cruz County—declare itself a "nuclear-free zone."

In the short 150 years since the twilight of Junipero Serra's missions, the Central Coast has managed to nurture the past while protecting its privileged resources for the future. Thanks to a prized sense of self-reflectiveness on the part of those who came to stay, this part of the world still looks and feels remarkably untouched, even as it shimmers with creativity and joie de vivre. Today the names the Spanish forefathers gave the Central Coast still cling to the rivers, mountains and towns—Santa Barbara, Santa Ynez, Santa Maria, Guadalupe, San Luis Obispo, San Simeon, Morro Bay, Big Sur, Carmel, Monterey, Santa Cruz, Año Nuevo—reminding those who live here what a very new world it still is.

JOURNEY DOWN THE COAST

A drive down the Central Coast is a drive through California's historic past, through layers of distinctive landscapes shaped as much by generations of explorers, ranchers and wide-eyed pioneers as by wind and wave. Three hundred miles of spectacular seascapes, forests and atmospheric ranch lands, this region can best, and most intimately, be savored by skirting the ocean along Coastal Highway 1. The following section is a brief tour of these coastal pleasures, with more information about what to see and where to stay detailed in later chapters.

Half Moon Bay

Nestled squarely on the Central Coast's legendary Highway 1, this hamlet is known to locals as the halfway point between San Francisco and Santa Cruz. An arts-and-crafts emporium called "Spanishtown" pays tribute to the town's nickname circa 1840 when Baja Californian immigrants claimed this slice of the coast for their own. When Prohibition dried up the nation's official alcohol consumption, Half Moon Bay's many secluded coves did a brisk business harboring eager rum smugglers who supplied San Francisco with spirits enough to wait out the dry years.

Soothed by the arms of prevailing fogs, the hemispherical bay still nurtures the rich fisheries and moist growing season that attracted its Portuguese, Spanish and Italian settlers in the 19th century. From here fleets plumb the coastal waters for salmon, anchovies and herring, while surrounding fields boast countless Christmas tree farms and enough pumpkins to fuel a month of Halloweens. Artichokes, berries and brussels sprouts share the roomy hillsides with cattle and sheep, while greenhouses supplying cut flowers to the entire state line the highway leading south.

Linked to San Francisco by the nifty little mountain pass of Highway 92, the town of Half Moon Bay is in the process of reinventing itself as a condominium-studded bedroom community for the Greater San Francisco Bay Area. Leading hotel chains recently have joined a select number of charming bed & breakfast establishments, serving notice that Half Moon Bay is to be regarded as a destination tourist stop.

San Gregorio to La Honda

At the beach where the slender thread of San Gregorio Road turns inland is a plaque commemorating the brief pit stop made here by Portola's 1769 expedition. Nineteenth-century stagecoach roads cut across the Coast Range in these parts into sheltered farmlands, tiny villages and primeval redwood forest settlements. A few stores, including a 1880s general store restoration, mark downtown San Gregorio, a former stagecoach stop and pony express mail depot, whose main street winds upward into the northern reaches of the Santa Cruz Mountains.

Halfway up the mountain, San Gregorio turns into La Honda Road, gateway to hidden redwood thickets filled with vacation cabins from a century's worth of those wanting to get far from the madding crowd. Still rough, beautiful and sparsely settled, these redwood fastnesses and ridges that overlook the coast have been home to fabled bohemians, bikers and eccentrics alike. They still are. This was the infamous headquarters of Ken Kesey's Merry Pranksters and today is the home of rock star Neil Young. For a dose of classic Central Coast mountain funkiness, La Honda fits the bill in spades.

At the top of the mountain, La Honda Road swings straight into the 20th century in the form of Interstate 280—also named the Junipero Serra Highway—the Bay Area's prime commuter racetrack.

Pescadero

Ghosts of *Californio* ranchers, Portuguese whalers and Japanese fishing pioneers haunt this tiny one-street town, whose name means "fisherman" in Spanish. A gateway to redwood campgrounds, prime surf and the convoluted stretches of Pescadero State Beach, the town is populated by houses, barns and authentic general stores straight out of the 19th century. To drive the tiny town—hemmed in on all sides by year-round growing fields and steep slopes grazed by cattle—is to ride the old stagecoach trail into a time capsule of the frontier West.

The top destination here is Duarte's Tavern, so authentic you'd swear it's got swinging doors. Adjoining the restaurant is a saloon straight from central casting, heavily populated with real cowboys, migrant workers and other colorful types.

An idyllic 210-acre expanse of wildlife sanctuary faces Pescadero Beach across Highway 1. On one side of the road waves plunge against miles of wide tide pools, while on the other elegant egrets, mallards, blue herons and brilliantly colored wood ducks pose and sail blissfully on lagoons threaded by giant cattails. This is a favorite secret playground for northern California's hip young community and has been since the 1960s. Even before the Summer of Love, a young, slender Jerry Garcia regularly jammed with his newly formed Grateful Dead to the roar of huge bonfires on this beach.

Año Nuevo and Points South

In late January, when the velvety grasses of the Central Coast's "false spring" add a certain elegance to the rough-hewn land, this stretch of San Mateo and Santa Cruz counties offers irresistible driving pleasure. Propelled by slate-gray storms off the coast, the ocean churns itself into enormous lathers of surf and crashing waves, presenting postcard interpretations of heaving seas.

The winter months are also famous along the coast for whale-watching and, for those who join the guided tours at Año Nuevo State Reserve, elephant seal mating rituals. Año Nuevo—named by explorer Juan Rodriguez Cabrillo—plays host each winter to thousands of female elephant seals herded into harems by their amorous bulls. Here the soft, furry babies are born amid tide pool and sand in the protected setting of primeval outcroppings. Truly astonishing in vigor and sheer size (2 tons is normal), these marvelous behemoths have made the rocky outpost one of the great bastions of their species. The two-plus-hour guided tour (December through March) puts you up close and personal enough with these lusty creatures to see why their sumptuous coats were so prized—and led them to the very brink of extinction.

Coastways Ranch, famous for little Christmas trees and luscious kiwi and olallieberry orchards, lies on the other side of Highway 1. It's just one of the many rustic, rambling ranches and stables lending frontier atmosphere to this neck of the woods.

Redwood forests—many protected as part of Big Basin, Castle Rock and Butano State Parks—crown the coastal highlands, which momentarily fan out into verdant rivers of artichokes or brussels sprouts before plunging into the sea. It's perhaps this unique blend of redwood crests, deep canyons crosshatched with small pockets of cultivation and high wild limestone bluffs that defines this stretch of coast. For a little extra visual spin, obliging cows, horses and sheep straight from central casting pop up pastorally on cue along high ridges and curvaceous draws.

Two state beaches merit special attention. Just north of Davenport, the stately lagoon of Scott Creek sparkles like something out of an Arthurian legend. Ghostly pampas grass rims the steep ridges behind, and Canada geese, coots and mallards float noisily on pools fringed with cattails and tule. Across the road, sandy beaches curve out of sight around jutting limestone sentinels of the continental United States.

Waddell Creek

Down the road apiece, Waddell Creek finally spills out into the Pacific after tumbling down from its source high in Big Basin Park. Hang gliders and windsurfers have laid claim to this windy spot, and on most days spectators can watch their jewel-colored sails dipping in and out of the waves like playful birds. Nearby, waterfowl stake out their plots in saltwater marshes and freshwater lagoons. This is a magic location for year-round beachcombing (look for gnarled driftwood and sea-smoothed rocks). Coastal access is available via plenty of well-marked paths, as well as trails worn over the years by legions of die-hard surfers. Use trails through private property with discretion, since trespassers, however innocent or athletic, do not amuse many local farmers.

But if you feel the need to take your shoes off and gambol in the ebb tide with someone you love—this is the place. On the romantic scale of 1 to 10, Waddell Creek is a 12.

At the adjoining state beach is a sign indicating Rancho del Oso—the onetime home of former President Herbert Hoover's brother and currently an undeveloped arm of Big Basin State Park. It is filled with scenic hiking possibilities.

Davenport

The tiny village of Davenport was, since shortly after the turn of 20th century, a company town built, owned and operated by and for the Portland Cement Company. Everything and everyone in it was white from cement dust—houses, cars, people and gardens. All of that was cleaned up in the 1960s, but, if one squints, imagination can do the rest. There are still signs of the past in some of the original, identical houses, one of which, the Bath House, turned saloon, then sporting house and is now part of the New Davenport Cash Store.

Across the street from the bustling Cash Store—where there are a bed & breakfast, restaurant, community core and global arts-and-crafts emporium—the whale-watching is as good as it gets. From here, whalers from all over the world came in the mid–19th century to fill their ships with precious oil and line their pockets with gold. One of those adventurous souls was Rhode Island's John Davenport, who came in 1850 and ended up

Crucifer from Another Planet

Stretching from Half Moon Bay down through Monterey County, mighty portions of the Central Coast lie cultivated with miles of brussels sprouts, which flourish in the lengthy growing season and cool summer fog of this moist seaside climate. Like an exotic and primitive cabbage, the brussels sprout is, indeed, a crucifer and a distant relative of the mustard family. Almost extraterrestrial in appearance, the stalks are studded with miniature cabbage heads, gray-green knobs growing the entire 2-foot length. Harvested when the little heads are still tiny and tender, brussels sprouts provide luxurious eating, simply steamed and bathed in butter, wine vinegar and kosher salt.

Grower Steve Bontadelli holds aloft a stalk of brussels sprouts, an important Central Coast crop.

running not only a major whaling operation but also a lumber wharf. (In those days, you were nobody unless you had your own wharf.)

Today the town that Davenport settled is still distinguished by two primary landmarks: the spouts of gigantic gray whales as they migrate south and the tall stacks of the cement plant, both visible for miles. Davenport is charm itself, easily circumnavigated on foot in under half an hour, a tour that rewards visitors with glimpses into world-class glassblowing, boatbuilding and knife-making studios.

Bonny Doon to San Lorenzo Valley

Just south of Davenport, Bonny Doon Road invites the lover of winding mountain roads to motor through some classic redwood country. Once at the top, the road turns into Empire Grade, which follows the rocky ridge north. Dotted with old orchards and farmhouses, this area has been settled since the mid-1900s, when grapes grown in this tough limestone soil made wines that wowed European critics. Vineyards are again popping up in this remote and secluded country, and the tasting room of Randall Grahm, Bonny Doon Vineyards' maverick winemaker, stands at the intersection of Bonny Doon and Pine Flat Roads. The tasting is superior—Grahm's wines have found their way into the country's finest restaurants and cellars—and the setting atmospheric.

Descending Empire Grade into the small town of Felton, the road leads up the San Lorenzo River Valley via Highway 9, a road so precariously crafted that it regularly washes out each winter. But a rewarding road it is. Forests filled with moss-covered bay trees, madrones and redwoods all but blot out the sun, forming a long green cathedral corridor. In the 19th century, logs from this area filled ships headed 'round the world. While most of the remaining trees are second growth, a thrilling exception lies just south of Felton on Highway 9, where protected groves of the oldest first-growth giants remain at Henry Cowell Redwoods State Park.

Highway 9 continues up the redwood valley through a series of tiny villages and fashionable summer homes owned since the 1930s by wealthy city folks from San Francisco and Hollywood. Just past the charmingly preserved frontier town of Boulder Creek is the entrance to Big Basin Redwoods State Park, home to massive virgin redwoods. The perfect place to escape the summer heat, these thousands of acres of primeval forest were protected in 1902, becoming the first in the California state park system. The popular camping and hiking spot has expanded to over 15,000 protected acres of wilderness, extending from the 2,000-foot summit all the way down to the beaches of Waddell, Scott and Gazos Creeks.

Wilder Ranch

Between Davenport and Santa Cruz, you'll notice the rows of cars seemingly abandoned on either side of the highway. This is evidence of the superior surfing found in these parts, attracting the faithful in even the foulest weather. You're almost in Santa Cruz when you can see the cluster of weathered buildings and prominent red-roofed stable of Wilder Ranch on your right. This graceful relic of the dairy barons of the 1880s occupies a special place in the hearts of area residents.

Covering over 5,000 acres of the most sumptuous and varied terrain on the Central Coast, the ranch (a former dairy ranch turned cattle ranch turned state park) sprawls from its seaside tide pools and plover sanctuary all way up to redwoods at the mountaintop of Bonny Doon. Along the way, Wilder encompasses magnificent meadows, ponds, springs and myriad wildlife habitats (blue heron rookeries, fox and coyote enclaves).

At the foot of the property is the beautifully maintained Victorian compound of the Wilder dairy ranch. All the buildings—including the long barn that housed the state's first cream separator, Wilder family house and stables adorned with handsome carved wood detailing—are open to the public. Nearby are the tumbled down remains of the original adobe, the house in which Russian Jose Bolcoff married Spanish land-grant heiress Maria Castro back when the ranch was part of the 10,000-acre Rancho Refugio.

The full exhilaration of this land is enjoyed by strapping on some sturdy shoes, a day pack filled with food and water, a camera and binoculars before heading up along the ranch's many hiking and biking trails. It's a trip back into the solitude and open grandeur of the Old West. The view of Monterey across the bay—from halfway up the highlands—is worth the sweat you'll spend getting there.

Santa Cruz

Long one of the state's most appealing and popular seaside resorts, the seductive town of Santa Cruz supports an eclectic population of artists, writers, winemakers, restaurateurs and rabble-rousers. Originally settled by the Franciscan fathers who established the Mission La Exaltación de la Santa Cruz in 1791, the town initially flourished thanks to the nearby large Branciforte Pueblo, the center of town life in Spanish days, then by Mexican land-grant ranchos that followed the pueblo's breakup and, finally, by American entrepreneurs attracted by the matchless setting of mountains descending into the hemispherical Monterey Bay.

While the original mission was twice destroyed by an earthquake and exists today as a one-third-scale replica, the past persists in the city's tree-lined streets of impeccably

On this site above the Santa Cruz coast, lighthouses have warned ships at sea of dangerous rock outcroppings since 1887. Buz Bezore

maintained Victorian mansions and classic examples of Craftsman bungalows. The work of ubiquitous early-20th-century California architect William Weeks—whose handsome public buildings, schools, libraries and courthouses literally dot the face of the state—is showcased throughout Santa Cruz. Most notable are the stately high school, the Spanish Revival Darling House bed & breakfast and, most prominently, the 1920s Palomar Hotel, whose scalloped roofline is the dominant landmark in the compact downtown.

Devastated by the 1989 earthquake (centered a mere 8 miles away), downtown Santa Cruz lost many of its historic commercial buildings. The rebuilding effort is nearly complete, and a restoration of the 19th-century St. George Hotel, the early-20th-century Cooper House and the splendid art deco Del Mar Theatre, as well as the erection of a nearby cinema complex, has pumped blood back into the cultural heart of the town.

For well over 100 years, the expansive main beach of Santa Cruz has hosted throngs of visitors, many flocking to the massive amusement park of the Santa Cruz Beach Boardwalk. Snuggled in between the beach and the arcades at one end, the Victorian ballroom of the Cocoanut Grove once hosted the best of Big Band orchestras and today regularly features hot Latin American and rock music groups. In addition to a colorful assortment of death-defying rides, the Boardwalk is graced with the Giant Dipper (the oldest wooden roller coaster in the country) and an enchanting 1879 carousel bedecked with hand-carved painted horses.

Lined with stately summer homes and the graceful shade of Monterey pines and cypress, West Cliff Drive curves along the coast, linking the end of the Santa Cruz Municipal Wharf with the wild cliffs of Natural Bridges State Park a few miles northward. In the middle, just at the point where the sheltered Monterey Bay gives way again to the turbulent Pacific Ocean proper, is Lighthouse Point. Since 1887, a lighthouse on this site has warned ships at sea of dangerous rock outcroppings. Today's tiny beacon, which replaced the badly undermined original in 1967, still warns fishing fleets at dawn and houses the state's first surfing museum.

Close to this spot, late in the 19th century, Hawaiian princes first commissioned long planks of redwood to be shaped into the first surfboards ever navigated in the New World. The surfing is still world class at Steamers Lane, home to a bevy of international surfing competitions and a place where perfect sets of waves beckon visitors and locals of all ages every morning.

Following the uphill curve of High Street past historic Mission Plaza, visitors arrive at the former ranch of lime and cattle potentate Henry Cowell. This grand 2,000-acre site, whose sweeping fields are alive with deer and coyote and framed by thick stands of red-woods, is now the home of the Santa Cruz campus of the University of California. Clustered in the English Oxbridge tradition into 11 self-contained colleges, the campus is a showpiece of contemporary architecture, crowned by an evolving arts complex and even larger groupings of science and engineering laboratories and classrooms, all built in harmony with the encircling landscape. The original limestone quarry and many of Cowell's limekilns, barns and ranch buildings are still scattered scenically throughout the campus. The sweeping view of the entire Monterey Bay from this academic vantage point is worth the drive.

Nestled beneath the lofty hills of the university sit 600 pristine acres of greenbelt known locally as the Pogonip. Purchased by the City of Santa Cruz, with the help of the State of California, this exhilarating hilltop setting once played host to international superstars of the 1930s when it formed the polo fields of the Pogonip Golf and Country Club. Spencer Tracy and his guests joined royalty and top polo players from around the world at this exclusive playground.

Capitola and Soquel

Once the intersection of Victorian-era commerce and well-worn stage lines, these sister cities face each other across diminutive Soquel Creek, which empties peacefully into a broad, sheltered beach at Capitola. Today, Capitola-by-the-Sea (named in a failed bid to be the state's first capital) attracts sunbathers to its sheltered children's beach and shoppers to its warren of galleries, crafts shops and boutiques. Both the beach and the shopping area adjoin the airy Esplanade, where trendy watering holes jostle with seafood restaurants for patrons.

Across the creek and Highway 1 lies sleepy Soquel, founded by Yankee merchants, settled by ambitious loggers and peopled by generations of cattle ranchers and horse trainers. Country roads wind away from the ocean and up into the Santa Cruz Mountains through endless pastures, small organic farms and thriving microwineries. This is also begonia country, where nurseries breed the large, luscious blooms sold to dealers and florists around the world.

Well tended and packed to the rafters with antiques shops, Soquel offers a surprising diversity of fine restaurants all built on the same small scale as the town itself. Soquel is home to the region's oldest winery, Bargetto, whose tasting room on Main Street is packed with history extending to the days before Prohibition when the enterprising Bargetto brothers kept frontier restaurants well stocked with sturdy vintages.

Aptos and Rio Del Mar

Sugar beet king Claus Spreckles made such a fortune in the fields near Aptos Creek that the imprint of his private polo grounds can still be seen lying just outside the entrance to 10,000 pristine acres of redwood lands that form the Forest of Nisene Marks. Made infamous in recent years as the epicenter of the Loma Prieta earthquake of 1989, this otherwise undisturbed forest offers endless hiking and horseback trails extending far into the interior of the Coast Ranges. The slender stretch of Highway 1 occupied by Aptos Village offers some of the most picturesque dining in the Central Coast.

At the coast, Aptos yields to the seaside community of Rio Del Mar, an attractive amalgam of beach homes abutting a short esplanade and miles of wide beachfront that includes spacious camping, barbecuing and seaside roaming possibilities. In the middle of Seacliff State Beach (a short stroll away) sits the wreck of a vintage World War I cement ship, the *Palo Alto*. Accessible by a slender pier, the hulk is a popular surf-fishing attraction. In addition to camping, hiking and fishing opportunities, the primarily residential areas of Rio Del Mar and Seacliff offer secluded sunning, surfing and, for the young and hardy, swimming conditions in water that remains just a few degrees too cool for most adults without wet suits.

A few miles down the coast lies Seascape, an upscale vacation community equipped with a fine golf course, popular swim/racquet club, attractive shopping complex, adventuresome dining and conference center. Farther south, the state beaches of La Selva and Manresa offer broad expanses of sand and surfing and unhurried beachcombing invitations. Another turnoff takes travelers through acres of strawberry fields and straw flowers destined for national markets and passes the pillowy dunes of Sunset State Beach.

Pajaro Valley to San Juan Bautista

Prime orchard and agricultural land leads from the fertile Pajaro Valley, site of one of Portola's historic landings, to one of California's most graceful and authentically preserved mission towns. Turning inland from Highway 1, Route 152 meanders past the lettuce and strawberry fields surrounding Watsonville, up a short but steep mountain pass and into the golden fields surrounding San Juan Bautista. The mission was founded in 1797 by Junipero Serra's hardy successor, Father Lasuen. The peaceful local Indians encountered by the Franciscan missionary not only inspired his choice of site but also labored in the building of the gracefully photogenic mission, the largest constructed by the Spanish padres in Alta California.

Today the mission's large plaza skirts the entire 184-foot length of the graceful arched portico, whose thick walls keep the dark mission interior, its restored dormitories and workrooms cool in the blazing heat of summer. Olive and cypress trees encircle the small Indian burial ground behind the mission, the view from which affords a dramatic panorama of the San Andreas Fault zigzagging through Hollister in the distance. The lofty beams of the chapel interior are crowned by an ornate baroque altar and graced with delicately painted stenciling. The whole conspires to make this place a remarkable window into the early days of Spanish occupation.

The small town of San Juan Bautista preserves its frontier feel in gracefully walled casas, adobes, landmark gardens, Mexican restaurants and the memorabilia-bedecked Plaza Hotel, built in 1868 to entertain the town's cross section of land-grant barons and cowboys. The Plaza Stable now houses a substantial collection of period wagons, stagecoaches and carriages. Alive with California's Spanish past, the town is a living museum, populated with historic homes, most handsomely restored and authentically furnished. Indeed, the houses, stables, adobes and mission are now protected as the San Juan Bautista State Historical Park. Inviting antiques shops line streets dotted with the occasional tumbleweed.

Amid the time-travel charm, each summer the adventurous Cabrillo Music Festival fills the plaza and the acoustically perfect mission interior with the sounds of the living present. The innovative Hispanic performance troupe El Teatro Camposino makes its home base in this bastion of early California heritage. And it should not be forgotten during a visit to San Juan Bautista that a movie star of major proportions is always in your midst: The mission's adjoining bell tower—now closed to the public—figured prominently in the climactic conclusion of Alfred Hitchcock's *Vertigo*.

Moss Landing

Marking the midway point of the Monterey Bay, where the Salinas River bisects the low-lying artichoke fields between Santa Cruz and Monterey, Moss Landing lies just south of the sensational bird-watching mother lode of Elkhorn Slough. The slough's 2,500 acres of salt marsh and tidal flats not only provide sanctuary for tens of thousands of waterfowl, but also teem with plankton rich enough to nurse oyster and shrimp farms supplying Central Coast restaurants.

In 1864, this scene bustled with activity. Established as a whaling station by Captain Charles Moss, a busy harbor soon serviced schooners loaded with produce from the Salinas Valley and whaling ships from around the world. Today, Moss Landing is essentially a faded postcard of a fishing village—a collection of piers, docks and duck-filled lagoons without a town in sight. Curiously enough, what Moss Landing does have is scores of vintage antiques stores lining the one road that twists through its ramshackle collection of docks.

Cooled by coastal fog, Castroville—near Moss Landing—is the Artichoke Capital of the World.
Shmuel Thaler

Global Matters

The artichoke, a Mediterranean native and member of the thistle family, was widely culti-vated by Italian immigrants attracted by the climatic and scenic resemblance of the Central Coast to their European homeland. Thriving along the Central Coast—most espe-cially in Monterey and Santa Cruz Counties—artichoke fields spill down to the very edge of bluffs overlooking the ocean in some places. The distinctive plant grows in round "islands" of feathery leaves, crowned by the fat globe that is the edible prize. The ultimate finger food, steamed artichoke leaves are simply pulled off, dipped in a lemon-butter mixture or dragged through garlic-infused mayonnaise and scraped clean of the tender meat with one's teeth. Nestled in the thistled interior lies the succulent heart, favored by Califor-nians and prepared in myriad ways. Roadside produce stands offer artichokes fresh from the fields and, like all roadside produce stands, these are hard to resist.

A drowsy fishing community par excellence, Moss Landing is also home to the man-made landmark that is the huge Pacific Gas & Electric steam-generating plant. Its twin towers visible from every spot on the Monterey Bay, the benign (though unsightly) plant holds a certain magic at twilight when its steel scaffoldings shimmer with twinkling lights.

The drive inland from Moss Landing wanders through a silver-green sea of artichokes that extends as far as the eye can see. In the middle of it all sits Castroville, a heartland ranching and agricultural settlement with one foot in the 1880s. Comprised of a single street and fortified by produce stands, tiny Castroville proudly clays claim to the title of Artichoke Capitol of the World. None dare argue. Encircled by fields of the globe variety of edible thistle, this cowboy town retails freshly harvested artichokes in every conceivable condition—from deep fried to candied.

Monterey

Monterey is an impeccably maintained fabric of historic old sections, waterfront wharves and piers, Cannery Row tourism and well-groomed conference hotels and seaside lodg-ings, all ringed by the teeming natural kingdom of the Monterey Bay. Fisherman's Wharf—originally built in 1846 and once bursting with international whaling traffic—offers a galaxy of seafood dining and souvenir shopping as well as fine sportfishing amid the nets, boats and paraphernalia of today's busy tuna, bonita and salmon industries. This is a prime vantage point for observing the antics of sea otters and for watching the fat harbor seals sun themselves.

Poised at the tip of the bay as it begins to yield to the open waters of the Pacific Ocean, the first fort of the Spanish empire in California, the Monterey Presidio, still maintains a military watch over the harbor. From its commanding position, the old bastion marks the beginning of Cannery Row, in its prime a cheek-by-jowl amalgam of sardine canneries and processing plants, colorfully chronicled in the 1940s by the pen of John Steinbeck. Today, the canneries offer their atmospherically ruined foundations to the seagulls and kelp beds. Many former canneries now house galleries, gift shops, wine-tasting rooms and fine restaurants.

The centerpiece of this seafront revival is the spectacular Monterey Bay Aquarium, where visitors come from all over the world to wonder at innovative natural habitat exhibits—some several stories high and literally carved out of the rock and underwater sanctuaries of the bay itself. Giant kelp forests teem with otters, octopi and sharks, and baby rays and starfish are available on a one-on-one level at the aquarium's Touch Tide Pool.

Pacific Grove

Founded in the 1870s as a seaside retreat for the Methodist Church, this quiet gem adjoining the northern edge of Monterey proper boasts incomparable Victorian homes turned into inviting, often luxurious bed & breakfast accommodations. On abalone-rich shores, ministers erected a suitable Christian meeting and recreation headquarters observed by Robert Louis Stevenson in 1879 to be modestly populated by those in search of "teetotalism, religion and flirtation." Long a popular conference site, Pacific Grove houses the landmark Asilomar meeting center, designed by Julia Morgan, whose architectural abilities also shaped the monumental whimsy of the Hearst Castle at San Simeon.

At Asilomar State Park, sand dunes give way to a wildly dramatic expanse of prime tide pools reaching tentatively into surf crashing wildly on the rocks of Point Pinos—alleged to be the first Central Coast location spied by Cabrillo. The spot still boasts a tiny searchlight of the Point Pinos Lighthouse, which has steered ships away from the treacherous rocks since 1856 (it is open for tours). Local abalone divers continue to search the waters off the point for the prized sea delicacy, whose huge, discarded iridescent shells formed great mounds, marking Native American habitation.

Each November, Pacific Grove captures its fair share of the limelight when the orange-and-black magic of hundreds of thousands of monarch butterflies fill the trees of the town's main avenue with a glory of quivering color.

Pebble Beach and 17 Mile Drive

Even before Bing Crosby's annual clambake, landed gentry flocked to this area of incomparable cliffs, churning surf and occasional movie crews. Winding between Pacific Grove and Carmel is an extraordinary stretch of road affording fabulous ocean vistas and glimpses of the lifestyles of the rich and famous. Here some of California's founding families laid down their own versions of great European country homes, most designed by the leading architects of the early 20th century.

The 5,000-acre Del Monte Forest is a sanctuary for the rare Monterey cypress, including that most photographed of Central Coast trees, the Lone Cypress. Its ancestors gave shelter to the landing party headed by Portola during his 1769 exploration of Alta

California. The waters along this circuitous drive have been the graveyard of countless cargo ships, dashed to bits during the past three centuries on the razor-edged rocks.

At each turn of this popular drive, some new, yet strangely familiar estate pops into view through the Monterey pines and stone gatehouses. Hitchcock's *Rebecca* was among the many Golden Age of Hollywood films set in these monuments to conspicuous, if tasteful, consumption. One especially noteworthy mansion is the Byzantine Palace—visible at Cypress Point—built at great cost of imported Italian marble in the 1920s for a Crocker banking heiress.

In addition to truly spectacular coastal vistas, this stretch of top-drawer real estate is a testament to lavish country club living. For the nominal toll charge to drive 17 Mile Drive, visitors can take a gander at the action on some of the world's most famous golf courses. Every January and February, the AT&T Pebble Beach National Pro-Am attracts the biggest names in the game and on the Hollywood set to such legendary courses as Pebble Beach (the Holy Grail for golf fanatics) and Spyglass Hill.

Carmel

Carefully nurtured artistic ambiance and romantic windswept cypresses share the borders of Carmel, one of the gems of early Spanish mission architecture. Here, photographer Ansel Adams flourished, Clint Eastwood became mayor and eating isn't allowed on the streets. Neon signs and telephone poles also are banned. Preserving its quaintness with a vengeance has paid off for this diminutive village, a slice of almost English country refinement perched on the edge of the continent. Tidy and almost impossibly tasteful in its collection of landscaped cottages, elegant lodgings and upscale restaurants, Carmel still exerts its undeniable, if conservative, appeal.

History has left its mark most vividly in the nearby Mission San Carlos Borromeo del Rio Carmel, established in 1771 by Father Junipero Serra, who later fell in love with its encircling adobe walls, gardens and view of the sea. Such was his attachment to his favorite mission that the padre was buried here, awaiting the canonization for which his New World supporters are currently petitioning. With its barrel-vaulted ceiling and Moorish tower, and authentically replicated kitchen, sleeping quarters and refectory, the mission well rewards visitors seeking a taste of Spanish occupation in the New World. The mission restoration also contains the first library in California—600 hand-bound volumes shelved in the original study used by Serra. In the gardens, the graves of over 3,000 Christianized Indians lie under the shade of vintage olive trees.

Bohemian painters, writers, photographers and bons vivants arrived here at the turn of the 20th century, drawn by the magnanimous deal of land barons James Devendorf and Frank H. Powers: dirt-cheap land to anyone actively engaged in the fine arts. The offer, plus fragrant pine forests at the edge of a serene beach, attracted the likes of Upton Sinclair, Jack London, George Sterling and Edward Weston, as well as hundreds of their best friends, hangers-on and lesser-known (though similarly talented) colleagues. Robinson Jeffers found the peaceful inspiration that he sought in the amazing Tor House and Hawk Tower, built in 1914 completely of rounded, native stone—an intrepid landmark not to be missed by visitors.

Each year the Monterey Jazz Festival spills sparkling into Carmel's streets and the brilliant brass and contrapuntal melodies of the baroque masters fill the town each year during the Carmel Bach Festival. And everybody—tourist and local alike—stops for a cocktail at Clint Eastwood's Hog's Breath Inn watering hole.

Carmel Valley

Across from the mission, Carmel Valley Road threads its way along the tiny Rio Carmel, climbing into the hills through lands once graced by enormous land-grant ranchos. Much of Carmel Valley continues to be owned by the very wealthy—Doris Day maintains a compound here—and has been immaculately groomed into an elegant patchwork of golf courses, country clubs and plush resorts. Thriving remnants of the early rancho period dot this Spanish-oak-drenched slice of the Coast Ranges, perhaps the purest taste of the *Californio* essence still to be found.

Orchards of pear, apricot and walnut line the verdant valley floor, which rises abruptly into slopes picturesquely studded with grazing herds of cattle. Up in chaparral country, Carmel Valley offers prime side road exploration through steep canyons and onto ridges offering stunning views of the ocean below.

One of the most famous continuations of Carmel Valley Road swings 20 miles inland from the coast to Tassajara Hot Springs. For those (preferably with four-wheel-drive vehicles) who can handle the sheer cliffs, hairpin turns and rocky conditions, the reward is wet release in rock tubs hollowed millennia ago by Indians who revered these waters. The earliest mineral springs in the West known to outsiders, the sulfur baths steam away in an idyllic oak grove setting shared with the Tassajara Zen Center. Guests who don't mind the center's rather spartan conditions can soak and meditate to their hearts' content.

Big Sur Coast and Backcountry

Most signs of human habitation disappear abruptly just south of Carmel. For the next 90 miles, the majestic coastal splendor of Big Sur reigns supreme. With few permanent residents and no towns to speak of, this pristine coastline still boasts its unspoiled, breathtaking grandeur. Here, Highway 1 earns its reputation as the most beautiful, if vertiginous, highway in the country. That the road exists at all—carved out of sheer cliffs dropping straight into the swirling tide below—is a miracle.

From nearly every vantage point, looking back toward the ocean, turquoise water, broiling surf and savage cliffs create the illusion of standing at the very dawn of creation. Twisting and turning for the next 30 miles, the highway swings down to any number of superb beaches, and then climbs to vista points, some of which are definitely not for the faint of heart.

Spectacular bridges defy gravity to span deep canyons and gorges—the best and most photographed of which is Bixby Creek Bridge, with a central span of over 300 feet. This is definitely a must visit. No matter how many times this stretch of the road has been traveled, the bridge still inspires even the most jaded to stop and stare.

From Bixby Creek, two noteworthy side roads, Palo Colorado and the Old Coast Road, take inquiring drivers deep into the interior of the coastal mountains, through fern canyons and up to windswept hilltops, affording stunning views of the entire Monterey Bay.

The Ventana Wilderness joins with the Los Padres National Forest at Big Sur, offering close to 2 million acres of pristine hiking and riding trails and awe-inspiring forests, beaches, trails and hilltops, including the southernmost habitat of the giant redwoods. Immediately south of the "town" of Big Sur lie the beautiful beaches, caves and cliffs of Pfeiffer Beach. After the day of beachcombing and hiking, locals trickle in for a sunset cocktail at the legendary Nepenthe, a restaurant/arts complex situated almost 1,000 feet above the sea. A hangout since 1949 for local culturati, Nepenthe has since been joined by

Big Sur's spectacularly rugged seascape has lured travelers to the Central Coast for generations. Shmuel Thaler

other fashionable resort neighbors, including Ventana Inn across the road and Post Ranch Inn just down the highway.

On each side of the highway continuing southward, state parks, beaches and forests extend as far as the eye can see, working their way to the very end of Monterey County. Julia Pfeiffer Burns State Park haunts the coast beginning 10 miles south of Nepenthe, its border encircling waterfalls, creek trails and dizzying ridges. Henry Miller, bad boy of bohemian literature, called this area home during the last half of his life.

After a dip in the public-access hot springs and tubs at the New Age think tank of nearby Esalen Institute, visitors might continue southward to partake of the prime meandering possibilities of Sand Dollar Beach and Jade Cove. A steep cliff trail drops down to the smooth, pale green pebbled surface of this popular picnic spot, whose bounty of nephrite jade has been aggressively scooped up by collectors over the decades.

Throughout the southern Big Sur area, rugged side roads—many overlaying old ranch trails—lead from the coast through redwoods and chaparral, retracing the steps of early pioneers. One of the loveliest of these, Nacimiento Road, begins south of Lucia and ascends 3,000 feet through oak groves and brush-covered ridges. It ends in the isolated setting of Junipero Serra's third mission, the authentically restored Mission San Antonio de Padua, founded in 1771. Complete with stone mill, corrals and the ruins of orchards, this lonely outpost of New World Christianity casts a haunting spell. For many, just getting there is half the pleasure.

Unadulterated and spectacular, the Big Sur coast preserves its primal magnificence, an area where early explorers and latter-day seekers staked their claim to—and refined—the

California dream. Nowhere else on the Central Coast is so much unspoiled coastal wilderness available to the public. Especially demanding along the Big Sur coastline, Highway 1 has tempted more than one fast car off its beautiful cliffs. However, there are convenient pullouts and vista points available almost every mile of the way, and most travelers find themselves using them frequently. If ever one stretch of road demanded a camera and binoculars, the Big Sur stretch of the Pacific Coast Highway is it.

San Simeon

As Monterey County gives way to San Luis Obispo County, the steep and agitated landscape of Big Sur relaxes, gradually rambling downhill toward the beginnings of superb beach country. The Central Coast's Mediterranean climate blooms as you head farther south, the days jumping up in temperature a few more degrees, the evenings staying balmier longer. The Spanish presence continues to be clearly felt—in place-names, in huge rancho holdings turned into almost-as-huge present-day farmlands and in the presence of mission restorations, culminating in the Spanish baroque splendor of Mission Santa Barbara.

The most graphic reminder of Old World influence, though, is that fantastical version of the Spanish Renaissance, William Randolph Hearst's amazing architectural wonder, La Cuesta Encantada (The Enchanted Hill). Hearst inherited hundreds of thousands of acres of San Simeon land grant from his indomitable mother, Phoebe, and senator father ,George. But it was William who made millions of dollars speculating on Comstock silver, using a portion of those gains to develop vast cattle ranch holdings overlooking what is now San Simeon State Beach.

Between 1919 and 1947, the newspaper magnate unleashed his massive fortune and passion for architectural overstatement on the superb hillside setting framed by the Santa Lucia Ranges. With architect Julia Morgan to temper his pipe dreams, Hearst proceeded to construct a tile, marble, wood and gilt complex filled with 37 bedrooms, fabulous indoor swimming pools, fountains, endless gardens and even a zoo.

To this fabulously costly hideaway came the famous and beautiful of the day—everyone from George Bernard Shaw and Winston Churchill to Charlie Chaplin and Carole Lombard. The unofficial hostess of Hearst Castle was screen star Marion Davies, the not-so-secret mistress of its owner. Richly satirized in Orson Welles's *Citizen Kane*, San Simeon is a kingdom unto itself and must be witnessed to be believed. Fortunately, most of its acres were deeded to a land trust in 2002 to ensure the public has access forever.

Cambria and Cayucos

South of San Simeon, Highway 1 slides through gentle beach country to the artists' colony of Cambria, which also serves as the lodging center for visitors to the Hearst Castle a few miles up the road. Settled in the 1860s by Welsh miners attracted by news of copper and quicksilver prospects, Cambria's lumber industry, dairy farming and superb swimming beaches have maintained the community's popularity up to the present.

Highway 1 moves inland here, through the rolling dairy and cattle country that first attracted Swiss and Italian immigrants to the Cayucos region in the 1880s. Even before that, Yankees had come and bought up land, eventually dividing the old *Rancho Moro y Cayucos* into real estate for development. The town's name comes from the Spanish version of an Indian name for indigenous canoes, *kayak*, with which the Chumash plied local waters for swordfish, marlin and tuna. In keeping with that tradition, the pier at Cayucos State Beach provides ample and popular fishing.

All along this section of coastline, great stands of blue-green eucalyptus dominate the hillsides and saturate the air with a heady, mentholated perfume. Imported from Australia in the last century under the misguided impression that they would provide fast-growing timber for construction, the eucalyptus has long since gone native, in some places choking out the original flora. Though their lumber proved unsturdy, these distinctive trees crop up along the entire Central Coast as ranch land windbreaks and as the region's signature ocean backdrop.

Morro Bay and Los Osos

Crowned by a formidable volcanic peak, the extensive beaches of this popular playground are home to abundant shellfish and spectacular processions of windswept dunes. A busy fishing port, the bay is one of the major waterfowl habitats in the country. Before that, this 12-mile stretch of coast, extending from Morro Strand State Beach down to Montaña de Oro State Park, was a prized harbor and hub of the shipping industry. By 1879, coastal steamers regularly put in at its sheltering bay. Protected by a slender sand spit of high dunes, the curvaceous bay is chockablock with waterfront development, pleasure and commercial fishing boat docks and every possible amenity catering to the visitors who stream to this outdoor sport magnet.

In every sense, the pinnacle of this portion of the San Luis Obispo coast is dramatic Morro Rock, highest of a dozen volcanic plugs still visible in the area along Highway 1. At almost 600 feet, the miniature Gibraltar commands the entrance to the bay and was formed by the same volcanic eruptions that produced the intricate stratifications of Montaña de Oro State Park's tide pools. Hikers and beachcombers are free to explore the base of the rock, but its upper cliffs and crags—a sanctuary protecting the nests of peregrine falcons—are off limits to humans.

Exposed at low tide, the vast mudflats around this monolithic boulder on steroids provide a smorgasbord of tiny crustacean snacks for 250 species of shorebird. Outstanding variety and quantity of wildlife combine with the recreational possibilities of dunes and surf to make this area a hit with vacationing Californians. Fine camping opportunities abound at Morro Bay State Park, the site of protected heron rookeries high in eucalyptus groves where the stately birds nest for half the year beginning in January.

While Highway 1 veers slightly inland from Morro Bay until it joins the ocean again south of Solvang, visitors can enjoy the seaside sanctuary of Montaña de Oro State Park by driving south along Pecho Valley Road. Acquired by the State of California in 1965, this undeveloped 8,000-acre setting occupies a former land-grant rancho used for cattle grazing since the end of the 19th century. Coyotes, foxes, deer and mountain lions still roam

---

All You Need to Know About Pismo Clams

The prized pismo clam finds a devoted following in Morro Bay vacationers. An entire culture devoted to clamming in the sand at low tide emphasizes proper digging technique and proper clam fork usage and engages in lively debate over the virtues of steaming vs. grilling the harvested shellfish. Wily veterans will gladly give advice upon any aspect of clamming if approached, but all that one really needs to know is that the obliging pismo clam spends most of its time burrowing less than 6 inches into the sand. Licenses for clamming are required and are available at every roadside attraction. Areas of state beaches where clamming is off limits are all clearly marked.

these chaparral plateaus overlooking the ocean, once the domain of the California grizzly bear.

The grizzly's colorful heritage lives on in nearby Los Osos Valley, where the Portola party of 1769 observed the abundance of the bears in the area. Indeed, when three years later the mission population at Carmel experienced crop failure and imminent starvation, a party led by Monterey presidio commander Pedro Fages was sent to bring back bear meat provisions from the valley. Fages and his men were so successful bagging Los Osos grizzlies that they sent back almost 10,000 pounds of jerked bear meat to the hungry fathers, soldiers and Indian neophytes of the northern Central Coast.

Many years later, dairy farmers arrived and thrived, leaving a legacy of rolling hills pocketed with browsing Bessies that still survives. In 1919, an enterprising developer bought 3,000 lots in what was then El Morro, changed its name to Morro Bay and began aggressively advertising his seaside paradise. Happily, the world failed to answer his call in droves. Consequently, the entire region remains today a haven for the seasonal visitor.

San Luis Obispo

An eclectic blend of frontier ranching, intensive agriculture, Spanish mission memories and Victorian vernacular, this often overlooked community nestles against the velvety Santa Lucia Mountains 10 miles from the ocean. San Luis Obispo is another coastal town that owes its existence to the industrious Father Serra, who established his fifth outpost of Christian civilization here among the Chumash people in 1772. One of the richest missions in the California chain, Mission San Luis Obispo boasted thousands of head of cattle, huge wheat harvests and eight sheep farms on and around its fertile fields.

Twenty-five years later, Serra's successor established the chain's 16th mission— Mission San Miguel Arcángel—to the northeast. The two Franciscan compounds are nicely preserved examples of the world of the fathers and their ranching abilities, an expertise continued today in the best tradition of hell-for-leather land-grant cattlemen.

Almost 100 years ago, the State of California established a technical college in the rambling ranch lands once cultivated by Spanish settlers. Nowadays, San Luis Obispo maintains its lively pulse thanks to the presence of California State Polytechnic College (affectionately known as Cal Poly) and posthippie baby boomers who have settled in and maintained the area's considerable appeal. San Luis also enjoys its share of well-preserved adobes and historical buildings. Clustered together in the heart of the small downtown are the mission and its grassy plaza, the two-story Sauer-Adams Adobe, the region's first Episcopal church, built in 1867, and the circa-1874 Ah Louis Store—a reminder of the strong Chinese presence here during the railroad-building period.

Southern Beach Towns and Dunes

Tiny secluded coves and bluffs covered with Day-Glo-hued ice plant and coreopsis merge southward into small communities at Avila Beach, Pismo Beach, Grover Beach, Oceano, Nipomo and Guadalupe Dunes Beach. Several piers providing top fishing vantage points extend out into the curve of San Luis Obispo Bay. At Avila Beach—one of the prettiest beaches imaginable in what seems like an endless procession of the prettiest beaches imaginable—the sybaritic pleasures of mineral springs bathing can be added to your list of required play.

One giant, 15-mile-long recreation area, the town, beaches and voluptuous sand dunes of Pismo (named for the mighty clam) seem to exist only for life in the great outdoors.

Seclusion and Retreat

The Central Coast of California is as famous for its free-spirited way of thinking as it is for its pictur-esque locations, and visitors flock to the area not only for the sensual, but for the spiritual as well. For the civilization-weary, there's a host of retreats and spiritual centers for those needing to sit back, relax and begin the search for inner peace. **St. Clare's Retreat House** (831-423-8093, 2381 Laurel Glen Rd., Soquel 95073) is a completely silent mountain retreat founded in 1950 by two Franciscan sisters. Now the sprawling commune attracts up to 90 guests each weekend for silent contemplation and specific concerns, such as alcoholism. Catholics run St. Clare's, but the staff is quick to point out that not all guests are Catholic.

The postcard view of the mountain-perched **Mount Madonna Center** (831-847-0406, 445 Summit Rd., Watsonville 95076) adds to the charm of this facility that offers private, individual and group retreat facilities along with weekend and weeklong seminars, such as "A Retreat for Lawyers," "The Energetics of Relationships" and "The Perils and Promises of the Spiritual Path." The center appeals to the body as well as the mind with hiking trails, volleyball, tennis courts, a spa and massage therapists.

The mineral springs and idyllic oak grove setting of the Buddhist-oriented **Tassajara Zen Mountain Center** (Tassajara Springs Rd., Carmel Valley 93924) is a prime spot for meditation or to participate in workshops like "Introduction to Zen" or "Zen/Yoga." The redwood or Japanese-style cabins, in-cluding a private bath and three meals a day, cost around $200 a weekend. For reservations, write to the Zen Center (415-431-3771, 300 Page St., San Francisco 94102).

In addition to providing a laid-back cutting edge to the West Coast's human potential movement, the sybaritic sanctuary **Esalen Institute** (reservations 831-667-3005, general info 831-667-3000, Big Sur 93920) became famous in the consciousness-raising 1960s. Now the "center for experimental education" allows visitors to take courses designed to heal and expand, while settling into the hot springs bath. Lodgings are much sought after—the best route is to sign up for one of Esalen's workshops.

On the site of a former stagecoach and railroad depot, rustic **Sycamore Mineral Springs Resort** (800-234-5831, 805-595-7302, 1215 Avila Beach Dr., Avila Beach 93424), with its own swimming pool and California cuisine restaurant, caters to those seeking spiritual rejuvenation without the help of meditation, religion or workshops. Sycamore Springs offers massage therapy, hot tubs and outdoor pepper- and sulfur-scented, 110-degree mineral waters to ease visitors into the world of relaxation.

Beach rentals and mobile homes cluster together to form the heart of the town of Pismo Beach, an appropriately ramshackle assortment of lodgings and conveniences saved from the mundane by its voluptuous stretch of sand dunes. The mountains of pale soft sand are home to the brown pelican, snowy plover and other curious native fauna.

Increasingly, the dunes comprising the Oceano Dunes Preserve south of Pismo Beach are shattered by the raucous sounds of dune buggies, those unlovable all-terrain vehicles with huge tires that usually turn up just over the next sand dune, where you least expect or want them.

Down the highway near the Santa Barbara County line wait the spectacular and peace-ful—400-foot undulating Guadalupe Dunes. Where today's recreationists play, a maverick group of artists, musicians, hedonists, bums and bohemians who called themselves "Dunites" once roamed. During the 1930s, these alternative lifestylers, for whom clothing was often optional, constructed lean-to huts on the dunes and proceeded to do their thing until the Depression finally reached their piece of coastal paradise. There are few remains of their colorful presence, though for the price of a beer, old-timers will oblige with colorful tall tales.

Even before the Dunites, Hollywood mega-producer Cecil B. DeMille spotted the cinematic potential of the mighty Nipomo dunes and cast them as the Sahara Desert in his epic *The Ten Commandments.* It was a heavenly role.

Lakes, sand dunes, lagoons and coastal canyons converge at Nipomo, which also marks an inland twist in Highway 1. Though the highway swings away from the ocean in order to avoid the sensitive missile testing operations of Vandenberg Air Force Base, there is plenty of coastal access to fishing areas and rocky points teeming with shore life.

Lompoc

Turning right abruptly at Point Conception, the Central Coast heads into the Santa Ynez Mountains at the town of Lompoc, a sprawling land-grant rancho whose latter-day growing fields produce more flower seed than anywhere else in the world. During the summer and autumn, when the brilliantly patterned fields blaze with near-neon color, it's easy to believe that this town produces almost half of the United States' annual flower crop.

Besides flourishing as a bedroom and support community for the Vandenberg military base, Lompoc also tempts inquiring visitors with one of the most complete restorations of any mission complex in the state. Founded in 1787 by Father Lasuen, Mission La Purísima Concepción had been reduced to ruins by neglect and earthquake until the State of California purchased the dilapidated relic in the 1930s and placed it in the capable hands of Civilian Conservation Corps workers to restore to glory. So seamless is the restoration that visitors practically can sample mission life on tours of the gardens, tannery, reservoir, soap factory, residences, workrooms and main church.

Solvang and the Santa Ynez Valley

Continuing on, Hans Christian Andersen would feel right at home in Solvang, a little taste of Denmark located 10 miles from the coast in the prime dairy country of the Santa Ynez Valley. Settled by Danes attracted to pasturelands that mimicked the Old Country, Solvang defined itself with the establishment of Atterdag College in 1911. This began the perpetuation of Danish folk customs, architecture and language that make the town a small, commercial Scandinavian theme park. Though it boasts its own restored Spanish mission and museum—Santa Inés, founded in 1804 as the 19th in the Franciscan chain—Solvang draws the lion's share of its visitors with the allure of half-timbered shops, picturesque Old World windmills, thatched roofs and cobblestone streets. A monument to all things Danish, Solvang is a bright-yet-shameless tourist trap, its citizens even dressing in Old Country garb on weekends and special occasions.

Solvang is also the gateway to several dozen wineries tucked into the transverse hillsides and valleys of the Santa Ynez Mountains. Here the temperate climate produced by sea breezes and coastal fog conspires to yield distinctive handmade wines rapidly attracting the attention of international connoisseurs. The tiny hamlets of Santa Ynez, Ballard, Los Olivos and Buellton beckon with their small-town charms and luxurious lodging and dining possibilities. The scenic hills stretching up to Santa Maria and down to Santa Barbara are literally alive with worthwhile tasting rooms, places where exceptional chardonnays and other fruits of the 10,000 acres of vineyards planted here will reward the inquiring wine buff.

2

TRANSPORTATION
The Freeway & the Right Way

The international airports of San Francisco, San Jose and Los Angeles form gateways to the tourism treasures of California's celebrated Central Coast. Since this region cries out to be seen up close, most visitors take to cars to wander the coastline's spectacular scenery before settling into their destinations. California Highway 1, often called the Pacific Coast Highway or Coast Highway, is the ultimate visual thoroughfare, claiming some of the most enjoyable stretches of blacktop anywhere in the continental United States. Plus, the coastal mountains are laced with connecting scenic highways, many following original stagecoach routes.

Highway 1 is easily connected to California's primary north–south freeway system and its two main arteries: US 101 (which follows the El Camino Real—the 18th-century "King's Highway" laid down by Franciscan fathers and their military protectors) and Interstate 5.

Scoring a perfect 10 on the boring meter, Interstate 5 is far and away the fastest way to get up and down the length of the state. It's also the main route used by truckers, recreational vehicles and lead-footed commuters. Straight, fast and unencumbered by scenic vistas, this freeway is considered dangerous by many locals, some of whom have fallen asleep at the wheel during long, monotonous journeys.

Running much closer to the coast, Highway 101 adds a few curves to slow down the traffic and throws in ample scenery and a smattering of isolated wineries, as well as opportunities for food and lodging along the way. Highway 101 fuses with Highway 1 for the short coastal jaunt between San Luis Obispo and Pismo State Beach.

For those who come to feast their eyes on the incomparable scenery of the Central Coast, there is only one road. However tortuous the turns, steep the cliffs or slow the traffic during summer weekends, Highway 1 is the most beautiful road in the world to many who have driven it. It certainly reigns supreme in California. Often it's a snug fit just to find room enough for two cars to pass each other safely in narrow corridors tunneled out of solid rock. This isn't the route for those in a hurry, but it is the royal road of coastal panoramas.

GETTING TO THE CENTRAL COAST

By Car
Unless you're entering the state from due north or due south, all roads to the Central Coast lead west. Out-of-state visitors immediately encounter the major topographical features of

Bad Road Conditions Hotline

Travelers can call **CalTrans Information Network** (800-427-7623) for recorded details of adverse highway conditions, updated as they change. Don't call for anything else because no humans are around.

this 1,000-mile-long edge of the western United States: the formidable Sierra Nevada Mountains, the broad Central Valley (known as the San Joaquin in the north, the Imperial in the south) and the slender, but persistent, uplift of the Coast Ranges. One way or another, all major interstate highways entering California to the coast take you over these natural landmarks.

Entering the state from Arizona, motorists manage to miss the high Sierra passes by following Interstate 10 through the Mojave Desert to Los Angeles, hooking up there with the Pacific Coast Highway for all points north. Travelers from southern Nevada and Las Vegas will find Interstate 15 the fastest route to the middle-of-nowhere crossroads of Barstow. From that dusty way station, Highway 58 heads through the tail end of the Sierras, over the 4,000-foot Tehachapi Summit, to connect with I-5.

Visitors driving to the coast via northern Nevada will find Interstate 80 a fabulous passage through the Sierras. It travels through the infamous Donner Pass (7,227 feet) before dropping to Sacramento and the San Francisco Bay Area. All of these east–west highways are fast, multilane, state-of-the-art thoroughfares. All intersect with mighty I-5, the widest and fastest, if not prettiest, of them all. For all of its shortcomings, I-5, which begins at the Canadian border and blazes all the way down to Mexico, provides driving convenience in a straight northwest shot through the center of California. From there, visitors can negotiate the coastal pass of their choice to arrive at seaside destinations from Half Moon Bay all the way down to Santa Barbara.

FROM SAN FRANCISCO

It is tempting to approach Santa Cruz and parts south from San Francisco via the corkscrew turns and sweeping vistas of Highway 1. But that would be the farthest thing possible from a shortcut. A better idea—one utilized morning and evening by Central Coast commuters—is to take Highway 280 south from San Francisco (always referred to as "The City" and never as "Frisco" by locals) and then cut across the Coast Ranges via Highway 92, connecting with Highway 1 at Half Moon Bay. A more circuitous route, but one rife with primeval redwood glens, fern canyons and small wineries, is La Honda Road, which exits Highway 280 farther south than Highway 92 and eventually connects with the Coast Highway at Pescadero.

FROM SACRAMENTO

Ringed by freeways, the state capital provides easy access to I-5, the mother of all California highways. From that concrete ribbon, the easiest way to connect with the Monterey Bay is by turning west at Highway 152 near the agricultural mecca of Los Banos and crossing Pacheco Pass (2,772 feet) to Watsonville and coastal Highway 1. Highway 156 branches southward from 152 just after Pacheco Pass and winds through the sleepy mission town of San Juan Bautista before slicing through the artichoke fields of Castroville and joining the Pacific Coast Highway. The *Californio* charms of San Juan Bautista are well worth the diversion.

FROM SAN JOSE

Many roads—some over scenic mountain passes, all of them extremely rural—lead from San Jose and the broad Santa Clara Valley south of San Francisco into various portions of

Santa Cruz and Monterey Counties. One pastoral stretch of Highway 101 skips through Morgan Hill and Gilroy (big-box-stores-meets-plebeian-vineyards) before cutting across acres of cultivated grapes, strawberries and lettuce at Highway 156 to join the ocean at Moss Landing.

From San Jose, Highway 17 (a daredevil's dream that offers 23 miles of nonstop twists and turns) traverses the Santa Cruz Mountains to connect with Highway 1 at Santa Cruz, affording fine views of the Monterey Bay and Loma Prieta Mountain, which lent its name to the massive, psyche-rattling 1989 earthquake. Many savvy drivers take Summit Road near Highway 17's Santa Cruz Mountain midpoint and drop down through the redwoods, gurgling streams and horse ranches along Old San Jose Road before hitting the Coast Highway at Soquel and the coast proper at Capitola.

The quickest way into the heart of California's 19th-century ranching country is Highway 101, which leads south 100 miles from San Francisco to King City and beyond. By turning west on rustic Nacimiento Road, adventurous drivers can tack the ridges and canyons of the Santa Lucia Mountains, winding through classic cattle country and groves of superb Spanish oaks all the way to the southern Big Sur coast. Though slow, challenging going, this gorgeous back road is worth the extra time it takes to navigate.

FROM FRESNO

From Fresno, travelers to the Central Coast journey through the agricultural heartland of California. To avoid spending half a day behind the ubiquitous slow tractors that ply two-lane farm roads, head north on Highway 99, which is densely planted with pink oleander and dotted with diners. Turn off on Highway 152 and follow the white line to the coast.

A more scenic route, albeit an hour slower, begins at Fresno, travels up to Madera via 99 and then shimmies down through the San Joaquin Valley via tiny Highway 145. At I-5, this slender road becomes Highway 198, which leads westward through the rolling hill country of the Diablo Range to Highway 101. It's then a smooth ride through Spanish California vistas to San Luis Obispo.

FROM BAKERSFIELD

There are two favored routes to the Central Coast involved here, one fairly straightforward but boring, the other brimming with eye-popping mountain views and verdant valleys. The scenic route involves heading west on Highway 119, which becomes Highway 166 at Cuyama. From there, 166 traipses through the Cuyama Valley, neatly tucked inside the Sierra Madre Mountains, until encountering Highway 101 at Santa Maria. Heading northward, Highway 101 merges with Highway 1 at Pismo Beach and diverges from at San Luis Obispo. Heading southward, 101 leads to Gaviota, gateway to the beaches of Santa Barbara.

FROM LOS ANGELES

The place where freeways were born, Los Angeles is a driver's dream, or worst nightmare, depending on your mood and blood sugar level. It is possible, however, to locate the threads through this labyrinth and get to the coast. One obvious route is to head toward the ocean until you find Highway 1 at Santa Monica and then work your way north. Another possibility is to take the queen of gridlock, Highway 405, until it bumps into Highway 101 northwest of the metropolitan area. Highway 101 connects with the Pacific Coast Highway at Ventura, just south of Santa Barbara. Then you're on your way to the good stuff on the Central Coast.

Central Coast Access

Listed below are the estimated miles and traveling times to the four major destinations on the Central Coast. It is assumed that drivers will perform bat-out-of-hell duties to get their passengers to the sea or the vineyards as quickly as possible. Consequently, the approximate times listed are a rare hybrid cross-pollination of the leisurely trek with the gas-pounding autoshot (the speed limit is 65 mph).

To Santa Cruz

City	Miles	Hours
Albuquerque	1,090	22:00
Big Sur	75	1:30
Denver	1,380	28:00
Fresno	210	4:15
Half Moon Bay	60	1:15
Las Vegas	580	12:00
Los Angeles	385	8:00
Monterey	45	1:00
Phoenix	770	15:15
Portland	750	14:15
Reno	315	6:30
Sacramento	175	3:45
Salt Lake City	835	16:45
San Diego	500	10:15
San Francisco	80	1:45
San Jose	35	0:45
San Luis Obispo	180	4:00
Santa Ynez	240	5:00
Seattle	915	17:30

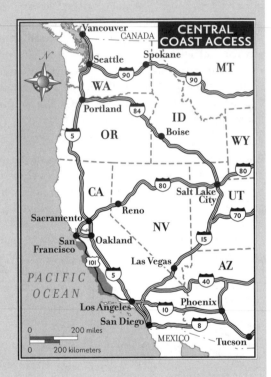

To Monterey

City	Miles	Hours
Albuquerque	1,045	21:00
Big Sur	105	2:15
Denver	1,425	29:00
Fresno	165	3:15
Half Moon Bay	100	2:00
Las Vegas	530	11:00
Los Angeles	340	7:00
Phoenix	725	14:15
Portland	795	15:15
Reno	360	7:30
Sacramento	220	4:30
Salt Lake City	880	17:45
San Diego	455	9:15
San Francisco	125	2:45
San Jose	80	1:45
San Luis Obispo	135	3:00
Santa Cruz	45	1.00
Santa Ynez	195	4:00
Seattle	960	18:30

To San Luis Obispo

City	Miles	Hours
Albuquerque	1,010	20:00
Big Sur	105	2:30
Denver	1,185	23:00
Fresno	120	2:30
Half Moon Bay	240	5:00
Las Vegas	425	8:30
Los Angeles	200	4:00
Monterey	135	3:15
Phoenix	590	11:15
Portland	930	18:15
Reno	495	10:30
Sacramento	360	7:45
Salt Lake City	1,020	20:45
San Diego	320	6:15
San Francisco	260	5:45
San Jose	215	5:00
Santa Cruz	180	4:15
Santa Ynez	62	1:15
Seattle	1,095	21:30

To Santa Ynez Valley

City	Miles	Hours
Albuquerque	872	16:50
Big Sur	172	3:50
Denver	1,122	21:50
Fresno	212	4:20
Half Moon Bay	307	6:20
Las Vegas	352	6:50
Los Angeles	57	1:20
Monterey	212	4:35
Phoenix	442	8:35
Portland	1,002	19:35
Reno	562	11:50
Sacramento	467	9:20
Salt Lake City	782	15:20
San Diego	82	1:35
San Francisco	332	7:05
San Jose	282	6:20
San Luis Obispo	62	1:15
Santa Cruz	252	5:35
Seattle	1,162	23:05

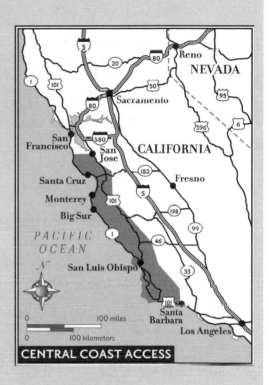

CENTRAL COAST ACCESS

By Bus

Any out-of-state or interstate bus traveler headed for the Central Coast must pass through either of two major hubs, Los Angeles or San Francisco, and connect to buses headed for their destinations. Here are the surest, fastest and most scenic options available on **Greyhound** (www.greyhound.com, 800-231-2222), the only line serving the entire state.

Greyhound travels between San Francisco and Santa Cruz four times daily in each direction ($11 one-way) and five times daily to and from Monterey ($18), stopping at San Francisco International Airport en route. From Monterey on the coast, buses veer inland to Salinas, another important hub. Buses leave San Francisco four times daily on their inland Los Angeles runs, reaching San Luis Obispo ($43) on the coast at mid-journey and, thereafter, following Highway 1 to Santa Barbara ($34—we know: It's cheaper to get to Santa Barbara than to San Luis Obispo, but we don't decide what's fair in fares).

From Los Angeles, Greyhound schedules 10 buses daily to Santa Barbara ($12) and 6 buses on its San Francisco route that hit San Luis Obispo ($27) before heading inland. The LA–San Francisco line also makes four stops at Monterey ($40) and six in Santa Cruz ($44).

Call Greyhound's San Francisco depot (415-495-1569) or Los Angeles station (213-629-8401) for exact departure and arrival times.

By Plane

Although most travelers will make their way to the Central Coast by car, a good portion will arrive via plane. Listed below are the state's major international airports and the regional fields that have connecting express flights to the primary hubs, as well as the airlines that serve the hubs.

United offers daily nonstop flights from both San Francisco and Los Angeles to Monterey Peninsula Airport and out again. **American** schedules nonstop daily hops between Los Angeles and Monterey. **American West** flies nonstop daily between Monterey and Phoenix. Daily flights to and from San Francisco, San Jose, Los Angeles and Phoenix lift off and touch down on United and American's San Luis Obispo tarmacs.

You might also call your local FAA flight service station for up-to-the-hour weather information regarding your destination.

Los Angeles International Airport (LAX) www.lawa.org, 310-646-5252, 1 World Way, Los Angeles 90045. Aer Lingus, Aero California, Aeroflot, Aerolitoral, Aeromexico, Air Canada, Air China, Air France, Air Jamaica, Air New Zealand, Air Pacific, Air Tahiti Nui, Airtrans, Alaska, All Nippon, American Airlines, American Eagle, American Trans Air, America West, Asiana, Aviacsa, Avianca, British Airways, Cathay Pacific, Champion Air, China Airlines, China Eastern, China Southern, Continental, Copa, Corsair International, Delta Airlines, El Al Israel, EVA Air, Frontier, Hawaiian, HMY Air, Horizon, Japan, KLM Royal Dutch, Korean, LACSA Air, Lan Chile, LTU International, Lufthansa, Malaysia, Mexicana, Miami Air, Midwest Express, Northwest, Omni Air, Philippine, Quantas, Singapore, Song, Southwest, Spirit, SQ Air, Sun Country, Swiss International, TACA International, Thai Airways, United, United Express, USAir, Varig Brazilian, Virgin Atlantic, VG Air, World,

Monterey Peninsula Airport (MRY) www.montereyairport.com, 831-648-7000, Hwy. 68 & Olmstead Road, Monterey 93940. American Airlines, American Eagle, America West, SkyWest, United, United Express.

Oakland International Airport (OAK) www.oaklandairport.com, 510-563-3300, 1 Airport Dr., Oakland 94621. Alaska, Aloha, American, America West Express, Continental, Delta, Jet Blue, Mexicana, Southwest, SunTrips, United.

San Francisco International Airport (SFO) www.flysfo.com, 650-21-5000, P.O. Box 8097, San Francisco 94128. Aeroflot, Air Canada, Air China, Air France, Airtrans, American, American West Express, ANA, Asiana, ATA, British Airways, Cathay Pacific, China Airlines, Continental, Delta, Eva, Frontier, Hawaiian, Horizon, Japan, KLM, Korean, LACSA, Lufthansa, Mexicana, Midwest, Northwest, Philippine, Singapore, TACA, Ted, United, United Express, USAirways, Virgin.

San Jose International Airport (SJC) www.sjc.org, 408-501-7600, 1732 N. 1st St., San Jose 95112. Alaska, American, ATA, America West Express, Continental, Delta, Frontier, Horizon Air, Mexicana, Northwest, Southwest, United, United Express.

San Luis Obispo County Regional Airport (SBP) www.sloairport.com, 805-781-5205, 901 Airport Dr., San Luis Obispo 93401. American Eagle, America West Express, United Express.

Santa Barbara Municipal Airport (SBA) www.ci.santa-barbara.ca.us/departments/airport, 805-967-7111, 500 Fowler Rd., Goleta 93117. American Eagle, America West Express, Delta, Delta Express, United Express.

Santa Maria Public Airport (SMX) www.santamariaairport.com, 805-922-1726, 3217 Terminal Dr., Santa Maria 93455. United Express.

By Rail

Getting railroaded can be a pleasant thing. **Amtrak**'s (www.amtrak.com, 800-872-7245) Seattle–Los-Angeles Coast Starlight makes a daily run up and down the California coast with stops in Oakland, San Jose, Salinas, Paso Robles, San Luis Obispo, Santa Maria and Santa Barbara. For armchair travel, the Starlight can't be beat. The Oakland–Santa-Barbara stretch costs $50 one-way, but the scenery that travelers enjoy from the train's windows is priceless. Crashing surf, smooth beaches, wetlands and sloughs, as well as rugged mountain peaks and canyons, glide by while you relax and appreciate it all.

Between San Luis Obispo and Santa Barbara, the Starlight threads its way through sand dunes and lagoons and provides breath-stopping vistas of Morro Rock and its neighboring volcanic peaks, plus glimpses of hard-to-get-to pristine coastal stretches. Visitors stopping in the city of San Luis Obispo can connect at the station by bus for tours of the stately Hearst Castle. Continuing south, the train follows the inside curve of the sand dunes stretching between Pismo Beach and Santa Maria, the gateway to the Santa Ynez Valley.

The Pacific Surfliner shuttles between Los Angeles and Paso Robles wine country (with stops in Santa Barbara, Lompoc, Santa Maria, Grover Beach and San Luis Obispo) seven times a day ($26 one-way). The bilevel cars feature panoramic windows, spacious dining areas and surfboard racks. Every seat sports a laptop computer outlet.

Central Coast Town Access

Here are the approximate driving distances from the Central Coast's four main destinations to selected towns and cities of interest within the distinct regions. Travel time may vary depending on weather, road conditions, the traveler's pace (the speed limit is 65 mph) and how many stops one makes along the way. The listings are the vehicular equivalent of a no-pause, straight-as-an-arrow forced march, but we encourage everyone to slow down and enjoy the scenery.

From Santa Cruz

City	Miles	Hours
Half Moon Bay	57	1:00
Pescadero	40	0:48
Davenport	10	0:14
Bonny Doon	15	0:18
Boulder Creek	13	0:16
Los Gatos	20	0:24
Capitola/Soquel	4	0:05
Rio Del Mar/Aptos	7	0:08
San Juan Bautista	34	0:41
Moss Landing	23	0:28
Monterey/Pacific Grove	45	0:55
Pebble Beach	53	1:05
Carmel	50	1:10
Big Sur	75	1:30
Lucia	100	2:00
San Simeon	140	2:48
Cambria	148	2:58
Cayucos	162	3:14
Morro Bay	168	3:22
Los Osos	173	3:28
San Luis Obispo	181	3:37
Avila Beach	191	3:49
Pismo Beach	193	3:52
Oceano	194	3:55
Santa Maria	225	4:15
Lompoc	231	4:37
Santa Ynez Valley	243	4:52
Santa Barbara/Goleta	286	5:43

From Monterey

City	Miles	Time
Half Moon Bay	101	2:04
Pescadero	84	1:41
Davenport	58	1:10
Bonny Doon	61	1:13
Boulder Creek	59	1:11
Los Gatos	66	1:19
Santa Cruz	46	0:55
Capitola/Soquel	42	0:50
Rio Del Mar/Aptos	39	0:47
San Juan Bautista	31	0:37
Moss Landing	23	0:28
Pebble Beach	7	0:08
Carmel	4	0:05
Big Sur	29	0:35
Lucia	55	1:06
San Simeon	94	1:53
Cambria	102	2:02
Cayucos	116	2:19
Morro Bay	122	2:26
Los Osos	128	2:34
San Luis Obispo	135	2:42
Avila Beach	145	2:54
Pismo Beach	147	2:56
Oceano	149	3:00
Santa Maria	166	3:30
Lompoc	185	3:43
Santa Ynez Valley	197	3:56
Santa Barbara/Goleta	242	4:50

From San Luis Obispo			From Santa Ynez Valley		
City	**Miles**	**Time**	**City**	**Miles**	**Time**
Half Moon Bay	239	4:47	Half Moon Bay	345	6:54
Pescadero	222	4:26	Pescadero	328	6:34
Davenport	194	3:53	Davenport	300	6:00
Bonny Doon	197	3:56	Bonny Doon	303	6:04
Boulder Creek	195	3:54	Boulder Creek	301	6:01
Los Gatos	202	4:02	Los Gatos	308	6:10
Santa Cruz	182	3:38	Santa Cruz	288	5:46
Capitola/Soquel	178	3:34	Capitola/Soquel	285	5:43
Rio Del Mar/Aptos	175	3:30	Rio Del Mar/Aptos	281	5:37
San Juan Bautista	167	3:20	San Juan Bautista	273	5:28
Moss Landing	159	3:11	Moss Landing	265	5:18
Monterey/Pacific Grove	136	2:43	Monterey/Pacific Grove	240	4:48
Pebble Beach	133	2:40	Pebble Beach	241	4:49
Carmel	132	2:38	Carmel	238	4:46
Big Sur	107	2:08	Big Sur	213	4:16
Lucia	81	1:37	Lucia	187	3:44
San Simeon	41	0:49	San Simeon	147	2:56
Cambria	33	0:40	Cambria	139	2:47
Cayucos	19	0:23	Cayucos	125	2:35
Morro Bay	13	0:16	Morro Bay	118	2:30
Los Osos	7	0:08	Los Osos	112	2:23
Avila Beach	9	0:11	San Luis Obispo	105	2:15
Pismo Beach	12	0:14	Avila Beach	101	2:01
Oceano	14	0:18	Pismo Beach	94	1:53
Santa Maria	40	0:45	Oceano	92	1:50
Lompoc	50	1:00	Santa Maria	60	1:20
Santa Ynez Valley	62	1:14	Lompoc	50	1:00
Santa Barbara/Goleta	106	2:87	Santa Barbara/Goleta	38	0:40

GETTING AROUND THE CENTRAL COAST

By Car

Highway 1 is the majestic lifeline caressing the Central Coast and connecting all points surveyed in this book. Stretching the length of California, it links the major cities of San Diego, Los Angeles and San Francisco and feeds into the freeways of the interior via scenic mountain back roads.

By Rental Car

Although car culture originated elsewhere, it hit its stride in California. Gifted with pliant, scenic highways, the Central Coast offers plenty of wheels-to-rent options. Here are listings of the top reliable agencies in the region:

Advantage www.arac.com, 800-777-5500.

Alamo www.alamo.com, 800-462-5266.

Avis www.avis.com, 800-831-2847.

Budget www.budget.com, 800-527-0700.

Dollar www.dollar.com, 800-800-4000.

Enterprise www.enterprise.com, 800-325-8007.

Hertz www.hertz.com, 800-654-3131.

National www.nationalcar.com, 800-227-7368.

Payless www.planetpayless.com, 800-729-5377.

Rent-A-Wreck www.rent-a-wreck.com, 800-944-7501.

Thrifty www.thrifty.com, 800-847-4389.

U-Save www.usave.net, 800-272-8728.

Automobile Club Hotlines

Members can call these 24-hour emergency telephone numbers for immediate road service and assistance: **AAA—California State Automobile Association** (800-400-4222), **National Automobile Club** (800-622-2130).

None
None

3

SANTA CRUZ

The Eden at World's End

Crisscrossed by the infamous San Andreas Fault, Santa Cruz has enjoyed its occasional date with destiny since the mid-1700s when Spanish conquistadores and padres marched up from Mexico to see what riches New Spain might hold. Redwood forests that had stood since the pre-Christian era, splendid seashores teeming with marine life and tide pools and a climate straight from the Mediterranean greeted the newcomers.

Between the establishment of a mission and a military garrison, the tiny community of Holy Cross (Santa Cruz) was off to a rousing start, even before Yankee captains of industry arrived in the early 1800s to take advantage of the natural riches—and, naturally, to get rich themselves. Those who might have passed through the area on their way to the Gold Rush ended up staying to romance the incomparable scenery. Once the Golden Spike was driven in Utah in 1869 linking railroads across the continent, settlers rushed to Santa Cruz County from all over the country.

Glowing magazine accounts touted the glories of taking the salt air and—thanks to entrepreneur Fred Swanton—a fabulous Brighton-style resort casino, dance palace and amusement park sprang up at the water's edge near the turn of the 20th century.

Even today, Santa Cruzans are justly famed for, and proud of, their recreational opportunities. Surfing rules along the superb coastline, where world-class surfers come to test the heaving winter waves or to cruise the long, slow summer swells. It was at Steamer Lane, just north of the Santa Cruz Municipal Wharf, that two Hawaiian princes caught a few waves in the late 1880s and began a craze for this potentially dangerous sport. Surfing still attracts youthful adventurers from far and near—sometimes from as near as the University of California–Santa Cruz, which established its ninth campus here 30 years ago.

Like all university towns, Santa Cruz prides itself on more than its fair share of diversity. Multiculturism plays itself out in a continuous world beat of music, fashion and food, while the UCSC campus inflects the sophisticated accents and tastes of the small community, and the famed Cabrillo Music Festival and Shakespeare Santa Cruz conclave draws globe-trotting culturati to the area every summer.

The redwood communities up in the mountains, overlooking the magnificent Monterey Bay, have long attracted artists, writers, composers and movie stars. Alfred Hitchcock summered here, Spencer Tracy played polo on the hillside below the present-day university and composer Lou Harrison works his musical magic from a studio south of town. Glassblowers, ceramists, filmmakers and computer animators all have found out that they can enjoy creative freedom—yet still have access to a far-flung market—from this little spot of Eden.

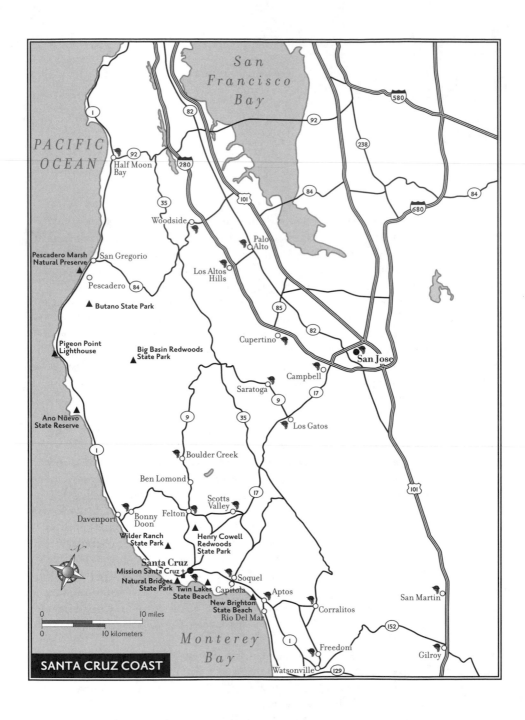

PACIFIC OCEAN

San Francisco Bay

Half Moon Bay

Woodside

Palo Alto

Los Altos Hills

Pescadero Marsh Natural Preserve

San Gregorio

Pescadero

Butano State Park

Cupertino

San Jose

Pigeon Point Lighthouse

Big Basin Redwoods State Park

Campbell

Saratoga

Los Gatos

Ano Nuevo State Reserve

Boulder Creek

Ben Lomond

Scotts Valley

Davenport

Bonny Doon

Felton

Wilder Ranch State Park

Henry Cowell Redwoods State Park

Santa Cruz

Mission Santa Cruz

Natural Bridges State Park

Twin Lakes State Beach

Capitola

Soquel

Aptos

New Brighton State Beach

Rio Del Mar

San Martin

Corralitos

Freedom

Gilroy

Monterey Bay

Watsonville

0   10 miles

0   10 kilometers

SANTA CRUZ COAST

Time flies when you're having fun in Santa Cruz, long recognized as the playground of the Central Coast.
Bob Hill

Today, during the summer and fall, the seaside blooms with holiday travelers anxious to unwind on the series of clean, white beaches and to try out their sense of adventure on the oldest wooden roller coaster in the world. The proximity to Silicon Valley has made the area a bedroom community and recreational outlet for new millionaires. Yet it's the quiet cliffs that gather into gold at sunset, the primeval silence of the magnificent old redwoods and the small-town camaraderie that cast the most enduring spell.

Santa Cruz is infused by a laid-back sense of play. Nothing is taken too seriously with weather this good. It's an idyllic setting for sipping one of the many fine locally made wines—the Santa Cruz Mountains appellation creates a variety of award-winning chardonnays, merlots and zinfandels—while sampling some of the fresh seafood caught from the bay.

Bussed by morning fog in the summer, as well as some serious rains in the winter, Santa Cruz bathes its visitors and residents alike in that famous Mediterranean sunshine seven months of the year.

The only caveat about this Central Coast community just 70 miles south of San Francisco: It's very, very difficult to leave. Just ask any local. Chances are that he or she is among the huge transplant community who just passed through town . . . and never left.

LODGING

No visit to this seaside playground would be complete without an overnight near the beach, where accommodations present panoramic views of the blue Pacific and the sensation of waves ushering you into the soundest night's sleep. Along the shore and in the redwood forests are many carefully appointed B&Bs that also offer an eclectic blend of architectural styles.

Credit cards are abbreviated as follows:
AE: American Express
  D: Discover Card
MC: MasterCard
  V: Visa

The area code for all Santa Cruz County lodgings is **831**. It is **650** for those north of the county line in Pescadero and Half Moon Bay.

APTOS
APPLE LANE INN
www.applelaneinn.com
Innkeepers: Trent & Diane Wong
800-649-8988, 831-475-6868
6265 Soquel Dr., Aptos 95003
Price: $100–$200, includes full breakfast
Credit Cards: AE, D, MC, V
Children: With limitations
Pets: With limitations
Handicap Access: Yes

Located at the end of a country lane between the villages of Soquel and Aptos and a few minutes from the ocean, this graciously restored Victorian farmhouse offers warm hospitality in the form of five cozy rooms—all with private baths—decorated with vibrant period antiques, fabrics and lighting fixtures. A true stunner is the basement Wine Cellar Room, a burgundy-and-French-vanilla-toned hideaway with stainedglass windows, private garden entrance, tiled-floors, dining table, refrigerator, sitting area and wine bottle racks. The mood is pure country charm, and the peace and quiet of the surrounding hills belie this inn's location as central to the area's top beaches and sights. Afternoon refreshments are served in the lovely sitting room, which boasts a player piano and an adjoining library, but guests have been known to take their drinks out to the pretty white gazebo that offers sumptuous views of the surrounding orchards and meadows. Breakfast is a gourmet affair, featuring food fresh from local growers' fields and pens.

Some frequently available items include buckwheat crêpe fruit bowl with honey lime yogurt dressing, egg-in-the-hole with mango maple lacquered bacon, slow-roasted herbed turkey hash with poached quail eggs, and crème brûlée French toast with maple syrup crème anglaise. Games are available in the sitting room, but most guests slip outside for horseshoes and croquet, or a tour of the Victorian rose garden.

✪ SAND ROCK FARM B&B
www.sandrockfarm.com
kris@sandrockfarm.com
Innkeepers: Kris & Lynn Sheehan
831-688-8005, fax 831-688-8025
6901 Freedom Blvd., Aptos
Price: $185–$225, includes full breakfast
Credit Cards: MC, V
Children: Yes
Pets: No
Handicap Access: No

This historic Arts & Crafts lovely, sitting amid a beautiful swath of redwoods and flower gardens, remains a pristinely quiet retreat while being still close enough to fine culture, dining and recreation opportunities to provide guests the high life if they so desire. Owner Kris Sheehan is a B&B pro, having won her stripes in the tough Napa/Sonoma market, and she has not only rebuilt the 1910 mansion to its former glory but also added some modern conveniences and comforting touches like up-to-date showers and Jacuzzis in some rooms. Daughter and business partner Lynn is a world-class chef who was groomed by some of the Bay Area's greatest culinary lights. Her afternoon wine and fruit and savory snack spread and full deluxe breakfasts are appointment meals not to be missed. The charming two-story home features five large antiques-splashed rooms, all with great views, private baths, polished hard wood floors and comfy feather beds, and some with original wallpaper. A spacious dining room, cozy reading porch and inviting sitting rooms reflect memories of everyone's favorite grandmother's house. The great staff also makes every moment here a casual, relaxing holiday. This is the perfect escape for couples or solitary souls looking for peace and quiet but high-level appointments and exquisite food. A hot tub also invites late-night intimacy beneath trees and stars on the back porch. Just down the hill, a lovely forest meadow awaits the next wedding ceremony, and a unique open-air barrel aging cellar (circa 1887) serves as an outdoor dining area for special events or celebrations. Even locals periodically book rooms here for a bit of R&R.

CAPITOLA
INN AT DEPOT HILL
www.innatdepothill.com
depothill@innsbythesea.com
Innkeeper: Claire DeVos
800-572-2632, 831-462-3376,
fax 831-462-3697
250 Monterey Ave., Capitola 95010
Price: $185–$385, includes full breakfast
Credit Cards: AE, D, MC, V
Children: With limitations
Pets: No
Handicap Access: Yes

Crowning a knoll within a few minutes' stroll of the sparkling beach and downtown Capitola Village, this stalwart 1901 railway station has been lavishly transformed into a spiffy B&B. In keeping with the architectural features of this former depot, the elegant appointments showcase an Orient Express–style theme. Each room bears the name of a glamorous destination and appropriately sophisticated appointments selected by a San Francisco interior decorator. The rooms are shamelessly sybaritic, like the sophisticated Paris Suite, whose black-and-white marble bathroom features a spacious two-person shower and French doors leading to the outdoor garden. The sky-blue Delft Room offers a sumptuous feather bed draped in linen and lace, plus a sitting room and Jacuzzi tub for two in its private garden. The Railroad Baron's Room—ablaze with deep red velvet upholstery, damask wall treatment and a dramatic domed ceiling—re-creates the feel of a Victorian Pullman coach and provides its own enormous soaking tub under a skylight that opens to the stars. In sunny weather, breakfast is taken on an outdoor brick patio whose sheltering shrubbery walls and musical fountain create the illusion of being in a Mediterranean villa, rather than two blocks from one of the area's most popular playgrounds. At the end of the day, guests are treated to a selection of fine wines and hors d'oeuvres laid out on a marble sideboard in the beautiful public rooms, which are filled with antique furniture, a vintage baby grand piano and a wall of well-stocked bookshelves running to the very top of the 16-foot ceilings. A luscious dessert is served each evening with coffee. The skillful innkeepers and staff minister to your every need, and all 12 suites come with telephones, private baths, fireplaces, fresh flowers, TVs, VCRs, stereo systems, fax/modem connections, bathrobes and hair dryers. Off-street parking—always scarce in this bustling beach town—is included in the price of your room.

DAVENPORT
DAVENPORT INN
www.davenportinn.com
inn@swanton.com
Innkeepers: Bruce & Marcia McDougal
800-870-1817, 831-425-1818,
fax 831-423-1160
31 Davenport Ave., Davenport 95017
Price: $115–$155, includes complimentary continental breakfast or full breakfast with discount
Credit Cards: AE, D, MC, V
Children: With limitations
Pets: No
Handicap Access: Yes

At the heart of this picturesque village, a former whaling port just north of Santa Cruz, is the eclectic New Davenport Cash Store, a tile-floored, high-ceilinged restaurant with full bar, plus a fine international and local arts emporium that also offers fine B&B facilities. The 12 rooms with private baths occupy two distinctive locations, one a charming, former turn-of-the-20th-century bathhouse attractively appointed with antiques, the other offering bracing ocean vistas on the floor above the Cash Store. The upstairs rooms have been decorated with ethnic treasures gathered from the global travels of artist-owners Bruce and Marcia McDougal, and the wraparound porch provides prime viewing of the migrating gray whales that cruise just offshore from January to May. A bountiful continental breakfast features delectable pastries from the Cash Store's bakery. The downstairs restaurant's sensuous breakfasts are the stuff of local legend. Cove beaches beckon just across Hwy. 1.

HALF MOON BAY
BEACH HOUSE
www.beach-house.com
Innkeeper: Kevin Scanlon
800-315-9366, 650-712-0220,
fax 650-712-0693
4100 N. Cabrillo Hwy., Half Moon Bay 94109
Price: $165–$395, includes continental breakfast
Credit Cards: AE, D, MC, V
Children: Yes
Pets: No
Handicap Access: Yes

All of the 54 suites that comprise the seven-year-old Beach House sit perched on a seaside bluff that affords unobstructed panoramic views of the rugged Central Coast. The loft studios are enriched with natural sunlight, and each provides a private balcony, separate bedroom and living areas, wood-burning fireplace, wet bar,

refrigerator, goose down comforter, organic cotton robes, free local phone calls, complimentary high-speed Internet access, cable TV and CD stereo. A full range of spa treatments awaits, just a phone call away, and the heated pool is inviting regardless of the weather. Plenty of nearby outdoor activities can be enjoyed by the hearty, but cultural and dining and wine options also await the sophisticate. Though relatively new, this refined inn and its well-trained staff have wowed seasoned travelers with both its graciousness and attention to fine detail.

CYPRESS INN
www.cypressinn.com
cypressinn@innsbythesea.com
Innkeeper: Mark Colman
800-832-3224, 650-726-6002,
fax 650-712-0380
407 Mirada Rd., Half Moon Bay 94019
Price: $160–$385, includes full breakfast
Credit Cards: AE, D, MC, V
Children: With limitations
Pets: No
Handicap Access: Yes

Romantic, relaxing and nestled on the sprawling sands of the Pacific Ocean shore, this converted beach house located 2 miles up the coast from downtown Half Moon Bay offers plush comfort and attentive service in a beautiful setting. Eight rooms in the

Well-lighted rooms with a view are featured at the Cypress Inn in Half Moon Bay. Cypress Inn

main building, six new oceanfront rooms across the street and four elaborate suites in the back beach house are all decorated in early California and contemporary motifs. All rooms boast fireplaces, private patios and quite possibly the world's most decadent feather beds, and a few rooms come complete with in-room Jacuzzis. The innkeeper keeps a roaring fire going and offers a constant flow of coffees, teas and hot chocolate in the main room throughout the day. A spread of wine, sparkling cider and hors d'oeuvres appears at sunset and indulgent homemade desserts and coffee at night. A full breakfast can be taken in the dining area or in your room, where you can savor the sight, smell and sound of the rolling ocean while you dine. Staff members are more than happy to recommend sightseeing excursions and to make restaurant reservations.

LANDIS SHORES

www.landisshores.com
luxury@landisshores.com
Innkeepers: Ken & Ellen Landis
650 726 6642, fax 650-726-6644
211 Mirada Rd., Half Moon Bay 94019
Price: $195–$345
Credit Cards: AE, D, MC, V
Children: With limitations
Pets: No
Handicap Access: Yes

Of all the newly constructed B&Bs popping up and down the Central Coast, this is definitely the most modern and the nicest. Despite its proximity to the Miramar Restaurant and Bar, the area around the Landis Shores gets barely any traffic. Only strollers, bicyclists and the occasional raccoon use the roadway separating the inn from the shoreline. The foods served in the morning and during the wine-and-appetizer spread at sunset are tasty. Ken is a fine chef, and Ellen actually works as a sommelier at the Ritz-Carlton up the coast. All

eight rooms are decorated in the manner of—and given names of—different wine districts from around the world, and they have excellent vistas of sand and sea. When night falls outside, the glittering harbor lights and soothing coo of the foghorns make this a very romantic and peaceful retreat. All rooms also sport private decks, luxurious robes, marble bathrooms, enveloping Sealy Posturepedic mattresses, radiant heated stone floors, high-tech tubs, refrigerators, spiffy entertainment centers and gas fireplaces.

Enjoying the sea from a deck is one of the many pleasures at Landis Shores Oceanfront Inn, among the most modern and most romantic of the newer inns in Half Moon Bay. Landis Shores Oceanfront Inn

MILL ROSE INN

www.millroseinn.com
info@millroseinn.com
Innkeepers: Eve & Terry Baldwin
800-900-7673, 650-726-8750,
fax 650-726-3031
615 Mill St., Half Moon Bay 94019

Price: $190–$360, includes full breakfast
Credit Cards: AE, D, MC, V
Children: With limitations
Pets: No
Handicap Access: Limited

Sheer indulgence in a vibrant garden setting is the motif of this wonderful retreat, which features four rooms and two suites with TV/VCR, well-stocked refrigerators and amenities like liqueurs, fruit basket, coffeemaker and hair dryer. Five of the rooms boast fireplaces, and all are decorated with English antiques, as well as down comforters and feather beds. All rooms have private entrances, and the front organic garden pays colorful tribute to the horticultural expertise of the innkeepers, who've filled this blooming sanctuary with hundreds of varieties of fragrant roses, poppies, irises, delphiniums and lilies. A garden in back showcases yet more flowers, an inviting brick patio and a romantic gazebo outfitted with a whirlpool spa. A champagne breakfast can be brought to your room, or you can indulge in multicourse morning offerings, including hot chocolate, fresh fruit drinks, soufflés and hot dishes. Wine and light appetizers are provided at sundown. This B&B just seems to do everything right. The place has class, and nothing seems strained or a stretch. The historic village of Half Moon Bay, in which the inn is set, offers fine dining and shopping possibilities, plus splendid coastal scenery and beaches a short drive away.

OLD THYME INN
www.oldthymeinn.com
innkeeper@oldthymeinn.com
Innkeepers: Rick & Kathy Ellis
800-720-4277, 650-726-1616,
fax 650-726-6394
779 Main St., Half Moon Bay 94019
Price: $130–$320, includes full breakfast
Credit Cards: AE, D, MC, V
Children: With limitations

Pets: No
Handicap Access: No

The innkeepers at this restored 1899 Queen Anne Victorian have infused their California village establishment with Old World hospitality and a sweet-scented garden, whose 80 varieties of herbs invariably end up perfuming teas and freshly made dishes at the inn's complimentary full breakfast. All seven rooms are decorated and wallpapered in turn-of-the-20th-century style and offer private baths. Three rooms have fireplaces, and three boast whirlpool tubs big enough for two. One detached room has its own private garden entrance and is

Old Thyme Inn offers Victorian comfort perfumed by a lush herb garden. Stan Cacitti

equipped for a romantic stay with fireplace, oversized whirlpool tub, TV/VCR and plush four-poster canopy bed. Evening champagne, wine and sherry are all the more relaxing taken in front of the main room's blazing fireplace. The innkeepers are happy to provide local sightseeing tips and restaurant recommendations.

✪ RITZ-CARLTON HALF MOON BAY

www.ritzcarlton.com/resorts/half_moon_bay
Innkeeper: Paul Racchford
650-712-7000, fax 650-712-7070
1 Miramontes Point Rd., Half Moon Bay 94019
Price: $265–$900
Credit Cards: AE D, MC, V
Children: Yes
Pets: No
Handicap Access: Yes

Sometimes, charming just won't do. Often, intimate doesn't have the right charge. Periodically, cozy just falls flat. There are times—not often, mind you—when the wonderful inns and bed & breakfast lodging options just aren't quite enough. Sometimes you feel like "puttin' on the Ritz." Fortunately, for those special times, a Ritz-Carlton resort has sprouted on a ruggedly beautiful piece of coast just south of Half Moon Bay that will meet the splendor and indulgence of the most luxe fantasy. The panoramic views from most of the 261 rooms will make you glow with a sense of having "arrived." From the covered Olympic swimming pool and lighted tennis courts to the glories of the two golf courses that lie in the midst of the Ritz-Carlton's verdant grounds, active elegance is the theme. The gorgeous Greco-Roman-inspired spa affords every special body care treatment imaginable (try the pumpkin wrap), and both Navio restaurant and the Conservatory's light-meal menu deliver healthy world-class cuisine. Thoroughly trained staff members hum like bees in a

When the sky's the limit, the Ritz-Carlton at Half Moon Bay offers every imaginable amenity, from its two golf courses to its spa facilities to unbelievably spectacular views. Ritz-Carlton

well-coordinated dance as they go about making the honey of hospitality for an international roster of guests. Everything sparkles and glows in the soft embrace of the evening fog swirling around the hot-tub gazebo and the fire rings set around the grounds for starry cocktails. For a very nominal surcharge, you can indulge in all the superb offerings of the Club level, a hotel within a hotel. The entire fifth floor has been given over to 52 special rooms and a comfortable lounge (with five gourmet spreads a day) as part of the Club program, and at least once, Central Coast travelers should spent a night in this wonderland of luxury.

ZABALLA HOUSE

www.zaballahouse.net
innkeeper@zaballahouse.net
Innkeeper: Sue Ball

Zaballa House offers overnight lodgings in one of the oldest houses in Half Moon Bay. Stan Cacitti

650-726-9123, fax 650-726-3921
324 Main St., Half Moon Bay 94019
Price: $115–$275, includes full breakfast
Credit Cards: MC, V
Children: Yes
Pets: Yes
Handicap Access: Yes

Welcoming visitors to the historic district of this seaside village is what claims to be Half Moon Bay's oldest structure, built by Estanislao Zaballa in the mid-1800s and today refurbished into a cheerful inn with five rooms in an annex, eight guest rooms in the main house and three additional suites outside. Appointed with antiques and boasting 10-foot ceilings, the rooms are equipped with private bathrooms, some with old-fashioned claw-foot soaking tubs and others with luxuriously modern whirlpool tubs built for two. Comforts extend to pre-dinner sherry and wine in the parlor, and breakfast is bountifully family-style, including hot breads and muffins, fresh juices, fruit and cereals, all taken in the friendly kitchen. The inn is surrounded by a courtyard and offers ample shopping and dining opportunities all along tiny, straight-from-a-Western-movie Main Street. Your family pet is even welcome.

PESCADERO
✪ COSTANOA

www.costanoa.com
Innkeeper: Laura Moran
877-262-7848, 650-879-1100
2001 Rossi Rd. at Hwy. 1, Pescadero 94060
Price: $95–$350, includes full breakfast
Credit Cards: AE, D, MC, V
Children: Yes
Pets: No
Handicap Access: Yes

When every turn affords a million-dollar ocean or forest view and all staff members look and dress like surfers or hikers or X-sport enthusiasts, adventuresome travel lovers know they have come to the right place. The unforced enthusiasm and warmth of the employees indicates that everyone on salary is happy to be there and you should be, too. A lodge and camp tucked into the hills and valleys of a pristine stretch of land on Highway 1, an hour south of San Francisco, Costanoa is a well-developed and yet barely developed wonderland. Its undisturbed shores and rolling countryside sit adjacent to four state parks, a wildlife reserve and 30,000 acres of trails, so it isn't surprising that visitors feel that they've been dropped magically into a dream world of flora and fauna unmatched on the Central Coast. Outdoor activity options arranged and led by resort staff include hiking, biking, kayaking, windsurfing, horseback riding and tide pooling, while short excursions to redwood forests, waterfalls, marshes, secret picnic spots and historic stagecoach-stop villages are a short hop away. The accommodations, from the tidy tent villages (with their heated beds) to the top drawer lodge suites, are appointed with deluxe touches that mean you aren't roughing it, even if you think you are. The slate fireplaces, walk-in glass showers, large sunken tubs, top-of-the-line cosmetic freebies, and prints of local wildlife on the walls fit the back-to-nature theme of the place without surrendering one creature comfort of the pampered lifestyle. A complimentary full breakfast is available in the large General Store, which offers healthy and very tasty lunch and dinner selections every day (the dining room is open to the general public). Snacks and drinks, including premium local wine and beer, are available with minimum markup. Sauna, steam room and spa treatments are part of the course here, but just lounging about with a good book is a popular pursuit as well. There's a kids' playground and outdoor barbecue area for family gatherings, but Costanoa is such a special romantic retreat that we recommend you dump your offspring with friends or relatives and selfishly share this spot with no one but your special loved one.

PESCADERO CREEK INN

www.pescaderocreekinn.com
Innkeepers: Ken & Penny Donnelly
888-307-1898, 650-879-1898
393 Stage Rd., Pescadero 94060
Price: $155–$195, includes full breakfast
Credit Cards: AE, D, MC, V
Children: With limitations
Pets: No
Handicap Access: No

A few years ago, former commercial insurance agent Ken Donnelly fell in love with a dilapidated building sitting on Pescadero Creek, and he was so moved by its possibilities that he chucked his career and undertook a decade-long building project that turned the dilapidated 1898 home into a sterling example of the innkeeping arts. Where others saw a dump, he saw the soul of a B&B. The three rooms inside and the garden cottage beyond the verdant gardens and large porch are love letters to fine craftsmanship and demonstrate a refined eye for the selection of antiques. The color schemes are invigorating, and period details throughout the house are spot-on perfect. The communal living area is both inviting and formal, its giant fireplace warming both the room's overstuffed chairs and the nearby dining room's great table. A full breakfast of organic offerings and an afternoon wine-and-cheese hour specializing in the organic foodstuffs and wines from the immediate area are worth the price of admission on their own. With Duarte's just down the street, myriad biking trails crisscrossing the countryside and cottage industries throwing open their doors up and down the main drag, the Pescadero Creek Inn, while a bit off the beaten path, is a short detour that will not be regretted.

SANTA CRUZ
BABBLING BROOK
BED & BREAKFAST INN

www.babblingbrookinn.com
babblingbrook@innsbythesea.com
Innkeeper: Claire DeVos
800-866-1131, 831-427-2437,
fax 831-427-2457

Not far from downtown Santa Cruz, the Babbling Brook B&B is a convenient and homey pied-à-terre for the discerning traveler. Babbling Brook Inn

1025 Laurel St., Santa Cruz 95060
Price: $165–$295, includes full breakfast
Credit Cards: AE, D, MC, V
Children: With limitations
Pets: No
Handicap Access: Yes

A great getaway boasting a central location in between residential and downtown Santa Cruz, the Babbling Brook is charm itself. The innkeeper has made each of the 13 temptingly decorated guest rooms a secluded oasis. The rooms are clustered around a central, multilevel cedar building whose stone foundation dates from the late 19th century, when the property was a gristmill. The soft sounds of the creek flowing through the property's lovely gardens serenade each room. All rooms have fireplaces, private baths, telephones and TVs and are decorated in a French country theme. Many offer private decks, and the Honeymoon Suite's deck even overlooks a waterfall. The Artist's Retreat at the highest point of the inn provides a full view of the garden and brook, plus a large deck and recessed hot tub. An elegant full breakfast is served in the charming living room, and a blazing, sitting room fireplace forms the center-

piece of early-evening wine-and-cheese tastings. The gardens and the white gazebo are a favorite wedding site.

CASABLANCA INN

www.casablanca-santacruz.com
casabeach@aol.com
Innkeepers: Glyn & Ray Luttrell
800-644-1570, 831-423-1570, fax 831-423-0235
101 Main St. (at Beach St.), Santa Cruz 95060
Price: $95–$375
Credit Cards: AE, D, MC, V
Children: Yes
Pets: No
Handicap Access: Yes

This red-tile-roofed, former seaside retreat of a San Francisco judge (circa

The view from Casablanca Inn overlooks Santa Cruz's main beach, pier and nearby Boardwalk. Buz Bezore

1920) has long been one of Santa Cruz's most distinctive landmarks. Located just across the street from the popular Santa Cruz Main Beach, colorful Boardwalk and vintage Cocoanut Grove Ballroom, the Casablanca offers bountiful ocean views and the soothing sounds of the waves to lull guests to sleep. Over the years, innkeepers Glyn and Ray Luttrell have combed antiques emporia for the attractive, unpretentious furnishings of each distinctive room. Some rooms retain the original bathroom tilework and fixtures, and spacious Room 22 sports a fireplace, four-poster bed and private terrace overlooking seacoast sites. The Luttrells purchased the rest of Judge Cerf's estate in 1997, giving the inn six more suites in the original ballroom, carriage house and servants' quarters. Essentially a small hotel ringed with a satellite of attractive motel units, the multi-level, Mediterranean-style main building hangs on the hillside just above its own Casablanca Restaurant, long regarded as one of the best in town, where contemporary seafood specialties and California cuisine are freshly prepared with an eye to innovative seasonings and elegant presentation. The restaurant's astonishing wine list—the most extensive in the area—regularly wins *Wine Spectator* awards for comprehensiveness, and it's a great place to sample locally made vintages. The dining room is utterly romantic, offering unparalleled views of the waterfront and a justifiably popular Sunday brunch.

CHAMINADE AT SANTA CRUZ
www.chaminade.com
chaminadeinfo@benchmarkmanagement
.com
Innkeeper: Tom O'Shea
800-283-6569, 831-475-5600,
fax 831-465-3415
1 Chaminade Ln., Santa Cruz 95065
Price: $159–$359, includes complimentary

continental breakfast or full breakfast
discount
Credit Cards: AE, D, MC, V
Children: Yes
Pets: No
Handicap Access: Yes

Located on the site of a former private school, this contemporary conference center, equipped with state-of-the-art lodgings, surrounds a lovely pink neo-deco warren of meeting rooms, terraces and dining rooms, set high on a eucalyptus-scented hill overlooking the Santa Cruz Yacht Harbor and Monterey Bay. Handsome overnight rooms, all with private patios opening on to a surrounding 300-acre forest of towering oaks, are equipped with full amenities. The grounds include outdoor Jacuzzis, a swimming pool, lighted tennis courts and hiking trails through the redwoods. Both the Sunset Dining Room and the plush Linwood's cocktail lounge offer spectacular sunset views and are just a stroll down landscaped paths, but the fully equipped 14,000 square-foot spa and fitness center—pampering body and beauty care, aerobics room, basketball court, weight room, sauna and enormous whirlpool—is this retreat's secret weapon. A few minutes from beaches and charming coastal villages, Chaminade feels like it's a million miles away from the madding crowd.

CHATEAU VICTORIAN BED & BREAKFAST INN
www.chateauvictorian.com
Innkeeper: Alice June
831-458-9458
118 1st St., Santa Cruz 95060
Price: $125–$155, includes continental breakfast
Credit Cards: MC, V
Children: No
Pets: No
Handicap Access: No

Located near the sea, on a hillside overlooking Santa Cruz's harbor, the Chateau Victorian responds appropriately with a nautical motif in this country-rustic yet opulent guest room. Chateau Victorian Inn

A true "painted lady" located only a block from Santa Cruz's main beach and famous seaside amusement park, this turn-of-the-20th-century Victorian was coated with dazzling berry hues and opened as a charming B&B in the early 1980s. The hospitable innkeeper has lovingly decorated the seven private rooms with fine antique armoires, lush upholstery and bed linens, and each room boasts its own bath, queen-sized bed and fireplace. The inn, located on a hillside affording an ocean view, cleverly conceals a secluded patio garden and several decks where sunset can be enjoyed over afternoon wine and cheese. The location is absolutely ideal for those seeking the salt-air action of the nearby Boardwalk, with its historic Giant Dipper roller coaster, and the inviting municipal wharf. Breakfast involves an expanded continental menu of fine coffees and teas, fruit, croissants and pastries, and wine and other refreshments are served in the late afternoon. Many fine restaurants and shops are within short walking distance.

CLIFF CREST BED & BREAKFAST INN

www.cliffcrestinn.com
innkpr@cliffcrestinn.com
Innkeepers: Adriana Gehriger Gil & Constantin Gehriger
831-427-2609, 831-252-1057, fax 831-427-2710
407 Cliff St., Santa Cruz 95060
Price: $175–$245, includes full breakfast
Credit Cards: AE, D, MC, V
Children: With limitations
Pets: No
Handicap Access: Yes

The beautiful interiors of this lovely Queen Anne Victorian—a historic landmark home built by California's Lieutenant Governor William Jeter in 1887—immediately cast a spell on visitors. Period details like Oriental rugs and antique furniture blend with the small mansion's abundant stained and beveled glass and intricate built-in woodwork. Only two blocks from the Santa Cruz Main Beach, each of the inn's five rooms offers a private bath, TV and CD player, and two rooms sport fireplaces. The charming Pineapple Room is named for its queen-sized four-poster bed, whose bed-posts feature an artfully carved pineapple design. The spacious Empire Room offers 19th-century ambiance, with 12-foot ceilings, king-sized canopy bed, double armoire and a soothing view of the garden through lace-covered windows. Most guests are further charmed by the lush estate gardens, created by John McLaren, the man who designed San Francisco's Golden Gate Park. At sunset, regional wines and cheeses are offered in the antiques-filled parlor. Breakfast in the garden solarium involves multiple courses that can include fresh juices and fruits, muffins, coffee cake, egg dishes, quiche, French toast, pancakes and sausage.

DARLING HOUSE

www.darlinghouse.com
ddarling@darlinghouse.com
Innkeepers: Darrell & Karen Darling
800-458-1958, 831-458-1958
314 W. Cliff Dr., Santa Cruz 95060

Price: $95–$260, includes continental breakfast
Credit Cards: AE, D, MC, V
Children: Yes
Pets: No
Handicap Access: Limited

The beveled-glass windows and red-tiled roofs of this distinguished Mission Revival mansion overlook a spectacular view of the Santa Cruz coast, municipal wharf and Monterey Bay beyond. Built as a private home in 1910 by revered California architect William Weeks, this gorgeous home—graced with a hardwood interior, Tiffany lamps and tile-decorated fireplace—is situated at the foot of Santa Cruz's scenic West Cliff Drive. Each of its eight rooms (two with private baths) has been attractively appointed with period antiques by innkeepers Darrell and Karen Darling, who preside over hearty continental breakfasts each morning in the ornate dining and sitting rooms. Sherry is served in the late afternoons, and savvy guests quickly learn that the expansive, ocean-view veranda is the top spot to take in the sights of sailboats and surfers dotting the sunsets. Each guest room is appealing, but especially note-worthy is the large second-floor chamber

The Darling House on West Cliff Drive in Santa Cruz was designed by celebrated architect William Weeks.
Christina Waters

In contrast to the many Victorian B&Bs in Santa Cruz, the Pleasure Point Inn offers a funky modern charm.
Pleasure Point Inn

overlooking the ocean, offering its own fireplace and a resident telescope for viewing the abundant marine life of the Monterey Bay. One of the shared bathrooms boasts an enormous, vintage clawfoot "bordello" tub, great for extended soaking for two. A small cottage nestling in the mansion's back gardens sleeps four, and an outdoor hot tub spa offers a pampering soak after a day on the beach.

PLEASURE POINT INN

www.pleasurepointinn.com
inquiries@pleasurepointinn.com
Innkeepers: Tara Forrest & Jill Johnson
831-475-4657
2-3665 E. Cliff Dr., Santa Cruz 95062
Price: $198–$265, includes continental breakfast
Credit Cards: MC, V

Children: No
Pets: No
Handicap Access: Yes

This thoroughly modern upscale inn offers the gracious accoutrements of the traditional deluxe bed & breakfast, but with amenities more closely in line with the great boutique hotels of Europe. Here the savvy traveler will find not only digital cable, DMX music, private dedicated phone lines and digital safe, but also polished hardwood floors, an elegant enveloping bed, gas fireplace, tasty expanded continental breakfast, a relaxed knowledgeable staff and some of the best views of the Santa Cruz coast from both your room and the rooftop viewing and hot-tub area. While sleek and trendy, the place also has lots of funky personality, which it draws from its grand location. The Pleasure Point coast right across the street, and the world-class surfing spots running its mile length provide hours of recreational activities and plenty of visual delights. In addition, the classy custom-made furnishings, tongue-and-groove oak work and heated Mediterranean tile floors—as well as the spacious luminous bathrooms with their large Jacuzzi tubs—whisper a siren's song to all those seeking care and comfort and a great escape with a special someone. By the way: The innkeepers can arrange private surfing lessons for one or two during your stay (go ahead, catch a wave).

SEA & SAND INN

www.santacruzmotels.com/sea_and_sand
.html
Innkeeper: Lisa King
831-427-3400, fax 831-466-9882
201 W. Cliff Dr., Santa Cruz 95060
Price: $99–$359, includes continental
breakfast
Credit Cards: AE, MC, V
Children: Yes
Pets: No
Handicap Access: Yes

Twenty cozy rooms and suites, some with hot tubs, all prettily decorated with comforters and upholstery in colors echoing the blue Pacific Ocean, are tucked into what looks like a long, white cottage situated on a bluff overlooking the white sandy beach just north of the Santa Cruz Boardwalk. A tiny lawn dotted with chaise lounges fronts the private, ocean-view expanse of this centrally located facility, whose every room boasts stunning coastal vistas. A favorite romantic getaway for locals and their visiting guests, the inn provides a continental breakfast, late-afternoon wine-and-cheese soirees and a terrific location for strolling West Cliff Drive, watching the world-class surfing action at Lighthouse Point and taking in beaching

and shopping. Sea & Sand also boasts newly remodeled cottages, all featuring fireplaces and private patios with hot tubs overlooking the bay.

DINING

Dining Price Code

The price range below includes the cost of a single dinner that includes an entrée, appetizer or dessert, and glass of wine or beer. Tax and gratuities are not included. Note: Smoking is not allowed in any restaurant or eatery in the state of California.

Inexpensive	Up to $15
Moderate	$15–$30
Expensive	$30–$50
Very Expensive	$50 or more

Credit cards are abbreviated as follows:
  AE: American Express
   D: Discover Card
MC: MasterCard
   V: Visa

The area code for all Santa Cruz County restaurants is **831**. It is **650** for those north of the county line in Pescadero and Half Moon Bay.

APTOS

✪ BITTERSWEET BISTRO

www.bittersweetbistro.com
831-662-9799
787 Rio Del Mar Blvd., Aptos
Open: Dinner nightly
Price: Expensive
Cuisine: California Continental
Full Bar: Yes
Reservations: Recommended for weekends
Credit Cards: AE, MC, V
Handicap Access: Yes

Bittersweet may not be an intimate bistro, but it preserves bistro attitudes toward robust, direct flavors via beautiful contemporary dishes. Banquette and booth seating provide a cozy arena for people-watching, but the menu of utterly fresh, expertly prepared California bistro fare is the top draw. Starters involve the spicy grilled prawn "martini" and delectable carpaccio of beef tenderloin over immaculate mesclun greens topped with fruity extra-virgin olive oil, Locatelli cheese, capers and diced sweet red onions. Main courses include classic rib-eye steaks grilled with a shallot merlot sauce, sand dabs and roasted chicken, thyme-crusted mahimahi and grilled wild sturgeon—all served with exceptional vegetables, highlighted by the house signature scalloped potatoes. Chef-owner Tom Vinolus, trained in intricate pastries, creates a warm apple bread pudding in which a cascade of diced apples springs forth from a tier of bread, moist and fresh from the oak fire—so sculptural, especially topped with a scoop of vanilla ice cream, another scoop of barely sweetened whipped cream and festooned everywhere with cookie topknots and powdered sugar. Destination bread pudding, make no mistake. Also not to be missed are the Winemaker Wednesday food-and-wine soirees, where world-class appetizers and small pizzas are created by Chef Tom to the delight of the local crowds who fork over $25 for great evenings in the annals of happy-hour food and beverage deals. And next door to the mother ship bistro resides the quaint, inviting Bittersweet Express, where many of the same dishes served in the formal dining room are available at reduced prices, either to go or to eat in the casual dining area.

CAFE SPARROW

831-688-6238
8042 Soquel Dr., Aptos
Open: Lunch Mon.–Sat., dinner nightly, brunch Sun.
Price: Moderate to Expensive
Cuisine: Bistro

Full Bar: No
Reservations: Recommended for dinner
Credit Cards: MC, V
Handicap Access: Yes.

Updated Continental classics find a lovely home in this small, prettily decorated café. Very popular with residents of the village and beach communities surrounding Aptos, Cafe Sparrow turns gourmet sandwiches and vibrant salads into memorable experiences. The dinner entrées are an eclectic assortment of Continental variations and include an excellent peppered Angus filet mignon, rich New Zealand venison in a brandied cherry demiglaze, as well as bistro fare like grilled chicken and breaded oysters with a lemon-caper crème. The pretty desserts and an award-winning wine list heighten the luster of this charming eatery.

MANUEL'S

831-688-4848
261 Center St., Aptos
Open: Lunch & dinner daily
Price: Inexpensive
Cuisine: Mexican
Full Bar: Yes
Reservations: Recommended for dinner
Credit Cards: MC, V
Handicap Access: Limited

Talented artist Manuel Santana would be a local legend even if he hadn't founded this vivacious Mexican restaurant overlooking Seacliff State Beach. But he did, and for 30 years the rich and the humble have given thanks over bottles of ice-cold Corona, tangy margaritas and plates of rich refried beans. Always crowded and alive with a convivial group of regulars who all seem to have grown up together, Manuel's feels like a culinary fiesta, with artwork on the darkwood walls and plenty of south-of-the-border tilework accenting the decor. Menu highlights include the soothing chiles rellenos, fruity enchiladas tropicales and

Hearty drinks and a convivial atmosphere are as important as the spicy dishes at Manuel's.
George Sakkestad

snapper smothered in chile and sour cream sauce. The guacamole and hot sauce are addictive, as are the house salads topped with guacamole, tomato slices, garbanzo beans and a very vinegary vinaigrette. Innovation isn't the point—Mexican comfort food with lively ambiance is.

PALAPAS

www.palapasrestaurant.com
831-662-9000
21 Seascape Village, Aptos
Open: Lunch & dinner daily
Price: Moderate
Cuisine: Mexican/seafood
Full Bar: Yes
Reservations: Recommended on weekends
Credit Cards: AE, D, MC, V
Handicap Access: Yes

The feel of a contemporary hacienda with a view of the Pacific has settled into this attractive, skylighted dining room in the middle of an upscale resort community. With enormous booths, lots of tilework and boldly colored textile decorating, the beautiful dining room serves skilled and imaginative Mexican seafood specialties. The entire Pacific Rim, from Mexico to Asia, fills the menu with dazzling fresh seafood sided with salsas and tropical produce. Not to be missed are the butterflied gulf prawns with guajilla sauce. Also wonderful are succulent grilled chicken tostadas topped with world-class guacamole and house made tomatillo sauce. The fresh fish entrées are sumptuous, even the sashimi is perfection, but the menu also includes some interesting vegetarian selections, like enchiladas filled with marinated tofu (and it's terrific), guacamole or creamy cheese. The attractive full bar pours a terrific selection of aged tequilas, and the whole place feels like a quick trip to the Mexican Riviera.

CAPITOLA/SOQUEL
PARADISE SUSHI

www.paradisesushi.com
831-464-3328
200 Monterey Ave., Capitola
Open: Lunch & dinner daily
Price: Moderate
Cuisine: Japanese
Full Bar: No
Reservations: No
Credit Cards: AE, MC, V
Handicap Access: Yes

Encircled in curved picture windows that offer an ocean view, Paradise Sushi sits high above Capitola Village and treats its clientele to an oceanful of Pacific Rim possibilities. The sleek sushi bar and alcove rooms make for a handsome Japanese dining experience. Green textile banners punctuate the pale-wood room dividers, and a psychedelic aquarium creates happy vibes in the center of the main dining room. Chefs create both classic and experimental sushi, catering to traditionalist and

One of Capitola Village's gastronomic lures is Paradise Sushi and its rock-and-roll sushi offerings. George Sakkestad

West Coast tastes. It's sushi with an edge—tempura soft-shell crab rolled with tobiko and cilantro or a spicy salmon, avocado, cilantro and nopalito cactus combination. Pair it with sake or a Sapporo draft, and this lunch or dinner could be paradise found.

SHADOWBROOK

www.shadowbrook-capitola.com
831-475-1511
1750 Wharf Rd., Capitola
Open: Dinner nightly, brunch Sun.
Price: Expensive
Cuisine: American
Full Bar: Yes
Reservations: Recommended
Credit Cards: AE, D, MC, V
Handicap Access: Yes

Proof that even long-standing restaurant legends can maintain their reputations, the Shadowbrook is not only de rigueur for out-of-town visitors and special occasions, it's also on the cognoscenti's short list of consistently fine dining experiences. This rustically elegant sprawl of multilevel stone and wood-beamed dining rooms turns out expert American cuisine served by an unerring wait staff. From the full bar upstairs, guests wander down past the central stone fireplace to a favorite private booth or round oak table overlooking Soquel Creek below. Fresh seafoods are a specialty, but many swear by the stellar prime rib served with horseradish-laced sour cream. Sunday brunches out on the patio involve inventive seafood Benedict, a grilled chicken on penne pasta and a marvelous Italian-style roast beef sandwich piled high with sweet red peppers and Fontina cheese. Ride the charming funicular down from street level to the restaurant below, and then stroll back through waterfalls and lush gardens. It's all shamelessly romantic.

✪ THEO'S

www.theosrestaurant.com
831-462-3657
3101 N. Main St., Soquel
Open: Dinner Tues.–Sat.
Price: Expensive
Cuisine: New American
Full Bar: No
Reservations: Recommended
Credit Cards: AE, MC, V
Handicap Access: Yes

Arguably one of the finest dining rooms on the Central Coast, Theo's offers the sort of deeply satisfying experience that only skill, quality and devotion can achieve. Touring these splendid, green flowery mazes takes the quality of the dining experience to the next level. Chef Nicci Tripp's menu teams American classics like roast duck on a creamy rich confit with nouvelle offerings, such as a barely seared, sashimi-grade Japanese yellowtail resting in a bed of cucumber "noodles," and all are always orchestrated beautifully, flecked with herbs and seductively matched with edible flowers. Try the supernaturally tender lamb with micro-chopped ratatouille, or wild boar tenderloin slices fanned out over a bed of sensational Yukon gold gnocchi (the tender baby spinach wilted over the boar and a spectacular sauce of roasted figs infused with pan juices and vanilla display a willingness to work with flavors outside their usual context). The wine list is extensive, and the desserts—like custard parfait perfumed with rosewater, surrounded by a pool of raspberries and a knob of whipped cream, and the deep dish of summer figs, blueberries and peaches, all topped with a voluptuous late-harvest zinfandel sabayon are sinfully satisfying. An aesthetic dining experience.

DAVENPORT
✪ LA CABAÑA TAUQERIA
831-425-7742
500 Hwy. 1, Davenport
Open: Daily 9–9
Price: Inexpensive
Cuisine: Mexican
Full Bar: No
Reservations: No
Credit Cards: No
Handicap Access: Yes

On a perfect morning, cobalt skies and sparkling waves seem to gravitate up the coast to the sleepy village of Davenport. You have already hiked the cliffs and beaches accompanied by crowds of Queen Anne's lace and soaring pelicans. But your appetite is at full throttle. What to do? Well, head over to the sheltered courtyard next to the tiniest post office on Hwy. 1 and stake out a table by the calla lilies. La Cabaña, beloved of German tourists, Italian bikers and buffed surfers, is about to make you a lunch offer you can't refuse.

La Cabaña looks like a tourist joint (a sign even proudly proclaims WELCOME TRAVELERS!), but in fact it's an authentic full-service Mexican restaurant whose menu runs the gamut from chicken mole to myriad burritos and tacos. Prominent among these is the rare regional specialty, the artichoke taco. Here you are sitting in the open air, gazing at the ocean, surrounded by what? By artichoke fields. Finally, you are afforded the opportunity of actually taking a little bite of the land itself. Grilled artichokes, tender and pliant, are tucked into freshly warmed corn tortillas and then all topped with a combo of muy picante salsa fresca, diced cilantro and a delicious tomatillo sauce. No froufrou sour cream, no designer garnish—simply the real deal, with a wedge of lime. You might be sitting at the beach in Zihuatanejo, the flavors are that convincing. Just as good are the nopalito (prickly pear cactus) tacos, in which succulent shreds of the delicious cactus (tastes like a ripe green bean) are treated to the same salsa and tomatillo topping and presented in a double wrap of soft, warm tortillas. La Cabaña has all manner of other goodies, from quesadillas, crisp tacos, nachos, chiles rellenos and tamales to full-on seafood dinners involving camarones mojo de ajo (madre de Díos!) and charbroiled red snapper. But the wise among us can't get past those emerald tacos of artichoke and nopalito. Oh, by the way: They cost $1.79 each.

FELTON
LA BRUSCHETTA
831-335-3337
5447 Hwy 9, Felton
Open: Breakfast Sat.-Sun, lunch Mon-Fri, dinner nightly
Price: Moderate
Cuisine: Sicilian
Full Bar: No
Reservations: Recommended for large parties
Credit Cards: MC, V
Handicap Access: Yes

Authentic Sicilian cookery joins up with Mediterranean classics at this gloriously warm and friendly dining room in the heart of the redwoods. The cooks burst forth in torrents of Italian as they work their passionate magic in view of admiring locals. Magnificent authentic pasta sauces—from spicy arrabiatta to voluptuous sun-dried tomato ragus—add to a menu adorned by intriguingly seasoned meat classics, such as the *filetto al basilico* as well as organic vegetable side dishes and salads. The house made ravioli are celestial, as is the special antipasti featuring grilled porcini and eggplant. Many dishes showcase the exotic cross-cultural flavor influences that make Sicily a mecca for epicureans, such as the ravioli stuffing of pine nuts and rosemary, or agnolotti filled with sausage and almonds. The desserts are seductive enough to ruin any diet, especially the creamy tiramisu. Charmingly neo-hippie ambience and a warm wait staff make any visit worthwhile.

Half Moon Bay
✪ CAFÉ GIBRALTAR
www.cafegibraltar.com
650-560-9039
425 Palma Ave., El Granada
Open: Dinner nightly
Price: Moderate
Cuisine: World fusion
Full Bar: No
Reservations: Recommended
Credit Cards: AE, MC, V
Handicap Access: Yes

Chef-owner Jose Luis Ugalde, his wife/business partner Liam and the very happy. savvy and chef-supporting staff make this open-kitchen trip through the Trans-Mediterranean a glorious adventure. Located a couple of miles north of Half Moon Bay proper, the restaurant is well worth the short hop up the coast. The servers are well versed on what the kitchen turns out and give impeccable descriptions of every dish. And what dishes they are. The chef's deep, thoughtful takes on rustic home cooking are a humdinger hybrid of African, Turkish and Caribbean cuisines. Don't pass on the amber, plum-glazed scallops with Moroccan sausage, which here are understatedly labeled coquilles St. Jacques, but in fact are so much more. The gnocchi con fungi in a spiced tomato and onion broth brings tears to the eyes of gastronomes. And the crusty, sumac-coated grilled octopus and calamari salad is redolent of lemon, mint and peppercress. But the confit of Dungeness crab and heirloom tomatoes could be the star of the evening: Slow-cooked to perfection with artichokes and roasted garlic, it could not be any fresher (after all, the ingredients were plucked from sea and field just that morning).

CETRELLA BISTRO AND CAFÉ
www.cetrella.com
650-726-4090
845 Main St., Half Moon Bay
Open: Dinner nightly, brunch Sun.
Price: Expensive
Cuisine: Californian
Full Bar: Yes
Reservations: Recommended
Credit Cards: AE, MC, V
Handicap Access: Yes

Long recognized by the serious food press as one of the best dining establishments on the Central Coast, Cetrella whips up great regional dishes from the abundance of local farms and ranches. Not to be missed is the Catalonian shellfish stew packed with Dungeness crab, mussels, shrimp and tomatoes in an almond-saffron broth. The grilled fresh catches of the day are always pristinely and inventively prepared, and the way the cooking crew treats the bounty of orchards and fields brings smiles to the eyes of greengrocers everywhere. The fritto misto of artichokes and royal trumpet mushrooms is as earthy and delicious and

Cetrella bustles with a sophisticated clientele, evidence of its rank as one of the finest restaurants on the Central Coast of California. Cetrella Bistor and Café

simple a dish as one can get these days and proves that one should not mess too much with Mother Nature. The Sunday morning spread is unusual but always tastebud-tickling. From the seviche of sweet Maine shrimp and mango, through the Provençal-style wood-oven-baked eggs and caramelized fennel soup, to the house-made fruit sorbets and Spanish-influenced crème brûlée, this is not your grandmother's Sunday brunch. The elegant bar provides a jazzy music retreat most weekend nights.

MEZZA LUNA
650-712-9223
3048 Cabrillo Hwy., Half Moon Bay
Open: Dinner daily
Price: Moderate
Cuisine: Italian
Full Bar: No
Reservations: Recommended
Credit Cards: MC, V
Handicap Access: Yes

A comfortable, raucous trattoria, Mezza Luna is a little slice of Italy located up the coast from downtown Half Moon Bay. Bustling, boisterous and complete with charming Italian waiters who've perfected the art of gracious service, it's an obvious local favorite. It offers an extensive array of fresh pastas, seafood and chicken and a wine list featuring both California wines and Italian varietals. The bruschetta is a classic, with slices of tomatoes and basil leaves smothering the crusty bread. The seafood linguine—a stewy combination of enormous mussels, clams, prawns and linguine—is a seafood lover's treat. Finish with a strong espresso and biscotti dipped in dark or white chocolate.

PASTA MOON
www.pastamoon.com
650-726-5125
315 Main St., Half Moon Bay
Open: Dinner daily
Price: Moderate
Cuisine: Californian/Mediterranean
Full Bar: No
Reservations: Recommended

Credit Cards: AE, MC, V
Handicap Access: Yes

Innovative and made-before-your-eyes pasta dishes are the signature of this smart, cafe-style eatery located at the end of Half Moon Bay's tiny Main Street. Service is accommodating and knowledgeable, and the tiny tables are located close enough together to allow plenty of menu comparisons with fellow diners, trattoria-style. Their creative salads involve intriguing herb blends and baby lettuces, but the traditional Caesar salad is also first-rate. But the homemade sauces and sausages, ripe tomatoes and ethereal pastas that make up the main creations are truly stunning. An entrée cioppino, packed with shellfish, could feed three hungry adults. A selective wine list—long on bright, young Italians and vintage Californians—complements the sassy cuisine, and the art-lined ambiance is vibrant. Terrific value for the money.

✪ ROGUE CHEFS
www.roguechefs.com
650-712-2000
Open: Lunch & dinner Mon.–Sat.
Price: Moderate
Cuisine: Eclectic Californian
Full Bar: No
Reservations: No
Credit Cards: MC, V
Handicap Access: Yes

Chef Kevin Koebel and some pals couldn't keep their jobs in the dining biz and also follow their muses, so they concocted this unusual outpost of creativity and impishness. This is as much a cooking school, wine bar, art salon and to-go deli as a restaurant: One look in the cases at the foods prepared on any particular day immediately communicates to hungry patrons just exactly what is going on here. The kitchen has only one rule: No recipes. Everything has to be guided by the ingredients at hand and the inspiration of the moment, be it pastry, appetizer or entrée, relying always on the training and wisdom the chefs have accumulated over the years. The results are staggering, from the meat and fish dishes to the sushi, vegetarian and fruit creations. Stop by anytime from noon till dusk and see—and taste—what's cooking. You won't be disappointed.

SUSHI MAIN STREET
www.sushimainst.com
650-726-6336
315 Main St., Half Moon Bay
Open: Lunch Mon.–Sat., dinner nightly
Price: Moderate
Cuisine: Sushi
Full Bar: No
Reservations: For four or more
Credit Cards: MC, V
Handicap Access: Yes

An elegantly ornate Japanese restaurant, Sushi Main Street pays as much attention to the details of its decor as it does to its food. With dark, cool chocolate ribbon slate gilded walls, whimsical tables, comfortable banquettes with very forgiving pads and a low-sprawling sushi bar, this small restaurant presents an extensive roster of sushi and tempura. Creative rolls, such as the hot tuna roll with tempura tuna, spicy sauce, avocado and daikon sprouts, and the sashimi and nigiri are expertly prepared. The menu also offers a wide array of designer sakes and a selection of delicious clay-pot soup dishes, such as the warm seafood nabeyaki (scallops, mussels, shrimp, clams, snapper, mushrooms and udon). The staff is knowledgeable and accommodating.

PESCADERO
DUARTE'S TAVERN
www.duartestavern.com
650-879-0464
202 Stage Rd., Pescadero
Open: Breakfast, lunch & dinner daily
Price: Inexpensive
Cuisine: Classic Central Coast

Full Bar: Yes
Reservations: Recommended on weekends
Credit Cards: AE, MC, V
Handicap Access: Yes

A local legend for over 50 years, this dark-wood roadhouse (and its classical bar straight out of a Hollywood Western) is justly popular with locals who can't get enough of the flavorful house cuisine. There's an outstanding abalone sandwich and a bevy of intensely flavored soups highlighted by the legendary artichoke soup made from the ubiquitous agricultural staple that flourishes along this stretch of coast. If you eat at the counter, you can watch cooks preparing your order of simple luxuries like fresh crab sandwiches, flavor-running steaks and some of the finest omelets in the land. Among the major listing of fresh berry pies, the locally grown olallieberry (a variety of blackberry) version is absolutely unforgettable. A regional treasure.

SANTA CRUZ
CARNIGLIA'S
www.carnigliasseafood.com
831-458-3600
Santa Cruz Municipal Wharf
Open: Lunch & dinner daily
Price: Expensive
Cuisine: Seafood/Italian
Full Bar: Yes
Reservations: Recommended
Credit Cards: AE, D, MC, V
Handicap Access: Yes

From its wharf perch, Carniglia's provides uninterrupted vistas of sand, sea and mountains through panoramic picture windows. Its kitchen matches the location by delivering equally picturesque plates of beautifully presented pastas and Mediterranean classics. Noteworthy are the good-looking spinach salad bordered with dollops of Harley Farms goat cheese and choice bits of crisp pancetta, and orders of calamari fritti big enough to fuel a soccer team. The tender strips of calamari are lightly floured, pan-seared, and then tossed with lots of grated Parmesan and a confetti of astringent fennel and red bell peppers. Especially tasty entrées include rack of lamb grilled with a sauce of prosciutto, white wine and cipollini onions, and linguine and prawns bathed in an arrabbiata sauce enhanced by Dungeness crab and porcini mushrooms. Both are terrific. If you have a designated driver, go ahead and succumb to the Carniglia's listing of grappas, the refined white lightning that can take the chill off in under five seconds. If that's not the direction your party is headed in, then enjoy the bracing espressos and tasty desserts.

CASABLANCA RESTAURANT
www.casablanca-santacruz.com
831-426-9063
101 Main St., Santa Cruz
Open: Dinner nightly, Sun. brunch
Price: Expensive
Cuisine: Californian
Full Bar: Yes
Reservations: Recommended
Credit Cards: AE, D, MC, V
Handicap Access: Yes

"Romantic" is the word for this fine dining room set in a 1920s Mediterranean estate-turned-inn perched on the hillside over the main Santa Cruz beach and wharf. Lots of gleaming brass, candlelight and enormous picture windows frame a captivating view of the water, all the prettier at night. Enhanced by an award-winning list of over 400 wines, Casablanca has creative fun with contemporary California cuisine. Superior fresh seafoods, rack of lamb with couscous and fig confit and the house signature filet mignon with a demiglaze of forest mushrooms are standards. An appetizer of roasted ancho chile stuffed with cheese and served with a red bell pepper sauce is wonderful, as is a grilled ahi steak on a bed of couscous ringed with a complex, shocking-pink dried-cherry mole and topped with a magenta gratin of pickled daikon. The house salad of baby butterhead lettuce and Dijon vinaigrette is a standout, and all of the fresh fish ideas work brilliantly, especially a linguine with prawns, sea scallops and clams in lemon thyme and fresh tomato cream. Elegant desserts feature special treats like pumpkin cheesecake dotted with whole walnuts and fresh mint and served in a pool of gossamer nutmeg crème anglaise, or a warm walnut-studded chocolate tart topped with a scoop of vanilla ice cream (which tastes like an X-rated brownie), as well as the seasonal purity of fresh local berries. The Sunday brunch, by reason of both the beachfront view and the superlative egg specialties served with lots of champagne, is justly popular.

CLOUDS

www.cloudsdowntown.com
831-429-2000
110 Church St., Santa Cruz
Open: Lunch & dinner daily
Price: Moderate
Cuisine: Californian/Asian fusion

Full Bar: Yes
Reservations: Recommended
Credit Cards: AE, D, MC, V
Handicap Access: Yes

Call it the linchpin of downtown Santa Cruz or call it the culmination of Lou and Christy Caviglia's evolving dining vision, but make no mistake—Clouds Downtown is one hoppin' joint. A magnet to veteran downtown habitués who order up martinis and scotch on the rocks like there's no tomorrow, Clouds' sleek copper-topped bar, black spiral chandeliers and colorful abstract canvases provide a distinctively modern backdrop to homey, American culinary classics and New American items with Asian accents. You'll find real men and women ordering pot roast and garlic mashed potatoes, rotisserie turkey swathed in fresh and tangy cranberry relish, lobster pot stickers, shrimp and soba salad, seared scallop salad and Dungeness crab cakes. In addition to its generously stocked bar, Clouds also boasts an impressive wine list, so it can indulge any libational whim with the greatest of ease.

Besides its reputation as an egalitarian watering hole, Clouds Downtown also serves Santa Cruz as a dinner palace and gathering spot for woman who lunch. George Sakkestad

The Crow's Nest is a required dining adventure for visitors to Santa Cruz's scenic Yacht Harbor. Frank Barbieri

CROW'S NEST

www.crowsnest-santacruz.com
831-476-4560
2218 E. Cliff Dr., Santa Cruz
Open: Lunch & dinner daily
Price: Moderate
Cuisine: American/seafood
Full Bar: Yes
Reservations: Recommended
Credit Cards: AE, D, MC, V
Handicap Access: Yes

The Crow's Nest and its incomparable Yacht Harbor location never fail to deliver a textbook beachfront experience. Many devotees of this handsome, split-level establishment situated right on the beach make tracks upstairs to the extremely popular bar, where attractive singles and live music on weekends heat up the recreational possibilities. There's also an oyster bar in the upper level and some outdoor seating. Downstairs and out on the glass-enwrapped decks, a menu of seafood standards is served along with the area's most comprehensive and inviting salad bar. The fresh grilled fish is fine, especially the local salmon and halibut, as are the fat sirloin steak sandwiches at lunch and aged filet mignon at night.

EL PALOMAR

www.elpalomarrestaurant.com
831-425-7575
1336 Pacific Ave., Santa Cruz
Open: Lunch & dinner daily, brunch weekends
Price: Moderate
Cuisine: Mexican
Full Bar: Yes
Reservations: Not required
Credit Cards: AE, D, MC, V
Handicap Access: Yes

This wildly popular dining room that has it all—inventive Mexican cuisine, world-class margaritas and the charismatic setting of an historic 1930s Spanish Revival hotel, whose lofty ceilings encompass the nonstop activity. While fine cocktails are served under the light and airy skylighting of the adjoining lounge, the main dining room best showcases the exciting food. The warm, fresh corn tortillas are the real thing and wrap perfectly around tender chile Colorado pork and shredded chicken in outstanding tacos. For less than $10, you can fill up on crisp puffy sopes, filled with chicken, vegetables, shredded cabbage and sour cream, or work through something grander in the form of fresh garlic-grilled prawns bathed in cilantro-laced, fiery hot guajilla chile sauce. Late brunches of voluptuous refried beans topped with a fried egg are without peer, and the house pozole—a rich pork-and-hominy soup topped with lime, cabbage and cilantro—will cure the worst cold or hangover (keep an eye open for the house special salmon and seafood pozole, a real killer). Housed in the tallest building in downtown Santa Cruz, El Palomar is hard to miss and impossible to beat.

✪ HOLLINS HOUSE

www.pasatiempo.com
831-459-9177
20 Clubhouse Rd. (at Pasatiempo Golf Club), Santa Cruz
Open: Dinner Wed.–Sun.
Price: Expensive
Cuisine: New American
Full Bar: Yes
Reservations: Recommended
Credit Cards: AE, MC, V
Handicap Access: Yes

The sweeping vista of the Monterey Bay creeps right up to the front porch of golf matriarch Marian Hollins's graceful home, which now houses a club and restaurant bearing her name. Those who visit Hollins House—a short drive from downtown Santa Cruz but a million miles away in sybaritic isolation—will find showstopping starters like thyme-scented Serrano ham and chanterelle mushrooms in an eggy cheese

gratin, or chickpea and fresh corn fritters. These are matched in execution and flavor by entrées of buttery prime beef filet, fork-tender braised oxtail and roasted Liberty Farms duck breast and intense duck confit atop a tart huckleberry reduction. These are meat and game from some designer Oz. For visual dazzle not just equaled but surpassed by exhilarating flavors, the desserts are knockouts. From the dried fig and apple bread pudding, where a scoop of burnt-sugar ice cream offsets the flavors of the warm pudding and fresh figs and apple, to the densely decadent vanilla bean crème brûlée (what the chef calls describes as "an adult vanilla pudding"), these elegant variations on classic American comfort dishes are, quite frankly, brilliant. The vintage 1930s California-French dining room, with its high ceilings, candlelight and view-capturing windows, suggests formality, but the youthful staff and enlightened menu exude relaxed hospitality.

MOBO SUSHI

www.mobosushirestaurant.com
831-425-1700
105 S. River St., Santa Cruz
Open: Lunch Mon.–Fri., dinner nightly
Price: Moderate
Cuisine: Japanese/sushi bar
Full Bar: Yes
Reservations: Accepted
Credit Cards: MC, V
Handicap Access: Yes

Extremely well-crafted sushi, amplified by worthy side dishes, nurtures Mobo Sushi's zone of sophistication—this town wouldn't be the same without it. While the very young, skilled staff keeps the orders flowing, all the classic tekkamakis, nigiris and anari sushis find tasteful expression, as do variations that could only have been created on the Central Coast. For example, the Rock & Roll is filled with freshwater eel and avocado, while Sushi Rage combines avocado, garlic and macadamia nuts as well as buttery yellowtail hamachi and sticky rice. The Presto Maki Roll is a local favorite, packed with pungent fresh basil and hamachi tuna. Tiny daikon sprouts and a crisp mountain yam adorn many jewel-like creations, but the emphasis here is on adventurous dining rather than slavish traditionalism—nothing too pretentious and everything fresh, fresh, fresh.

OLITAS CANTINA & GRILLE

www.olitassantacruz.com
831-458-9393
Municipal Wharf, Santa Cruz
Open: Lunch & dinner daily
Price: Moderate
Cuisine: Mexican/seafood
Full Bar: Yes
Reservations: No
Credit Cards: AE, D, MC, V
Handicap Access: Yes

No visit to the Santa Cruz Wharf is complete without a stop at the beautiful Olitas. The contemporary Mexican cantina theme is

Diners and afternoon celebrants gather at Olitas Cantina to enjoy the incredible views, frisky drinks and bountiful seafood. George Sakkestad

enhanced by glorious burnished woodwork, and the friendly bar serves superior cocktails and fine local wines. Afternoon drinks here are a religion. The bar offers clear panoramas of the waves and surfing activity at Lighthouse Point. From one of the main dining rooms, the vista is filled by the main beach, colorful boardwalk attractions and the Santa Cruz Mountains beyond. The menu has its charms, long on fresh seafoods with touches of southwestern and Pacific Rim inspiration, but the true draws here are the visuals. The pretty young things that crowd the bar area and views of marine life, ubiquitous gulls and pelicans, seals and the occasional dolphin and whale all fuel the waterfront ambiance.

✪ O'MEI RESTAURANT

831-425-8458
2316 Mission St., Santa Cruz
Open: Lunch Mon.–Fri., dinner nightly
Price: Moderate
Cuisine: Contemporary Asian
Full Bar: Yes
Reservations: Recommended but not required
Credit Cards: AE, MC, V
Handicap Access: Yes

From merely wonderful to off-the-scale celestial, this kitchen is gloriously consistent in delivering some of the finest flavors on the planet. The Pacific Rim culinary genius of Roger Grigsby has made the sleek, serene dining rooms of O'Mei one of the area's most popular and consistently excellent restaurants since its opening over 20 years ago. Regular trips to the Far East recharge Grigsby's inventive menu palette, translated through contemporary California emphasis on light, fresh presentation. The results are disarming. Tiny dishes of intriguing appetizers are brought around to each table (a godsend for cranky low-blood-sugar travelers), and diners can choose from baby ears of pickled corn, an addictive tangle of green beans spiked with garlic, chile-infused carrots, vinegary straw mushrooms or fermented wheat gluten, which as many of us know tastes better than it sounds. The seasonally transmuting menu is always tantalizing, and standouts from the appetizer menu invariably involve the sumptuous red oil dumplings and fabulous slender green beans tossed with fermented shrimp. Vegetables like the yu xiang eggplant, vibrant with the haunting perfume of Szechuan peppercorns, or asparagus in garlicky black bean sauce are meals unto themselves. More complex, but equally accessible, are special creations like mala corn chicken, crispy Taiwan-style rock cod, tea-smoked sea bass, calamari in black bean sauce, lemon pipa tofu balls (as delicious as its name) and black pepper beef with watercress. The listing of wines provides access to the finest from area microwineries, and a savvy beer buyer has marched the world in search of the best brews to accompany the sometimes fiery foods. Desserts are inventive and the nifty O'Mei apple blossom—warm diced apples, creamy vanilla ice cream, crisp pastry and a serious dusting of cinnamon—always delivers an enlightening finish. A favorite with visiting celebrities, politicos, artists, members of the UC Santa Cruz power structure and just plain folks.

✪ OSWALD

831-423-7427
1547 Pacific Ave., Santa Cruz
Open: Dinner Tues.–Sun.
Price: Moderate to Expensive
Cuisine: Californian
Full Bar: No
Reservations: Recommended
Credit Cards: AE, D, MC, V
Handicap Access: Yes

This local treasure continues to astonish with its intention and seasonal savvy. A smart, urban bistro with few pretensions under the guidance of culinary genius

Damani Thomas, Oswald is one of the top culinary sensations in Santa Cruz. The menu explores seasonal ingredients served with generous eye appeal and a sense of culinary style. An extensive wine list, bold on local and California wines, offers choice accompaniment for pan-roasted yellowtail with black chanterelles, portobellos and sweet potatoes, or a Provençal fish soup deepened with a variety of shellfish stocks, fennel and saffron crème fraîche. Other winners are the pork tenderloin fanned across a bed of tender micro-spaetzle and sautéed red cabbage, and the house spice-encrusted langoustines surrounded by a pool of electrifying tangerine vinaigrette containing a dice of shallots and pears. Desserts are original and decadent, like a seasonal trio of sorbets flavored with blood oranges, mandarin oranges and Meyer lemon. Try the napoleon of warm Meyer lemon custard.

PARWANA

831-458-1988
1209 Soquel Ave., Santa Cruz
Open: Lunch & dinner Tues.–Sun.
Price: Inexpensive
Cuisine: Afghani
Full Bar: No—no alcohol allowed
Reservations: No
Credit Cards: D, MC, V
Handicap Access: Yes

Parwana is, surprisingly, the first Afghan restaurant in the Central Coast's melting pot of ethnic eateries. Judging by its instant popularity, Santa Cruz is way overdue for the fragrant pilaus, simmered vegetable stews and grilled meats of this faraway region (think Indian curries, Kurdish spiced yogurts and Pakistani kebabs). The restaurateurs have transformed the former breakfast landmark Bea's with the voluptuous rhythms of Middle Eastern music, whose aural calligraphy is matched by faux tile wainscoting, silk sari tablecloths and hanging hexagonal chandeliers reminiscent of ones I've seen in the bazaars of Cairo. It's all very fresh and welcoming, right down to the red runner dividing the room's dozen tables. Even if you don't quite know what you're ordering, the menu offers clear descriptions of familiar and unusual entrées and all-star appetizers like buranee kaddu, an addictive creation of garlicky sautéed pumpkin topped with a tart sour cream dressing, and aushak, steamed dumplings filled with leeks and topped with sensuous and very non-Western meat sauces. Do not miss this dish! It is so wonderful that it is wisely offered in an expanded entrée-sized portion as well.

PEARL ALLEY BISTRO & WINE BAR
www.pearlalley.com
831-429-8070
110 Pearl Alley, bet. Pacific Ave. & Cedar St., Santa Cruz
Open: Dinner nightly
Price: Moderate to Expensive
Cuisine: Global bistro
Full Bar: Yes
Reservations: Recommended
Credit Cards: AE, D, MC, V
Handicap Access: No

Exquisite ingredients and inventive, unpretentious presentation distinguish one of the top dining rooms in the area. Before culinary wunderkind Marc Westburg opened this accessibly chichi bistro on the site of a longtime favorite wine bar, he'd cooked all over the world and done a stint as Trader Vic's personal chef. The multicultural flavor, texture and seasoning ideas gleaned from this extensive experience power some of the most innovative dishes on the Central Coast. The small dining room, whose hardwood floors accentuate the convivial hubbub, offers a constantly changing menu long on small dishes. The fiery Pacific Rim haunts such dishes as an exquisite fresh kimchee salmon served with the house pickled cabbage and toasted nori,

while more European are signature dishes such as tournedos of lamb in a rose geranium jelly glaze, and seared halibut with lavender, white peach and viognier coulis and grilled white corn. All have developed cult followings. Special menus featuring the cuisine of different parts of the globe headline for a week each month, so adventuresome gourmands can eat everything from kangaroo to antelope when their timing is right. And only a fool would bypass dessert at Pearl Alley. Try the blueberry soufflé with mango or a warm pear crisp, pooled with crème anglaise, dotted with fig slices and covered with a cinnamon crumb topping. The long wood bar attracts solo diners as well as connoisseurs of Pearl Alley's lengthy listing of outstanding Central Coast and French vintages, most available by the glass.

REAL THAI KITCHEN
831-427-2559
1632 Seabright Ave., Santa Cruz
Open: Lunch & dinner daily
Price: Inexpensive
Cuisine: Thai
Full Bar: No
Reservations: Recommended for weekend dinner
Credit Cards: AE, MC, V
Handicap Access: Yes

Fans of the brilliant flavor complexities of Thai cuisine have made this small, colorfully decorated restaurant their second home. Using the freshest local produce and seafoods as a primary base, chef Prasit Saranyaphiphat expertly applies the traditional seasonings of chiles, garlic, basil, lemongrass and lime to a wide range of authentic dishes. The creamy pad Thai stir-fried rice noodles beautifully support a flotilla of shrimp, chicken, egg, tofu and ground peanuts. Southern Thai curries, richly layered with sweet basil, fiery chiles and satiny coconut milk, are unforgettable, especially those involving roasted duck or fresh seafoods. Many people come simply for sensuous appetizers like the fine spicy shrimp soup filled with mushrooms, lemongrass and coconut milk or the chicken larb (minced poultry, toasted rice powder, lime, chiles, basil, cilantro and shredded lettuce), which puts to shame any other chicken salad that you could contemplate. Don't miss the barbecued pork ribs paired with an icy Singha beer. Vivacious hostess-partner Ellen Saranyaphiphat is a gem.

✪ RISTORANTE AVANTI

831-427-0135
1711 Mission St., Santa Cruz
Open: Lunch Mon.–Fri., dinner nightly
Price: Expensive
Cuisine: Italian
Full Bar: No
Reservations: Recommended
Credit Cards: AE, MC, V
Handicap Access: Yes

If one word could be used to describe the work and vision of Brian Curry and his crew, it would be integrity. They are committed to providing customers with amazing, organic food, most of which is grown within a 50-mile radius of the restaurant. Curry, former chef de cuisine at Highlands Inn, also worked at Bernards Inn and Sent Sovi before being hired by Avanti owners Paul and Cindy Geise. For over a year now, Ristorante Avanti faithful have been noticing the menu tweaks and changes: small things, like the selection of olives offered at the start of the meal, and more dramatic changes, such as removing the half-portion option on selected entrées. There's a new refinement in the presentation. Main dishes and vegetables arrive on individual plates, with unique saucing and seasoning identities, rather than being served on a single plate. Sourcing ingredients through local growers and producers has taken top priority. And meats are being given star treatment along with organic salads and heirloom vegetables. If listed on the ever-changing menu, the succulent, baked meatballs and house-made papardelle noodles are an excellent choice, or try the wild roasted sturgeon festooned with peas, red bell pepper and fennel and served over a bed of Yukon gold potatoes. And never pass up the pan-seared day-boat scallops or creamy polenta and chicken cacciatore—a fantasy dish seemingly from the hands of an Italian grandmother. Newcomers and veterans alike all secretly feel that Ristorante Avanti has rolled out its cozy wine bar and acres of Mediterranean flavors just for them. The prices are reasonable, and the camaraderie is irresistible.

✪ SESTRI RESTAURANT & BAR

www.sestrisantacruz.com
831-479-0200
655 Capitola Rd., Santa Cruz
Open: Dinner nightly
Price: Moderate to Expensive
Cuisine: Italian
Full Bar: Yes
Reservations: Recommended
Credit Cards: AE, MC, V
Handicap Access: Yes

A beautiful suite of rooms, an exhibition kitchen, alfresco seating and a vivacious full bar are highlights at Sestri, Santa Cruz's newest Mediterranean restaurant. But chef Jamie Smith's beautifully presented Italian-accented entrées and appetizers are the true stars here. Fresh local produce, seafoods and organic ingredients are provided professional panache by the French Culinary Institute grad who earned his stripes in top San Francisco and Menlo Park restaurants. Salads are a house specialty and show off Smith's passion for fresh herbs and unusual flavor alliances. Ripe figs and bitter dandelion can share a place with almonds, pecorino cheese and 16-year-old balsamic vinegar. Pastas are heightened with house-made sausage and fire-roasted tomatoes. The wood-burning ovens of Sestri produce not only exceptional pizzas but specialties like the oven-roasted halibut, shrimp and smoked duck breast with toasted fresh corn. Desserts are stellar, from authentic Italian panna cotta to tarts showcasing heirloom fruits. Lots of fine ingredients add up to lots of flavor excitement.

✪ SOIF

www.soifwine.com
831-423-2020
105 Walnut Ave., Santa Cruz
Open: Dinner nightly (small plates from 3pm weekends)
Price: Expensive
Cuisine: Californian/Continental
Full Bar: No
Reservations: No
Credit Cards: D, MC, V
Handicap Access: Yes

The smart wine bar in downtown Santa Cruz exudes metropolitan ambiance while making locals and visitors alike feel completely at home. Spare interior design flatters the wine lovers who flock to the bar to sample over 50 intriguing vintages by the 2-ounce pour or glass. Chef Chris Avila's expert small plates are designed to romance the wines, and reflect both regional and seasonal highlights. Tiny samples of everything from perfect bruschettas and roasted fingerling potatoes to tender calamari salads and intensely flavored tiny meatballs in almond sauce all show off culinary confidence as well as a sense of seasoning playfulness. Here tapas nod to the Mediterranean but aren't afraid to cross over into both California as well as Europe. A terrific listing of full dinner items can include variations on wild local salmon, classic duck breast with peaches or authentic brasserie dishes like braised veal cheeks with chard and polenta. A revolving menu, both of foods and wines, delights enthusiastic foodies, plus there's a wisely stocked wine shop just beyond a room partition.

STAR BENE

831-479-4307
2-1245 E. Cliff Dr., Santa Cruz
Open: Daily
Price: Moderate
Cuisine: Italian
Full Bar: No
Reservations: Recommended
Credit Cards: AE, MC, V
Handicap Access: Yes

At Star Bene, Italian is not only spoken and eaten, it fills the air with unhurried ambiance. Charmingly decorated with sparkling white linens and a sheltered courtyard for alfresco dining in the warmer months, Star Bene provides a shimmering glimpse of the Mediterranean right on the Central Coast. The menu doesn't attempt to reinvent. Instead it enhances delicate salads, antipasti, pastas and some meat and fish dishes simply and elegantly. A classic appetizer like prosciutto and melon becomes an elegant experience—wedges of sweet cantaloupe are finessed with cured Parma ham and a trio of kalamata olives. The osso buco, literally falling off the bones and dotted with porcinis and carrots, offers earthy goodness. Cornish game hens and fresh fish are perfect choices, but Star Bene's girello vegetariano—three elegant pinwheels of handmade vegetable-layered pasta splashed with bright red and béchamel cream sauces, then flecked with parsley—could easily be the ultimate luxury vegetarian dish.

SUKEROKU

831-426-6660
1701 Mission St., Santa Cruz
Open: Lunch & dinner Tues.–Sun.
Price: Moderate
Cuisine: Japanese
Full Bar: No

Reservations: No
Credit Cards: MC, V
Handicap Access: Yes

Since the late 1970s, this tiny Japanese restaurant and even tinier sushi bar have satisfied the cravings for soy, sake and sushi on the part of neighbors and university regulars in this Westside Santa Cruz community. Blond wood tables and the occasional travel poster make up the spare decor, but the real star here is the wonderful food. Exceptional bowls of fat udon noodles filled with shiitakes, prawns and vegetables are available at dinner, as are consummate teriyaki salmon and pork, and feather-light tempura. The sushi is first-rate, served up with friendly flair, as is the occasional outburst of song by legendary chef-owner Isao Hamashi. A local treasure.

THAI NOODLE HOUSE
831-457-0238
2106A Mission St., Santa Cruz
Open: Lunch through dinner to closing daily
Price: Inexpensive
Cuisine: Pan-Pacific homecooking
Full Bar: No
Reservations: No
Credit Cards: AE, DC, MC, V
Handicap Access: Yes

A cozy hole-in-the-wall in one of the busiest Westside Santa Cruz neighborhoods, this is a haven for fans of luscious noodle specialties as well as the classic curries and stir-fries of Thailand. Ten tiny tables laden with hot and spicy condiments fill the charmingly cluttered interior. Walls are adorned with sequined textiles and carved tracery. Service is personal and friendly. Low prices and freshly created dishes provide a non-stop draw for university types and lovers of ethnic cuisine. Fueled by chiles, garlic, lemon grass, ginger and cilantro, the house specialties cover spice-laden territory from the heady Tom Yum hot and sour soup to vibrant curries

and grilled seafoods. Noodles rule here, in the four of salads, appetizers and over two dozen soups. The glass noodle salad with chicken and shrimp is a knock-out, as are the gigantic bowls of noodles in fragrant broths. Easy and spicy does it at this unpretentious ethnic eatery.

VASILI'S
831-458-9808
1501 Mission St., Santa Cruz
Open: Dinner Tues.–Sun.
Price: Moderate
Cuisine: Greek
Full bar: No
Reservations: A good idea
Credit Cards: No
Handicap Access: No

If you're looking for an energetic backdrop to international dining, this place is nothing less than a gift from the Greek gods. Owner and chef Vasili Karagiannopoulos has a bountiful exuberance for food, and it's always evident in his simple taverna. The warm hearth is lined with photos, pottery and faux frescoes of Zorbaesque dancers and is always packed with jubilant regulars digging into platters full of fragrant country-style pork shish kebabs, roast lamb shank, piles of delicately sautéed calamari and Greek salad, mounds of chopped tomatoes, Bermuda onions, cucumbers, peppers and feta liberally adorned with capers. No visit to a Greek restaurant would be complete without a few swills of pine-scented retsina or some sweet, hearty rice pudding. Saturday nights are particularly jovial, as Vasili and his crew do traditional dances to rowdy live music. The top-drawer staff is knowledgeable and friendly.

WATSONVILLE
✪ FIESTA TEPA-SAHUAYO
831-724-3492
15 1st St., Watsonville
Open: Daily 9am–9pm
Price: Moderate

Cuisine: Mexican
Full Bar: No
Reservations: No
Credit Cards: AE, D, MC, V
Handicap Access: Yes

Holding down one end of a tiny shopping strip off Riverside Avenue near downtown Watsonville, Tepa-Sahuayo is crammed with simple tables and chairs surrounded by a floor-to-ceiling homage to the arts and crafts of Mexico. Hand-painted pottery, dried chiles, back-strap loom tapestries and carved wooden Oaxaqueño flowers adorn every inch of wall and table space, while a jukebox fully loaded with Mex-pop adds to the aromatic dining room. The plastic place mat menu proclaims "hard to find dishes," and it isn't kidding. You don't run across too much huitlacoche outside of Mexico, but there it is, stuffing a delicate enchilada along with squash blossoms and mole sauce (part of a lunch combo plate and bigger than Monte Alban). Enchiladas come with every possible sauce: red, white, green, even a pink one made from rose petals—an old Oaxacan recipe. A galvanized bucket of beer, iced fresh juices (try the tamarindo) in their own pottery pitchers, great chips and sassy dip keep you company until the handmade food starts to arrive. A chile relleno the size of a Barcalounger is sheer melted-cheese comfort, while a crisp taco filled with achiote-rubbed pork tastes like a Mayan barbecue. If it is available, always order a special of poblano chiles stuffed with pomegranate seeds, turkey and almonds and topped with a hot/sweet nogada sauce of puréed walnuts and spices. Accompanying all the entrées here—joining the main course on plates the size of a Vera Cruz moon—are oceans of saffron-tinted rice, cabbage salad with salsa fresca and guacamole, whole pinto beans and a central bowl of seriously hot sauce. It would be hard to tell that you weren't somewhere near Oaxaca, so unpretentiously authentic is the mood and welcome at this tiny jewel of a dining spot.

FOOD PURVEYORS

Bakeries

Aldo's 831-476-3470, 4628 Soquel Dr., Soquel. Featured here are fragrant, rustic, fresh-baked breads and pastries, including the mighty Italian raisin fugasa.

The Buttery 831-458-3020, 702 Soquel Ave., Santa Cruz. The Buttery bakes great breads, but the sumptuously frosted cakes and elegant cookies are even better. Don't miss the zucchini muffins and pecan sandies.

Emily's Good Things to Eat 831-429-9866, 1129 Mission St., Santa Cruz. Emily's cooks up such aromatic attractions as pumpkin muffins and round, fragrant sourdough bread, plus brews some of the strongest coffee this side of Colombia.

The Farm 831-684-0266, 6790 Soquel Dr., Aptos. A local baking institution, The Farm is the place to settle in for a cappuccino, tarts, soups or a vast selection of homemade breads. Cozy, atmospheric and satisfying.

Gayle's Bakery & Rosticceria 831-462-1200, 504 Bay Ave., Capitola. The grandmommy of local artisan bakeries, Gayle's has been a destination for early-morning workers and vacationers for three decades, and the afternoon crowds come for the haute deli selections and the blue-plate special meals. Great tarts, breads, cookies and atmosphere.

The bounty of French bread has put Kelly's on the map. Paul Schraub

HMB Bakery 650-726-4841, 514 Main St., Half Moon Bay. HMB is a traditional bakery with a wide assortment of cakes, cookies, pastries and its famously rich and sticky Hot Cross Buns.

Heather's Patisserie 831-662-3546, 7486 Soquel Dr., Aptos. The latest addition to Santa Cruz's pantheon of female bakers, Heather churns out delicious breads, cookies, morning pastries, cakes, tortes, chocolate concoctions and a killer mango-passion mousse cake.

Kelly's French Pastry 831-423-9059, 402 Ingalls St., Santa Cruz. Authentic French breads, cakes and pastries, killer pear tarts and pain d'amande have put this institution on the map.

Moonside Bakery 650-726-9070, 604 Main St., Half Moon Bay. Pastries, cookies, fresh-baked bread, plus breakfasts make this downtown bakery a perfect stop for a quick fix or a languorous morning.

Coffeehouses

120 Union 831-459-9876, 120 Union St., Santa Cruz. A 1960s-style, neohippie hangout featuring weathered couches, big leafy plants and terrific caffe latte, this is a favored destination for locals.

Caffe Pergolesi 831-426-1775, 418 Cedar St., Santa Cruz. The Perg attracts young and aggressively avant-garde students and artists who congregate to swill industrial-strength coffee and wait to be discovered.

Chocolate 831-427-9900, 1520 Pacific Ave., Santa Cruz. A caffeine-infused meeting spot housed in the front of Bookshop Santa Cruz, Chocolate's is wildly popular with outdoor cafe types and seekers after the luscious intoxicant that gives the place its name.

Half Moon Bay Coffee Company 650-726-3664, 20 Stone Pine Rd., Half Moon Bay. Upscale and full-service, this coffeehouse offers a full range of fresh coffee, espresso drinks and unique teas, as well as soup, sandwiches and desserts. The best desserts on the coastal side of San Mateo County are served here.

Java Junction 831-423-5282, 519 Seabright Ave., Santa Cruz. This seaside caffeine haven, with its sunny patio, is beachy in ambiance. It offers all kinds of coffee drinks and smoothies, plus goodies like bagels, muffins and sinfully gooey cinnamon rolls.

La Di Da Jazz Cafe 650-726-1663, 500C Purissima St. at Kelly Ave., Half Moon Bay. The self-proclaimed "coolest cafe on the coast" serves up special coffee drinks, whimsical desserts, sandwiches and art, plus the tastiest fruit-flavored water on the coast.

Lulu Carpenter's 831-429-9804, 1545 Pacific Ave., Santa Cruz. Lulu's dubs itself "a fine eating and drinking establishment," but it really is a coffeehouse—a charming coffeehouse, but a coffeehouse nonetheless. A quaint front patio on the city's main drag and a cloistered bricked patio behind make for either lively passerby interaction or sedate privacy while you imbibe your frothy brews and homemade pastries.

M Coffee 650-726-6241, 522 Main St., Half Moon Bay. Cozy and cute, M comes complete with round, paisley-print tables, pastries, sandwiches and delicious lattes.

Mr. Toots 831-475-3679, 221 Esplanade, Capitola. A lovely coffeehouse that offers an ocean view and upper room, dark-wood ambiance, Toots has a long-standing following and wonderful mochas.

Pacific Coffee Roasting Company 831-685-2520, 7554 Soquel Dr., Aptos. A lovely patio is communal space for joggers, students and workers on break, who come to enjoy the sun or light fog. Good coffee and sweet treats provide the fuel.

Peet's Coffee & Tea 831-457-8170, 1409 Pacific Ave., Santa Cruz. A purveyor of tasty coffees and fine teas since 1967, Peet's is an 80-store chain home based in the San Francisco Bay Area that keeps its footprint light in hip coastal communities and blends well (sorry) with its small-town neighbors. The loose and rare teas are very special indeed.

Santa Cruz Coffee Roasting Company 831-459-0100, 13309 Pacific Ave., Santa Cruz. This breezy landmark has it all: outdoor tables, local art/photo shows on the walls, a ragtime-y piano, chessboards, bagels, muffins, cookies and very comfy booths. Oh yes, and excellent coffee, half of which is certified both organic and fair trade.

Farmers' Markets

Aptos Certified Farmers' Market 831-728-5060, 6500 Soquel Dr., Cabrillo College lower parking lot, Aptos. Considered the granddaddy of the area's open-air produce emporia, the Aptos Market vends everything organic in Mother Earth's cornucopia, year-round, every Sat. 8am–noon.

Capitola Farmers' Market 831-454-0566, Capitola Theatre parking lot, Capitola Village. May–Nov. Thurs. 2:30–6:30pm.

Coastside Farmers' Market 650-726-1249 or 650-726-4090, Cetrella parking lot, 845 Main St., Half Moon Bay. Everything from organic fruits and vegetables to lavender, wild king salmon and artisanal goat cheese from world-famous Harley Farms is available. May–Oct. Sat. 9am–1pm.

Felton Farmers' Market 335-9364, 6090 Hwy. 9, Felton. May–Nov. Tues. 2:30–6:30pm.

Live Oak Farmers' Market 831-454-0566, corner of E. Cliff Dr. & 15th Ave., Santa Cruz. May–Nov. Sun. 9am–1pm.

Our Lady of the Pillar Church Farmers' Market 650-726-4674, Church & Mill, Half Moon Bay. May–Oct. Sun. 9am–1pm.

Santa Cruz Community Farmers' Market 831-454-0566, corner of Cedar & Lincoln Sts., Santa Cruz. This organic market bounces with friendly, festive, folksy atmosphere, laced with live music and street entertainment every Wed. 2:30–6:30pm year-round, come rain or come shine.

UCSC Farm & Garden 831-459-3240, corner of Bay & High, foot of UCSC campus, Santa Cruz. June–Oct. Tues. & Fri. noon–6pm.

Downtown Santa Cruz comes vibrantly alive every Wednesday afternoon when local growers bring their bounty to the colorful block-long farmers' market. George Sakkestad

Watsonville Certified Farmers' Market 831-726-7266, Watsonville Plaza on the corner of Peck & Main, Watsonville. May–Oct. Fri. 3–7pm.

Westside Farmers' Market Swift Street Courtyard 402 Ingalis St., Santa Cruz. Fri. 2–6pm.

Frozen Desserts

Gelato Mania 831-426-7117, 110 Cooper St., Suite B, Santa Cruz. Top-of-the-line gelato scooped in myriad flavors, some found in nature, others from someplace else. Because this is, after all, Santa Cruz, the shop shares space with an oxygen bar boasting over a dozen aromas on tap.

Marianne's 831-458-1447, 1020 Ocean St., Santa Cruz. A landmark for decades, opulent with sinful creaminess like vanilla bean milk shakes, this parlor serves sugar cones filled with California 17, a killer version of Rocky Road. Alfred Hitchcock used to stop by daily when he lived in the hills nearby.

Polar Bear Ice Cream 831-425-5188, 1224 Soquel Ave., Santa Cruz. Polar Bear is known for fine espressos and delectable ice creams, including good berries and a superior pumpkin flavor.

Saturn Cafe 831-429-8505, 145 Laurel St., Santa Cruz. For 30 years, this has remained a destination for cool dessert lovers of all ages. Everyone should experience this funky restaurant's infamous Chocolate Madness at least once in life.

Culture

Architecture

In the carefully groomed residential streets surrounding downtown Santa Cruz, rows of pastel-hued cottages and mansions preserve the aura of the 19th-century boom in this seaside mecca. City fathers filled Walnut St. with the curved archways, steep gables and ornate turrets marking the high point of Stick, Gothic Revival and Queen Anne styles, all of which flourish today surrounded by historic landscaping and vintage trees. Wealthy land and cattle barons filled the town's Beach Hill district with majestic Victorian mansions, while the Oceanview Ave. district overlooking the city is literally lined with fine, ornate Queen Anne beauties. The ubiquitous architect William Weeks was just hitting his stride in the 1920s, peppering the entire state with memorable schools, libraries, courthouses, hotels and public buildings. The colorful tiles, Mission Revival polychromed ceilings and curved roofline of Santa Cruz's Palomar Hotel carry on his legacy. A half mile away, on W. Cliff Dr. overlooking the Santa Cruz Boardwalk, one of Weeks's rare private homes still boasts its arched terrace, red-tile roof and copper flashing details as the exquisite Darling House Bed and Breakfast Inn.

Cinema

41st Avenue Playhouse 831-475-3504, 1475 41st Ave., Capitola. Mid-county four-plex offers a digital sound system and comfortable rocking chair seating. Mainstream Hollywood movies are the standard here.

✪ **Del Mar Theatre** 831-469-3220, 1124 Pacific Ave., Santa Cruz. Lovingly restored art deco palace sports three screens and some luminous 1930s architecture to welcome you to its Golden Age of Cinema bosom. The latest foreign, art house and midnight classic flicks ignite its large, plush auditorium and two lesser screening halls. Staffed by bright, young filmmies.

Nickelodeon 831-426-7500, 210 Lincoln St., Santa Cruz. This four-screen complex specializes in the best current independent films from the U.S. and abroad. A favorite with area culturati and the university crowd, who relish the good popcorn (freshly made with real butter) and fresh fruit juices. A local institution.

✪ **Rio Theatre** www.riotheatre.com, 831-423-8209, 1205 Soquel Ave., Santa Cruz. A large vintage movie palace with plush seats, tiled restrooms and an upstairs "crying room" for youngsters or others in distress. Usually screens international, independent, X-sport or avant-garde productions, but also plays host to live world beat or alt-rock concerts and edgy spoken-word and art-crowd cultural high jinks.

Santa Cruz Cinema 9 Theatres 831-460-2599, 1405 Pacific Ave., Santa Cruz. This classy multiplex features a wide selection of mainstream movies, especially big-budget blockbusters. The large physical plant—complete with neon lights and a huge snack bar that offers espresso drinks, pastries and frozen drinks—creates a high-tech feel very different from most local theaters.

Signature Riverfront Twin 831-460-2599, 155 S. River St., Santa Cruz. Renovated in 1997, this old-time showcase features two theaters and stadium seating to catch mainstream fare. Biscotti and espresso are available at the snack bar.

✪ **Skyview Drive-In Theatre** 831-475-3405, 2260 Soquel Dr., Santa Cruz. Skyview remains the area's sole reminder of the glory days of the drive-in. This open-air Americana throwback offers a choice of double features (often thrillers) on two giant screens to be enjoyed the old-school way.

Gardens

Half Moon Bay Nursery 650-726-5392, 11691 San Mateo Rd., Half Moon Bay. An eye-popping panorama of colorful perennials fills the greenhouses of this florists' nirvana. Open daily 9–5.

University of California–Santa Cruz Arboretum www.ucsc.edu/arboretum, 831-427-2998, 1156 High St., Santa Cruz. Experimental and showpiece gardens, both emphasizing indigenous plants, are on display along the arboretum's many trails. Amid the groves of various eucalyptus trees, the collections of native California plants from Australia, New Zealand and South Africa are considered among the best in the world. The displays include 10 genera of redwood trees, a California garden and a Mediterranean garden. Open for self-guided tours daily 9–5. The Jean & Bill Lane Library is open Wed.–Sun. 1–4.

University of California–Santa Cruz Farm and Garden Project www.ucsc.edu/casfs, 831-459-4140, off Coolidge Dr., Santa Cruz. A working farm/agroecology project nestled at the foot of the hilltop campus, this 25-acre meadow filled with vegetable and flower beds, orchards and row crops was founded by French-intensive master gardener Alan Chadwick, whose students have continued to experiment with organics in these fertile fields. The project provides a vivid opportunity to observe one of the hotbeds of ecologically correct Central Coast growing techniques. Open daily dawn to dusk for self-guided tours. Docent tours are offered Thurs. at noon and Sun. at 2pm.

Historic Places
EVERGREEN HISTORICAL CEMETERY
831-429-1964, ext. 17
Evergreen & Coral Sts., Santa Cruz 95060
Open: Daily dawn to dusk, docent-led tours 10am first Sat. of the month Mar.–Nov.
Admission: Free, donations appreciated

One of the earliest non-Catholic cemeteries in the state, this verdant hillside became a final resting place in 1850 for area settlers, from judges to courtesans. Beneath the weathered and tottering headstones lie Civil War veterans, Freemasons and civic fathers, plus a few civic mothers sprinkled among the boys. An entire section devoted to the graves of Chinese immigrants marks the burial site of those who came to build the region's railroads, bridges and roads.

JAMES JOHNSTON HOUSE & WILLIAM JOHNSTON HOUSE
No telephone
Higgins Purissima Rd., Half Moon Bay 94019
Open: Daily dawn to dusk
Admission: Free, donations appreciated

The only remaining example of a New England saltbox-style dwelling on the northern Central Coast, the two-story, white clapboard house built in 1853 by one of the original 49ers, Ohio-born James Johnston, remains one of this area's most important and earliest structures. Built in the 1860s, the neighboring home of William Johnston still shows off its wooden peg construction and original shutters and corner boards. The lovely country road itself curves for almost 10 miles through old Santa Cruz Mountain farms, pastures and meadows before rejoining Highway 1.

MISSION LA EXALTACIÓN DE LA SANTA CRUZ
831-426-5686
126 High St. at Emmet St., Santa Cruz 95060
Open: Tues.–Sat. 10–4, Sun. 10–2
Admission: Free

Founded in 1791, Mission La Exaltación was the 12th California mission. With a seemingly unlimited and willing population of Native Americans, rich grazing lands and proximity to ocean trade, the setting promised to be one of the richest in the Franciscan empire. But all turned sour when the civilian Pueblo of Branciforte sprang up across the river, populated by a rough crew of former convicts, pirates and opportunists, hard men who lured the Ohlone converts away with the temptations of drink, gambling and gold. After falling into disrepair during the early 19th century, the original mission was leveled by an earthquake in 1857. Today, the mission site is occupied by a Catholic church built in 1889. Across the street, a one-third-scale replica of the mission and its domed tower houses a chapel and the mission's original paintings and statues.

PURISSIMA TOWN SITE
No telephone
Verde Rd., Half Moon Bay 94019
Open: Daily dawn to dusk
Admission: Free

One of the earliest American settlements in Half Moon Bay, this ghost town was a lively stagecoach stop and mercantile center in the 1870s. Today, its rustic cemetery and remodeled schoolhouse still exude the spell of yesteryear.

The New England–style James Johnston House has stood watch over the Half Moon Bay coastline since the middle of the 19th century. Stan Cacitti

The narrow-gauge railroad and General Store at Roaring Camp in Felton. John Poimiroo/Roaring Camp Railroads

ROARING CAMP RAILROADS
www.roaringcamp.com
831-335-4484
Graham Hill Rd. off Mount Hermon Rd., Felton 95018
Open: June–Aug. daily 10–6, Sept.–May weekends 10–6
Admission: Sun Tan Special round-trip train rides, adults $20, children 3–12 $15, under 3 free, parking fee $6 (Steam Train slightly cheaper)

Ensconced near the stately, old-growth redwoods of Henry Cowell State Park, this color-fully re-created steam-railroad depot town continues to delight visitors with its Old West flavor and scenic, narrow-gauge train rides. Shops, concessions and sawmill re-creations all bustle with attendants clad in vintage-1870s attire. However, two historic train rides are the real attraction here. Hour-and-a-quarter rides, involving round-trip odysseys through the primal redwood forests of the Santa Cruz Mountains on the narrow-gauge Steam Train, begin here twice a day. Also coursing up steep grades and down through the logging country of days past, the Sun Tan Special follows original tracks descending from Roaring Camp to the sunny oceanfront activity of the Santa Cruz Beach and Boardwalk twice a day on three-hour round trips.

SANTA CRUZ MUNICIPAL WHARF
www.ci.santa-cruz.ca.us/pr/wharf
831-420-6025
W. Cliff Dr. & Front St., Santa Cruz 95060
Open: Daily dawn–2am
Admission: Free (except parking)

The incessant bellowing of the resident colony of harbor seals that lounge among the wharf's huge pilings welcomes visitors to this shop- and restaurant-lined fishing pier. Offering terrific wraparound views of the surfing action at Steamer Lane and the turn-of-the-20th-century Boardwalk casino and arcade, the wharf buzzes with open-air fish markets and gift and sporting boutiques, as well as bay excursion crafts for hire. Constructed in 1914, this fishing and pleasure pier extends out into Monterey Bay near where four earlier versions were built, the first one in 1853 to fill sailing ships with the produce of the fertile Santa Cruz Mountain countryside. Today, the casual pace begins at dawn for local anglers and winds down with sunset cocktails for locals and visitors alike.

✪ WILDER RANCH STATE PARK

www.santacruzstateparks.org/parks/wilder
831-426-0505 (visitors center), 831-423-9703 (ranger)
1401 Old Coast Rd. off Hwy. 1, Santa Cruz 95060
Open: Daily 8am–dusk; visitors center and dairy Thurs.–Sun. 10–4
Admission: $6 per vehicle parking fee, $5 for 62 years and older, $3 disabled with state pass

This graceful relic of the dairy barons of the 1880s occupies a special place in the hearts of area residents. Stretching over 5,000 acres of the most sumptuous and varied terrain on the Central Coast, the ranch—a former dairy ranch turned cattle ranch turned state park—sprawls from its seaside tide pools and plover sanctuary all the way up to redwood groves crowning a 2,000-foot mountaintop. Along the way, the spread encompasses magnificent meadows, ponds, springs and myriad wildlife habitats, including blue heron rookeries and fox and coyote dens.

At the foot of the property is the beautifully maintained Victorian compound of the Wilder dairy ranch. All of the buildings, including the long barn that housed the state's first cream separator, the antique stable, the workshop with original water-driven machinery, the bunkhouse and the owners' large, period-furnished, Victorian manor house, are open to the public. Nearby stand the worn remains of the original adobe, the house in which Russian Jose Bolcoff married Spanish land-grant heiress Maria Castro back when the ranch was part of the 10,000-acre Rancho Refugio.

The full exhilaration of this land is best enjoyed by strapping on some sturdy shoes and by filling a day pack with food, water, a camera and binoculars before heading up along the ranch's many hiking, biking and equestrian trails. It's a trip back into the solitude and open grandeur of the Old West.

Historic Walking Tours

HALF MOON BAY/PESCADERO HISTORIC WALKING TOURS

A self-guided tour brochure of some of the vintage 19th-century dwellings built by fishing and ranching settlers is available from the local **chamber of commerce** (650-726-5202, 225 S. Cabrillo, Hwy. 1, Half Moon Bay 94019). Highlights include Spanishtown landmarks of the first Spanish and Portuguese settlements, the Half Moon Bay community Methodist Church (built in 1872), 1853 Johnston House (one of the finest examples extant of the New England saltbox style) and the 1820 Pilarcitos Catholic Cemetery.

SANTA CRUZ MISSION PLAZA WALKING TOUR

In addition to boasting a historic mission adobe, the plaza surrounding the Santa Cruz Mission State Historic Park (831-425-5849, 144 School St. at Adobe St., Santa Cruz) enjoys the distinction of being the first area populated by the earliest influx of American settlers. Built in 1822 to house native inhabitants who worked at Mission Santa Cruz, the adobe is the only authentically restored Native American residence in the California mission chain. The seven rooms are set up to show how the occupants lived over the years and are open Thurs.–Sun. 10–4 (tours Sun. at noon). Impressive early homes are still to be seen on a self-guided walking tour of the area, including Santa Cruz's oldest house, the 1850 Francisco Alzina home (107 Sylvar St.), an intricate Stick-style villa (207 Mission St.) built in 1883 and a splendid Gothic home with classical railings and gable (127 Green St.) built in 1867.

Kids' Stuff

Mystery Spot 831-423-8897, 465 Mystery Spot Rd., Santa Cruz. A wacky local landmark where trees grow at weird angles and buildings defy the laws of physics. People seem to change size and balls roll uphill. Is it due to the mysterious force of some buried meteor, or is it simply an optical illusion? Whatever it is, this wooded 150-foot plot offers lots of gee-whiz, brain-tickling fun. Open daily 9–7. Adults $5, children 5–11 $3, under 5 free.

Pacific Edge 831-454-9254, 104 Bronson St. #12, Santa Cruz. For the kid in everyone, Pacific Edge offers a chance to experience the thrill of rock climbing in an indoor, safe environment. Learn the skills of safe climbing or perfect your technique. Special kids classes available, as are day passes. Open daily 10–10.

✪ **Pigeon Point Lighthouse** Necessity and technology conspired in the erection of brilliant beacons clinging to the rockiest edges of the Central California coast during the 19th century. Armed with the high candlepower of the French Fresnel lens, which ingeniously utilized over 1,000 pieces of cut glass to magnify its light, the slender lighthouses and their stalwart attendants kept faith with mariners until the coming of automation and the computer. Always a charming sight, a few of these curved towers continue to shed light along the Central Coast. The Pigeon Point Lighthouse, located just south of Half Moon Bay, was built in 1872 on a murderous outcropping of rocks and contains a Fresnel lens that was first used on Cape Hatteras during the Civil War. It still manages to pierce the often pea-soup fog that clings to the North Central Coast and now functions as both a Coast Guard outpost and a hostel run by American Youth Hostels.

A youth hostel is lodged inside the 1872 Pigeon Point Lighthouse, the second tallest lighthouse on the California coast. Shmuel Thaler

✪ **Santa Cruz Beach Boardwalk** www.beachboardwalk.com, 831-423-5590, 400 Beach St., Santa Cruz. More than 34 exciting rides, including an old-fashioned wooden roller coaster, the Giant Dipper, make this heaven for youngsters. Rides at either end of the Boardwalk, including a

The dolphin tank at Long Marine Lab in Santa Cruz keeps inquisitive kids on their learning toes. Shmuel Thaler

mellow Ferris wheel, bumper cars, "underground" train excursions and a colorful vintage-1911 carousel, will please the very young. Wilder rides, including the state-of-the-art, stomach-churning, mind-melting Typhoon will test the endurance of teenagers and impress even the most jaded thrill seeker. Neptune's Kingdom, an indoor pirate-theme amusement center with a video arcade, historical displays, snack bars and a two-story miniature golf course, is perfect for the entire family.

Seymour Marine Discovery Center at Long Marine Lab 831-459-3800, 100 Shaffer Rd., Santa Cruz. Docents lead tours through the public aquarium and touch tanks, where visitors can get up close and personal with hermit crabs, sea anemones and more. They also teach about the marine environment of the Monterey Bay. Open Tues.–Sat. 10–5, Sun. noon–5 (site tours at 1, 2 and 3pm). Adults $5, seniors, students or youths $3, children 5 and under free. First Tues. of each month is free.

Museums

COASTAL ART LEAGUE GALLERY
www.art.net/thegallery/calm
650-726-6335
520 Kelly Ave., Half Moon Bay 94019
Open: Thurs.–Mon. 11–5
Admission: Free

A nonprofit, cooperative gallery, this "artists' gallery" treats all of its artwork as museum quality and exhibits it as such. Shows are installed every five weeks and showcase the best in traditionalist, regional and incisive art from Half Moon Bay and Bay Area artists.

MARY PORTER SESNON GALLERY
831-459-3606
Porter College, UCSC, Santa Cruz
Open: Tues.–Sun. noon–5
Admission: Free.

Innovative schedule of exhibitions in two small galleries highlight contemporary California, Native American and Latin American artists. Cutting-edge installations in a friendly setting.

MUSEUM OF ART AND HISTORY
www.santacruzmah.org
831-429-1964
705 Front St., Santa Cruz 95060
Open: Tues.–Sun. 11–5
Admission: Adults $5, students & elders $2, 17 and under free; everyone free first Fri. each month

One of the cornerstones of post-earthquake-of-1989 Santa Cruz, this joint cultural venture of the Art Museum of Santa Cruz County and the Santa Cruz County Historical Trust offers revolving exhibitions highlighting regional history and contemporary artists. A permanent installation, packed with heirloom clothing, tools, trunks and telegraphs on the second floor of the main building, accesses the entire history of human habitation in the area, from the Ohlone people through the frontier logging boom to the boardwalk fantasy world. The museum presents talks, tours and films on art and history-related themes and features a rental gallery of work by area artists.

SANTA CRUZ ART LEAGUE
www.scal.org
831-426-5787
526 Broadway Ave., Santa Cruz 95060
Open: Wed.–Sat., 11–5, Sun. noon–4
Admission: Donations

A showcase for revolving exhibitions of top California and Monterey Bay artists, including invitational and juried collections.

✪ SANTA CRUZ CITY MUSEUM OF NATURAL HISTORY
www.santacruzmuseums.org
831-420-6115
1305 E. Cliff Dr., Santa Cruz 95062
Open: Tues.–Sun. 10–5
Admission: Adults $2.50, elders $1.50, 18 and under free

Housed in a graceful seaside mansion overlooking the Monterey Bay, the museum offers visitors an eyeful in the way of exhibits detailing the natural and cultural history of the northern Central Coast area. Ohlone artifacts share space with illustrated specimens of local flora and fauna and fossil remains. Docent-led museum tours, field trips, classes and workshops are available, as well as year-round classes for youngsters on natural history topics. Not to be missed are January's Fungus Fair and June's Native Animal Day.

✪ SANTA CRUZ SURFING MUSEUM

831-420-6289
Mark Abbott Memorial Lighthouse, W. Cliff Dr., Santa Cruz 95060
Open: Wed.–Mon. noon–4
Admission: Free (donations accepted)

Billing itself as the only surfing museum in the world, this eclectic collection of vintage longboards, videos, photographs and memorabilia, including the first wet suit, tracks the history of surfing in Santa Cruz. The tiny collection housed inside the Mark Abbott Memorial Lighthouse, perched above the world-class surf activity of Steamer Lane, features a sweeping view of the Santa Cruz Beach and Boardwalk. On this spot in the late 1900s, Hawaiian princes first brought the ancient Polynesian sport to the New World.

Music

✪ **Bach Dancing & Dynamite Society** 650-726-4143, P.O. Box 302, El Granada 94108. Jazz nut and self-proclaimed beach bum Pete Douglas has run this homey, nonprofit music emporium on Miramar Beach for over 30 years. $16 to $20 will get you great music (often from touring headliners or up-and-coming Young Turks between gigs in San Francisco and Los Angeles) and incomparable ocean views. For a few dollars more, you can partake of a buffet. Attention: Bring your own wine. Classical music on most Saturdays, jazz on Sunday at 4pm. A mailer of coming attractions is available upon request

Cabrillo Festival of Contemporary Music www.cabrillomusic.org; e-mail: ellen@cabrillo music.org, 831-426-6966, 104 Walnut Ave., Suite 206, Santa Cruz 95060. Affectionately known by locals as the CabMuFest, this four-decade-old, internationally acclaimed two-week summer festival of new, adventurous and avant-garde music takes the Santa Cruz cultural community by storm, usually during the first weeks of August. The award-winning festival orchestra is led by music director and conductor Marin Alsop, and guest artists have included John Cage, Nadja Salerno-Sonnenberg, Lou Harrison, Phillip Glass, Keith Jarret, the Kronos Quartet, Aaron Jay Kernis and John Adams. The highlight of the season is the closing day of performances in the acoustically charmed Mission San Juan Bautista.

New Music Works www.newmusicworks.org; e-mail: pmcomp@cruzio.com, 831-724-7010, P.O. Box 2266, Santa Cruz 95063-2266. Supported in part by the Aaron Copland Fund for New Music, this music ensemble, comprised of professional musicians and composers, showcases the best in contemporary classical music during its fall–spring season. Conductor Phillip Collins takes the group through myriad chamber music and musical-theater pieces, including its annual Night of the Living Composers, and culminates with the whimsical Avant Garden Party in June.

Santa Cruz Baroque Festival www.scbaroque.org; e-mail: info@scbaroque.org, 831-457-9693, P.O. Box 482, Santa Cruz 95061. Gifted soloist and cultural arts impresaria Linda Burman-Hall lures top baroque interpreters and virtuosos of harpsichord, forte piano and vocal repertoire from the San Francisco and Monterey Bay areas to perform in this stellar series of early masters concerts. Bach, Vivaldi, Mozart, and Scarlotti are brilliantly represented by solo, chamber and baroque specialists during its February–May season.

Santa Cruz Chamber Players www.scchamberplayers.org, 831-425-3149, UCSC, Santa Cruz. Stocked with local musicians with an appreciation of unusual chamber music, featuring traditional and contemporary masterpieces, this local musical institution plays venues around the county and on the university campus during its fall–spring season.

Santa Cruz County Symphony www.santacruzsymphony.com; e-mail: sccs@santacruz symphony.org, 831-462-0553, 200 7th Ave., Suite 225, Santa Cruz 95062. Under the leadership of music director John Larry Granger, this aural talent bank stages a dynamic series of classical and contemporary orchestral masterworks performed by resident symphony and guest virtuosos in the acoustically renovated, art deco Santa Cruz Civic Auditorium and Watsonville's Mello Center during a fall–spring season.

Nightlife

120 Union 831-459-9876, 120 Union St., Santa Cruz. Neobopster hangout where poets and radicals gather to spread the political and lit word. Good coffees, good beers and sometimes some good jazz jams.

99 Bottles of Beer 831-459-9999, 110 Walnut Ave., Santa Cruz. The perfect bar for those who love their suds, 99 Bottles has a warm, brick-and-hardwood interior that just begs patrons to settle in for the long haul. As the name implies, there's a huge selection of the frothy stuff, from local microbrews to foreign beers—drink 'em all (not at one sitting, of course) and you'll find your name on the wall of fame. Features an upstairs gaming room and a ton of pub food to complement all that beer.

Anchor Tap 831-477-0749, 209 Esplanade, Capitola Village. Catch live dinner music on Wednesday night, DJ spinners on weekends and an occasional National Championship of Karaoke on some Sunday early evenings at this pub overlooking Capitola's cozy beachfront.

The Aptos Club www.aptosclub.com, 831-688-9888, 7941 Soquel Dr., Aptos. Good old-fashioned rock and roll takes command of the stage every night of the week and doesn't give it up (except to karaoke on Wednesday). A roadhouse without much socially redeeming value.

The Avenue Bar 831-426-3434, 711 Pacific Ave., Santa Cruz. Renovations include nicely appointed private booths, a wood floor and a tasteful back patio sporting an outdoor bar. It's a place where urban professionals in their early 30s would feel quite comfortable—though it's more akin to a working-class rumpus room. As the plethora of video games and tight shirts would suggest, young college kids looking for love still fill the place on a Friday night.

✪ **Blue Lagoon Cocktail Lounge** 831-423-7117, 923 Pacific Ave., Santa Cruz. The Blue Lagoon remains the best place in town to get down to techno and disco music. Its full bar offers an amazing selection of libations, and a celebration of any sort isn't the same without one of the bar's famous Flaming Dr Peppers. Expect a diverse crowd, from the leather-clad to those in velour hip-huggers. Don't be shocked if there's a line out the door—more and more people (of all sexual persuasions) have come to know and love Santa Cruz's oldest gay bar.

Bocci's Cellar 831-427-1795, 140 Encinal St., Santa Cruz. Classic Big Band swing music aficionados will call this place home. The small cellar stage area is filled to overflowing with quality interpreters of jazz and pop of the last 50 years. Some sweet rocker types also squeeze in some nights of the week. A hidden gem.

Brookdale Lodge www.brookdalelodge.com, 831-338-6433, 11570 Hwy. 9, Brookdale. A San Lorenzo Valley tradition, the lodge lures old hippies and rock-and-roll greats in the twilight of their careers (think Leon Russell) and a lot of local talent, too. Open mic and a prime rib dinner command attention in the world-famous Brook Room (a stream runs directly through it) every Thursday night. Late-night food and overnight rooms are also available for those turned off by driving home down snaky Highway 9 after the heavy-drinking gig is done.

✪ **The Catalyst** www.catalystclub.com, 831-423-1336, 1011 Pacific Ave., Santa Cruz. One of the coast's top venues, the friendly dance hall, affectionately nicknamed the "Cat" by locals, offers a billiards room, three bars, a great sound system and a massive dance floor. Every form of rock and world-fusion music is booked, including area artists and some of the biggest names in the biz like Emmylou Harris, Pearl Jam and Neil Young. The Catalyst serves food daily, has three full bars, multiple pool tables and a tropical, vine-ensconced atrium where smaller acts sometimes play.

Cayuga Vault 831-421-9471, 1100 Soquel Ave., Santa Cruz. Some of the best folkies on the rise, loopers on the edge and experimental musicians slightly out of their orbits pack this small, intimate venue with the sounds of tomorrow. The local avant-garde scene is alive and well at this comfy, safe house for all things weird yet melodic.

Cetrella www.cetrella.com, 650-726-4090, 845 Main St., Half Moon Bay. Spiffy crowds and talented singers blend at this hip and sophisticated venue. Some of the best jazz practioners in northern California make this a regular stop on their tours. Always hopping Thursday through Saturday night. It closes early, so hit this place before the music stops around 11pm.

Club Caution www.clubcaution.net, 516 Front St., Santa Cruz. The newest club on the local scene seems like it could have it all when it throws open the doors as 2005 dawns: outdoor patio, long wooden bar, game room, restaurant, Wi-Fi hot spot, record store, dance floor, performance stage and DJ booth. The owners promise "all the lights and power of New York City, the theatrics of Hollywood and the personality of our own San Francisco." Wow. Can they pull it off? Only time (and booze and prosperous boy–girl relationships) will tell.

Club Dakota 831-454-9030, 1209 Pacific Ave., Santa Cruz 95060. DJ spinmeisters get their groove thang on most nights of the week, and sexy young (and not so young) things offer a rainbow of sexual-oriented possibilities on the dance floor and intimate booths. Women's night rules every Wednesday.

Cocoanut Grove Ballroom 831-423-2053, 400 Beach St., at the Boardwalk, Santa Cruz. A little bit of cultural history thrives in this Boardwalk institution. Built back in the 1940s, the elegant ballroom has seen its share of big names, magical nights and frolicking patrons. Glenn Miller, Tito Puente, David Crosby and James Brown are just some of the acts who've done their magic on the retro bandstand. Still headlines some fair talents.

Crow's Nest www.crowsnest-santacruz.com, 831-476-4560, 2218 E. Cliff Dr., Santa Cruz Yacht Harbor. Like a grand old galleon, this venerable drinking (and eating) establishment keeps sailing right along, only stopping to pick up devoted new passengers. It's a one-size-fits-all spot, though definitely not a Gen X place. The Nest caters to the yachting—or wannabe yachting—crowd. Good drinks, loud rocking local bands, seasoned atmosphere and plenty of pretty people upon whom to feast your roving eyes.

Fog Bank 831-462-1881, 211 Esplanade, Capitola. A rocking pickup voodoo room with a loud, boisterous bonhomie that doesn't fade till the doors are padlocked and everyone is turned out into the night. All things and all others still unattached look better near closing time, so be forewarned: Morning could bring mourning.

Henfling's www.henflings.com; e-mail: tmm@cruzio.com, 831-336-8811, 9450 Hwy. 9, Ben Lomond. This great grub, grog, dance floor and roots Americana music roadhouse in the San Lorenzo Valley books some of the best up-and-coming folkie, blues and rock performers before they hit the big time, as well as some of the classic acts that can't quite fill the big halls anymore. The music and vibes are excellent and as local as you can get. A musical outdoor barbecue is featured every Saturday and Sunday afternoon.

Hoffmann's Bakery Café 831-420-0135, 1102 Pacific Ave., Santa Cruz. Some nice scones to go with that jazz classic, sir? Good smells, great tastes and elegant jazz riffs team up for a free, mellow downtown Santa Cruz pit stop, almost every early evening of the week.

Ideal Bar & Grill 831-423-5271, 106 Beach St., Santa Cruz. Best known as a restaurant, Ideal also has a bar located right at the mouth of the Santa Cruz Wharf. Settled seductively along the sand, Ideal's interior is as light and breezy as the beach air—viney greenery winds its way around the nooks and crannies, and surfboards and surfer pix adorn the walls. There's a square bar chock-full of all of the libations that one could hope for and a small, live-music stage. Almost every night, smooth jazz, rock and pop accompany the drinking and dining.

✪ Kuumbwa Jazz Center www.kuumbwajazz.org, 831-427-2227, 320-2 Cedar St., Santa Cruz. A Santa Cruz institution for nearly 30 years, Kuumbwa attracts some of the top names in both classic and experimental jazz. A nonprofit club propelled mostly by the success of big-name, sellout shows, donations and grants, it offers an outlet for both local performers and those of worldwide acclaim. Thursday nights and weekends tend to see area artists playing world-beat, trance and acid jazz, and some traveling folk and rock icons dropping by on their way to LA or San Francisco. The Monday Night Concert Series boasts the crème de la crème of the jazz world, seemingly headlining every legend still working the jazz-club and concert-hall circuits. Nothing but the best is the motto here. Nestled in between downtown SC's Bagelry and Poet & Patriot, it's an intimate venue that attracts appreciative, knowledgeable audiences. Wine, beer and tasty grub are served in the back.

Margaritaville www.margaritaville.com, 831-476-2263, 231 Esplanade, Capitola. DJs provide the music, and good-looking fellas and gals provide the eye candy and possible romantic futures. Expect some good, clean weekend fun with fresh and frolicking young adults.

Mediterranean www.themedfly.net, 831-688-7004, 265 Center St., Aptos. The epicenter of local punk and alternative-rock music scenes. This intimate little club usually features three bands churning out powerful original material every night of the week. The Med has experienced some sound-bothers-neighbors dustups in the past, so it's best to give a call before showing up for a night of drinking, dancing and stage diving.

✪ Moe's Alley www.moesalley.com, 831-479-1854, 1535 Commercial Way, Santa Cruz. Moe's has all of the makings of a classic roadhouse joint: smoky, dimly lit and appealing to all walks of life, from aging hippies, old-time bluesmen and cowpokes to college kids, hipsters and singles. It's a clean, comfortable spot to enjoy live music any night of the week. Local bands, plus nationally recognized blues powerhouses like Joe Louis Walker, Charlie Musselwhite, Chris Cain and Duke Robillard, play the best in funky covers and original material.

Mr. Toots 831-475-3679, 221 Esplanade, Capitola. Some mighty fine bluegrass and folk practioners sit in the Toots spotlight any given night of the week. Mellow sounds to accompany sips of beer, wine or java con coctions.

Poet & Patriot Irish Pub 831-426-8620, 320 Cedar St., Suite E, Santa Cruz. When Celtic musicians aren't fiddling and drumming in the front room, the Poet overflows with university types tossing back pints and talking about their goatees and the revolution—in that order. The other room is dedicated to darts, which gets a little serious at times, and the bar stools belong to old hippies and card-carrying Irishmen. Dark, low-ceilinged, smoky-aired and sticky-tabled, this is a bar that feels like an old friend with interesting opinions. Word to the curious: Reading the walls is good "edutainment."

A true own-and-dirty roadhouse, Moe's Alley attracts some of the best blues musicians alive to its comfy confines. George Sakkestad

Chris Matthews, owner of the Poet & Patriot in Santa Cruz. The pub offers Celtic music and other entertainment. Robert Scheer

● **Red Room** 831-426-2994, Santa Cruz Hotel, 1003 Cedar St., Santa Cruz. Easily the loudest, most irritating, most forgiving place to get a drink in town. The multiply-pierced, the almost retired, the grunged, the lifted, the alternatively gendered, the manic—they all come here, sooner or later, and form an immediate pod of evening camaraderie. After 9pm, laughter at this bar becomes a collective bonding ritual. Even the socially deficient leave with new best friends. A rite of passage. A way of life.

Seabright Brewery www.seabrightbrewery.com, 831-426-2739, 519 Seabright Ave., Santa Cruz. One of the most popular spots on the Eastside, the brewery boasts beers brewed on-site, a menu of appetizers, burgers and salads and one of the finest outdoor patios for sun-soaked afternoons and heater-warmed nights. Tuesday marks the famed "Neighborhood Night"—those from outside the burg are also

Allison Smith is recognized as the personable Princess of the Patio at Eastside Santa Cruz's award-winning Seabright Brewery. George Sakkestad

welcomed with open arms—for a night of discount pitchers from 3pm until closing. Seabright ushers in the weekend with live music every Friday evening.

Severino's www.seacliffinn.com, 831-688-8987, 7500 Old Dominion Court, Aptos. The Seacliff Inn's very own restaurant, bar and dance spot, Severino's is a sexy watering hole for well-heeled, cultured adults looking to let loose for a night. Don those spiffy clothes, be on your best behavior (at least until you've downed a few martinis) and soak in the sights. There's live jazz and pop standards Wednesdays through Saturdays, an outdoor patio and a trickling waterfall. It's a comfortable, attentive nightspot.

Shadowbrook 831-475-1511, 1750 Wharf Rd., Capitola. Mellow songsters and jazz-influenced musicians grace this small and cozy bar space with a world-famous restaurant just a few steps away. For decades now, this cool listening room has employed some of Santa Cruz's most gifted music makers on their nights off from their regular bands and gigs, and the sounds seem like they'll just go on forever, thanks to wise management and loyal local followers of the jazz muse.

Vets Hall 831-454-0478, 846 Front St., Santa Cruz. This funky old auditorium still packs 'em in for traveling punk shows and big-name reggae splashes. Something wicked or fringe seems to be happening here at least one night a week, sometimes more during summer.

Windjammer 831-688-4433, Rancho Del Mar Center, Aptos. Old-fashioned rock and roll and some streetwise country rock are the mainstays at this quarter-century-old destination hot spot. Lots of good local talent still kicking out the jams for rowdy weekend bacchanals.

Stage
Actors' Theatre www.openstage.org, 831-425-7529, 1001 Center St., Santa Cruz. Dramatic and musical performances, plus a series of readings of new plays, are offered by this lively, local, year-round production company in a small theater venue.

Bay Shore Lyric Opera Company www.bslopera.com, 888-496-7372, 831-462-3131, 120 Monterey Ave., Capitola. Around for nearly a decade, the Bay Shore Lyric Opera performs some of the world's classic operas like *Die Fledermaus*, *Carmen* and *La Bohème*. The company's full productions, complete with a 26-piece orchestra, are staged in the vintage Capitola Theater.

✪ **Shakespeare Santa Cruz** www.shakespearesantacruz.org, 831-459-2121, 831-459-2159 tickets, Theater Arts Center, UCSC, 1156 High St., Santa Cruz. A vivacious professional theater company of top American and British actors hosts innovative and critically acclaimed productions of Shakespeare and related contemporary dramatic works. The four-play summer festival holds forth in repertory performances on the large Performing Arts Theater stage, as well as in the outdoor redwood glen.

Tandy Beal & Company 831-429-1324, 740 Front St., Santa Cruz. Santa Cruz is the home base of this nationally acclaimed troupe, an innovative touring ensemble that peforms its engaging blend of soaring contemporary choreography and witty multimedia work several times each year in Santa Cruz and Monterey, as well as in major big-city venues.

This Side of the Hill Players 650-726-0998, 1167 Main St., Half Moon Bay. The local theater company stages three full productions a year, including original and classic plays like *The Great Toy Conspiracy* and *The Fantasticks*.

UCSC Presents 831-459-2826, UCSC, Santa Cruz. The campus's arts and lecture series books top multicultural troupes from around the world and innovative dance faculty choreographers to dance on the university's Performing Arts Theater stage.

Paul Whitworth as Richard III, in a production by Shakespeare Santa Cruz, a professional company comprising British and American actors.

Shakespeare Santa Cruz

RECREATION

Obsessed with the outdoors and drawn to the sea, Santa Cruzans relish reinventing ways to play in the open air. No stretch of scenic road is without its walkers, runners and cyclists. Rain or shine, beaches bloom with tide pooling and volleyball enthusiasts. Beyond the edge of the land, the ocean simmers with surfers, swimmers and sailors. Parasailers, windsurfers and hang gliders tempt the fates at myriad sites. Fishing enthusiasts find reverie and fuel for tall tales in wave, pond and stream. Camping along the coast and in its forests and valleys is de rigueur for all. Whatever the recreational itch, Santa Cruz has the exact pastime to scratch it.

Beaches

These beaches are described in the order you will encounter them traveling southward down the Pacific Coast Highway from San Francisco, the best jumping-off point.

El Granada Beach Bet. E. Breakwater & Mirada Rd., Half Moon Bay. A seawall keeps this sheltered, sandy stretch particularly peaceful. Come prepared for cool, foggy conditions. Parking and restrooms are available. No entrance fee.

Dunes Beach Off Young Ave., Half Moon Bay. A dirt road provides access to this prime setting for horseback riding on the beach. Horse rentals are nearby just off Hwy. 1. Ample parking. No entrance fee.

Venice Beach Venice Blvd., Half Moon Bay. Adjoins Dunes Beach by way of a dirt road. Offers luxurious sand, perfect for horseback riding and all-day beachcombing. No entrance fee.

Francis Beach Kelly Ave., Half Moon Bay. One of the fishing village's main beach areas, this spot offers 50 campsites and RV slots, with picnic tables on bluffs overlooking the beach. Restrooms and beach alike are wheelchair accessible. Fees for camping and day use.

Laguna Creek Beach Hwy. 1 at Laguna Creek. Another of this stretch of the coast's many hidden, cliff-hewn cove beaches. Undeveloped, to the delight of privacy-conscious sun worshippers. No entrance fee.

Martin's Beach Hwy. 1, 6 miles south of Half Moon Bay. Prime surf fishing, especially for smelt, is the top attraction of this privately developed cove beach. Restrooms and picnic tables are available. Toll road with entrance fee.

San Gregorio Beach Hwy. 1 & San Gregorio Rd., San Gregorio. At the intersection of old stagecoach roads, this idyllic cove setting is framed by encircling coastal hills and rolling farmlands. The spot marks one of the campsites of Portola's 1769 Spanish expedition to the San Francisco Bay. Watch out for rip currents. Restrooms and picnic tables supply all-day comfort. Day-use entrance fee.

Pomponio State Beach Hwy. 1, 3 miles north of Pescadero Rd., Pescadero. A luscious stretch of beach offers prime driftwood-gathering possibilities, thanks to the confluence of a scenic creek and the sea. Many facilities, including restrooms, picnic tables, cooking grills and ample parking, are available. Day-use fee.

Pescadero State Beach Hwy. 1 at Pescadero Rd., Pescadero. This mile-long beach offers an irresistible diversity of terrain, from soft dunes to highly explorable tide pools. Just across the Coast Highway from the sights and sounds of the wildlife preserve of Pescadero Marsh and offering lots of restroom facilities and picnic sites, this is a top all-day destination. Plenty of parking and hiking trails. No entrance fee.

Bean Hollow State Beach One mile south of Pescadero Rd. on Hwy. 1. A little gem of curved beach and lagoon offers a view of pounding waves and dangerous surf. Parking, restrooms and picnic tables are available. No entrance fee.

Pebble Beach Hwy. 1, bet. Hill Rd. & Artichoke Rd., 1.5 miles south of Pescadero Rd., Pescadero. Pebbles worn round and smooth by the waves are the specialty here, including varieties of agate. Tiny but inviting, there is a self-guided nature trail leading south to Bean Hollow State Beach. Restrooms and picnic tables are available. No entrance fee.

Año Nuevo State Reserve Hwy. 1 & New Years Creek Rd., Pescadero. Hiking trails lead along the northern bluffs, dunes and tide pools of this famous sanctuary. Gray whale sightings are legion during winter months, but the prime attraction remains the boisterous breeding ritual of the elephant seals, which gather here to mate and bear their soft, endearing young. Parking, restrooms and a wheelchair-accessible path and viewing platform are available. Named by the explorer Sebatian Vizcaino on January 3, 1603, this fascinating peninsula and offshore island contains tide pools filled with sea urchins, hermit crabs, anemones and other intertidal life-forms, while shell mounds left by Ohlone residents thousands of years ago still dot its rugged marsh, scrub and dunes. The Año Nuevo State Reserve protects colonies of northern elephant seals, which annually populate the sandy reaches of the reserve's more than 1 million acres during the winter breeding season. On guided walks, visitors may observe the enormous creatures at close hand from December to March. Highly popular, the three-hour tour requires advance reservations (650-879-2025). Entrance fee.

Waddell Creek Beach Hwy. 1, 1 mile south of San Mateo–Santa Cruz County line. Adored by those who live here, this is the quintessential northern Central Coast beach. At the southwest tip of Big Basin State Park, this beautiful setting offers prime beachcombing and leisurely walks. Hang gliders love to soar overhead, and the surf beyond is invariably flecked with the multicolored sails of windsurfers. Coastal access is available via plenty of well-marked paths, as well as trails worn over the years by legions of die-hard surfers. Use trails through private property with discretion, since many of the local farmers are not amused by trespassers, however innocent or athletic. But if you feel the need to take your shoes off and gambol in the ebb tide with someone you love, this is the place. On the romantic scale of 1 to 10, Waddell Creek is a 12. Restrooms and parking are available. No entrance fee.

Scott Creek Beach Hwy. 1 north of Davenport Landing, Davenport. The broad expanse of sand offers plenty of room for sunbathers and beachcombers. An intertidal reef and numerous tide pools teem with marine life. Rest rooms and parking are available. No entrance fee.

Davenport Beach Hwy. 1 at Davenport. Undeveloped and sheltered, this beach roams along cliffs and bluffs. Parking only on highway shoulders and in the town of Davenport. No entrance fee.

Panther Beach Hwy. 1, 1 mile north of Bonny Doon Rd., near Davenport. Accessible only by a trail through artichoke fields, this secluded setting remains undeveloped and heavily frequented by die-hard surfers and boozing teens from the Santa Clara Valley. Fistfights and car break-ins compete with the crashing waves for visitors' attention.

Bonny Doon Beach Hwy. 1 at Bonny Doon Rd., south of Davenport. Hidden from view, this stretch is a cult favorite with surfers throughout the northern Central Coast. No facilities, no entrance fee.

Red, White & Blue Beach Hwy. 1 at Scaroni Rd., 5.5 miles north of Santa Cruz. A red, white and blue mailbox marks the spot south of Davenport for fans of clothing-optional sunbathing. Long a private beach, this naturists' mecca offers picnic tables but frowns on cameras and dogs. Day-use and camping fee.

Natural Bridges State Beach 2531 W. Cliff Dr. off Hwy. 1 (Mission St.), Santa Cruz. At the northern edge of Santa Cruz proper, rugged cliffs and sandstone rock formations sculpted by wind and wave create an enchanting setting. Unfortunately, the graceful arches that gave the beach its name have succumbed to the elements. Features over 50 acres of cypress and eucalyptus groves, to which the brilliant orange monarch butterflies migrate each year. On weekends from October to February, guided tours of the Butterfly Natural Preserve are available. Natural Bridges is famous for tide pools filled with pink-tentacled anemones, black turban snails, prehistoric-looking mossy chiton and purple sea urchins. Sandy beaches adjoin picnic sites, and much of the lovely property is wheelchair accessible. Restrooms and ample parking are available. No entrance fee.

Lighthouse Field State Beach W. Cliff Dr. & Pelton Ave., Santa Cruz. Just north of Lighthouse Point, this broad stretch of beach offers fine swimming and is accessible by walkways down to the sand. The basic theme here is "endless summer," with plenty of impromptu musical and drumming sessions, frolicking dogs and kids. Across the street is an undeveloped park of wildflowers and trees crisscrossed by walking and biking paths and studded with picnic tables. This is a favorite local spot for early-morning and sunset walking rituals, cycling, in-line skating and front-row viewing of the surfing just off Lighthouse Point. Parking is available. No entrance fee.

Cowell Beach W. Cliff Dr. & Bay St., Santa Cruz. Stairways lead down to this prime day-use location at the top of Santa Cruz's main beach, featuring volleyball during the summer and year-round surfing at Steamer Lane, one of the legendary sites on the Pacific Ocean. A paved walkway leads to restrooms, and wheelchair access to the shore is provided during the summer season. Parking and lifeguard on duty during the crowded summer season. No entrance fee.

Santa Cruz Main Beach and Boardwalk Beach St. near Front St., Santa Cruz. The Boardwalk with its vendors, games and rides is the last remaining oceanfront amusement park in California. On a hot day, the adjoining Santa Cruz and Cowell Beaches are where the action is—whether it's surfing, sunbathing, swimming, volleyball or strolling on the pier. Ample pay parking. No entrance fee.

Seabright Beach E. Cliff Dr. & Seabright Ave., Santa Cruz. Known to locals as Castle Beach, this wide, sandy shoreline abuts the wonderful Santa Cruz Museum of Natural History. Good water sport spot. Limited parking. No entrance fee.

Twin Lakes State Beach 7th Ave. at E. Cliff Dr., Santa Cruz. Warm, wide and sheltered, this inviting expanse of sand curves around the mouth of a lagoon abundantly populated with ducks, geese and native waterfowl. Popular with lovers, sunbathers, families and fishing buffs who patrol the nearby harbor jetty. An irresistible stretch of powdery white sand, the beach offers lots of windsurfing and volleyball action, plus the eye appeal of boats weaving in and out of the yacht harbor. Restrooms are available. Parking is on roadway shoulders (a bit dicey during the summer). No entrance fee.

Corcoran Lagoon Beach E. Cliff Dr. at 21st Ave., Santa Cruz. Frequented by the local beach community, this undeveloped cove is accessible by stairs at 20th Ave. and offers some fine tide pools, as well as sand. No entrance fee.

Pleasure Point Beach E. Cliff Dr. & 41st Ave., Santa Cruz. A number of rocky trails lead to this surfing, swimming and clamming spot. The bluffs above the beach offer spectacular views of Monterey Bay, and several tide pools invite exploration. No entrance fee.

Privates/Key Beach E. Cliff Dr. south of 41st Ave., Santa Cruz. Some of the top surfers in the country haunt this charming pocket beach, accessible via walkway through private property. Undeveloped, it offers minimal parking. No entrance fee.

The sheltered sands of Capitola City Beach offer a haven for beach lovers and sandcastle builders of all ages.
Shmuel Thaler

Hooper Beach Capitola Wharf, Capitola. Peacefully out of the way from Capitola's main beach, this secluded stretch is perfect for undisturbed wave-watching and picnicking. Parking is available but usually a challenge. No entrance fee.

Capitola City Beach Esplanade & Monterey Sts., Capitola. Restaurants, shops and galleries line the esplanade framing this popular swimming, sunbathing and people-watching area. A safe play area for children is formed by the curve of Soquel Creek as it meets the sea, and nonstop volleyball is practically a religion. Parking is almost impossible, so take the shuttle located at the Hwy. 1 & Park Ave. exit. No entrance fee.

Seacliff State Beach Seacliff exit off Hwy. 1., Rio Del Mar. You'll find a natural history center, covered picnic areas and 26 RV sites along this long, sandy, 85-acre beach, which stretches below picturesque bluffs. The swimming is good, and fishing is allowed from a pier where the concrete-hulled freighter *Palo Alto* (a user-friendly curiosity left over from World War I) is docked. Showers are available. Entrance fee.

New Brighton State Beach Hwy. 1 Park Ave. exit, 4 miles south of Santa Cruz. Pristinely sheltered, these 68 sandy acres are crowned by bluffs of fragrant eucalyptus and offer myriad trails through beachfront forests and beach access by stairway. A good waterfowl viewing area, the long sandy beach offers restrooms that are wheelchair accessible, 115 campsites, showers and bicycle camping sites. Fire pits along the beach make this a popular location for alfresco cookery. A splendid view of the Monterey coastline, just across the bay, makes this a favorite with vacationers and day trippers alike. Entrance fee.

Rio Del Mar Beach South end of Seacliff State Beach, take Seacliff exit off Hwy. 1, Rio Del Mar. An esplanade well stocked with convenience stores and a fine seafood restaurant and bar fronts this wide expanse of sand that offers lots of privacy and long stretches of strolling during the week. On the weekends, the secret is poorly kept. Gentle waves make it attractive for bodysurfing during the late summer and early fall. A bike path/walking trail connects with nearby Seacliff State Beach. Restrooms and ample parking are available. No entrance fee.

Manresa State Beach Hwy. 1 to San Andreas Rd. exit, La Selva. A treasure in this stretch of the coast, Manresa is accessible via stairway and paths from the main parking lot and by Sand Dollar Dr. walkway. Lovely for strolling and wading with the abundant shorebirds. Swimmers beware: Manresa possesses formidable rip currents. Restrooms and 63 camp-sites for tent camping are available. Entrance fee.

Sunset State Beach San Andreas Rd. off Hwy. 1, Watsonville. Diverse flora and fauna, huge sand dunes and a pine-forested, 90-tent site and RV campground distinguish this long expanse of beach. Located in a rural area just south of Manresa State Beach, its 7 miles of sandy shoreline are great for beachcombing, picnicking, fishing and clamming. Showers are available. Entrance fee.

Palm Beach Hwy. 1 to Hwy. 129 exit then to Beach Rd., Watsonville. Encompassing a drift-wood mother lode at the mouth of the Pajaro River, this is a lovely getaway beach boasting wheelchair-accessible restrooms, a picnic area and a fitness trail. Day-use fee.

Bicycling

BICYCLE RENTALS
Bicycle Shop of Santa Cruz www.bicycleshopsantacruz.com, 831-454-0909, 1325 Mission St., Santa Cruz.

Bicyclery 650-726-6000, 415 Main St., Half Moon Bay.

Bike Works 20 Stone Pine Rd., Suite G, Half Moon Bay, 650-726-6708.

Electric Bike Rentals 831-459-7235, 115 Cliff, Santa Cruz.

Electric Sierra Cycles www.electricrecbikes.com, 831-425-1593, 302 Pacific Ave., Santa Cruz.

Family Cycling Center www.familycycling.com, 831-475-3883, 914 41st Ave., Santa Cruz.

TOP RIDES
Bonny Doon to San Lorenzo Valley Bonny Doon Rd. invites the lover of winding mountain roads to pedal through some classic redwood country. After a fairly serious climb, the road turns into Empire Grade, which follows a rocky ridge north through a level road dotted with old orchards, farmhouses and vineyards. Descending Empire Grade into the small town of Felton and Hwy. 9, the cyclist encounters forests filled with moss-covered bay trees, madrones and redwoods that all but blot out the sun and form a long, green cathedral corridor.

East Cliff Drive This pleasant route runs along both sides of E. Cliff Dr., offering spectacular views of Monterey Bay.

On a clear day the hills of Monterey across the bay are visible to savvy bicyclists enjoying the bluffs above Santa Cruz. Shmuel Thaler

Natural Bridges State Park Myriad bike paths traverse this 54-acre forest and beach area.

New Brighton State Beach All ages can easily ride through this 68-acre beach located 4 miles south of Santa Cruz.

Pescadero Road Wonderfully flat ride on old stagecoach road through true California backcountry. The charming town of Pescadero is a great stop for lunch and meandering among the quirky shops.

San Lorenzo River Bikepath Bike paths run along both sides of the San Lorenzo River levee from Front St. to Santa Cruz Beach.

UC Santa Cruz Campus This scenic campus is crisscrossed with bike paths and affords cyclists a spectacular view of Monterey Bay.

West Cliff Drive A popular, flat ride from Natural Bridges State Park to the Boardwalk that meanders along the coast past surfers, beachcombers and joggers and through fields of wildflowers and native grasses.

Wheels of Instruction

To immerse yourself immediately into Santa Cruz cycle culture, you could do worse than contacting the folks at the **Santa Cruz County Cycling Club** (www.santacruzcycling.org, 831-438-0706) to find out what's spinning on local roads, where to join group excursions and get their skinny on upcoming races, events and training programs. Neophytes, outsiders and travelers are welcome. Another option would be to contact the **Santa Cruz County Regional Transportation Commission** for its wonderful map of bike paths and lanes that web this very bike-friendly county (www.sccrtc.org, 831-460-3200, 1523 Pacific Ave., Santa Cruz 95060).

Bird-Watching

Pescadero Marsh Natural Preserve Hwy. 1 north of Pescadero Rd., 15 miles south of Half Moon Bay. Over 160 species of birds regularly visit and breed in this beautiful, undeveloped sanctuary, the largest coastal marshlands between Marin County and Elkhorn Slough. Magnificent blue herons and egrets are among the most charismatic. The finest bird-watching seasons are late fall and early spring when the waters teem with loons and grebes, visually stunning additions to the resident community of egrets, herons, kites, hawks, mallards and cinnamon teal. Bird-watching is allowed along Pescadero Rd. and on marked interpretive trails off Hwy. 1. Tread lightly since this is a sensitive spot.

Scott Creek Hwy. 1 north of Davenport. An idyllic vision of tule-lined wetlands is gracefully encircled by the sandy beach on one side and the canyons and redwood-topped slopes of the Santa Cruz Mountains on the other. Wood ducks, cinnamon teals, mallards and coots keep company with grebes, herons and egrets in this languid oasis, especially beautiful in the early morning when mists rise from the surface of the deep green water.

Twin Lakes State Beach E. Cliff Dr. near 7th Ave., Santa Cruz. The lagoon that spills over onto the white sandy beach originates across the slender roadway as Schwan Lagoon, a eucalyptus-ringed wildfowl refuge enjoyed via a wooded path around the park. Here pied-billed grebes and black-necked stilts glide in company with long-billed curlews and marbled godwits. Loons may be heard in the tall grasses, and a wide variety of ducks and geese are happy to be fed by those who come supplied with bags of bread.

Each winter huge numbers of monarch butterflies migrate south for the winter, blanketing eucalyptus groves throughout the Central Coast. Shmuel Thaler

Monarch Butterfly Migration

Great clouds of brilliant orange-and-black wings descend upon the Central Coast each winter as neon-hued monarch butterflies migrate south for the winter. Especially fond of wintering while packed tightly together in astonishing clusters, monarch butterflies literally enshroud entire groves of eucalyptus as they wait in semidormancy for the warmth of spring. Starting in October, the delicate yet hardy long-range travelers are visible all over the coastline, but several spots are renowned for their annual populations of hundreds of thousands. The eucalyptus groves in the sheltered forests at Natural Bridges State Park (just north of Santa Cruz) are prime viewing spots for this annual autumn influx of Lepidoptera. Look, but don't touch. Docents at the park (831-423-4609) lead "butterfly walks" during the fall and winter.

Boating
CANOEING & KAYAKING

Adventure Sports Unlimited www.asudoit.com, 831-458-3648, Sash Mill #15, 303 Potrero St., Santa Cruz 95060. Instruction, classes, rentals, sales, tours of Big Sur and Carmel.

Kayak Connection www.kayakconnection.com, 831-479-1121, Santa Cruz Yacht Harbor, 413 Lake Ave., Santa Cruz 95062. Guided tours, long- and short-term kayak rentals, retail sales.

Venture Quest Kayaking www.kayaksantacruz.com, 831-427-2267, 831-425-8445, 125 Beach St., Santa Cruz 95060. Kayak rentals, sales, lessons and guided tours.

CHARTERS & CRUISES

Chardonnay Sailing Charters www.chardonnay.com, 831-423-1213, Santa Cruz Small Crafts Harbor, Santa Cruz 95060. Ecology excursions to the Monterey Marine Sanctuary, astronomy and sunset cruises, as well as Taste of Santa Cruz and private charters, available aboard a 70-foot racing yacht. Ask about the wine- and beer-maker cruises. Trips depart from Santa Cruz Small Craft Harbor.

Huli Cat www.hulicat.com, 650-726-2926, Pillar Point Harbor, Half Moon Bay. Whale-watching trips, nature cruises and bird outings are the specialty, but team-building outings are also easily arranged.

Lighthall Yacht Charters www.lighthallcharters.com, 831-429-1970, 934 Bay St., Santa Cruz. Participate on Tuesday and Wednesday night races or just enjoy the Saturday afternoon sake tasting or sunset cruise. Dinner cruises also are available.

Pacific Yachting & Sailing www.pacificsail.com, 831-423-7245, 790 Atlantic Ave., Santa Cruz. Choose from two-, four- or six-hour cruises.

Fishing
CHARTERS, RENTALS

Capitola Boat & Bait 831-462-2208, Capitola Wharf, 1400 Wharf Rd., Capitola. Mooring, equipment and boat rentals, bait and tackle, live bait, snacks, novelties and gifts are available.

Chartle Charters www.chartlecharters.com, 831-336-2244, P.O. Box 4202, Santa Cruz. Captain Joe Stoops shares his 25 years of professional fishing experience with serious and casual fishing folk seeking salmon, halibut, rockfish and tuna.

Huck Finn Sportfishing 650-726-7133, Pillar Point Harbor, 1016 Bancroft Ave., Half Moon Bay. Open-party and charter trips for salmon and rockfish aboard a 60-foot boat. Bait, tackle and rental gear are available.

Riptide www.riptide.net, 888-747-8433, 415-469-8433, H Dock, Johnson Pier, Pillar Point Harbor, Half Moon Bay. Fishing for rockfish all year is the call here, but salmon and tuna trips are planned in season. Whale-watching and nature trips also are available.

Santa Cruz Sportfishing www.santacruzsportfishing.com, 831-426-4690, P.O. Box 5235, Santa Cruz. Group and individual fishing trips for salmon, rock cod and albacore in both deep and shallow waters. Whale-watching tours and boat cruises are also available. Fishing equipment, licenses and bait rentals are available. Reservations recommended.

Shamrock Charters www.scurfslanding.com/shamrock.html, 831-476-2648, Santa Cruz Yacht Harbor, 2210 E. Cliff Dr., Santa Cruz. Open boats or private charters for salmon, rock cod, ling cod, and albacore fishing in season. Complete tackle shop and deli sandwiches. Licenses, bait and rod rentals are available.

Stagnaro's Fishing Trips www.stagnaros.com, 831-427-2334, Santa Cruz Municipal Wharf, P.O. Box 7007, Santa Cruz. Daily, half-day and evening trips for salmon and bottom fish, with bait provided. Fish cleaning and ice packing are available. Full-service wharf shop, bait, tackle, rentals, snacks and beer.

PLACES TO FISH

Capitola Fishing Wharf End of Wharf Rd., Capitola. Pier fishing. Bait and tackle shop is available.

Cement Ship 831-685-6444, 831-688-3241, State Park Dr., Aptos. The cement ship *Palo Alto* serves as a whimsical pier. Perch, halibut, flounder, sole and white croaker are caught here.

El Granada Beach runs along Hwy. 1 near Pillar Point Harbor, outside Half Moon Bay. Good surf fishing. The east breakwater is good for rockfishing, and surf perch, white croaker and starry flounder are also abundant.

Greyhound Rock 831-462-8333, Davenport. A favorite and beautiful local fishing spot.

Johnson Pier Half Moon Bay. Open 24 hours a day to catch rockfish and starry flounder.

Martin's Cove Private beach 6 miles south of Half Moon Bay. Small fee for surf fishing and smelt netting. Nets are available for rent.

Pomponio Beach Hwy. 1 south of Half Moon Bay at Pomponio Creek. Surf perch, white croaker, starry flounder and rockfish are caught here.

San Gregorio Beach Hwy. 1 & San Gregorio Rd., San Gregorio. Surf perch, white croaker, starry flounder and rockfish abound. Restrooms and a picnic area are available.

Santa Cruz Municipal Wharf 831-429-3628, Beach St., Santa Cruz. Bonito, croaker, flounder, halibut, ling cod and shark lead the seafood hit parade.

Santa Cruz Small Crafts Harbor 831-475-6161, Eaton St. at Lake Ave., Santa Cruz. Good fishing is available from the east jetty at the entrance. Boat rentals and supplies are available.

Sunset State Beach 831-763-7063, 201 Sunset Rd., Watsonville. Fishing and clamming. Restrooms, picnic areas and showers are available.

Twin Lakes State Park Portola Dr. near 7th Ave., Santa Cruz. Surf fishing is excellent. Restrooms are available.

Golf

De Laveaga Golf Course www.delaveagagolf.com, 831-423-7212, 401 Upper Park Rd. & De Laveaga Dr., Santa Cruz. Taking in spectacular views of the Monterey Bay in the near distance from its hilltop perch above the city of Santa Cruz, this busy course has thrice

Poison Oak Prevention

As if to even up the score in the stunning Central Coast, Mother Nature liberally populated the hills, fields and coastline with that three-leafed devil: poison oak. The oils contained in the leaves and stems of *Rhus diversiloba* are highly toxic to most people, and the allergic rash produced by contact is highly uncomfortable. The rash, with its redness, burning and excruciating itching, can last for weeks, though calamine lotion can provide some relief. The best course is to avoid any cross-country detours and stick to cleared areas and trails. Don't be fooled into thinking that you're safe clambering down the bluffs leading from Hwy. 1 to the shoreline below. In the rocky pockets and dense grasses right on the edge of the ocean wait some of the worst stretches of poison oak in the state. Find out what this plant looks like and memorize its shiny, three-leafed outline. It's unmistakable in the fall, when the leaves turn to a blaze of red and orange glory.

hosted the California State Open Tournament. The entire enterprise just underwent renovation, so some of the following numbers are based on the pre–May 2005 design. Public; 18 holes, 6,010 yards, par 72, rated 70.0. Pro shop, cart rental, night-lighted driving range, bar, restaurant.

Half Moon Bay Golf Links www.halfmoonbaygolf.com, 650-726-4438, 2000 Fairway Dr., Half Moon Bay. Public; 18 holes, 7,100 yards, par 72, rated 71. Pro shop, cart rental, bar, restaurant.

Pasatiempo Golf Club www.pasatiempo.com, 831 459 9155, 18 Clubhouse Rd., Santa Cruz. This beautiful slice of high-links heaven was created by renowned golf architect Alister MacKenzie (he also designed Augusta and Cypress Point) and offers inspiring vistas of the Monterey Bay below. Semiprivate; 18 holes, 6,131 yards, par 70, rated 71.2. Pro shop, cart rentals, driving range, bar, restaurant.

Seascape Golf Club www.seacapegc.com, 831-688-3213, 610 Clubhouse Dr., Aptos. This lovely club prides itself as a "step back in time" experience, where the cypress, Monterey pine and eucalyptus tree protected fairways are guaranteed to be playable for golfers of nearly every skill level. Semiprivate; 18 holes, 6,034 yards, par 71, rated 69.2. Pro shop, cart rentals, driving range, bar, restaurant.

Spring Hills Golf Course www.springhillgc.com, 831-724-1404, 501 Spring Hills Dr., Watsonville. With a beautifully designed course striding a serene, picturesque setting, this rural secret offers streams meandering through the front nine and panoramic views of the Santa Cruz countryside on the back nine. Public; 18 holes, 6,218 yards, par 71, rated 68.7. Pro shop, cart rentals, driving range, beer/wine bar, snack bar.

Hiking

Big Basin State Park 14 miles north of Santa Cruz on Hwy. 9, extending to Hwy. 1, 30 miles north of Santa Cruz. Eighty miles of hiking trails embroider more than 18,000 acres of archetypal redwood forest stretching down to the rocky Pacific coastline. Founded in 1902, Big Basin was the first state park in the California system. Its crystal-clear streams, surging waterfalls, wildlife-rich meadows, fern canyons and towering, old-growth redwoods provide some of the finest hiking on the West Coast. Some trails are legendary. Berry

Creek Falls/Sunset loop begins at the park headquarters and threads through cathedral stands of redwoods to the 65-foot-high Berry Creek Falls, which cascades into a mossy pool in the heart of the forest. Experienced hikers who enjoy a variety of landscapes in a single, all-day trek will want to follow trails meandering along Waddell Creek and Gazos Creek. Leading from the park's mountain interior all the way down to the ocean at Hwy. 1, six- to eight-hour odysseys wind through stands of Douglas fir, madrone, tanbark oak, wild huckleberry, orchids, iris and western azalea. Maps for these and other tree-and-sea trails are available at the ranger's station at the park headquarters.

Butano State Park 5 miles south of Pescadero, 3 miles east of Hwy. 1. Tucked into the Santa Cruz Mountains just north of Big Basin State Park, these 2,200 acres of primeval redwood canyons offer 20 miles of fine hiking trails through dramatic landscape, kept magically moist year-round thanks to coastal fogs. The redwood understory brims with sword fern, trillium, sorrel, thimbleberry and huckleberry, and it's not unusual to spot coyote, gray fox, mule deer and even the occasional bobcat. Backpackers can negotiate a pocket of first-growth redwoods on a 5-mile hike to the 1,600-foot trail peak. Special guided nature walks through this natural sanctuary are offered in the summer.

Forest of Nisene Aptos Creek Rd. via Hwy. 1, Seascape exit. Ablaze with wildflowers during the spring and carpeted with velvety mosses and ferns during the lush, winter wet season, 10,000 acres of relatively undeveloped splendor showcase towering second-growth redwoods, vigorously reborn after the intensive logging of the late 19th century. Hiking trails lead for miles into deep canyons and up to bluffs that afford views of the ocean—the most popular of which follow Aptos Creek Canyon past the ghost town remnants of mining and logging camps. Quail, opossum and mule deer thrive here, and in the spring, the forest floor explodes with exquisite trillium, toothwort and starflowers. A monument to the revitalizing power of nature, the forest cradles the epicenter of the recent 1989 Loma Prieta earthquake, marked by a sign on the Aptos Creek Trail. The forest offers myriad possibilities for day walks, picnics, horseback riding, bicycling and overnight camping at six rather primitive sites along West Ridge Trail.

Gazos Creek Hwy. 1, 20 miles north of Santa Cruz. The Gazos Creek Road leads uphill, eventually becoming a trail that follows the creek through rugged fern canyons and meadows and ends high in the Santa Cruz Mountains at Big Basin State Park. Uphill and all-day, this hike rewards those with sturdy shoes and strong legs with fine views of the coastline and pristine, protected terrain.

Henry Cowell Redwoods State Park 831-335-4598, main entrance 1 mile south of Felton on Hwy. 9. Four thousand acres of magnificently forested redwood preserve were once the home of the Ohlone people. Today, miles of trails lead through impressive stands of oak, madrone, digger pine and chaparral terrain on sunny ridge tops. The ancient heart of this sanctuary is the stand of soaring, old-growth redwoods, easily enjoyed via the 1-mile Redwood Grove Nature Trail loop near the main picnic area. The oldest and most beautiful remaining on the Central Coast, this grove reduces even the jaded to genuine awe.

New Brighton State Beach Hwy. 1 at Park Ave. exit, Aptos. Interpretive nature trails provide prime waterfowl viewing, and sandy trails thread the beachfront, eucalyptus groves and panoramic bluffs of these 68 secluded acres that front a splendid curve of the Monterey Bay. There is ample beach parking for those who want to explore the day away and 115 campsites with restrooms for those with a longer idyll in mind. For information, call 831-475-4850.

Wilder Ranch State Park Coast Rd. at Hwy. 1, 5 miles north of Santa Cruz. Purchased by the State of California, this former dairy ranch still houses authentically restored barns, stables, corrals and Victorian residential structures as part of an interpretive site celebrating ranch life on the 19th-century Central Coast. Hiking trails comb the park's 5,000 acres, which stretch from plover sanctuaries on the shoreline to heron rookeries, meadows and redwood bluffs at the 2,000-foot summit. Invigorating views of the ocean from the park's windswept bluffs are part of the reward for a day's walking. Open daily, 8am–sunset. For information about visitors center facilities, call 831-426-0505.

Horseback Riding

Big Basin Stables www.bigbasin.org, 831-338-8860, Hwy. 236 off Hwy. 9, Boulder Creek.

Costanoa Coastal Lodge www.costanoa.com, 650-879-1100, 2001 Rossi Rd., at Hwy. 1, Pescadero.

Redwood Riding Adventures 831-335-1334, 5028 Hwy. 9, Felton.

Sea Horse/Friendly Acres Ranch 650-726-8550, 2159 Hwy. 1, Half Moon Bay.

Willow Pond Horse Ranch www.willowpondranch.org, sharonray@willowpondranch.com, 831-464-2276.

Surfing

26th Ave. Off E. Cliff Dr., Santa Cruz. Reef/sand bottom, lefts and rights; underappreciated spot popular with bodysurfers, intermediate to advanced.

Capitola Jetty Capitola Village. Reef bottom, both rights and lefts; best at low tides, needs a 6- to 8-foot swell before it fires off, good beginner spot; lifeguards on duty during the summer.

Cowells Beach In front of West Coast Santa Cruz Inn on W. Cliff Dr. near Santa Cruz Boardwalk. Sand bottom, very gentle rights; best at low tides, slow, easy peaks rolling onto a safe beach, perfect spot for beginners; lifeguards on duty during the summer.

Four Mile Beach Hwy. 1, 1 mile south of Davenport. Reef break, fun rights; intermediate to advanced spot; cars get broken into a lot, "red triangle" (great white sharks frequent area), not worth the risk to outsiders.

The Hook End of 41st Ave., south of Pleasure Point, north of Capitola. Reef bottom, rights and lefts; smaller but usually faster waves than Pleasure Point, gets crowded (and angers locals), intermediate to advanced spot; exit from water dangerous at high tides (prepare to paddle a half mile south to Capitola Pier).

Inside Pleasure Junction of E. Cliff Dr. & 41st Ave. Rocky reef bottom, all rights; good for beginners during small swell, really needs 6-foot swell to work for advanced; can be gnarly (read: dangerous) during large swells, difficult to exit during high tides.

Manresa State Beach Hwy. 1 to San Andreas Rd. exit, La Selva. Sandy beach break; best on smaller swells, large swells line up and close out, advanced; strong current during heavy surf.

California's Central Coast is famed for its safe, pristine and uncrowded surfing spots. Dan Coyro

Mavericks Off Pillar Point, Half Moon Bay. Known everywhere as the biggest, most treacherous waves in the world, Mavericks attracts serious surfers and daredevils. A sudden series of steep changes in depth pushes the swell up and out with explosive force, creating dangerous but exhilarating surfing conditions.

Natural Bridges Outer Reef End of Swift St. off Hwy. 1 at northern city limits of Santa Cruz. Reef bottom, right break; needs a minus tide and big swell to work, advanced spot; nasty currents when big but a nice place for a day on the beach.

Pleasure Point E. Cliff Dr. & 41st Ave., Santa Cruz. Reef bottom, rights and lefts; "sewer peak" has big bowls, supersteep, for the advanced; first peak and second have good longboard waves, work on any swell, intermediate to advanced.

Privates This is longboard paradise, with right lines gently peeling off toward Capitola Pier for sensual long rides. Pleasant place to spend the day with mellow fellows and talented gal-nicks.

Scott Creek Hwy. 1 north of Davenport Landing, Davenport. Reef bottom, beach break and a right point break; point break still ridable at 15 to 20 feet, unpredictable, lots of kelp, "red triangle" (sharky).

Shark's Cove Portola Dr. & 41st Ave., Santa Cruz. Reef bottom, mostly a right, left when it's small; fun, secondary waves that roll through the "hook" continue wrapping, best at low tide, larger waves line up and close out, beginner to advanced.

Steamer Lane W. Cliff Dr. & Bay St., Santa Cruz. Reef bottom, mostly a right, left when it's big; "outsides" holds any swell, big rights that peel along the cliff line, not a beginner break, advanced; "middle peak" lines up nearly 50 yards from the cliff, holds any swell; a haven for seals and otters, kelp gets thick in some spots at low tide, high tide poses difficulties for exiting the water.

Sunset State Beach San Andreas Rd. off Hwy. 1, Watsonville. Sand bottom, lots of peaks, lefts and rights; beginner spot when small, intermediate to advanced otherwise; can get big rips when there's a swell.

Tennis

PRIVATE (FEE FOR NONMEMBER WALK-INS)

Colony Club Tennis 650-726-2849, 330 Purissima St., Half Moon Bay.

Imperial Courts Tennis Club 831-476-1062, 2505 Cabrillo College Dr., Aptos.

Seascape Sports Club 831-688-1993, 1505 Seascape Blvd., Aptos.

Tennis Club of Rio Del Mar 831-688-1144, 369 Sandalwood Dr., Rio Del Mar.

PUBLIC (FREE, FIRST COME FIRST SERVED)

Cabrillo College 6500 Soquel Dr., Aptos.

Derby Park Woodland Way at Natural Bridges School, Santa Cruz.

Harbor High School 300 La Fonda Ave., Santa Cruz.

Highland County Park Hwy. 9 & Glen Arbor Rd., Ben Lomond.

Jade Street Park 4400 Jade St., Capitola.

Santa Cruz High School 415 Walnut St., Santa Cruz.

Soquel High School 401 Old San Jose Rd., Soquel.

SHOPPING

The thoroughly Californian concept of shopping as entertainment remains alive and well in Santa Cruz and Half Moon Bay. Shops here are not so much patronized as inhabited by gregarious locals who set up cafe colonies wherever the spirit moves them. From the area's many resident artisans come contemporary glass, jewelry, pottery and hand-sculpted furniture, sharing the modern shopping scene with top designer names in leather, silk and wool from around the world. You will find no mall or major retailers suggested here, only the best home-grown merchants the area offers.

Antiques & Collectibles

Downtown Santa Cruz Antique Fair & Collectibles 831-429-8433, Lincoln St., bet. Pacific & Cedar Sts., Santa Cruz. On the second Sunday of each month, expert collectors from the area set up shop and display a wide range of vintage goodies through the late morning and early afternoon.

Judi Wyant Antiques 831-426-3215, 1532 Pacific Ave., Santa Cruz. This is a treasure trove of classy antique jewelry—many of them one-of-a-kind—and quality reproductions celebrating accessories' golden oldies. A beautifully arranged shop; the staff is most patient and helpful.

Miss Jessie May's Antiques and Collectibles 1533 Pacific Ave., Santa Cruz. Crazy yet classy collectibles in a rambling spread attract both the serious and casual explorer.

Mr. Goodie's Antiques 831-427-9997, 1541 Pacific Ave., Santa Cruz. Awaiting the sharp-eyed collector are loads of wonderful stuff from bygone eras, including lavish antique and vintage costume jewelry, Depression glass and Fiestaware, classic Hawaiian shirts and nostalgic prints.

Mr. Goodie's in downtown Santa Cruz offers loads of wonderful stuff from recent bygone eras. George Sakkestad

Shen's Gallery www.shensgallery.com, 831-457-4422, 2404 Mission St., Santa Cruz. Perfumed by incense, this beautiful shop imports burnished Chinese furniture, jade and coral jewelry, ceramics, carvings, prints and Hsing teapots—antiques every one.

Soquel Village Antiques 831-476-4747, 4700 Soquel Dr., Soquel. Treasure hunters think they've arrived in the Promised Land when they enter the portals of this discerning shop.

Tiffany's Antiques www.tiffanysflowers.com, 831-477-9080, 3010 Center St., Soquel, and 831-427-9086, 1540 Pacific, Santa Cruz. Two locations share some high-end discoveries from the owners' walkabouts to ritzy estate sales and Midwest shopping sprees.

Trader's Emporium 831-475-9201, 4940 Soquel Dr., Soquel. A popular browsing spot with local antiques and collectibles buffs, this gigantic old Quonset hut houses 26 distinct shops offering antique items of every possible description.

Village Fair Antiques villagefair.net, 831-688-9883, 417 Trout Gulch Rd., Aptos. See the collections of 25 dealers under one roof.

Wisteria Antiques 831-462-2900, 5870 Soquel Dr., Soquel. A globe-trotting buyer hauls back caches of vintage country French and European pine armoires, dining sets, rare occasional pieces and imaginative furniture. Together they stylishly populate this labyrinth of gardens and showrooms.

Arts & Crafts

Annieglass www.annieglass.com, 831-427-4260, 110 Cooper St., Suite F, Santa Cruz, and 831-762-2041, ext. 21, 310 Harvest Dr., Watsonville. Downtown's fine crafts boutique explodes with bright wall-to-wall glasswork, serving pieces and home accessories. The

Watsonville factory/outlet store offers behind-the-scenes tours of its facilities and the colorful secrets behind the housewares-making process.

Artisan's Gallery 831-423-8183, 1364 Pacific Ave., Santa Cruz. An engaging collection of the very finest in locally produced ceramics, woodwork, hand-loomed textiles, glassware, lamps, innovative toys and games, plus walls studded with local paintings and prints, distinguishes this local treasure.

Aumware Glass www.aumwareglass.com, 831-429-5307, 500 Hwy. 1, Davenport. The creative dinnerware and other sparkling pieces of artist Josef Bear light up any room in which they are placed. These colorful, elegant and sensuous creations refuse to let your eyes leave them once they've caught your attention.

Coastal Gallery 650-726-3859, 424 Main St., Half Moon Bay. Since 1987, this spacious gallery has brought work by some of the best emerging artists from around the world to the Central Coast. Lots of originals. Limited-edition etchings and knockout sculpture.

Courtyard Gallery www.courtyardgallery.net, 650-712-1114, 643 Main St., Half Moon Bay. This outpost of contemporary sculpture is especially noteworthy for its wonderful hangings by sculptor Yael Kahanov, who was nurtured at the renowned "Atelier 17" in Paris. Her fantastic, whimsical glass-on-copper wall sculptures of dancers and musicians possess so much bundled kinetic energy and colorful dash that they threaten to leap from the wall and turn the room into a Technicolor dance party. Not to be missed.

Craft Gallery www.craftgallery.net, 800-331-4476, 831-475-4466, 126 San Jose Ave., Capitola Village. Largest selection of handcrafts on Monterey Bay.

Gallery M www.gallerym.net, 650-726-7167, 328 Main St., Half Moon Bay. Displays fine functional art furniture, unique sculpture, pottery, handwoven rugs and two-dimensional art handcrafted by well-known and emerging artists.

Gravago 831-427-2667, 111 Cooper St., Santa Cruz. Packed with fabulous finds from exotic corners of the Far and Middle East, from tapestries and antique copper and brass to Indonesian carvings and African trade bead jewelry.

L. H. Selman Ltd. www.theglassgallery.com, 800-538-0766, 831-427-1177, 123 Locust St., Santa Cruz. What a dazzling hall of delights Larry and Marti Selman have created. The caliber of glass artists represented here is unsurpassed on the Central Coast. One-of-a-kind glass sculptures, limited-edition paperweights and other creations of fine glass should not be missed. Call for a private tour and appointment. A collection of fine jewelry is available next door at **The Glass Gallery II** (103 Locust St.)

Lundberg Studios www.lundbergstudios.com, 831-423-2532, 131 Old Coast Rd., Davenport. Showrooms for this internationally acclaimed art glass studio offer a world-class selection of Tiffany reproduction lamps, vases and iridescent lusterware bowls. The fabulous glassblown paperweights have found their way into the Smithsonian and Louvre gift catalogs.

New Davenport Cash Store 831-426-4122, 1 Davenport Ave., Davenport. The finest tableware from local Santa Cruz Mountain potters shares floor-to-ceiling displays with Guatemalan hand-loomed textiles, elegant tie-dyed silks, Mexican Day of the Dead figures and antique ivory and amber, as well as stunning contemporary art jewelry.

Petroglyph www.petroglyph.com, 831-458-4278, 125 Walnut St., Santa Cruz. Creativity oozes from this brightly colored ceramics studio, the newest addition to the local arts-and-crafts scene. Petroglyph provides ceramics and paints, and then turns customers lose with their imaginations. Kids love it.

Spanishtown Arts & Crafts Center 650-726-7366, 501 San Mateo Rd., Half Moon Bay. Colorful cluster of unique and high-quality regional arts and crafts in a dozen shops featuring revolving exhibits. Some shops are open during the week, but all are open on the weekends.

Books

Bookshop Santa Cruz 831-423-0900, 1520 Pacific Ave., Santa Cruz. Many locals consider this sprawling, inviting store the heart of downtown Santa Cruz. Major news and magazine rack, ample seating for browsing and a lively in-house cafe make coming here an all-day event.

Bookworks 831-688-4554, 36 Rancho Del Mar Shopping Center, Aptos. A wide selection of books for all interests, with a special emphasis on young minds. Magazines and newspapers, as well as cards and gifts, and a small cafe with cookies, coffee and tea round out the sprawling Aptos bookshop and cafe.

Capitola BookCafe 831-462-4415, 1475 41st Ave., Capitola. A major selection of national and international magazines highlights this well-stocked cultural mecca, graced by an in-house espresso and dessert cafe.

Gateways Books & Gifts www.gatewaysbooks.com, 831-429-9600, 1531 Pacific Ave., Santa Cruz. Metaphysical and New Age offerings of every sort fill this engaging retreat, which also features motivational CDs and cassettes, incense and crystals. Very Santa Cruz.

Literary Guillotine 831-457-1195, 204 Locust St., Santa Cruz. The rarest and best in small press and university press literature cram this tiny haunt for inquiring browsers and book lovers.

Logos Books & Records 831-427-5100, 1117 Pacific Ave., Santa Cruz. Two huge floors are filled with used and rare books, including major science fiction, gothic paperback and women's sections. Used CDs, tapes and collectors'-quality LPs make this place a hot, must-visit spot.

Moon News 650-726-8610, 315 Main St., Half Moon Bay. Sleek, smart new bookstore and newsstand offers magazines and newspapers from around the world, plus good recent fiction and nonfiction.

Ocean Books E-mail: oceanbooks@earthlink.net, 650-726-2665, 416 Main St., Half Moon Bay. New and used books with an emphasis on California and local history, sci fi, mysteries and rare out-of-print books.

Resource Center for Nonviolence Bookstore 831-423-1626, 515 Broadway, Santa Cruz. This progressive boutique sells music and books of a politically correct persuasion. Guest speakers periodically drop by to cheer the troops. Expect sincere, homey ambiance, lively conversation and a bit of pamphleteering.

Zamzam 831-425-7264, 1537 Pacific Ave., Suite 101, Santa Cruz. Tucked in a corner of a downtown office building, this intriguing nook is stocked with Islamic literature.

Fashion

Bunny's Shoes 831-423-3824, 1350 Pacific Ave., Santa Cruz. The smart, the trendy, even the avant garde in women's footgear are displayed in this appealing boutique for the enlightened foot fetishist. Some bags are also displayed, but the bottom line here really is shoes, shoes, shoes. Across the street (1349 Pacific), a second Bunny's merchandises body care products, some clothing, hats and gloves, plus cool retro housewares.

Cotton Tales Natural Fibers 831-429-1956, 1201 Pacific Ave., Santa Cruz. This Santa Cruz tradition has always provided quality children's clothing to the ecologically conscious community. The store also carries some baby toys and accessories and locally made quilts.

Cruz'n 831-476-2533, 127 Monterey Ave., Capitola. Geared to the young outdoorsy set, this shop features bold and sassy beachwear and resort apparel.

European Children's Clothing 831-479-9062, 110 Stockton Ave., Capitola Village. Clothes for newborn to 12-year-olds.

Galla Cabana www.gallacabana.com, 831-423-7575, 1364 Pacific Ave., Santa Cruz. Starting as a lingerie and swimsuit shop, Galla Cabana has branched out into quality casual (yet not cheap) European wear. Clothing from Italy and France mix and match with Brazilian hand-mades and major U.S. labels recognized for the crafting of their signature creations.

Hat Company 831-458-9585, 1346 Pacific Ave., Santa Cruz. Get a head of the trends at a store devoted entirely to haberdashery. This shop features every hat style imaginable, from the practical to the zany.

Hot Feet 831-476-3960, 219 Capitola Ave., Capitola Village. An all-encompassing shoe haven, this beachside shoe store stocks the trendy, the sensible and all of the footwear in between, plus socks, gloves and sunglasses.

Jade 831-425-2244, 1128 Pacific Ave., Santa Cruz. The motto here is: exotic, exquisite essential. And this high-end boutique just about pulls it off. Featured are unique locally made jewelry and finely turned casual women's wear—good for either the fresh-air weekend or sensual party night—produced by small California design companies for Jade's stylish 30-something clientele.

Jewels on Pacific 831-345-7431, 1535 Pacific Ave., Santa Cruz. This wonderful boutique specializes in locally made jewelry, plus antique evening wear and clothing reproductions that echo the art nouveau and art deco eras. Some of the fresh yet vintage-appearing dresses have exquisite beadwork and design motifs inspired by early 20th century works of art. Especially alluring is a line of hand-dyed silk shibiri (folded and creased silk) from Boulder Creek's Cloudforest Design. (Ask for Michele.)

Lauren's 831-462-5245, 120 San Jose Ave., Capitola. Well-chosen California sportswear and contemporary outfits, all in natural fibers, fill this tiny boutique by the beach.

Pacific Trading Company 831-476-6109, 504 Bay Ave., Capitola, and 831-423-3349, 1224 Pacific Ave., Santa Cruz. Elegant, contemporary apparel, plus plenty of jewelry and accessories, have made this company popular with locals for the past 15 years.

Om Gallery www.omgallery.com, 831-425-1184, 805 Pacific Ave., Santa Cruz, and 831-475-1836, 111 Capitola Ave., Capitola. Owner Max Halterman designs clothing, handbags, shoes and stupendous traditional Vietnamese lamp shades, and then has five Vietnam families (all friends of the proprietor) produce the items for both wholesale and retail distribution. Halterman's choices of materials and construction techniques ensure that the goods, tweaked for American lifestyles and sizes, are both aesthetically pleasing and durable.

Rouge 831-454-0675, 110 Cooper St., Suite 100C, Santa Cruz. This men's and women's (mostly women's) fashion destination stocks casual and carefree clothing from small Los Angeles design firms and hip European labels. Some jewelry is displayed for the 25- to 45-year-old target audience.

Shandrydan 831-425-8411, 107 Walnut Ave., Santa Cruz. A spacious boutique filled with California easy-living styles, local designer outfits and a bonanza of contemporary designer jewelry, it attracts the 35- to 60-year-old fashion-savvy.

Shoe Fetish 831-454-0287, 110 Cooper St., Suite G, Santa Cruz. Sporting a stylish leather-and-slate floor and art photographs on the wall, this footwear nirvana offers high-end leather boots and shoes fine-crafted in Spain and Brazil. Surprisingly modest prices for such well-designed and -manufactured goods.

Sockshop & Shoe Company www.sockshopandshoeco.com, 831-429-6101, 1125 Pacific Ave., Santa Cruz. Frisky, stylish sportswear and footgear for men, women and kids.

Star Nine 831-457-9999, 719 Pacific Ave., Santa Cruz. Popular with budget-minded hipsters, Star Nine attracts 20-somethings with its wild and wacky clothing and accessories.

Unique Clothing 650-726-6062, 407 Main St., Half Moon Bay. Owner Margo Christiansen joins with other area designers to create—well, as the name explains—unique clothing.

Velvet Underground 831-469-9401, 1543 Pacific Ave., Santa Cruz. This women's fashion shop features clothing, jewelry and female-oriented fun and games.

The Wardrobe: Selected Consignment 831-429-6363, 113 Locust St., Santa Cruz. Quality resale clothing.

Jewelry

Latta www.lattajewelry.com, 831-475-1771, 120 Stockton Ave., Capitola. Contemporary variations on art nouveau themes distinguish the handsome, handmade jewelry created by local goldsmith Jay Latta. Set with polished and faceted gemstones, the rings are of special beauty.

Main Street Goldworks www.mainstreetgoldworks.com, 650-726-2546, 542 Main St., Half Moon Bay. The custom-designed jewelry is superb. The master jewelers can be seen at work behind a small partition, and the cases are aglow with sparkling diamond and fine metal creations.

Many Hands Gallery 831-429-8696, 1001 Center St., Santa Cruz, and 831-475-2500, 510 Bay Ave, Capitola. These two shops feature visual feasts of handblown glass, ceramics, leather, fiber and especially handcrafted gold, silver and cloisonné jewelry from over 125 top Californian artisans, 80 percent of whom are local. Owner Kate Nolan creates much of the jewelry in-house from antique crystal and semiprecious gemstone beads from around the world.

Precious metals meld with semiprecious stones in the wide array of jewelry available at Many Hands Gallery, located both in Capitola and downtown Santa Cruz. Robert Scheer

Santa Cruz Pawn and Time Pieces www.santacruzpawn.com, 831-469-8458, 117 Walnut Ave., Santa Cruz. Great old clocks overhang the entrance, and cases are packed with quality jewels and antique accessories. A very cool place.

Thomas Mantle Designs 831-429-8234, 1001 Center St., Santa Cruz. A talented, resident goldsmith and jewelry designer creates one-of-a-kind contemporary mounted pieces in this engaging studio and showroom.

The Vault Gallery www.thevaultgallery.com, 831-426-3349, 1339 Pacific Ave., Santa Cruz. A stunning inventory of imaginative contemporary gold and silver jewelry, grouped into opulent display cases according to gemstones, makes a visit to this shop feel like a stroll through a museum. In the back, a small boutique trades in exclusive silk blouses, gowns and sweaters.

Specialty & Eclectic

Angel Moon 650-726-2133, 433 Main St., Half Moon Bay. Quintessentially Central Coast, this is a quirky, celestially oriented store filled with gifts, cards and books.

Arcangeli Grocery Company 650-879-0147, 287 Stage Rd., Pescadero. This family-style bakery and market, founded in 1929, is stocked with goods like salsas, vinegars and oils, California wines, fresh-baked French breads and deli items.

Atlantis Fantasyworld www.atlantisfantasyworld.com, 831-426-0158, 1020 Cedar St., Santa Cruz. Joe and Dottie Ferrara's store has been in business for 29 years and remains a godsend for the hard-core comic book and trading card aficionado. Look for collectors' items issues, plus the new and unusual for kids of all ages.

Camouflage 831-423-7613, 1329 Pacific Ave., Santa Cruz. This cozy store features a wide array of massage oils, sensual toys and books—a clean, well-lighted place to shop for lingerie and sleek women's clothing.

Cedanna Artful Living 650-726-6776, 400 Main St., Half Moon Bay. Stocked with modern furniture, art, housewares, mirrors, jewelry and one-of-a-kind inventions by local and regional avant-garde artists, this eclectic store is one-stop shopping for home decoration.

Chefworks 831-426-1351, 1527 Pacific Ave., Santa Cruz. A recreational chef's dream, this store is stocked to the gills with top-of-the-line pots, pans, woks, dishes, utensils and culinary accessories, plus cookbooks, olive oils, sauces and more.

Cunha's General Store 650-726-4071, 448 Main St., Half Moon Bay. The time trip starts when you enter this unique store packed with cowboy gear, dry goods and deli items. It ends when you leave, having overheard tall tales of resident farmers and local fishermen.

Cowboy paraphernalia and an eclectic variety of dry goods set an old-fashioned tone at Half Moon Bay's historic Cunha's General Store. Stan Cacitti

Recently rebuilt following a devastating fire that destroyed the original building, it still has history and looks nearly the same, but it also has a few modern touches that make shopping easier.

Eco Goods 831-429-5758, 1130 Pacific Ave., Santa Cruz. For a little store, this downtown shop offers more ecologically correct goods than you can imagine. Eco Goods carries hemp clothing, natural fibers and environmentally friendly supplies for the entire family. An alternative general store.

Half Moon Bay Wine and Cheese 650-726-1520, 604 Main St., Half Moon Bay. A grand selection of great cheeses and international and regional wines, available for testing before purchasing. A cool wine bar area is perfect for tastings and discussions with visiting experts and winemakers.

Harbor Seal Company 650-726-7418, 406 Main St., Half Moon Bay. This quirky emporium showcases unusual bird- and sea-life toys, puzzles, books, toys and educational games. It's neat for big people as well as for children.

Havana Village 831-464-0662, 208 Monterey Ave., Capitola Village 95010. More cigars, pipes, humidors than you'll see in a lifetime, crowded into one tight little space.

Jones N' Bones 831-462-0521, 621 Capitola Ave., Capitola. An eclectic collection of specialty-flavored olive oils, vinegars, hot sauces, scone mixes and more, plus baking and cooking accessories, is nestled in a charming old house with a lovely garden area in the Capitola Village.

Kaleidoscope www.kaleidoscope-pts.com, 831-475-0210, 828 Bay Ave., Capitola. "The parent teacher store" says it all: books, tapes, quality toys, educational materials, art supplies for kids.

Museum Shop 831-454-9986, 118 Cooper St., Santa Cruz. The Museum of Art and History's gift shop features great books of local artists, quirky knickknacks and collector's items.

Nuestra Tierra www.nutierra.com, 888-992-0008, 650-712-9135, 421 Main St., Half Moon Bay. This charming, surprising art-filled emporium has gathered the work of some of Mexico's finest artists for its unusual collection of folk art, textiles, jewelry, pottery and sculpture. The area's exclusive outlet for the incredible work of Sergio Bustamante.

Paper Vision 831-458-1345, 1345 Pacific Ave., Santa Cruz. Books of all types are available, plus the most witty, comprehensive and mesmerizing selection of fine greetings cards in the area.

Pipeline 831-425-7473, 818 Pacific Ave., Santa Cruz. This head shop is one of the last downtown reminders of Santa Cruz's hippie heydays, the 1960s. Pipeline carries pipes and hookahs, posters, incense burners, music-related clothing, tobacco and tobacco accessories, as well as Indian and other Asian imports.

Rhythm Fusion www.rhythmfusion.com, 831-423-2048, 1541C Pacific Ave., Santa Cruz. Pound for pound, this is the noisiest place in town. Specializing in handmade percussion instruments, the store has a sterling reputation, which attracts some of the most famous musicians working today to this small, hole-in-the-wall enterprise. But neophytes are always welcome. Off-the-shelf or custom designed, you can get anything you want to help you keep that world beat.

San Gregorio General Store www.sangregoriostore.com, 650-726-0565, corner of Stage Route & Rte. 84, San Gregorio. In existence since the 1890s, this store has served its small community with just about everything the locals need: (in the owners' words) "seeds, cast-iron cookware, advice, aspirin, wines (fine to rot gut), western and work clothing,

The Old Rock Guy

Clark Hansen is a rail-thin, cowboy-outfitted rock hound with a causal demeanor and a keen eye. Out of his ramshackle store/home off a dusty side street in downtown Pescadero, behind Duarte's Tavern, emerge some of the most beautiful gems and minerals in the world: fluorite, rose quartz, amethyst, agate, appopolite, selenite crystal, petrified wood. He handpicks his items from sources he's cultivated for decades (most from Siberia, Russia and Morocco). Clark spins tales about his favorite pieces and knows the backstory on just about every valuable stone in his collection. His bookends and fine jewelry stun the uninitiated, but the lamps, bowls and animals are all intriguing. Prices start around $15 and climb into the thousands of dollars, but looking is free. These days, candleholders are his most popular item for sale. He's open for business every day (till he decides to go to bed). As he says, "If you're talking to me, then I'm open" (650-879-1919, P.O. Box 471, Pescadero 94060).

groceries, no TV, shoat rings, hardware, bullshit, lanterns, coal hods, books, crockery, posters, weather analysis, toys, beeswax, piano in tune, cowperson hats and boots, international beers, cards, homemade sandwiches, homegrown tomatoes, garlic and apples in season." Also serves as a post office and saloon and features live music on the weekends.

Santa Cruz Harley-Davidson & Buell 831-421-9600, 1148 Soquel Dr., Santa Cruz. Northern California's only dealership also sports a museum of antique hogs and memorabilia.

Sense of Peace www.senseofpeace.com, 650-712-8900, 604 Main St., Suite C, Half Moon Bay. This tranquil and meditative shop is given over to all things calming. Asian influences abound, and customers emerge with zero angst after a slow walk around the premises. From tapes and books to waterfalls and comforting home furnishings, the Om factor is quite high here.

Soif www.soifwine.com, 831-423-2020, 105 Walnut Ave., Santa Cruz. A sibling to the wonderful Soif Wine Bar next door, Soif "the Merchants" has myriad rare and difficult-to-find bottlings from around the globe. The proprietors have earned their stripes working at some of the area's best wineries (Bonny Doon, for one), and their frequent trips to Europe and other spots on the world map mean juicy discoveries for local patrons.

Squid Row Behind Santa Cruz Art Center, just off Center & Union, Santa Cruz. A charming alley covered with blossoming plants, this one-block-long street has been a traditional local center for unique arts and collectibles. It is often a site for special pottery sales featuring local artists' creations.

Streetlight Records www.streetlightrecords.com, 831-421-9200, 941 Pacific Ave., Santa Cruz. A deep selection of both new and used record albums, CDs, videos, DVDs and video games are available at this downtown shop that buys, sells and trades. Streetlight proudly features local, underground music releases, and every employee is seemingly an expert in some musical microniche, whether it be classical, industrial, punk, soul, gothic or *rock en español*. An eclectic taste of Santa Cruz.

Sports

Bugaboo Mountain Sports 831-429-6300, 1521 Pacific Ave., Santa Cruz. Boldly displayed paraphernalia for outdoor adventure—backpacking, climbing, cross-country skiing, biking and white-water rafting—top off this emporium.

Old School Shoes 831-423-2700, 1017 Pacific Ave., Santa Cruz. Throwback athletic shoes and snazzy re-creations of casual shoe classics are available for men, women and kids. Converse is well represented, and a large bags-and-backpacks section also claims some wall space.

O'Neill's Surf Shop www.oneill.com, 831-475-4151, 1115 41st Ave., Capitola, and 831-469-4377, 110 Cooper St., Suite 100D, Santa Cruz. Founded by wet-suit inventor Jack O'Neill, this is the Banzai Pipeline of North Central Coast surf shops, with everything from sunglasses and baggies to surfboards and wetsuits.

Outdoor World, Inc. 831-423-9555, 136 River St., Santa Cruz, and 831-479-1501, 1440 41st Ave., Capitola. Everything that you'll need to enjoy the great outdoors is here: sunglasses, snorkeling gear, insect repellent, racquets, balls, bathing suits, fins, goggles, canteens, compasses, shoes and shirts.

Paradise Surf Shop, near Pleasure Point in Santa Cruz, was created to service woman surfers. Robert Scheer

Pacific Wave www.pwavc.com, 831-458-9283, 1502 Pacific Ave., Santa Cruz. For the serious surfer or just the fashionable wannabe, this converted bank holds a treasury of surf, skate and boogieboards, as well as quality active wear for the hip and young at heart.

Paradise Surf Shop 831-462-3880, 3961 Portola Dr., Santa Cruz. Catering primarily to female surfers, this women-run surf shop features a choice selection of sporty clothes and swimwear, plus a fine array of surfboards.

Santa Cruz Surf Shop 831-464-3233, 753 41st Ave., Santa Cruz, and 811 Pacific Ave., Santa Cruz. One block from the beach and just down the road from top surfing conditions at Pleasure Point, this "locally grown" shop features a huge selection of surfboard and skateboard equipment, top brand names and locally designed Santa Cruz surfboards.

SEASONAL EVENTS

January
Fungus Fair 831-420-6115, Santa Cruz.
Heritage Day Festival 650-726-2418, Half Moon Bay.

February
Clam Chowder Cook-Off 831-420-5273, Santa Cruz.
Cultural Council's Hearts for the Arts 831-688-5399, Santa Cruz.
Natural Bridges Monarch Butterfly Migration Festival 831-423-4609, Santa Cruz.

Each January, Santa Cruz-area mycologists gather to trade notes, sample wild mushrooms and don silly costumes at the Fungus Fair. Robert Scheer

April

Big Basin & Castle Basin State Parks Trail Days 831-968-7065, Santa Cruz.
Masters' Cup Open Disc Golf Tournament 831-423-7214, Santa Cruz.
Rhododendron Show 831-475-3024, Santa Cruz.
Spring Wildflower Show 831-429-3773, Santa Cruz.

May

Bluegrass Art, Wine & Music Festival 831-335-4441, Felton.
Boulder Creek Art & Wine Festival 831-338-7099, Boulder Creek.
Celebrate Santa Cruz 831-429-8433, Santa Cruz.
Chamarita Festival 650-726-2729, Half Moon Bay.
Flower Festival 650-726-3194, Half Moon Bay.
Heritage Day Festival 650-726-2418, Half Moon Bay.
Industrial Hemp Expo 831-425-3003, Santa Cruz.
Longboard Invitational 831-425-8943, Santa Cruz.
Santa Cruz Blues Festival 831-479-9814, Aptos.
Strawberry Festival 831-728-6183, Watsonville.

June

Japanese Cultural Fair 831-462-4589, Santa Cruz.
Native Animal Day 831-420-6115, Santa Cruz.
Vintners' Festival 831-479-9463, Santa Cruz.
Woodies on the Wharf 831-420-5273, Santa Cruz.

July

Fat Fry Summer Music Festival 831-420-2800, Aptos.
Firecracker 10K Race 831-420-5273, Santa Cruz.
Fourth of July Celebration 831-429-3477, Santa Cruz.
Hot and Cool Jazz Festival 831-474-7407, Santa Cruz.
Old-Fashioned Fourth of July 650-728-3313, Half Moon Bay.
Wharf to Wharf Race 831-475-2196, Santa Cruz.
World's Shortest Fourth of July Parade 831-688-2428, Aptos.

August

Arts & Fun Festival 650-879-0848, Pescadero.
Cabrillo Music Art & Wine Festival 831-420-5243, Santa Cruz.
Dickens Universe 831-459-2103, UCSC.
Fig Fest 831-427-3554, Santa Cruz.
Jose Cuervo Pro Beach Volleyball Tour 800-793-TOUR, Santa Cruz.
Roughwater Swim 831-429-3477, Santa Cruz.

September

Begonia Festival 831-476-3566, Capitola.
Capitola Art and Wine Festival 831-475-6522, Capitola.
Fat Fry Blues Festival 831-420-2800, Aptos.
Greek Festival 831-429-6500, Santa Cruz.

The Nautical Parade is the highlight of the Begonia Festival that occurs each September in Capitola. Robert Scheer

Harbor Days 650-726-5727, Pillar Point.
Santa Cruz County Fair 831-688-3384, Watsonville.

October
Apple Butter Festival 831-722-1056, Watsonville.
Fireworks Spectacular 831-420-5273, Santa Cruz.
Hallcrest Vineyards Harvest Fair 831-335-4441, Felton.
Hot Rods at the Beach 831-427-2323, Santa Cruz.
Italian Heritage Festival 831-423 5590, Santa Cruz.
Mission Fiesta 831-425-5849, Santa Cruz.
Open Studios Tour 831-688-5399, Santa Cruz.
Pumpkin and Art Festival 650-726-9652, Half Moon Bay.
Sentinel Triathlon 831-423-4242, ext. 301, Santa Cruz.

November
Christmas Crafts and Gifts Festival 831-423-2053, Santa Cruz.
Women's Surfing Contest 831-475-6522, Capitola.

December
Christmas Bird Count 831-427-2288, Davenport.
First Night Santa Cruz 831-425-7277, Santa Cruz.
Harbor Lighting 650-726-4723, Pillar Point.
Lighted Boat Parade 831-475-6161, Santa Cruz.

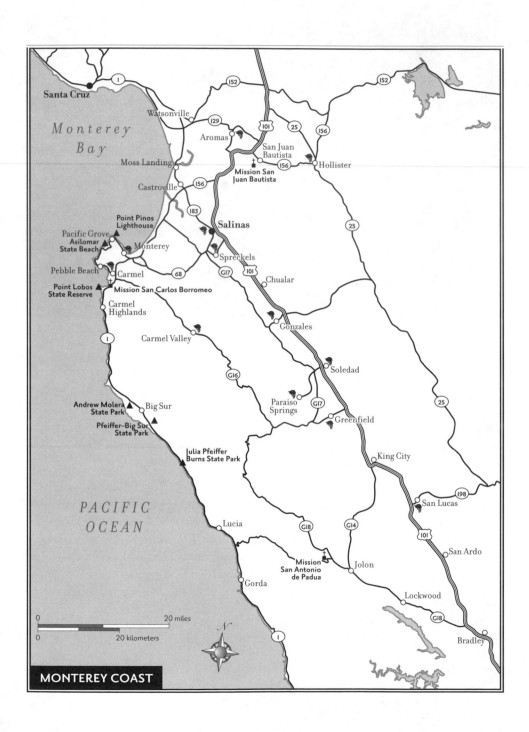

MONTEREY COAST

4

MONTEREY, CARMEL & BIG SUR

Head of the Class

From whaling heydays past to state-of-the-art aquarium, Monterey has exerted on visitors a magnetic pull as constant as its spectacular tides. A patchwork of historic landmarks, waterfront lodgings and fishing activity, the area burst into the settlers' consciousness when busy padre Junipero Serra joined Spanish explorer Portola in the founding of the mission and presidio of what was part of New Spain in the late 1700s. Surrounded by "Steinbeck country," the town of Monterey is still haunted by the ghosts of Doc Ricketts and the heroes of Cannery Row, today a pastiche of boutiques, bistros and tourist crafts galleries showcasing local artisans.

The adobes that marked the Mexican era share the limelight of careful restoration with the 18th- and 19th-century residences of sea captains and writers, such as Robert Louis Stevenson, who were attracted to the whaling and shipping milieu that enfolded Monterey. The Presidio—the first fort of the Spanish empire in California—still stands watch over the hemispherical Monterey Bay, though the spectacular exhibits and open-air wildlife sanctuaries of the Monterey Bay Aquarium now claim more visitors' attention. Embraced by the Coast Ranges to the east and the wild cliffs, rocks and tide pools that mark the crossroads of the bay and the Pacific Ocean, Monterey continues to lure outdoors enthusiasts as well as artistic entrepreneurs.

At its geographical gateway, the tiny delta of the Salinas River, Monterey is edged by the abundant waterfowl colonies of Elkhorn Slough, visited by bird-watchers and ecologists from all over the world. The soothing coastal fogs that lend Monterey its moody ambiance also create unique habitats for rare flora, such as the Monterey cypress, and fauna, like the snowy plover and brown pelican. To its south, the town of Monterey is hugged in by the Carmel Highlands, a froth of forest and fern-laced undergrowth that announces the beginning of the challenging Big Sur coast, where the geologically youthful Coast Ranges are still lifting their way out of the ocean floor.

A pleasant architectural braid of Mediterranean terra-cotta and Iberian adobe with New England Victoriana, the texture of the entire Monterey region is permeated with the influence of the ocean. Thanks to its temperate influence, the area is embraced by a latticework of fields bearing greens—artichokes, broccoli, lettuces, strawberries—into America's markets. The town's long history as one of California's earliest settlements is balanced with its

Historic Fisherman's Wharf has long drawn crowds to the town of Monterey. Shmuel Thaler

contemporary sheen as a world-class convention and conference center. Major hotel chains join scores of charming bed & breakfasts to house meetings and rendezvous of every sort. Restaurants vie with those of larger sister cities, San Francisco and Los Angeles. Dozens of local estates create handmade wines of national repute—Monterey County is increasingly the source for premium grapes in the entire state.

Tasteful, upscale, yet never far from the roots of its coastal attractions, Monterey is a vibrant emblem of the immigrant spirit that cultivated the Central Coast.

LODGING

Monterey and its coastal neighborhoods have been hosting guests since the Spanish first settled here at the end of the 18th century. The sheer number of high-quality overnight possibilities testifies to the region's charisma as a destination for visitors from all over the world. The conference trade thrives in this spectacular waterfront setting, and contemporary hotel giants offer up rooms with a view and all the amenities. Aficionados of the well-turned Victorian B&B consider Pacific Grove a treasure amounting to the mother lode. Carmel's abundance of irresistible overnight inns is as legendary as its haunting shoreline. And world-class resorts dot the coastal hills along Big Sur and are tucked into the crags and twists of Carmel Valley. The following are must-visit lodging destinations in the Monterey area.

Credit cards are abbreviated as follows:
  AE: American Express
   D: Discover Card
 MC: MasterCard
   V: Visa

BIG SUR

✪ DEETJEN'S BIG SUR INN

www.deetjens.com/home.htm
Innkeeper: Bruce Need
831-667-2377, fax 831-667-0466
Hwy. 1, Big Sur 93920
Price: $75–$195
Children: With limitations
Pets: No
Handicap Access: Limited

California casual pushes rusticity to the
point of funk in this thoroughly Big Sur
landmark, which specializes in weathered
wood, sheltering redwoods and cozy overnight comfort. The Norwegian-style lodge—
listed on the National Register of Historic
Places—offers a central vantage on the
spectacular natural setting. It's also just
down the road from that bohemian outpost,
Nepenthe, a famous watering hole housed
in the former residence that Orson Welles
bought for his bride, Rita Hayworth. A fine
wine list accompanies candlelight dining in
the inn's restaurant, which also offers hearty
breakfasts. The 20 overnight rooms are
simply but freshly decorated. Some share
bathrooms, some have fireplaces, and the
down comforters add coziness. A fire is
always lit in the main lodge, where the
friendly staff will help visitors find gorgeous beaches and the best redwood canyon
hiking.

POST RANCH INN

www.postranchinn.com
E-mail: res@postranchinn.com
Innkeeper: Dan Priano
800-527-2200, 831-667-2200,
fax 831-667-2824
Hwy. 1 (P.O. Box 219), Big Sur 93920
Price: $495–$1,085, includes continental
breakfast
Credit Cards: AE, MC, V
Children: No
Pets: No
Handicap Access: Limited

If luxury were tangible, it would feel just
like the Post Ranch Inn. Set on 98 acres of
pristine, unbelievably gorgeous forestland
just south of Big Sur, the inn's treehouses,
ocean houses and massive suites are built
into the landscape so as not to disturb
Mother Earth. Environmental correctness
is the inn's middle name, from the strategically placed recycling bins right down to
the natural, environmentally sound toi-
letries. When you're not reveling in the elegantly austere pleasures of one of the 30
rooms' king-sized beds, expansive sky-
lights, sunken whirlpool tubs and wood-
burning fireplaces, you can hike the
property's many winding trails, relax in the
spa or pool, take advantage of the complimentary yoga classes and wine tastings, or
savor meals from the inn's four-star restaurant. The inn offers a designer breakfast
of seasonal fruits, killer granola and sinfully rich homemade pastries served either
in the ocean-view dining room or in your
own room. Private, romantic and utterly
unforgettable, the Post Ranch is worth
every penny.

*You can relax in a tub at the rustic-yet-refined Post
Ranch Inn and still take in the exquisite view of the
rugged Big Sur Coast.* Post Ranch Inn

Relaxing at Big Sur's Ventana Inn can be as simple as taking a hot tub on private decks adjoining guest rooms. Robert E. Bussinger

⭐ VENTANA INN & SPA

www.ventanainn.com
E-mail: concierge@ventanainn.com
Innkeeper: Paul O'Dowd
800-628-6500, 831-667-2331,
fax 831-667-0573
Hwy. 1, Big Sur 93920
Price: $340–$1,450, includes continental breakfast
Credit Cards: AE, D, MC, V
Children: No
Pets: No
Handicap Access: Yes

A collection of dramatic, weathered cedar lodges clinging to the ancient oak groves overlooking the wild Big Sur coastline form one of the most charismatic retreats on any resort horizon. Spreading across a summit ridge 1,200 feet above the coast, the Ventana Inn complex—including the landmark restaurant Cielo (from which many trace the origins of California cuisine), two swimming pools, a general store and fabulous tiled sunken spas—is one of the ultimate Central Coast resorts. The 60 guest rooms and suites (many with raised fireplaces and hot tubs sunk into private decks) are lavishly decorated with natural wood and tilework, including huge shower, bathing and dressing room areas, and they have stood the test of time, according to delighted returning guests. But the resort has not stood still. Overseer Paul O'Dowd has reconfigured the floor plan of some guest rooms into two-story villas, spa suites and fireplace suites. A wide range of materials were utilized in the redesign, including teak and slate, redwood for the floors, granite with an antique finish, glass tiles, mosaic slate tiles, wrought iron, pewter, bronze, bamboo, rich stained woods, and warm fabrics such as leather and chenille. Guests will now enjoy deeper soaking tubs, oversized showers with indirect natural light, more luxurious beds and bedding, plasma television monitors and Bose surround sound. Still, the feeling is distinctly rustic, harmonizing effortlessly with the mountain terrain that brings grazing deer to your door and ravens soaring through the nearby sheltering forests. Each room, suite and secluded cottage boasts TV/DVD and honor bar/refrigerator. The suite of central spas offers hot swirling water deep enough to swim in and private enough for honeymooners. The Allegria Spa gives new meaning to the concept of total spa: It works as much on the soul as it does on the body. Breakfast, taken before the main lodge's roaring stone fireplace, features fresh juices, fruit, home-baked coffee cakes and breads and pots of excellent coffee. The afternoon wine-and-cheese affair is unsurpassed in quality. And sign up for any and all excursions headed by wildlife guide and raconteur Steve Copeland. A walk through the woods with him is a life enhancer. Later, stroll or ride a golf-cart shuttle to the trendsetting restaurant, from whose enormous decks sunset takes on new meaning. And you have not grasped the concept of tranquility until you've partaken of the clothes-optional Japanese hot pools on a full-mooned night. All the cares of the world seep away and everything that worried you before now seem so unimportant. The visit is a success: You have finally slipped into Ventana consciousness.

CARMEL
CARRIAGE HOUSE INN
www.ibts-carriagehouse.com
E-mail: carriagehouse@innsbythesea.com
Innkeeper: Cathy Lewis
800-433-4732, 831-625-2585,
fax 831-624-0974
Junipero Ave., bet. 7th & 8th Aves.,
Carmel 93921
Price: $150–$395
Credit Cards: AE, D, MC, V
Children: Within limitations
Pets: No
Handicap Access: Yes

This former motel has made the giant leap forward into a real inn-*cum*-B&B, and it is to be commended for the accomplishment. Many such facilities dreamed of hopping on the B&B explosion when it hit last decade, but most didn't have the right stuff. Well, Carriage House does. Staffed by happy workers (the first sign that management is doing something right) and showcasing an emphasis on details and special amenities, this affordable accommodation in the heart of Carmel is well worth the money. Comfy king beds, in-room icemakers, vaulted ceilings, bay windows with built-in banquettes, deep hot tubs, mini-fridges, giant TVs and free videos, overstuffed chairs, free local calls, fresh flowers, tile floors, CD players, lush robes—everything has been thought of to make your stay comfortable and memorable. The wine and appetizer affair at dusk, the free treats and drinks in your room and the free espresso drinks all day are other finishing touches that make you want to book a return soon. Also, it's just a short walk down the hill to the best dining establishments of Carmel.

The English garden at the Cobblestone Inn invites you to relax, perhaps after a walk to the nearby shops in Carmel Beach. Cobblestone Inn

COBBLESTONE INN
www.cobblestoneinncarmel.com
E-mail: info@foursisters.com
Innkeeper: Sharon Carey
831-625-5222, fax 831-625-0478
Junipero Ave., bet. 7th & 8th Aves.,
Carmel 93923
Price: $125–$275, includes full breakfast
Credit Cards: AE, D, MC, V
Children: Yes
Pets: No
Handicap Access: Yes

An English garden collaborates with French country overnight appointments to create a thoroughly Continental atmosphere in this well-run inn. A cobblestone courtyard leads to the main living room and lounge, where tea, sherry, wine and appetizers are served each evening. Each of two dozen guest rooms has its own fireplace, antique decor, plump quilts, soft carpeting, private bath and TV. After a welcoming buffet breakfast of hot muffins and breads, fresh fruit, egg dishes, granola, yogurt and fresh coffee, guests can walk to Carmel Beach and the village's many charming shops and restaurants. This fine facility is another member of the impeccable Four Sisters Inns.

The Highlands Inn has been around since 1916, but it's up-to-the-minute in every modern creature comfort.
Highlands Inn

CYPRESS INN

www.cypress-inn.com
Innkeeper: Doris Day
800-443-7443, 831-624-3871,
fax 831-624-8216
7th Ave. & Lincoln St., Carmel-by-the-Sea
93921
Price: $125–$495, includes extended
continental breakfast
Credit Cards: AE, MC, V
Children: Yes
Pets: Yes
Handicap Access: Yes

This pet-friendly Mission Revival resort is as famous for its owner, Doris Day, as it is for its plush, elegant decor. Each room is delightfully different, and all the amenities are first-tier. Recent renovations have made the rambling building even more welcoming and beautiful. The staff is bright and cheery, and a wonderful cocktail bar with a tapas menu recently opened and has already become a favorite gathering spot for guests and Carmel locals. The quiet pool invites both the fit and those who may have played a bit too hard the night before, but the subdued classiness of the courtyards and sun-dappled balconies permeates the entire soft ambiance of one of Carmel's true gems.

HIGHLANDS INN

www.highlands-inn.com
Innkeeper: Andrew Davidson
800-682-4811, 831-620-1234,
fax 831-626-8105
120 Highlands Dr., Carmel 93923
Price: $205–$695
Credit Cards: AE, D, MC, V
Children: Yes
Pets: No
Handicap Access: Yes

A California landmark since 1916, this world-class resort perched in the Carmel Highlands overlooking the spectacular coastline of Point Lobos exudes natural wood and stone elegance. In 1984, a $40 million renovation transformed the accommodations into cozy, contemporary retreats with fireplaces and fully equipped kitchens. The 142 rooms are blatantly seductive, equipped with huge beds, fireplaces—stacks of firewood are strategically located all over the property—TV, spacious dressing area, plush terry robes, well-stocked refrigerators, coffeemakers with a variety of coffees and amazing king-sized whirlpool tubs built for two. Lavish landscaping—long on native shrubs like the elegant California wild lilac—hugs the network of walkways leading down to the magnificent stone lodge, headquarters for a bistro overlooking the swimming pool, cocktail lounge and the sparkling Pacific's Edge dining room with its breathtaking views of the swirling surf and tide pools below. The outstanding California cuisine here would alone be worth a visit. Just minutes away are the natural wonders of Point Lobos State Park—which you can even glimpse from your balcony through the binoculars provided in each room—but chances are you won't be able to tear yourself away from your room, except perhaps to dine. The room service menu, a miniature of the restaurant's, is outstanding.

LA PLAYA HOTEL
www.laplayahotel.com
E-mail: info@laplayahotel.com
Innkeeper: Tom Glidden
800-582-8900, 831-624-6476,
fax 831-624-7966
Camino Real at 8th Ave., Carmel 93921
Price: $175–650
Credit Cards: AE, D, MC, V
Children: Yes
Pets: No
Handicap Access: Yes

Built in 1904 for an heiress of the Ghirardelli chocolate family and fortune, this

dream of a Mediterranean villa—a member of Historic Hotels of America—is one of the lodging treasures of Carmel. A few steps away from the white sand beaches of this charming village, La Playa's 75 rooms, two suites and five storybook cottages combine ocean views with sumptuous terraced gardens set with a jewel of a swimming pool. All the guest rooms are quiet and close to the beach. Award-winning cuisine is served in the hotel's elegant Terrace Grill, and many of the plushly decorated rooms come with fireplaces and inviting patios. Decor is Old World elegant throughout, and Carmel's fabled shops, boutiques and galleries are but a short stroll away. Expert travelers claim the bungalows are preferable to the rooms.

✪ L'AUBERGE CARMEL
www.laubergecarmel.com
Innkeeper: David Fink
831-624-8578, fax 831-626-1018
Monte Verde St. at 7th Ave., Carmel 93921
Price: $225–450
Credit Cards: AE, D, MC, V
Children: No
Pets: No
Handicap Access: Yes

David Fink, owner of Carmel's highly praised Bouchée Restaurant, has opened Carmel's newest luxury inn and restaurant, L'Auberge Carmel. It is a glorious transformation of the former Sundial Lodge, located in the heart of Carmel, just four blocks from Carmel Beach. The 20-room inn was originally built in 1929, and the three story wood frame and stucco building has always reflected Carmel's artistic and elegant lifestyle. During the renovation, Fink's team retained the European feel of a quiet villa built around a classic brick courtyard, so the past slips sweetly into an embrace from the present. The entire property is reserved, peaceful and private. The pampering begins the moment you walk through the door of this wonderful retreat, which shares more with its siblings in southern France than its neighbors in Carmel. You are escorted to your room by a bright young staff member to find a plate of perfect figs and peaches, some chocolates and a glass of excellent wine waiting to help knock your journey's dust from your mind and palate. The room features a giant plasma TV, thick brocaded curtains, decadently soft chairs, wet bar and fridge, spectacular lighting, CD player, warm, rich-toned appointments throughout and spun honey walls. But the star of the room is the giant designer bed, as plush and soft as a mother's bosom, where you slip into a sleep as gentle as a babe's. The bathrooms are massive, with accoutrements of the top rank, radiant heating floors, massive tub (the best we've ever enjoyed) and whimsical art deco sink. The in-house restaurant features a 5,000-bottle wine cellar, and chef Walter Manzke heads the kitchen. An alfresco breakfast in the morning and evening meals in the 12-table dining room are prepared by the same staff as Carmel's Bouchée, simply one of the best restaurants on the Central Coast.

MISSION RANCH RESORT

Innkeeper: Teresa Johnson
800-538-8221, 831-624-6436,
fax 831-626-4163
26270 Dolores St., Carmel 93923
Price: $100–$275, includes continental breakfast
Credit Cards: MC, V
Children: Allowed with limits
Pets: No
Handicap Access: Limited

The lush ranchlands of this historic acreage near the Carmel Mission offer terrific views of meadows peacefully stocked with sheep, the fog creeping in atmospherically from the beaches of Monterey Bay and the comfort of a recently refurbished 31-room farmhouse

attractively upgraded by owner Clint Eastwood. Yes, *that* Clint Eastwood. This country spread combines rustic ambiance with contemporary comfort, especially attractive to guests who like to unwind yet stay close to sights, shopping and the dining attractions of Carmel and Monterey. Overnights come with continental breakfast and access to tennis courts and fitness facilities, with excellent hiking nearby. The property affords fine dining at its California cuisine restaurant, which includes a cozy '30s bar and sandstone fireplace.

QUAIL LODGE RESORT AND GOLF CLUB

www.quaillodge.com
E-mail: info@quaillodge.com
Innkeeper: Mike Oprish
888-828-8787, 831-624-2888,
fax 831-624-3726
8205 Valley Greens Dr., Carmel 93923
Price: $295–$975, continental breakfast
Credit Cards: AE, D, MC, V
Children: Yes
Pets: No
Handicap Access: Yes

The word "luxury" takes on fresh meaning at this Mobil 4-Star resort boasting gloriously designed overnight accommodations, a destination golf course, tennis courts, swimming pools, hot tubs, fine continental cuisine, trout fishing ponds and hiking trails that stretch 850 acres deep into the Carmel hills. It's run like a Swiss watch on a California timetable. The plush appointments and flawless service justify the price at what many consider a dream getaway. One hundred rooms and 14 suites pamper guests in designer trappings long on exquisitely tailored furnishings, mirrors, fireplaces, plants, private decks with wooden hot tubs and tiled fireplaces. Lodgings run the gamut from lakeside lodges with balconies and terraces to cottages with wet bars and villas straight from

Architectural Digest. A short walk through extraordinary plantings that blend in with the spectacular scenery leads to The Covey, one of the finest restaurants on the Central Coast. If you're discreet, you'll spy Doris Day—a Carmel Valley resident who dines here weekly—among the dinner guests.

SANDPIPER INN

www.sandpiper-inn.com
E-mail: sandpiperinn@yahoo.com
Innkeeper: Bill Lee
800-633-6433, 831-624-6433,
fax 831-624-5964
2408 Bay View Ave., Carmel 93923
Price: $95–$220, includes breakfast
Credit Cards: AE, D, MC, V
Children: Within limitations
Pets: No
Handicap Access: Limited

One hundred yards from Carmel Beach, this elegant country inn occupies a 1929 Prairie-style residence distinguished by spacious rooms, open-beam ceilings, wood-burning fireplaces and horizontal lines. The innkeepers run the attractively antiques-decorated, art-filled inn with Old World warmth, generating the feeling of staying overnight at a gracious private home. Peace and quiet reigns, with the exception of TV in the lounge. Tea and cookies are served in the fireside lounge at five o'clock each evening, and morning brings an expanded continental breakfast. The inn's lovely garden is filled with the rhododendrons, camellias and azaleas that flourish in the moist, coastal climate. There is a two-night minimum stay on weekends, three nights in the summer.

Water seems to define Quail Lodge Resort, heightening the excitement of its bold architecture and many amenities. Quail Lodge Resort

STONEHOUSE INN
www.carmelstonehouse.com
stonehouseinn@aol.com
Innkeepers: Terri & Kevin Navaille
877-748-6618, 831-624-4569,
fax 831-624-8209
8th Ave. below Monte Verde St., Carmel
93921
Price: $89–$244, includes full breakfast
Credit Cards: AE, MC, V
Children: With limitations
Pets: No
Handicap Access: No

Retaining the bohemian "artists' colony" flavor that attracted notable past guests like Jack London and Sinclair Lewis, this historic Carmel house (built in 1906) oozes charm in its stonework exterior, fetching gardens, old-fashioned glass front porch and white wicker furniture. Each of six overnight rooms—two with private baths—is uniquely decorated, some with four-poster beds and gabled ceilings. Some rooms present dramatic ocean views. The inn provides a breakfast of juices, coffee, fresh fruit, pancakes, French toast and omelets. The extraordinary living room stone fireplace is kept blazing, and evening wine and cookies may be enjoyed in the gardens, cozy interior or inviting porch area. The inn is within easy walking distance of shopping, restaurants and the beach.

TICKLE PINK INN
www.ticklepink.com
Innkeeper: Mark Watson
800-635-4774, 831-624-1244,
fax 831-626-9516
155 Highland Dr., Carmel Highlands 93923
Price: $289–$499, includes breakfast
Credit Cards: AE, MC, V
Children: Allowed with limits
Pets: No
Handicap Access: Limited

Despite the cute name, this popular getaway has been a fixture with savvy travelers since the 1950s, when the secluded hotel was established on the site of Senator Edward Tickle's private retreat. Sharing a main driveway off Hwy. 1 with the Highlands Inn, the facility's 35 rooms and suites line the Carmel Highlands cliffs overlooking both ocean and an exquisite hidden cove beach, and they boast ample amenities. Rooms are outfitted with bright floral comforters, tiled bathrooms and private balconies offering deluxe views. Coffeemakers, TVs, terrycloth robes and morning newspapers come with each room, and some suites feature wood-burning fireplaces and spa tubs. There is even a stand-alone cottage from the original Tickle estate that can accommodate two couples. A substantial continental breakfast and an evening wine-and-cheese spread on the terrace lounge are included in the price.

CARMEL VALLEY
BERNARDUS
www.bernardus.com
reservations@bernardus.com
Innkeeper: Jim Cicel
888-648-9463, 831-658-3400,
fax 831-659-3529
415 Carmel Valley Rd., Carmel Valley 93924
Price: $420–$1,690
Credit Cards: AE, D, MC, V
Children: Within limitations
Pets: No
Handicap Access: Yes

Bernardus Lodge, opened in 2000, is luxurious even by California's high standards. Every vacation detail has been considered, from the stone fireplaces and feather beds in the rooms, to relaxing spa packages, to the delicious cuisine at Marinus Restaurant—its wine list is already an "excellence award" winner according to *Wine Spectator.* Surrounded by Carmel Valley meadows and oaks, Bernardus's 57 guest rooms demand only serenity and rejuvenation. Take in a game of tennis, croquet or golf, plunge into the sparkling pool, indulge in the nearby wine region, or take a 10-minute drive to the Monterey Peninsula.

CARMEL VALLEY LODGE
www.valleylodge.com
info@valleylodge.com
Innkeepers: Diane & Peter Coakley
800-641-4646, 831-659-2261,
fax 831-659-4558
Carmel Valley Rd. at Ford Rd. (P.O. Box 93),
Carmel Valley 93924-0093
Price: $149–$339, includes continental breakfast
Credit Cards: AE, D, MC, V
Children: Yes
Pets: Yes
Handicap Access: Yes

Finding "rustic" and "dog-friendly" in the same accommodations isn't easy, but they cozily snuggle side by side in this country inn deep in the Carmel Valley. Poochie gets a welcome bag of treats on arrival, and you get s'mores in your room. Toast them in the many rooms equipped with fireplaces or in the lobby's grand stone fireplace. Open beams arch over all 31 rooms, setting off Shaker-style furnishings, wood-burning fireplaces, cable TV, original artwork and quilted bedspreads. Walk around the beau-

Dogs are welcome at Carmel Valley Lodge, but that does not prevent the rooms from offering the height of luxury for their owners, too. Carmel Valley Lodge

tifully landscaped grounds, relax by the pool and heated spa or take a three-minute walk to the center of Carmel Valley village for wine tasting or a leisurely meal. Each accommodation features a doggy hitching post on the patio, and a continental breakfast greets guests each morning. You also can enjoy a cup of French roast from the coffeemaker in your room anytime during the day or night.

CARMEL VALLEY RANCH RESORT
www.wyndham.com
Innkeeper: Martin P. Nicholson
800-422-7635, 831-625-9500,
fax 831-626-2574
1 Old Ranch Rd., Carmel 93923
Price: $260–$1,200
Credit Cards: AE, D, MC, V
Children: Yes
Pets: No
Handicap Access: Yes

Once a fruit farm in the late 1800s, the lush 1,700-acre spread nestled in Carmel Valley has been upgraded to the lavish standards of a Spanish-style ranch resort. Ideal for vacationers and business travelers alike, rooms and suites are tucked into the hillsides, offering views of stately oaks, gardens and an 18-hole championship golf course. Bedrooms with adjoining living rooms—decorated with antiques, woven rugs and artwork—include cathedral ceilings, woodburning fireplaces, balconies and bleached wood walls. An exclusive resort with world-class recreation, the ranch is most widely recognized for its golf and tennis facilities. Guests can also treat themselves to a variety of fitness and hiking activities. An on-property corral adds to the authentic ranch-style experience, with horseback rides through the Santa Lucia Mountains providing spectacular views of the property's rolling acreage. There are also two swimming pools and six whirlpool spas located throughout the resort. The main lodge, reminiscent of an old country estate, is airy and inviting, with stone fireplaces and ceiling-to-floor-length windows—a lovely spot to sip cocktails while watching the sunset. Also located in the main lodge, The Oaks dining room features fresh fruits and vegetables of Carmel Valley, fish caught along the coast and herbs from the resort's own garden.

LOS LAURELES LODGE

www.loslaureles.com
innkeeper@loslaureles.com
Innkeepers: Mike & Les Terry
800-533-4404, 831-659-2233,
fax 831-659-0481
313 W. Carmel Valley Rd., Carmel Valley 93924
Price: $90–$595, includes continental breakfast
Children: Yes
Pets: Yes
Handicap Access: Yes

This fascinating old hunting lodge has been completely remodeled, but it still proudly wears its glorious past in plain view. Comfortable guest accommodations have been fashioned from the former Vanderbilt thoroughbred horse stables (circa 1930), and knotty-pine-paneled walls and period antiques contribute to the genteel atmosphere of a time that sweetly lingers like a dream at the edge of memory.

The Hill House and Vanderbilt Cottage present a step or two up in residential elegance and spaciousness, and various junior suites circle the rambling grounds. The pool and cabana have long been a favorite daytime hangout for Carmel Valley residents, and the scene there is playful and simmering with the possibilities of amour. Come evening, the action shifts to the popular and quite legendary saloon, where everyone becomes friendly by the second round and the kitchen produces some enticing pub grub for the chattering

crowd. Also, the fine dining available at the Lodge Restaurant is the equal of any dining room in the Monterey area, and overseer Mario Beretti makes sure the quality of the food and the sense of camaraderie remain high.

MARINA

✪ MARINA DUNES RESORT

www.marinadunes.com
info@marinadunes.com
Innkeeper: Linda Dias
877-944-3863, 831-883-9478,
fax 831-883-9477
3295 Dunes Dr., Marina 93933
Price: $99–$449
Credit Cards: AE, D, MC, V
Children: Yes
Pets: No
Handicap Access: Yes

Marina Dunes Resort is the only oceanfront development allowed along Monterey Bay in more than two decades, and the effort and care owner John King took to nestle it amid

The way the Marina Dunes Resort fits comfortably into the Monterey Bay shoreline is a mark of its environmentally sensitive architecture.
Marina Dunes Resort

an important and environmentally sensitive shore (on the edge of the of Monterey Bay National Marine Sanctuary) proves that the permits were granted to the right person. All the rooms boast breathtaking views of either the Pacific Ocean or 19 acres of secluded, rolling dunes. Watching the sun set directly in front of our deck, the last rays of light playing a glowing farewell to the dunes below our room (illuminating crashing waves and small snowy plovers scurrying about), was pure heaven. As we sipped cocktails before the fireplace, the wind billowing the fine crêpe curtains as the full moon rose, the Big Dipper appearing, and a solitary fishing boat beating its way home along the horizon, we agreed the moment was one of the most special in our lives. The slate floors, stressed-leather couches and overstuffed chairs, the top-drawer appointments, mirrored bathroom, oversized tub, extraordinary lighting, two TVs, wet bar and giant cloud of a bed provided glorious accompaniment to our reveries. The staff is extremely well trained and helpful, and golf carts are provided so guests can unwind with a glide around the grounds. The giant pool, Jacuzzis and full spa also whisper luxury. An A. J. Spurs steak house and bar provides the on-campus dining and nightlife options, but the full range of the region's culinary genius is but a few miles away from this isolated oasis of calm.

MONTEREY

HOTEL PACIFIC

www.hotelpacific.com
reservations@innsofmontery.com
Innkeeper: Randy Venard
800-554-5542, 831-373-5700,
fax 831-373-6921
300 Pacific St., Monterey 93940
Price: $129–$329, includes continental breakfast
Credit Cards: AE, D, MC, V
Children: Yes
Pets: No
Handicap Access: Yes

The sparkling patio of the Hotel Pacific invites you to relax. Sun or shade—take your pick! Hotel Pacific

This elegant adobe hotel, with a design that harks back to Monterey's Spanish colonial legacy, manages to combine Old World charm with modern luxury in a way that makes guests feel as if they've entered a timeless world. The layout here lends itself to comfort, as does the attention to detail—each room has wood-shuttered windows, hardwood floors warmed with Berber wool rugs, a gas fireplace and a goose-down feather bed. On foggy mornings, you may have trouble tearing yourself away from your room to explore the delights of downtown Monterey, just two blocks away. The suites have their own terraces, many opening onto private, interior courtyards lush with flowering shrubs and burbling fountains. Breakfast in the salon features mounds of bagels and pastries, bowls of fresh fruit, cereal and coffee. Come back to the hotel for afternoon tea to relax and plan the night's adventures. Even at 105 rooms, Hotel Pacific has the cozy aura of a much smaller establishment. Perhaps it's the ever-present splash of water from the courtyard fountains, but a stay at Hotel Pacific conjures the tranquility of a bygone era, but with all the cutting-edge comforts of today.

JABBERWOCK

www.jabberwockinn.com
innkeeper@jabberwockinn.com
Innkeepers: Joan & John Kiliany
888-428-7253, 831-372-4777,
fax 831-655-2946
598 Laine St., Monterey 93940
Price: $145–$265, includes full breakfast
Credit Cards: D, MC, V
Children: With limitations
Pets: No
Handicap Access: No

Built in 1911 and once a convent, this Arts & Crafts home sits four blocks above Cannery Row and the Monterey Bay Aquarium. Charmingly homey with its *Alice in Wonderland*ish whimsical decor, hidden gardens and waterfalls, the inn offers seven rooms decorated with beautiful antiques, plump comforters, Victorian beds with lace-trimmed sheets, and fresh flowers. The Jabberwock's home-cooked breakfast may be taken in the privacy of overnight rooms or by the fireplace in the dining room. A bell rings at five o'clock each afternoon to announce freshly prepared hors d'oeuvres and sherry on the enclosed sunporch overlooking estate gardens and Monterey Bay. Bedtime milk and heavenly chocolate chip cookies await visitors returning from their evening activities. All seven of the lovely rooms boast private baths, and four have fireplaces. The huge Borogrove Suite has its own cozy fireplace and a picture window for viewing shore sights. Complete with an impressive Lewis Carroll library, the Jabberwock is a hidden treasure that could inspire fairy tales of its own. A

There's a lamp for reading beside your bed at the Jabberwock, but bedtime milk and chocolate chip cookies may put you to sleep before you can turn the first page. Jabberwock

two-night stay is required on weekends.

MONTEREY HOTEL

www.montereyhotel.com
Innkeeper: Maureen Doran
800-727-0960, 831-375-3184,
fax 831-373-2899
406 Alvarado St., Monterey 93940
Price: $69–$299
Credit Cards: AE, D, MC, V
Children: Yes
Pets: No
Handicap Access: Yes

The stately Monterey Hotel, constructed in 1904, boasts a magnificent facade and an interior to match. Located in the heart of downtown Monterey, where fine dining and shopping abound, the Monterey Hotel has been restored to its original splendor, with hand-carved furnishings, antique patinas, polished wood floors and leaded-glass chandeliers. Rooms feature plantation shutters and marble baths, while suites include the additional luxuries of fireplaces and wet bars. Recently acquired by Moonstone Hotel Properties—a privately owned family of boutique California properties—the Monterey Hotel is completing an $8 million expansion that will add needed amenities while preserving the hotel's early-20th-century detail and charm. Twenty-five rooms will be added to the current 45, as well as additional meeting space, extra parking and a 1,200-square-foot fitness facility. When expansion is complete in late 2005, the hotel's main entrance will be relocated from busy Alvarado Street to the more spacious Calle Principal.

✪ OLD MONTEREY INN

www.oldmontereyinn.com
omi@oldmontereyinn.com
Innkeeper: Pattie Vallarta
800-350-2344, 831-375-8284,
fax 831-375-6730
500 Martin St., Monterey 93940

There's no doubt that the venerable Monterey Hotel is a stately bastion of old-fashioned luxury, but its décor, while faithful to an earlier era, is recent and fresh, as seen here in the inviting lobby. Monterey Hotel

Price: $240–$450
Credit Cards: MC, V
Children: Within limitations
Pets: No
Handicap Access: No

Landscaped gardens and vintage oaks embrace this half-timbered English Tudor-style country home built in the 1920s within walking distance of historic Old Monterey. Each of 10 overnight rooms retains the gracious theme with antique and wicker furniture, fireplaces, skylighting and garden views. Special suites offer king-sized feather beds (as close to a floating on a cloud as most of us will get), high-thread-count linen, tiled bathrooms, wonderful amenities, a dressing room and a sitting room with fireplace and bay window. The separate cottage is distinguished by fine stained-glass detailing. A full breakfast is provided in bedrooms, or in the antiques-filled dining room at a table set with stunning Oriental china. Everything here is regal yet understated. An evening selection of wines and cheeses is laid out by the living room fireplace, and a carafe of port is provided for late-night imbibing so guests can prolong the golden night. One of the great accommodations in the area.

Commanding views and airy rooms are the hallmark of the Captain's Inn. Captain's Inn

MOSS LANDING
CAPTAIN'S INN
www.captainsinn.com
res@captainsinn.com
Innkeepers: Melanie & Captain Yohn Gideon
831-633-5550
8122 Moss Landing Rd., Moss Landing 95039
Price: $110–265, includes full breakfast
Credit Cards: MC, V
Children: Older okay
Pets: No
Handicap Access: Yes

Plunging completely into a nautical theme, the eight rooms of this unique inn built as the Pacific Coast Steamship Company in 1906 are appointed with artifacts from a life spent at sea (co-owner Yohn Gideon, a former U.S. Coast Guard captain, did just that). The four rooms in the main house are joined by six additional guest rooms in the old boathouse. The plush Queen Anne beds (one is even made from the remains of old fishing trawler), fireplace, luxury tub and either concrete/slate or hardwood floors guarantee relaxing comfort, and the airy rooms with their vaulted ceilings and prow-like plate-glass windows encourage bird-watching through the complimentary binoculars. The modern world is always a click away since the Dish TV, dataports and free-local-call phones share space with old trawler lights and classic oceangoing and wildlife art prints. A gourmet breakfast is prepared each morning by culinary wizard/co-owner Melanie Gideon. Hot appetizers and fruit are served around sunset and cookies at bedtime. The dreamy town of Moss Landing, with its myriad antiques shops and cozy dining spots, is just steps away from this little-known treasure.

PACIFIC GROVE
CENTRELLA HOTEL
www.centrellainn.com
centrella@innsbythesea.com

Innkeeper: Amrish Patel
800-233-3372, 831-372-3372,
fax 831-372-2036
612 Central Ave., Pacific Grove 93950
Price: $159–$299, includes full breakfast
Credit Cards: AE, D, MC, V
Children: Allowed in cottages
Pets: No
Handicap Access: Yes

Built in 1889 as a state-of-the-art private boardinghouse, this award-winning Victorian restoration has earned overnight admirers, as well as a place on the National Register of Historic Places. All of the 26 high-ceilinged, comfortably decorated rooms—including suites and cottages—have private baths and telephones. An expanded continental breakfast buffet greets visitors in the dining room each morning. Tea and hors d'oeuvres are served in the late afternoon, and the evening cookies and coffee are scrumptious. The Centrella is aptly named, being within walking distance of Monterey's Cannery Row and world-famous aquarium.

GATEHOUSE INN

www.gatehouse-inn.com
info@gatehouse-inn.com
Innkeepers: Steve Lucas & Ruby Rustan
800-753-1881, 831-649-8436,
fax 831-648-8044
225 Central Ave., Pacific Grove 93950
Price: $135–$220, includes full breakfast
Credit Cards: AE, D, MC, V
Children: Within limitations
Pets: Within limitations ($25 per night cleaning fee)
Handicap Access: Limited

Local lore has it that literary lion John Steinbeck regularly discussed historical trivia with the original owner of this Italianate 1884 residence. And the present-day charm of this magnificently decorated inn carries the torch high for its Victorian heyday. Many guests think it's just like staying at Grandma's house when they were kids. Much of the original decor—including lincrusta walls—has been enhanced with silk-screened period reproduction wallpaper, period antique furnishings and opulent themes, like one chamber that feels like a sultan's tent with mother-of-pearl inlaid headboard, Persian carpet and camel saddle chair. All come with private bath (yes, even claw-foot tubs), and five rooms boast gas potbelly stoves or fireplaces. A fine full breakfast is served in the morning, and afternoon wine and hors d'oeuvres are part of the endless charm. The location, 100 yards from the ocean, invites strolling and access to Monterey's top sights.

If you're old enough to have had a grandmother born in the Victorian era, then you'll feel right at home in the Gatehouse Inn's rooms stuffed with soft comforts of every kind. Whatever your age, a visit here will take you into more restful times. Gatehouse Inn

GOSBY HOUSE INN

www.gosbyhouseinn.com
info@foursisters.com
Innkeeper: Kalena Mittleman-Rojas
800-527-8828, 831-375-1287,
fax 831-655-9621
643 Lighthouse Ave., Pacific Grove 93950
Price: $100–$200, includes breakfast
Credit Cards: AE, D, MC, V

The Queen Anne Victorian stateliness of Pacific Grove's Gosby House has greeted overnight guests since 1887. Grant Huntington

Children: Yes
Pets: No
Handicap Access: Limited

The distinctive front door turret and pointed cupola announce this gracious gabled inn as a showpiece Queen Anne Victorian, circa 1887. Filled stem-to-stern with distinctive finery, antiques and charming whimsy from the 19th century, this beautiful facility was originally built as a boardinghouse and today offers lodgings in 22 rooms of varying sizes, some with fireplaces and all with private baths. The rooms all have refrigerators, and atmospheric fireplaces in 12 rooms provide coziness to match the antiques, period reproductions and plump bed linens. It's like spending a night in the 19th century, but with the convenience of a phone by your carved wooden bedside. Breakfast is substantial and unpretentious, with guests helping themselves to huge breakfast rolls, muffins, scones and hot egg dishes, and then moving out to the garden for the morning meal. The parlor, straight out of a Merchant-Ivory film, is the location for afternoon sherry and hors d'oeuvres. Bicycles are available to help maximize enjoyment of the nearby Pacific coastline and Cannery Row.

GREEN GABLES INN

www.greengablesinnpg.com
info@foursisters.com/inns/greengablesinn
Innkeeper: Lucia Root
831-375-2095, fax 831-375-5437
301 Oceanview Blvd., Pacific Grove 93950
Price: $120–$280, includes breakfast, wine and hors d'oeuvres
Credit Cards: AE, D, MC, V
Children: Yes, in Carriage House rooms
Pets: No
Handicap Access: Limited

One of oceanfront Pacific Grove's most magnetic landmarks, this multigabled Queen Anne mansion was built in 1888 by a southern California businessman for his paramour. The incredibly intricate results

The Green Gables in Pacific Grove features turn-of-the-20th-century atmosphere a stroll from the crashing surf. Grant Huntington

of the original owner's passion for bay windows, gingerbread and lavish stained-glass insets have been turned into a gracious inn, one of the prestigious Four Sisters Inns. Of the charmingly period-decorated 10 rooms and one suite, several boast ocean views with fireplaces and 7 provide private baths, some with spa tubs. Morning brings the day's newspapers with coffee and full, family-style breakfast buffet featuring fresh egg dishes, fruit, scones, pastries and pancakes served in the parlor. In the afternoon, wine and appetizers are served by helpful staff members, who'll be happy to provide bicycles for touring the dramatic coastline. One of the most romantic B&B establishments on the Central Coast, in the late 1990s it was named the number one B&B in North America by the Official Hotel Guide put out by U.S. travel agents.

✪ MARTINE INN

www.martineinn.com
don@martineinn.com
Innkeeper: Don Martine
800-852-5588, 831-373-3388,
fax 831-373-3896
255 Oceanview Blvd., Pacific Grove 93950
Price: $129–$329
Credit Cards: AE, D, MC, V
Children: Within limitations
Pets: No
Handicap Access: Yes

Martine Inn just does it all the right way. From its marvelously trained staff (helpers delicately walk that fine line between granting guests their privacy and being on hand when they seek information about anything the area has to offer) to the museum-quality antiques that fill the 24 rooms, top of the line is the motto. One room sports furnishings from the Edith Head estate, and another includes a mahogany bedroom suite exhibited at the 1893 Chicago World's Fair. The other rooms are nothing to turn up one's nose at. A full breakfast is served on

antique Sheffield silver, lace and crystal, and the evening wine, cheese, fruit and hors d'oeuvres spread is the talk of the building. In-room dinners are available, and the whirlpool spa and relaxing courtyard prove inviting long into the balmy summer nights. Besides a sitting/TV room, a game room filled with distractions, including a billiards table, is always humming, and owner Don Martine's restored MG collection provides a marvelous conversation starter. *Bon Appétit* proclaimed the inn "one of best B&Bs in historic homes," and one look out the front plate-glass window at the splendid views of crashing surf will have you nodding in agreement.

SEVEN GABLES INN

www.pginns.com
Innkeepers: Susan Flatley-Wheelwright &
Ed Flatley
831-372-4341
555 Ocean View Blvd., Pacific Grove 93950
Price: $175–$385, includes full breakfast
Credit Cards: MC, V
Children: Within limitations
Pets: No
Handicap Access: Yes

The 1886 Seven Gables Inn is an imposing and stately presence, commanding its share of the coastline in Pacific Grove. Seven Gables Inn

A stately 1886 confection of multigabled gingerbread, the grand mansion's exterior is more than matched by an inviting interior of museum-quality antiques, ornate rugs and gilded light fixtures. The inn houses 14 elegant guest rooms, including several in adjoining cottages. Each comes with private bath and a stunning coastal view, and the highly desirable second-floor Bellevue Room offers an especially sunny exposure and bay view from cozy window seats. A turn-of-the-20th-century fantasy, the inn's period theme extends to guest room appointments like antique sideboards, stained-glass windows, vintage rugs, huge armoires and comfortable viewing chairs or couches. Wine, tea and appetizers are served in the stately dining room each afternoon and a full breakfast greets guests in the morning. Innkeeper Susan Flatley-Wheelwright grew up in the showy mansion, and she and her staff can spin great yarns about the area's history, as well as offer suggestions on visiting Monterey's many historic attractions.

Pebble Beach
INN AT SPANISH BAY
www.pebblebeach.com
Innkeeper: Rod Schinnerer
800-654-9300, 831-647-7500,
fax 831-644-7960
2700 17 Mile Dr., Pebble Beach 93953
Price: $528–$2,100
Credit Cards: AE, D, MC, V
Children: Yes
Pets: No
Handicap Access: Yes

Located on fabled 17 Mile Drive at the edge of the brooding pines of Del Monte Forest and only a few hundred yards from the Pacific shore, this 236-acre Mediterranean-style enclave is embraced by some of the finest championship golf terrain on the planet. More than 270 luxurious rooms and suites—each boasting four-poster beds, marble baths, fireplaces, cable TV, and most with balconies, patios and stupendous ocean views—make this a matchless resort on arguably the most spectacular setting on the Central Coast. Guests are treated to preferred tee times at such world-class links as Pebble Beach Golf Links and Spyglass Hill Golf Course, as well as the Links at Spanish Bay, designed by Tom Watson, Robert Trent Jones Jr. and Frank Tatum. If golf isn't your bag, there's tennis, swimming, spa-going or simply soaking up magnificent views from any of four restaurants and lounges. Complete indulgence here tends to make every guest feel like one of the rich and famous . . . and many are.

THE LODGE AT PEBBLE BEACH
www.pebblebeach.com
Innkeeper: Janren Chicourrat
800-654-9300, 831-624-3811,
fax 831-644-7960
1700 17 Mile Dr., Pebble Beach 93953
Price: $595–$1,900
Credit Cards: AE, D, MC, V
Children: Yes
Pets: No
Handicap Access: Yes

Since 1919, this elegant retreat has catered to international celebrities, sports legends and those who crave the ultimate in pampering lodgings. The view through the lobby salon's windows is straight out of the Golden Age of Hollywood, overlooking the emerald expanse of the golf course's 18th hole and beyond to the white Pacific surf swirling along the craggy shoreline. In addition to golf, there are all those luxury tennis, swimming, horseback riding and fitness facilities. The Lodge's 161 spacious guest rooms continue the luxurious theme, with views of the ocean, fairways or vibrant gardens. In addition to fine restaurants, the Lodge boasts a dark-wood Tap Room sanctuary lined with a fascinating collection of golf memorabilia.

DINING

Fed by year-round harvests and the delicious influence of Pacific Rim neighbors, California cuisine has a vivacious reputation the world over. Food historians like to trace the origins of this bold, light culinary style to the Central Coast. After all, it was at Ventana Inn in Big Sur that California cuisine artist Jeremiah Tower roasted his first red bell pepper and launched the evolving trend toward mesquite grilling. It's no surprise that in this stretch of the Central Coast, seafood is king, especially the silken flesh of the Monterey spot prawn, farm-raised abalone and wild Monterey Bay king salmon. Italian cuisine, a legacy from the pioneering fishing families, is another great specialty.

Dining Price Code

The price range below includes the cost of a single dinner that includes an entrée, appetizer or dessert, and glass of wine or beer. Tax and gratuities are not included. Note: Smoking is not allowed in any restaurant or eatery in the state of California.

Inexpensive	Up to $15
Moderate	$15–$30
Expensive	$30–$50
Very Expensive	$50 or more

Credit cards are abbreviated as follows:
   AE: American Express
    D: Discover Card
  MC: MasterCard
    V: Visa

BIG SUR
✪ CIELO
800-628-6500, 831-667-2331
Hwy. 1, 28 miles south of Carmel, Big Sur
Open: Lunch & dinner daily
Price: Expensive
Cuisine: Californian/Mediterranean
Full Bar: Yes
Reservations: Required for dinner

Credit Cards: AE, D, MC, V
Handicap Access: Yes

Here in the heart of Big Sur is arguably the most beautiful setting for an inn and restaurant in the world. Perched 1,000 feet above the Pacific Ocean, framed by the Santa Lucia mountain range, Cielo seems hoisted atop the world. On a clear day, the view alone is worth the drive. The recently renovated restaurant, like the inn, is rustic, discreet and sophisticated, and under the direction of Tom Fichera, the inn's director of food and beverage, the dining room is hitting on all 16 cylinders. Both lunch and dinner menus play off the Central Coast "Riviera" setting and sport a classical French California theme. Chef Matthew Millea is one talented fellow, and his inspired menu showcases that gift. The ahi tuna tartare tostada and warm Dungeness crab salad are two sublime starters. In fact anything from the sea he touches becomes transcendent. Other appetizers include Sonoma foie blond pâté, lobster martini and the world's best Caesar salad. Entrées like the wild mushroom risotto, lemongrass and teriyaki braised pork shank with kaffir lime, wildflower honey roasted Sonoma duck breast, and slow-cooked rabbit with dried plums are complemented by an award-winning wine list and a knowledgeable staff. An in-house bakery produces a wide array of desserts, breads and pastries. The tab is rich, but so is the experience.

DEETJANS
831-667-2378
Hwy. 1, Big Sur
Open: Breakfast & dinner daily
Price: Inexpensive to Moderate
Cuisine: Healthy American home cooking
Full Bar: No
Reservations: Recommended for large parties
Credit Cards: MC, V
Handicap Access: Yes

A few cats have the run of the rustic dining rooms in this quintessential Big Sur restaurant, arguably the area's most charming, founded in the '30s by legendary Big Sur personality Grandpa Deetjans. The cozy, modest restaurant was always an adjunct to the inn, both now run by a nonprofit organization and neatly tucked into a tight canyon under graceful redwoods. The simple American menu changes occasionally at the whimsy of the chef, but generally includes at least one of each of the basics: lamb, beef, fresh fish, oak-grilled chicken, fresh pasta, and a vegetarian specialty. Highly recommended for breakfast.

NEPENTHE

831-667-2345
Hwy. 1, 30 miles south of Carmel, Big Sur
Open: Breakfast, lunch & dinner daily
Price: Moderate
Cuisine: Regional American
Full Bar: Yes
Reservations: Recommended for large parties
Credit Cards: AE, MC, V
Handicap Access: Yes

A legendary bohemian pit stop since the day that it opened in 1949, Nepenthe has always been a gathering spot for leading literary lights seeking escape from the urban jungle. Henry Miller was a regular denizen, and Orson Welles purchased a cabin on the property for his bride, Rita Hayworth. A central fireplace and lots of rustic woodwork add to the charm of this terraced establishment hugging the rocky coastline. The Kiva Restaurant serves a daily brunch and offers a tapas menu until dusk on its outdoor deck. The view from the terrace provides an unsurpassed glimpse of the wild beauty of this magic spot. Sooner or later everyone makes the pilgrimage here, sometimes for an evening cocktail (the Bloody Marys have few rivals), sometimes for the fine salads and exceptional burgers, but always for the view and the unique moody Central Coast atmosphere. Don't forget to bring your camera.

CARMEL

ANTON & MICHEL

831-624-2406
Mission St. & 7th Ave., Carmel
Open: Lunch & dinner daily
Price: Expensive
Cuisine: Modern French bistro
Full Bar: Yes
Reservations: Recommended
Credit Cards: AE, D, MC, V
Handicap Access: Yes

Tucked away among the shops of Carmel, this small bistro seems to evade time—the maître d' even changed the hands on the old grandfather clock to match our reservation. The view from the large glass windows is humble, overlooking a small fountain and several little shops, but like the decor—and the bronze embossed plates waiting at every table—it has an air of simple elegance. The wait staff is charming and helpful, and one could easily spend a day studying the extensive wine list. Anton & Michel's menu relies on top-quality seafood and meat paired with fresh, well-prepared vegetables. The cream of asparagus soup and warm spinach salad offer the perfect bridge into upscale comfort foods like filet mignon. Old favorites are a staple of the menu, but many dishes have a refreshing creative twist. A favorite is the almond rosemary encrusted Chilean sea bass with herb sauce served on a bed of lemony round pasta with asparagus. Chocolate definitely rules over their small selection of desserts, but unexpected treats like a light mango mousse with a crust of ladyfingers also offer the perfect complement to an expensive yet completely satisfying meal.

✪ BOUCHÉE RESTAURANT

831-626-7880
Mission St., bet., Ocean & 7th Aves., Carmel

Open: Dinner Tues.–Sun.
Price: Expensive
Cuisine: Californian
Full Bar: No
Reservations: Recommended
Credit Cards: AE, MC, V
Handicap Access: Yes

When David Fink opened Bouchée a few years ago, expectations were high. Fink, the former general manager of Highlands Inn and cofounder of the Masters of Food & Wine, teamed up with Walter Manzke, the former executive chef of Patina in Los Angeles, who earned his culinary medals by training with Joachim Splichal, Alain Ducasse and Ferran Adria. The duo then attracted a luminous beverage and wine star director, Chris Bradford. What the three have developed is, simply put, the top dining room in Carmel, and that, as they say, is a mouthful. The hip diner partakes of the four-course tasting menu and wine paring, one of the great deals of the new century. From the opening tomato salad with watermelon and white balsamic granite, through the second course of seared Maine diver scallops or Monterey Bay red abalone to the main entrée of olive-oil-poached South Pacific sea bass or Liberty Farm duck breast with foie gras mushroom strudel, not one false note is played by the kitchen. The rocky road candy crème brûlée was as decadent and sinful as any dessert has a right to be. Quail, lamb and chicken join every tasty creature from the sea on the regular menu, so anything you choose is a wise decision. When matched with the wines of the evening, a dinner at Bouchée becomes the linchpin of a special tale you will be spinning for years.

CAFE STRAVAGANZA
831-625-3733
241 Crossroads Center, Hwy. 1 & Rio Rd., Carmel
Open: Lunch & dinner daily

Price: Inexpensive to Moderate
Cuisine: Regional Mediterranean
Full Bar: No
Reservations: Recommended for dinner
Credit Cards: AE, MC, V
Handicap Access: Yes

This brightly decorated Mediterranean cafe offers casual dining in a comfortable atmosphere with a generous menu laced with the flavors of Greece, Italy and the Middle East. With a blend of Californian and Mediterranean cuisine, Cafe Stravaganza offers something for everyone. There's a long list of tempting appetizers, soups and salads. The garlic Portofino, one of the most tantalizing appetizers, is a roasted garlic head served with focaccia bread, Gorgonzola cheese and a basil marinade. Main dishes, including Stravaganza specialties like the chicken saltimbocca, a chicken breast layered with prosciutto and Fontina and covered with mushrooms sautéed in a wine sauce, come in sizable portions. In addition to the seafood, chicken and lamb dishes, a healthy variety of vegetarian options are available, including the vegetable penne, a dish of grilled eggplant, zucchini, mushrooms and sun-dried tomatoes covered in a lemon and wine sauce. There's also a wide array of interesting burgers, sandwiches, pizzas and calzones, as well as a succinct children's menu. Make sure to save room for dessert, as that's where this restaurant really shines, making each work of art with tender loving care.

CAFFE NAPOLI
831-625-4033
Ocean Ave., Carmel
Open: Lunch & dinner daily
Price: Inexpensive to Moderate
Cuisine: Southern Italian
Full Bar: No
Reservations: Recommended for dinner
Credit Cards: AE, D, MC, V
Handicap Access: Yes

This is the real Napolitana thing, with someone in the kitchen who obviously loves food and loves cooking. The menu, grounded in the fundamentals of garlic, basil, olives and artichokes, is strong on seafood, hearty pasta dishes, southern Italian-style risotto, pizza and lightened with a selection of seven salads. With the authenticity comes some Old Country clichés that have gone out of California restaurant vogue: checkered tablecloths, garlic braids, flags and maps from the mother country. But there's nothing passé about the award-winning wine list and the very trendy line out the door as visitors join regulars waiting for one of the few coveted tables. Popular demand led to the opening of Little Napoli around the corner, with the same prices and menu.

CASANOVA
831-625-0501
5th Ave., bet. Mission & San Carlos Sts., Carmel
Open: Lunch & dinner daily, brunch Sun.
Price: Moderate to Expensive
Cuisine: Country French/Italian
Full Bar: Yes
Reservations: Recommended for dinner
Credit Cards: MC, V
Handicap Access: Yes

Ambiance abounds in this former residence turned French Provençal dining room, consistently ranked as Carmel's most romantic restaurant. Even when the fog is in, the alfresco fountain patio is inviting, thanks to conveniently placed space heaters. Though portions are not large and the food is expensive, you get what you pay for: attentive service, classic country European fare with strong French and Italian overtones, a posh wine list. Specialties include herb-encrusted roasted rack of lamb with onion marmalade and an unforgettable paella Catalana. Lunch features similarly hearty fare, such as spaghettini

Mimmo di Capri with beef tips, fresh tomatoes, olive oil and herb sauce. Desserts, temptingly displayed, are made on the premises (the fruit tarts are standouts).

FLYING FISH GRILL
831-625-1962
Carmel Plaza, Carmel
Open: Dinner nightly (except Tues.)
Price: Moderate
Cuisine: Asian/Californian with emphasis on seafood
Full Bar: Yes
Reservations: Recommended for weekends
Credit Cards: AE, D, MC, V
Handicap Access: No

While many modern restaurants strive to create a high level of bustle and therefore a presumably comfortable habitat for fast-laners, Flying Fish offers a rarefied serenity. Warm redwood booths provide a sense of privacy, and the service is reliable and friendly. The creative fusion of Japanese-filtered-through-California cuisine is a rich cultural blend, harmonizing lively Asian flavors with home-grown culinary complements. A perfect example is the signature almond sea bass, encrusted in chopped almonds, grilled and served with mashed potatoes. The chef's flair for the unusual is evident in the parchment-wrapped salmon with black beans and several seafood clay pots, cooked at your table, in broth with vegetables and savory dipping sauces. The straightforward, rare peppered ahi is always recommended, and the visually oriented will appreciate the characteristic Asian flourishes of color and line.

✪ GRASINGS
831-624-6562
6th Ave. & Mission St., Carmel
Open: Lunch & dinner daily
Price: Moderate.
Cuisine: Coastal California/French

Full Bar: Yes
Reservations: Recommended
Credit Cards: AE, MC, V
Handicap Access: Yes

Nestled between a boutique and a terrace courtyard, this quaint little restaurant may be difficult to spot from the street, but that's what makes it one of Carmel's best-kept secrets. The mood is unpretentious and casual, a popular setting among locals. The dining room is small and airy with soft lighting and white linen tablecloths. With creative control over the menu, owner and chef Kurt Grasings offers an eclectic selection of tasty seafood and hearty pasta dishes. While French trained, chef Grasings instills his dishes with a subtle California coastal accent. Interesting starters include fried calamari with leek rings and spicy dipping sauce, scallops with leeks and onions in a white wine butter sauce or a salmon salad with warm, roasted potatoes and spinach. Dinner features herb-crusted sea bass with lentils, bacon and roasted garlic; paella with mussels, clams and shrimp; orzo pasta and spicy sausage; or medallions of pork with shiitake mushroom, bacon, peas and polenta. The creations are unusual, but earnestly prepared and outstanding in their own right. In contrast to the unique dinner combinations, the desserts are elementary, but satisfying. The warm brownie with vanilla ice cream and fudge sauce is always a sure winner.

THE GRILL ON OCEAN AVENUE
831-624-2569
Ocean Ave., bet. Dolores & Lincoln Aves., Carmel
Open: Lunch & dinner daily
Price: Moderate to Expensive
Cuisine: Gourmet grill
Full Bar: Yes
Reservations: Recommended in summer
Credit Cards: AE, D, MC, V
Handicap Access: Yes

Casual elegance is the name of the game at the modern-yet-cozy Grill on Ocean Avenue. Bridging the gap between European presentation and Asian spice, the restaurant's creative culinary minds pay about as much attention to gastronomical aesthetics as they do taste. A medley of appetizers is almost as strong and tempting as the main courses themselves—steamed clams bathed in chardonnay, garlic and herb broth, or seared ahi crusted in sesame seeds and paired with a garlic black bean vinaigrette and seaweed. The restaurant's oakwood-fired grill gives birth to such wonders as a Cajun walnut-crusted, pan-roasted Chilean sea bass in mango puree or an exquisitely delicate free-range chicken with a light mustard and rosemary cream sauce. And the desserts—this isn't typical tiramisù and ice cream territory. Pair a delicate summer fruit compote with a warming Irish coffee and you have a slice of culinary heaven.

IL FORNAIO
831-622-5100
Ocean Ave. & Monte Verde St., Carmel
Open: Lunch Mon.–Fri., dinner nightly, brunch Sat. Sun.
Price: Moderate to Expensive
Cuisine: Italian
Full Bar: Yes
Reservations: Recommended on weekends
Credit Cards: AE, D, MC, V
Handicap Access: Yes

With the Monterey area's dizzying abundance of dining options, Il Fornaio stands out for its inviting atmosphere: The sizable restaurant maintains the warmth of a much smaller eatery. Located in the historic Pine Inn, the tastefully designed space sets a tone that never gets tiring, especially when diners may choose from among four dining areas: the dynamic main dining room, the more intimate Sun Room, the counter at the open kitchen and wood-fired oven, or the bar. In addition, there's an adjacent rotunda housing a cafe, flooded with light and serving delicious house-made breads (available at many area stores), pastries and specialty coffees—a popular morning hang-out. The extensive menu draws from all regions of Italy, presenting wood-fired pizza, pasta, rotisserie chicken and meats, and seafood dishes, as the dedicated staff manages to keep the spirit of Italy alive in Carmel.

MISSION RANCH
831-625-9040
26270 Dolores Ave., Carmel
Open: Lunch Mon.–Sat., dinner nightly, brunch Sun.
Price: Expensive
Cuisine: California ranch
Full Bar: Yes
Reservations: Recommended
Credit Cards: MC, V
Handicap Access: Yes

In 1986, actor-director Clint Eastwood purchased and extensively remodeled this 22-acre inn overlooking Carmel Bay. The California ranch heritage is captured in both the decor and the menu of the restaurant. You'll find standards like baby back ribs, filet mignon and roast prime rib, but there's also a surprising amount of fresh fish. Everything is well prepared and full portioned, and the homemade desserts shine. The nightly piano bar enlivens the house, and the outdoor terrace is a great place to enjoy views, food and music during the Sunday Jazz Brunch Buffet, which features live acts, such as local recording artist Gennady Loktionov. There's a lot to like here, even if you don't see Clint.

✪ PACIFIC'S EDGE
831-624-3801
Highlands Inn, Hwy. 1, Carmel
Open: Dinner daily, brunch Sun.
Price: Expensive

Cuisine: New American/Central Coast Californian
Full Bar: Yes
Reservations: Recommended
Credit Cards: AE, D, MC, V
Handicap Access: Yes

You couldn't ask for more: the refined luxury of a world-class hotel, spectacular coastal views and a superior restaurant. The Pacific's Edge features regional California cuisine with an emphasis on organic local foods, backed by impeccable service and a 1,000-bottle wine list. Menu highlights include roasted day boat sea scallops and pancetta-wrapped loin of venison. In addition, each week executive chef Jeff Cox and cellar master Barnaby DeLuna create a four-course, prix fixe dinner menu that can be ordered with selected wines by the glass. In February, gourmands can take in the Masters of Food & Wine, which draws an international roster of celebrity chefs and vintners for a diverse, weeklong program that includes gourmet meals, wine seminars and cooking classes. If the award-winning food weren't ample excuse for a special dinner, the view from the windows is breathtaking.

RIO GRILL
831-625-5436
Hwy. 1 at Rio Rd., Carmel
Open: Lunch & dinner daily
Price: Moderate
Cuisine: American Southwest/Californian
Full Bar: Yes
Reservations: Recommended
Credit Cards: AE, D, MC, V
Handicap Access: Yes

This is the place for beautiful people—at the bar, behind the bar, even on the walls (the bar walls feature full-color caricatures of celebrities and friends). That's why the Rio constantly wins the "Best Place to Meet People" accolade. The restaurant wins on other points, too: excellent, friendly service and delicious New American food that mixes exotic (mustard-marinated rabbit with a balsamic vinegar rum reduction sauce) with casual (the best eggplant sandwich around). The daily blackboard specials are where the culinary action is. There are unique wines by the glass and a list chockfull of top flight California wines. The high-energy dining rooms emulate an open-air Santa Fe look—lots of stylish artwork, live cacti and kid-friendly butcher paper tablecloths with crayons. Book a table here in advance or expect a long wait at the door.

ROBATA GRILL & SAKE BAR

831-624-2643
3658 The Barnyard, Carmel
Open: Dinner nightly
Price: Moderate to Expensive
Cuisine: Japanese
Full Bar: Yes
Reservations: For large parties only
Credit Cards: AE, D, MC, V
Handicap Access: Yes

A crowded restaurant is always a good sign, especially when raw fish dominates the menu. Robata is always a public event, where the chefs' hands barely graze the fish, so quickly does it go from dock to kitchen to customer's plate. The decor could be defined as '70s Californian, primarily indicated by walls, tables and counters of natural redwood. Robata also has something most Japanese restaurants don't: a full bar. Margaritas and sushi? Why not? If tequila doesn't give you the courage to go raw, the menu offers many delicious cooked Japanese standards. The outdoor patio with a fire pit offers an alternative ambiance.

TERRACE GRILL

831-624-4010
La Playa Hotel, Camino Real & 8th Ave., Carmel
Open: Breakfast, lunch & dinner daily
Price: Moderate
Cuisine: Mediterranean/American Southwest
Full Bar: Yes
Reservations: Recommended
Credit Cards: AE, MC, V
Handicap Access: Yes

The neighborhood location is a little out of the way, but the Terrace Grill, located inside the La Playa Hotel, one of Carmel's oldest, is worth the trip. The dining room has a casual ambiance, complemented by colorful gardens and a peek at the ocean from the alfresco terrace. The menu, whether breakfast, lunch or dinner, is an unusually successful marriage of California, Asian, Southwest and Mediterranean cuisine. Highlights include homemade artichoke ravioli and tantalizing coconut-sesame shrimp served with wahani and arborio rice. The best part is that prices are very reasonable for the quality and the quantity offered. Another plus is the locally oriented wine list. Desserts, while homemade, don't always live up to their billing.

CARMEL VALLEY
THE COVEY AT QUAIL LODGE

831-620-8860
Quail Lodge Resort, 8205 Valley Greens Dr., Carmel Valley
Open: Dinner nightly
Price: Expensive
Cuisine: European/Californian
Full Bar: Yes
Reservations: Required
Credit Cards: AE, D, MC, V
Handicap Access: Yes

The dining jewel in the resort crown that is Quail Lodge, the Covey consistently covers itself with award glory for food, service, setting and wine list. Overlooking one of Carmel Valley property's many lakes and lawns, the restaurant gives new meaning to the words "fabulous" and "expensive." Those who don't mind being treated like

Superb Continental dining served in Carmel Valley's elegant, award-winning Quail Lodge has made The Covey a favorite site for celebrity guests. Quail Lodge

royalty can join celebrity residents of this exclusive area at sumptuously set tables, where brilliant creations long on updated classics are all heightened by fresh herbs grown in the dining room's gardens. Outstanding duck, lamb and veal dishes are not to be missed, the shrimp and scallop quenelle is feather-light, and the desserts are extravagantly satisfying. This place is elegant, catering to a very worldly set, and diners not dressed for the occasion will tend to feel out of place. But for a true taste of the luxurious, it's that very special spot.

SOLE MIO

831-659-9119
3 Delfino Pl., Carmel Valley
Open: Lunch & dinner Tues.–Sun.
Price: Inexpensive to Moderate
Cuisine: Italian islands
Full Bar: No
Reservations: Recommended
Credit Cards: AE, MC, V
Handicap Access: Yes

Sole Mio transports diners to the sunny isle of Capri, the homeland of chef-proprietors Sol and Domenico Vastarella. The rustic interior is accented by antiques, candle-light and lyrical Italian music. The Old World charm carries over into the friendly, efficient service, reasonable prices and a menu based entirely on family recipes. The emphasis is on pasta (the fettuccine Alfredo is exceptional) and meat-based dishes such as osso buco (slow-cooked lamb shanks) and saltimbocca (free-range veal). The compact wine list has impressive breadth. And desserts, though limited, include essential standards like tiramisù. A great place for those who enjoy leisurely meals.

WHITE OAK GRILL

831-659-1525
9 Carmel Valley Rd., Carmel Valley
Open: Lunch & dinner Thurs.–Sun.
Price: Moderate
Cuisine: Californian/French
Full Bar: No
Reservations: Recommended
Credit Cards: AE, D, MC, V
Handicap Access: Yes

It would be incorrect to say that the White Oak Grill is "worth the drive" when half of the thrill is the trip into Carmel Valley, 12 miles inland. The recent restoration of what was originally an old milk house, built in the 1890s for a dairy, takes advantage of both the old and the new. It's country all right, but sophisticated country. A limited but fine menu expresses the chef-owner's "California interpretation of Country French cuisine" and translates as flavorful, with sauces based on vegetable stocks rather than cream or butter, in the true

Provençal style. Local harvests of both seafood and produce and the owner's knowledge of complementary food and wine pairings make for a most pleasurable meal. In season, alfresco seating is available under live oaks.

WILL'S FARGO

831-659-2774
12 miles from Hwy. 1, in the center of Carmel Valley Village
Open: Dinner nightly
Price: Moderate to Expensive
Cuisine: American/Continental
Full Bar: Yes
Reservations: Recommended
Credit Cards: AE, D, MC, V
Handicap Access: No

A steak house, perhaps without peer on the Central Coast, Will's Fargo has been serving up bountiful portions of superbly prepared beef entrées since 1959. Patrons here select their main course in the butcher shop, a mini re-creation of what you might have found in a Midwest town during the 1950s. Steaks are cut to order and served with a house-made relish tray, soup or salad, hot cheese bread, stuffed baked potato and fresh vegetable. The warm, turn-of-the-20th-century dining room is studded with western relics and artifacts. The filet mignon, New York–cut steak, double-thick lamb chops and prime rib eye are standouts. Chicken and seafood are also offered. The wine list is quite good and predictably heavy on reds. The service is snappy, knowledgeable and friendly—many of the staff members are veteran employees. For just a quick bite, consider the lounge menu featuring pasta, Caesar salad and a superb French dip sandwich au jus. Desserts include many standards: cheesecake, strawberry shortcake, homemade apple pie and a delicately rich walnut pie. There's an excellent selection of after-dinner drinks at the bar and a friendly mix of patrons.

MONTEREY
CAFE FINA

831-372-5200
47 Fisherman's Wharf #1, Monterey
Open: Lunch & dinner daily
Price: Moderate to Expensive
Cuisine: Contemporary Italian
Full Bar: Yes
Reservations: Recommended for dinner
Credit Cards: AE, D, MC, V
Handicap Access: No

Energetic Italian spirit fills this waterfront trattoria equipped with its own wood-burning pizza oven imported from the Old Country and a full bar. Cafe Fina offers lighthearted atmosphere with zesty mesquite-grilled seafood, chicken and beef specialties. The fine pizzas come with inventive toppings and fragrant, fresh herbs, and the handmade pastas and raviolis reflect the warmth of the proprietors Dominic and Naida Mercurio, whose family portraits line the walls of this charming cafe. Don't miss the smoked salmon pizzettes with tomatoes and mozzarella and a goat cheese and black olive ravioli in cream sauce. Very cozy, terrific flavors and lots of fun.

EL PALOMAR

831-372-1032
24 Abrego St., Monterey
Open: Lunch & dinner daily, brunch Sun.
Price: Moderate
Cuisine: Mexican
Full Bar: Yes
Reservations: Recommended for weekends
Credit Cards: AE, MC, V
Handicap Access: Downstairs only

El Palomar is one of the most authentic Mexican seafood restaurants that you'll find this side of the border. Focusing on seafood specialties generously packed full of prawns, calamari, crab, octopus, oysters or fish, it also offers a variety of chicken, beef, pork and vegetarian options. You'll find authentic Mexican dishes, such as chicken mole, chile rellenos and pozole, and several tasty combination platters as well. The freshly made tortillas and tortilla chips are warm and hearty, and the salsa is positively divine. With a full bar, El Palomar boasts more tequilas than most gringos know exist, as well as six Mexican/Spanish beers, domestic and other imports and a modest wine selection featuring many wines from local vineyards. The service is polite, friendly and unobtrusive. The spacious, tiered floors and tasteful decor invite lounging in the comfortable chairs inside, as does the outside patio area, with heat lamps and a central fire pit to ward off the chill when the fog blows in. El Palomar is within walking distance of many area hotels and lodges, and it's close to downtown Monterey's lively Alvarado Street, where the locals like to bar-hop.

FRESH CREAM
831-375-9798
100C Heritage Harbor, 99 Pacific St., Monterey
Open: Dinner daily
Price: Expensive
Cuisine: French/Californian
Full Bar: Yes
Reservations: Recommended
Credit Cards: AE, D, MC, V
Handicap Access: Yes

When you want everything "just so" and you're willing to pay for it, go to Fresh Cream. Guests ascend a spiral staircase leading to a full-service bar and the dining rooms, three of which overlook Fisherman's Wharf and Monterey Bay. Original French château paintings and early California impressionist artworks contribute to the intimate setting in which to enjoy extraordinary service and inspired French-based cuisine. Everything is made from scratch—and it shows. The menu bal-

ances fresh fish, poultry and vegetarian fare, all richly flavored, but not heavy, and visually stunning. Signature dishes include lobster ravioli with shrimp butter, topped with two caviars. The equally impressive desserts include a sensational crème brûlée. A full bar is part of the attraction.

JUGEM
831-373-6463
409 Alvarado St., Monterey
Open: Lunch Mon.–Fri., dinner nightly
Price: Moderate to Expensive
Cuisine: Contemporary Japanese
Full Bar: Yes, especially of sakes
Reservations: Recommended on weekends
Credit Cards: AE, MC, V
Handicap Access: Yes

We always feel like we're out of town, in the chic heart of Tokyo perhaps, when visiting this contemporary sushi haven in the animated center of Monterey's Alvarado Street. The distinct urban style is rarely seen in small coastal towns, though it works, posing a playful contrast to its surroundings. Our sushi-snob friends from LA prefer Jugem for its wide selection, and for those requiring even more exotic fare, there are several daily specials. Freshness is essential for good sushi, and Jugem does not compromise. In addition, there's a full range of reliable Japanese standards such as tempura, teriyaki and udon noodle dishes. Start off with the edamame (steamed green soybeans) appetizer or the nasu (eggplant with sweet sauce).

LALLAPALOOZA
831-645-9036
474 Alvarado St., Monterey
Open: Lunch & dinner daily
Price: Moderate to Expensive
Cuisine: American
Full Bar: Yes

Reservations: No
Credit Cards: AE, D, MC, V
Handicap Access: Yes

Touted as a "Big American Menu & Martini Bar," this restaurant operates on the idea that you may eat or drink in either the restaurant or the bar, which flow together in a continuous lively scene. The sleek, modern design is tempered by country tables and a bit of outdoor cafe seating on spirited Alvarado Street, Monterey's nightlife center. The menu recalls a time when dishes had fewer ingredients, with names most people at least recognize. Choose among classic sandwiches, chili and meat loaf, as well as jambalaya, world championship smoked ribs, 10- to 24-ounce steaks and a slew of requisite pasta entrées—all in giant portions. The crowd tends toward 20- and 30-somethings, though families are encouraged. In contrast to the classic food menu, the bar menu is more daring, with contemporary cocktails and 14 martini selections.

✪ MONTEREY'S FISH HOUSE

831-373-4647
2114 Del Monte Ave., Monterey
Open: Lunch Mon.–Fri., dinner nightly
Price: Moderate
Cuisine: Seafood
Full Bar: Yes
Reservations: Recommended
Credit Cards: AE, D, MC, V
Handicap Access: No

A bit off the beaten path for most visitors, Monterey's Fish House is worth the five-minute drive from downtown Monterey to dine at one of the most popular local restaurants. A converted house and a staff of family and friends make for one of the most enjoyable dining experiences anywhere. The seafood is fantastically fresh, and the homemade pasta seems supernatural. Many specials are offered in appetizer or entrée portions, and you can ask for any dish to be sized accordingly. Highlights include any of the barbecued fish, the squid pasta, the Sicilian holiday pasta (described as cioppino over pasta) and, when available, the barbecued oyster appetizer and the Monterey prawns. If the Sicilian calamari is available, do not miss it. The place is always packed, and for good reason, so make a reservation.

MONTRIO

831-648-8880
414 Calle Principal, Monterey
Open: Lunch Mon.–Sat., dinner nightly
Price: Moderate
Cuisine: Modern Euro-American bistro
Full Bar: Yes
Reservations: Recommended
Credit Cards: AE, D, MC, V
Handicap Access: Yes

Montrio is a classic city restaurant—sleek, modern, multitextured with an airy, high-tech feel—fueled by lively, full bars on both upper and lower levels and a friendly, energetic staff. Like the ambiance, chef Tony Baker's food is interesting and eclectic, a cross of European bistro and modern American. The menu is vegetarian-friendly. The terrine of eggplant, roasted peppers and goat cheese is a great starter. Other winners include roasted chicken, braised veal cheeks and the oven-roasted portobello mushroom with crispy polenta. Portions are large, and lunch, at under $10, is a deal. The wine list is strong on alternative and rare wines. (If you're really into wine, ask to see the Back Room List.) No wonder Montrio took "Best New Restaurant of 1995" honors from *Esquire* magazine.

PARADISO TRATTORIA

831-375-4155
654 Cannery Row, Monterey
Open: Lunch & dinner daily

Price: Moderate to Expensive
Cuisine: Italian
Full Bar: No
Reservations: Recommended
Credit Cards: AE, D, MC, V
Handicap Access: Yes

There's an unmistakable air of magic filling this sleek oceanfront trattoria, especially for those lucky enough to get a table overlooking the cresting waves as they lap Monterey's beautiful coast. Appetizers include an impressive assortment of grilled vegetables, as well as standard seafood favorites accented with distinctive Italian twists. Paradiso presents deliciously delicate, California-style, wood-fired pizzas and a sumptuous, warm spinach salad. The modern trattoria features endless dishes from the grill and a wide array of pasta specialties. The service seems to get more and more friendly with each item ordered. But whatever you order, make sure that you leave room for Paradiso's notoriously decadent desserts.

THE SARDINE FACTORY
831-373-3775
701 Wave St., Monterey
Open: Dinner nightly
Price: Moderate to Expensive
Cuisine: Seafood/Continental
Full Bar: Yes
Reservations: Suggested
Credit Cards: V, D, MC, AE
Handicap Access: Yes

A maze of elegantly decorated rooms, the Sardine Factory offers five very different dining rooms in which to enjoy sumptuous, award-winning dishes. Some rooms have fireplaces, others have wingback chairs and chandeliers, and the most distinctive and inviting room is a solarium surrounded by trees and plants with white lights and a fountain. And the award-winning food? The rich and creamy abalone bisque created for President Reagan's inaugural can't

be beat. Appetizers also include fresh clams, oysters, mussels and a stellar smoked salmon with sardines, frisée and dill cream cheese. The kitchen is most recognized for its fresh seafood, aged beef and an extensive wine selection (there are over 25,000 bottles of wine in the cellar). Noted entrées include Dungeness crab on chicken with hollandaise sauce and green beans, salmon with mushroom risotto and asparagus, as well as abalone and lobster tail. The food is rich, but dessert tarts, custards and cakes can tempt even the strongest resolve. The lemon meringue with mango and chocolate is over the top, but delightful. Service is flawless, and the staff is graciously attentive.

✪ STOKES ADOBE
831-373-1110
500 Hartnell St., Monterey
Open: Lunch Mon.–Sat., dinner nightly
Price: Moderate
Cuisine: Northern Mediterranean
Full Bar: Yes
Reservations: Recommended
Credit Cards: AE, D, MC, V
Handicap Access: Yes

Stokes Adobe, as its name suggests, is housed in one of the more imposing examples of historical Monterey architecture, an adobe built in 1833 that was originally the home of Dr. James Stokes. It has housed a number of successful restaurants over the years, and its newest incarnation proves worthy of the space. Stokes Adobe is more than a quaint piece of tradition with some tasteful, modern embellishments, and it manages to be elegant without being the slightest bit stuffy. The eclectic country European menu is ambitious, and the well-composed dishes do not disappoint. The chef's platter of assorted small bites will launch your evening most impressively, followed by reputation-building entrées like the grilled, lavender-infused pork chop served with bread pudding and pear chutney and the rustic pasta tubes with homemade fennel sausage and fresh manila clams.

TARPY'S ROADHOUSE
831-647-1444
Hwy. 68 & Canyon Del Rey Rd., Monterey
Open: Lunch Mon.–Sat. dinner daily,
brunch Sun.
Price: Inexpensive to Moderate
Cuisine: American regional
Full Bar: Yes
Reservations: Recommended
Credit Cards: AE, D, MC, V
Handicap Access: Yes

Situated in a 90-year-old former Spanish ranch house, Tarpy's puts a modern spin on traditional American comfort food. There are five primary dining rooms plus outdoor dining in the European-style courtyard.

Besides full-portioned helpings of old-fashioned favorites like meat loaf with marsala mushroom gravy, chef-partner Michael Kimmel offers specials highlighting exotic game such as elk, moose and ostrich. Finish your meal with a classic dessert, like tapioca pudding or warm apple pie. The one drawback at this spacious, atmospheric restaurant is the proximity to the airport, which distracts alfresco diners. Prices are better at lunch, but expect a crowded dining room.

MOSS LANDING
PHIL'S FISH HOUSE & EATERY
831-633-2152
7600 Sandholdt Rd., Moss Landing
Open: Lunch & dinner daily
Price: Inexpensive
Cuisine: Seafood
Full Bar: Yes

Phil DiGirolamo's Phil's Fish House in Moss Landing features fresh seafood pastas and take-home locally caught salmon. Robert Scheer

Reservations: No
Credit Cards: AE, D, MC, V
Handicap Access: Yes.

Phil DiGirolamo is king of a domain of fish and seafood so fresh that they practically flirt. Legions of addicts trek, ice chests in hand, to Phil's Fish House to savor his fresh seafood pastas and to take home locally caught salmon, halibut and snapper. In a white-tablecloth joint, grilled yellowtail and garlicky pastas loaded with Monterey Bay spot prawns would cost $30. At Phil's, where the forks are plastic and the plates are paper, the dish is $10 and superb. Phil also loves sand dabs, his personal favorite fish. Phil always has the fattest salmon, the freshest flounder and often rare items, such as luvar. What Phil really deals in is hospitality. "I love people—ya gotta love people. We're a fish market," he admits, "but above all we're telling people how to eat fish, how to enjoy the best. The bay is alive." If the broad-shouldered Sicilian can't sell you a fish, you must be a vegetarian. The enormous tanks, coolers and central table—piled high with everything from baby octopus and slithery calamari to whole salmon and cod, slabs of opa, mahimahi and mountains of scallops—make an arresting display. Phil will help you choose and will send you home with a few cooking tips. You'll be back.

PACIFIC GROVE
FANDANGO
831-372-3456
223 17th Ave., Pacific Grove
Open: Lunch & dinner daily
Price: Moderate to Expensive
Cuisine: Mediterranean
Full Bar: Yes
Reservations: Recommended
Credit Cards: AE. D, MC, V
Handicap Access: Yes

The weathered wood exterior, brightened by flowers and a patio, welcomes you to the entrance of Fandango where owner Pierre Bain usually greets guests. Of five delightful dining rooms, at least one should match your mood, be it romantic or convivial. One room holds a single table, and the rest have some combination of the three fireplaces, two bars, two kitchens, and mesquite grill. The vibrant "Cuisine of the Sun" covers all points along the Mediterranean, from the saffron-infused paella to the bouillabaisse Marseillaise to the couscous Algerois. Fresh seafood, steak and pasta are well represented, and the rack of lamb is one of the area's best. The massive wine list of 550 vintages provides an enjoyable browse and has earned *Wine Spectator*'s top award. Though there is no dress code, there's an air of formality at dinner that might make you feel a bit less than comfortable in jeans and a T-shirt. Maybe it's only by contrast to Pierre's exquisite European suits. Then again, well-behaved dogs are welcome on the patio.

THE FISHWIFE
831-375-7107
1996 Sunset Dr., Pacific Grove
Open: Lunch & dinner daily
Price: Moderate to Expensive
Cuisine: Seafood
Full Bar: No
Reservations: Recommended
Credit Cards: AE, D, MC, V
Handicap Access: Yes

A supportive environment for fish fanatics, The Fishwife has two highly successful restaurants, though the Pacific Grove location offers a peek of the ocean and is recommended for visitors. Offering fresh seafood at fair prices, chef Julio Ramirez integrates flavors from his Latin American homeland into his exclusively seafood platters, sandwiches, pastas and salads. Entrées come with black beans, rice and steamed vegetables, plus your choice of a dozen piquant Fishwife sauces, such as cilantro-garlic and mango-avocado salsa. Loyal regulars favor the best freshwater tilapia in town, grilled snapper Cancún, the spicy cioppino and the seafood wrap with shrimp, crab and scallops. Try the air fries for a delicious fat-free accompaniment and the raspberry iced tea for cool refreshment at this award-winning establishment.

✪ PASSIONFISH

www.passionfish.net
831-655-3311
701 Lighthouse Ave., Pacific Grove
Open: Dinner nightly
Price: Moderate
Cuisine: American
Full Bar: No
Reservations: Recommended
Credit Cards: AE, D, MC, V
Handicap Access: Yes

The stars here are slow-roasted meats, line-caught local fish and organic vegetables and salad greens from local growers. The combos whipped up from these choice ingredients have locals filling the lively dining rooms every night, so always make your reservations early. Appetizers are treated with primo respect, and putting together a meal comprised only of these small plates is a smart way to go. The Caribbean spicy seafood chowder, the asparagus fries with sesame aioli, the celery and Mcdjool date salad with ricotta salata, the tuna and wasabi slaw in ginger vinaigrette are guaranteed crowd pleasers. But entrées also deliver. The Monterey Bay wild salmon cannot be beat, and the Maine sea scallops with balsamic butter are as fresh as the first sun rays of spring. Another winner is the duck confit with leatherwood honey sauce, and many regulars swear by the Kaua'i shrimp with spicy Vietnamese sauce. Great teas, fine high-end beers and a dazzling wine list also place Passionfish at the top of anyone's short A list.

✪ MAX'S GRILL

831-375-7995
209 Forest Ave., Pacific Grove
Open: Dinner Tues.–Sun.
Price: Moderate
Cuisine: Californian/Asian
Full Bar: No
Reservations: Recommended
Credit Cards: AE, D, MC, V
Handicap Access: Yes

In the time since celebrated chef Hisayuki "Max" Muramatsu and his hostess-wife Yuko opened his stylish eatery on the Monterey Peninsula, every foodie in northern California has made a pilgrimage to this mecca of remarkable cuisine. A Tokyo-born, French-trained, award-winning chef, Max trained at Maxim's of Paris and was former executive chef at the prestigious Anton & Michel in Carmel. This is his first solo venture, and he is succeeding marvelously. His confit of duck with house-made wild mushroom ravioli, sushi samba and tempura prawns, roasted Colorado rack of lamb in a lavender honey mustard crust, and pan-roasted wild Pacific salmon reach the pinnacle of the chefly arts, but don't pass on his rib-eye steak in Roquefort cheese, roasted garlic and wine reduction sauce, which is without doubt the best piece of meat either of us has enjoyed over the last 20 years. Max is well known for his desserts, especially his Hawaiian mango mousse cake, which is (and we are almost ashamed for trotting out these two words) ethereal and sublime. Come early for the sunset menu ($13.50 for three courses), but everything here is reasonably priced. Max's Grill is the best new restaurant on the Central Coast to open in the last two years.

OLD BATH HOUSE

831-375-5195
620 Ocean View Blvd., Pacific Grove
Open: Dinner daily
Price: Moderate

Cuisine: Continental
Full Bar: Yes
Reservations: Highly recommended
Credit Cards: AE, D, MC, V
Handicap Access: No

Many restaurants with built-in views simply ride the coattails, but not the Old Bath House. Enviably located at Lover's Point, overlooking Monterey Bay, this restored Victorian delivers top-notch Continental cuisine with a modern twist. The dining room is small (65 seats) and very narrow, but the surroundings more than compensate. The wait staff is confident and gracious, and the food speaks for itself. Try the grilled swordfish fillet over tomato sauce, apple-smoked bacon, green olives and arugula, or the lavender-thyme pork chop. The food-friendly wine list is complemented by 16 selections by the glass. The four-course, early-dining menu is a gourmet bargain.

✪ WHITE HOUSE

831-375-9626
649 Lighthouse Ave., Pacific Grove
Open: Dinner nightly
Price: Expensive
Cuisine: Californian/Mediterranean
Full Bar: No
Reservations: Required.
Credit Cards: MC, V
Handicap Access: Yes

One of the most talented chefs working the Monterey Bay area, Robert Kincaid has transformed a lovely 19th-century three-story house into a hotbed of California cuisine. His nightly three-course prix fix dinners utilize nothing but the most pristine local ingredients, and when combined with his old-school training, the dishes emerge not only deep and satisfying, but also lovely to look at. The tapas and second-course salads are things of delicious beauty, and taste-wise nothing on any other Monterey-region menu compares to the grace and complexity of the gratin of escar-gots in garlic parsley butter. One dish for which Kincaid is justly famous is his cassoulet à la Robert, wherein he combines confit of duck and garlic sausage with herbs and the earthiest white beans to ever pass a lip. The whole gentle yet flavorful concoction dissolves on the palate and lingers on the mind. A roast chipotle-glazed pork loin had neighboring diners nearly speaking in tongues with enthusiasm. Never pass on his Hungarian goulash soup, just about the heartiest elixir to hit our foggy coast in decades. His Holland Dover soul and filet of beef in sauce béarnaise are both consistent showstoppers.

PEBBLE BEACH
CLUB XIX

831-625-8519
Lodge at Pebble Beach,
17 Mile Dr., Pebble Beach
Open: Lunch & Dinner daily
Price: Expensive
Cuisine: Contemporary Continental
Full Bar: Yes
Reservations: Recommended for dinner
Credit Cards: AE, D, MC, V
Handicap Access: Yes

Adjacent to one of the world's most fabled sites—the 18th green of the Pebble Beach Golf Links—Club XIX takes its name from the age-old tease about what comes after the eighteenth hole. The answer: an unabashedly chic, airy dining room counterpointed by flawless service, stylish fabrics, fine china and crystal stemware. The outside patio, flanked by two fireplaces, provides maximum views and is best at lunch. The health-conscious cuisine of chef Lisa Magadini never fails to please. Signature dishes include handmade orecchiette pasta with a wild mushroom sauce and fresh thyme. In addition, two prix fixe menus, one of which is vegetarian, are offered daily. The full bar offers a host of luxury liqueurs to conclude the meal or complement dessert.

✪ ROY'S AT PEBBLE BEACH

831-647-7423
2700 17 Mile Dr., Pebble Beach
Open: Breakfast, lunch & dinner daily
Price: Expensive
Cuisine: Euro-Asian
Full Bar: Yes
Reservations: Recommended on weekends
Credit Cards: AE, MC, V
Handicap Access: Yes

Everything at Roy's is on a grand scale—the dramatic Pebble Beach location, the spacious, modern dining room, the sumptuous Euro-Asian fare. This is a place to indulge yourself, the kind of restaurant that can follow a superb day without risk of anticlimax. The bicontinental approach to cooking is well illustrated in the signature blackened ahi tuna, enhanced with both soy-mustard and beurre blanc sauces. Other popular dishes are the Szechuan charred short ribs and the ravioli with sun-dried tomatoes, garlic and ricotta cheese, but I find myself repeatedly ordering the lemongrass-crusted swordfish with a basil-curry sauce, one of the best dishes at any restaurant. Arrive a half hour before sunset to hear a bagpipe player who makes music outdoors in full Scottish regalia, with the Pacific waves keeping time in the background. Whether breezy or blustery, the outdoor patio and the music are sublime.

STILLWATER CAFE

831-625-8524
Lodge at Pebble Beach, 17 Mile Dr., Pebble Beach
Open: Lunch & dinner daily
Price: Expensive
Cuisine: Californian, with seafood emphasis
Full Bar: Yes
Reservations: Recommended
Credit Cards: AE, MC, V
Handicap Access: Yes

Inside the luxurious Lodge at Pebble Beach and overlooking the famed 18th hole of the Pebble Beach Golf Links, the Stillwater Cafe is striking and trendy. The artistic accents, from lamps to paintings to the stunning aqua-colored glass bar, are a rainbow of color that dazzles. The menu relies on seafood, with a few items for those preferring a more earthbound focal point. A fresh, raw start is suggested with in-season oysters on the half shell (we like the sweet kumomoto best). The abalone on angel-hair pasta, in appetizer or entrée portion, is delicious, and the steamed calamari is a pleasant change from the more common fried version. While the menu offers plenty of high points, some dishes attempt too much in their desire to please, obscuring, rather than enhancing, the primary flavors.

FOOD PURVEYORS

Bakeries

Fifi's Cafe & French Bakery 831-372-5325, 1188 Forest Ave., Pacific Grove. Fifi's is the crème de la crème of Monterey-area bakeries, famed for napoleons, cheesecakes, petits fours and berry delights to take out or to consume with espresso on the premises.

Sweet Elena's 831-393-2063, 465-D Olympia St., Sand City. The former sweetheart of the farmers' markets goes retail with this delicious outlet for her world-class scones, tarts, cookies, jams and assorted pastries. Savories, soups, sandwiches and quiches are also available for lunchtime fare.

Talented local performers appear at Morgan's Coffee and Tea in Monterey. Randy Tunnel

Wishart Bakery 831-624-3870, Ocean Ave., Carmel. Downtown Carmel's pastry heaven offers up fresh and heavenly muffins, scones and pastries (like a wonderful cherry-filled turnover) that, when paired with a cup of the house coffee, is a breakfast made in heaven.

Coffeehouses
Caravali Coffees 831-655-5633, 510 Lighthouse Ave., Pacific Grove. This popular java joint specializes in house-roasted cappuccinos, dark French roasts and special blends.

Morgan's Coffee and Tea 831-373-5601, 498 Washington Ave., Monterey. A funky spot in a funky building, clients and atmosphere make Morgan's Boho central. Talented local singer-songwriters appear nightly, and conversation here is as important as the food and exotic teas and coffees, including Turkish offerings.

Farmers' Markets
Old Monterey Farmers' Market 831-655-2670, Alvarado St., bet. Pearl St. & Del Monte Ave., Monterey. Features scores of growers' displays, plus live music and finger food booths. Tues. 4–7pm.

Frozen Desserts
Carmel Beach Cafe 831-625-3122, Ocean Ave., bet. Mission & San Carlos Sts., Carmel. This cafe serves sinfully delicious frozen yogurts and luscious Italian ice creams in a charming space.

Pieces of Heaven 831-625-3368, 3686 The Barnyard, Carmel. This shop offers samples of world-famous Ben & Jerry's ice cream flavors like Cherry Garcia.

CULTURE

The cultural tone of the Monterey Bay and Big Sur coast was set long ago by spectacular natural beauty and welcoming climate, factors that have beckoned to and informed the creativity of writers, mavericks and artistic freethinkers of every stripe for over 200 years. The inspiring and uncrowded landscape not only provided sanctuary for artists and, more recently, internationally acclaimed arts events, it also shaped and freed the uncluttered, often radical directions that creative life would take here.

If there is a single dominant theme, it is eclecticism. The same coastal splendor that inspired the pens of Robert Louis Stevenson, Robinson Jeffers, John Steinbeck, Jack Kerouac and Henry Miller now hosts the music masters of the world at the annual Monterey Jazz Festival. In a part of the country where filmmaking is literally part of the scenery, the cinematic nouvelle vague plays nightly at handsomely restored movie palaces. Contemporary artisans push the edges of handmade forms within the shadow of a Franciscan mission.

Continually reinventing its architectural environment in response to the natural rhythms of seismic temblors, this portion of the Central Coast takes visible pride in preserving the landmarks of its colorful history. Scarcely a town in the region is without tile-roofed homage to its Spanish ancestry. Victorian cottages from the boom years of the American Yankee settlement are carefully maintained as living—and lived in—postcards from the past. Here the historic coexists comfortably with culture's latest wave.

Architecture

The natural terrain and texture of this region is still punctuated with the earliest imports of Spanish settlers and the work of their native acolytes. The tone of thick adobe walls, sunny courtyards and Renaissance Spain's Moorish arches was set by the series of sturdy missions created by Franciscan padres in the late 18th century. Dotting the Central Coast, these landmarks of the first immigrant invasion of California still dominate the psychic landscape of the region, flavoring architectural thinking for generations since. Some of the jewels in this chain of Spanish influence remain, many restored over the centuries as centerpieces in Central Coast communities, most notably in Carmel.

After the missions were secularized following Mexico's divorce from Spain, their stylistic influence spilled over into adobe ranch houses and town homes, which today still exist in handsome profusion, especially in the heart of Old Monterey. When Mexico lost its claim to California, and Americans entrepreneurs enthusiastically made their move, clapboard homes, New England–style churches and white picket fences began fleshing out the spine of Monterey Bay's Spanish outposts.

At several moments in the life of this region, the Spanish influence ascended into the baroque, leaving one lavish example to be savored today. One is the Royal Presidio Chapel in Monterey. A gem of Spanish colonial baroque architecture, the ornate stone facade of the Royal Presidio Chapel was created in 1794 by master designers from Mexico City after the original wood-and-adobe structure—founded in 1770 by mission founder Junipero Serra—was destroyed. With its lyrical bell tower, original 18th-century statues and stations of the cross, this living legacy of the original Spanish capital in the New World remains one of the important windows on the founding spirit of the Central Coast.

Cinema

Century Galaxy 6 831-648-0123, 280 Del Monte Center, Monterey. As close to a Hollywood multiplex as this area gets, the Century Galaxy shows the newest movies in THX on six screens.

✪ **Lighthouse Cinema** 831-372-7321, 525 Lighthouse Ave., Pacific Grove. First-run screenings in an intimate, neighborhood movieland ambiance are the specialty of this main street theater.

Osio Plaza Cinema 831-644-8171, 350 Alvarado St., Monterey. This new multiscreen theater, built in the style of a nearby adobe, shows popular Hollywood films, foreign films, and art house features.

State Cinemas 831-372-4555, 417 Alvarado St., Monterey. Lamentably, this 1928 beauty was cleaved into a triplex and shows only Hollywood's latest.

Gardens

La Playa Hotel Gardens 831-624-6476, 8th Ave. & El Camino Real, Carmel. The gardens of this graceful Mediterranean-style hotel are lavishly maintained with formal plantings of Icelandic poppies, tulips, primroses and hyacinths, as well as enough attractively grouped beds of perennial plantings to make a visit here a romantic and fragrant experience all year round.

Monterey Museum of Art—La Mirada 831-372-3689, 720 Via Mirada, Monterey. Stroll through the lush gardens at this branch of the Monterey Museum of Art and you'll be transported through the vegetation of Australia, England, California and the tropics. Native Californian plants and perfumed rosebushes dominate the grounds of the museum.

Historic Places

CANNERY ROW
No telephone
Off Foam St., Monterey
Open: Continuously
Admission: Free

John Steinbeck romanticized the people of his *Cannery Row*—the madams, grocers, fisherfolk, cannery workers and bohemians—colorful characters long departed. What remain are "the quality of light, the tone, the habit, the dream" of this once thriving amalgam of canneries, which today still sports plenty of waterfront atmosphere. Souvenir shops, boutiques, galleries and other regional attractions now fill the looming cannery buildings, whose pilings reach into the very tide pools of the Monterey Bay.

CASA DEL ORO
831-649-7118
Corner of Scott & Oliver Sts. Monterey
Open: Daily 11–6
Admissions: Free

The adobe gained its Spanish name, "house of gold," from the prevailing rumor that miners stashed gleanings from their Gold Rush escapades in the resident safe. Originally built to service American sailors, the casa thrived as a general store during the Gold Rush boom of 1849. Still preserving its mercantile atmosphere, it is colorfully stocked with 19th-century dry goods, bolts of cloth and tableware, and burlap sacks filled with grains, beans and coffee.

CASA SOBERANES
831-649-7118
336 Pacific St., Monterey
Open: Daily
Admission: Free

Built during the 1840s by Custom House Warden Don José Rafael Estrada and later sold to Don Feliciano Soberanes, this lovely tile-roofed colonial adobe was Europeanized with a Mediterranean-style balcony. The interior, including what has long been thought to be the prettiest adobe salon in Monterey, is attractively decorated with period New England furniture and Mexican folk art.

COLTON HALL & OLD JAIL
831-646-5640
522 Pacific St., Monterey
Open: Daily 10–5
Admission: Free

Designed as a town hall by Yankee alcade (mayor) Walter Colton in 1847–49, this important historic landmark was quarried of local stone and housed the first Constitutional Convention of the State of California during the autumn of 1849. Over the years, it served as a school, county seat, municipal court and police headquarters and was handsomely restored in time to celebrate the Centennial of 1949. The tables and benches of the upstairs assembly hall are arranged as they were when the 48 delegates from around the new state gathered to design the emerging government. The original designs for the grizzly bear, which still adorns the state flag, are displayed here. At the next-door jail, desperadoes ruminating on a few final hours on earth carved their names into the walls, providing macabre entertainment for modern-day visitors.

COOPER-MOLERA ADOBE
831-649-7118
508 Munras Ave., Monterey
Open: Tours daily at 2, 3 & 4pm
Admission: Free

One of the largest extant adobes in the state, this structure was built in 1826 by English sea captain John Rogers Cooper, who converted to Catholicism and became a Mexican citizen in order to marry the renowned *Californio* beauty Encarnacion Vallejo, sister of General Mariano Vallejo. A successful businessman, Cooper added onto the original single-story adobe as his fortune from hides, tallow and sea otter pelts grew. Tours place the visitor dramatically in touch with affluent life in the early colonial period.

CUSTOM HOUSE
831-649-7118
1 Custom House Plaza, Monterey

Open: Daily 10–5
Admission: Free

The oldest public building in California, this 1814 adobe-and-tile structure flew the flags
of Spain, Mexico and the United States during its tenure as the most important port of
entry into Alta California. At this site, custom taxes were levied on all trading ships during
the Spanish rule, taxes that helped finance government expenses for the entire region.
Fandangos were danced here to celebrate the arrival of foreign trading vessels, many laden
with finery like Chinese silks. Under the direction of wealthy Yankee Thomas Larkin, the
facility was enlarged and renovated in 1841. Later, in 1846, Commander Sloat proclaimed
the takeover of California by the United States by raising the Stars and Stripes over what
was perceived then as a symbol of foreign domination. Today, this state historical monument is packed with reminders of Monterey's former shipping glory, including harpoons,
vintage portraits and brocade garments worn by the wealthy *Californios.*

LARKIN HOUSE

831-649-7118
510 Calle Principal, Monterey
Open: Tours daily at 11am, 2pm & 3pm
Admission: Free

In creating what was to be the first two-story adobe in the Spanish capital in 1835, leading
merchant Thomas O. Larkin invented the graceful Monterey style of Mexican adobe architecture. The encircling second-story veranda and low-hipped roofs that characterize this
house were Larkin's own design and represent a fusion of the Spanish-style adobe with
New England innovations, like the extensive use of glass in windows and symmetrical floor
plan. Today, the house is beautifully restored and decorated with period antiques, including much of Larkin's own furniture and belongings.

MONTEREY PRESIDIO

831-242-5000
Pacific St., north of Scott St., Monterey
Open: 24 hours daily
Admission: Free

Founded on June 3, 1770, when Gaspar de Portola claimed Monterey for the king of Spain,
the second military fort in Alta California first took shape as a structure of huts and crude
barricades. At the turn of the 19th century, the presidio was moved to its present site overlooking the majestic port immortalized by Richard Henry Dana in *Two Years Before the Mast.*
First the Mexican government (1822), then the Americans (1846) erected blockhouses
and gun sites, spots now commemorated with plaques. The Sloat Monument commemo-
rates the first raising of the American flag over Monterey by U.S. Naval Commodore John
Drake Sloat. Today, this oldest military reservation in the United States is one of the largest
army posts in the country and site of the Defense Language Institute (831-647-5000).
Historic markers dot the reservation, indicating Indian ceremonial rocks and the first
landfalls of Sebastian Vizcaino (1602) and Father Junipero Serra (1770). The view overlooking Monterey Bay is daunting.

OLD WHALING STATION
831-375-5356
391 Decatur St. at Heritage Harbor, Monterey
Open: Gardens open daily, dawn to dusk
Admission: Free

When adventurous Scotsman David White built this adobe residence in 1847, the walkway
leading up to the house was paved with whale vertebrae. This calcified evidence of the
sheer numbers of whales being dispatched from this busy Monterey Bay location was apt,
since, upon White's departure, the house was taken over by the Old Monterey Whaling
Company as headquarters for the lucrative, and messy, processing of whale oil. Restored in
1980, the Old Whaling Station shares its gardens with what is thought to be the first brick
building constructed in California.

✪ TOR HOUSE
www.torhouse.org
831-624-1813
26304 Ocean View Ave., Carmel
Open: Tours on the hour Fri. 10–3 & Sat. by phone reservation
Admission: $7

As ruggedly romantic as the poet's words, this charismatic stone house and tower was built
by Robinson Jeffers, who first came to Carmel with his wife, Una, in 1914. With its commanding view of the rocky coastline and stone Hawk Tower, which the poet built for his
wife, the house is a haunting, gothic presence in its quiet residential setting. Its stalwart
rockwork walls were raised with Jeffers's own hands and contain stones gathered from the
four corners of the globe, including one from the Great Wall of China, some from England,
lava from Hawaii, even a porthole from the ship that took Napoleon to exile on Elba. Lovely
gardens may be toured, as well as the burnished redwood interior filled with antique
Oriental rugs. Truly the retreat of an artistic maverick spirit.

Historic Walking Tours
Monterey's Path of History In the heart of Old Monterey, clustered near Fisherman's
Wharf, a score of fine 19th century casas, adobes and public buildings still exist as beauti-
fully restored landmarks to this city's rich historic past. A walking tour around this Path of
History provides an in-depth encounter with the abundant Spanish, *Californio* and early
American period. Administered by the Monterey State Historic Park (831-649-7118,
525 Polk St., Monterey), a two-day $5 admission pass ($3 youth, $2 kids) gains the visitor
access to over 20 sites. Maps and guided tour details are available at **Pacific House, Colton
Hall** and the **Cooper-Molera Adobe**.

 Pacific Grove Victorian House Tour Founded in the late 1870s as a Methodist summer
retreat, Pacific Grove quickly blossomed with stately Victorian mansions—many now open
to the public as bed & breakfast establishments. Ornate Gothic, turreted Queen Anne and
even a few turreted English castle styles dominate. Some of the loveliest of these are
located along Ocean View Blvd. and Lighthouse Ave., including the **Green Gables Guest
House**, the **Gosby House Inn**, **Hart Mansion**, the **Trimmer Home** and **Sea Star**. Each
year, usually in October, a **Victorian House Tour** (831-373-3304) gives visitors access to
some of the finest of these late-19th-century architectural beauties.

Dennis the Menace Playground in Monterey, a popular family recreation spot located by El Estero Lake, was designed by cartoonist Hank Ketcham, who created that little cartoon rascal Dennis the Menace. Shmuel Thaler

Kids' Stuff

Dennis the Menace Playground 831-646-3866, at the Camino El Estero Park, Monterey. Designed by cartoonist Hank Ketcham, who created that little cartoon and movie rascal Dennis the Menace. This is a fun spot for romping on slides, futuristic jungle gyms and a steam locomotive, or just soaking up the peaceful beauty of El Estero Lake.

✪ **Monterey Bay Aquarium** www.monterey bayaquarium.org, 831-648-4888, 886 Cannery Row, Monterey. With over 6,500 aquatic creatures and 100 exhibits, this multilevel facility is the big fish in the international aquarium pond. New and unusual exhibits abound, but children tend to fall in love with the Touch Tide Pool, where they can run their hands along the living surfaces of star fish, anemones and sleek bat rays. Another favorite is the sea otter exhibit, a two-story marine kingdom that opens onto the open air and coastal rocks, enabling a view of these playful swimmers in and out of water. The Portola Cafe, which offers a creative cafe menu, is open for snacks and lunches daily 10–5.

Monterey Youth (MY) Museum www.my museum.org, 831-649-6444, 601 Wave, Monterey. Kids of all ages can find something to do at this very interactive museum. Learning is fun in MY Grill, MY Boat, MY Media Center, the Creation Station, and the Magical Fingerpainting Machine, all hands-on exhibits where kids can "touch everything."

Lighthouses

✪ **Point Pinos Lighthouse** (Asilomar Ave. off Ocean View Blvd., in Pacific Grove) was built in 1855, the oldest continuously operating lighthouse on the West Coast. Necessity and technology conspired in the erection of these brilliant beacons during the 19th century, sending out their luminous message of jagged perils lurking in the fog. Armed with the high candlepower of the French Fresnel lens, which ingeniously utilized over 1,000 pieces of cut glass to magnify its light, the slender lighthouses and their stalwart attendants kept faith with mariners until the coming of automation and the computer. Always a romantic sight, a few of these curved towers—like the one at Point Pinos—continue to shed light along the rockiest edges of the Central California coast. Open weekends for self-guided tours between 1 and 4, Point Pinos Lighthouse is furnished with Victorian antiques and helpful explanations of its automated workings.

Missions
MISSION SAN ANTONIO
831-385-4478
Mission Creek Rd., Jolon
Open: Daily 10–6
Admission: Donations

Nestled in the Santa Lucia Mountains, the third mission in the chain built by the Franciscans was founded in 1771, and the present church was begun in 1810. Picturesquely situated, the mission recently had its arched walkways and adjoining compound buildings
restored. The isolated setting and full restoration-in-progress of the entire complex lend
this lovely Franciscan outpost a haunting, frozen-in-time atmosphere.

MISSION SAN CARLOS BORROMEO DEL RIO CARMELO
831-624-1271
3080 Rio Rd. & Hwy. 1, Carmel
Open: Mon.–Sat 9:30–4:30, Sun. 10:30–4:30
Admission: Donations

Though founded by Father Junipero Serra in 1771, the second mission in the wide-ranging
Franciscan enterprise was moved to its present location and completed with sandstone

The oldest continuously operating lighthouse on the West Coast, the Point Pinos Lighthouse was built in 1855.
Shmuel Thaler

blocks quarried from the Santa Lucia Mountains by Serra's successor, Francisco Fermen Lasuen, in 1797. In its prime, the compound on the banks of the Carmel River furnished the former Spanish capital of Monterey with the bounty from its orchards, fields and stables and was the official headquarters of the Franciscan missionary effort in Alta California. Buried within this mission he loved so well, Father Serra is now entombed in a splendid bronze sarcophagus near the sanctuary, where he awaits the canonization for which his faithful are currently petitioning. Two other great California Franciscans— Serra's able protégé Lasuen and expedition diarist Crespi—are buried here as well. The handsome mission interior boasts a vaulted, ribbed ceiling, baroque altar and beautifully restored, hand-carved doorway lintels. Its oval domed tower retraces Spanish architecture's debt to the conquering Moors, as does the sanctuary's star window. The adjoining museum displays the silver religious ware Serra brought from Mexico and California's first library, as well as a restored kitchen and the cell in which Serra lived and corresponded with his far-flung brethren. Planted with vintage olive and pepper trees, the garden and cemetery contain the graves of over 3,000 Indians, plus members of Monterey's pioneer families.

Mission San Juan Bautista thrives in its historic Old West setting. Shmuel Thaler

✪ MISSION SAN JUAN BAUTISTA
831-623-4528
2nd and Mariposa Sts., San Juan Bautista
Open: 9:30–4:30 daily
Admission: Donations

Founded in 1797, Mission San Juan Bautista basilica—located 10 miles inland from Monterey—is the largest in the California mission family. The 40-foot polychromed chapel walls were originally painted in 1818 by Bostonian Thomas Doak, a deserter from the ship *Albatross*. Today, the mission's large plaza skirts the entire 184-foot length of the graceful arched portico, whose thick walls keep the dark mission interior, as well as its restored dormitories and workrooms, cool in the blazing heat of summer. Olive and cypress trees encircle the small Indian burial ground behind the mission, the view from which affords a dramatic panorama of the San Andreas Fault zigzagging through Hollister in the distance. The lofty beams of the chapel interior are crowned by an ornate baroque altar. The atmosphere conspires to make this place a remarkable window into the early days of Spanish occupation. Each summer the adventurous **Cabrillo Music Festival** fills the plaza and the acoustically perfect mission interior with the sounds of the living present. The innovative Hispanic performance troupe **El Teatro Campesino** makes its home base in this bastion of early California heritage. And it should not be forgotten during a visit to San Juan Bautista that a movie star of major proportions is always in your midst: The mission's adjoining bell tower—now closed to the public—figured prominently in the climactic conclusion of Alfred Hitchcock's *Vertigo*.

Museums
CENTER FOR PHOTOGRAPHIC ART
www.photography.org
831-625-5181
San Carlos St. & 8th Ave., Carmel
Open: Tues.–Sun. 1–5
One of the finest galleries in Carmel was founded by pioneering local photographers such as Ansel Adams and Edward Weston. Housed in a wing of the Sunset Center, it contains fine photography exhibits by internationally known artists, plus permanent collections, and it is staffed by knowledgeable docents who can share the history of photography.

✪ HENRY MILLER LIBRARY
www.henrymiller.org
831-667-2574
Hwy. 1, Big Sur
Open: Tues.–Sun. 11–5
Admission: Free

Built in 1981 as a land trust and ode to the late Henry Miller, the Big Sur memorial library houses an extensive collection of rare and well-known works in the town Miller fell in love with when he was a struggling writer. It is also a community resource center and meeting place for local artists and poets, and it plays host to art exhibits, concerts and poetry readings. The library also boasts acres of picturesque land and ocean views.

LA MIRADA
www.montereyart.org
831-372-3689
720 Via Mirada, Old Monterey
Open: Thurs.–Sat. 11–5, Sun. noon–4
Admission: $3

This 1849 adobe, an extension of the Monterey Museum of Art, displays artwork and antiques of several historical periods. A 10,000-square-foot addition houses the Armin Hansen Collection of California art and a separate Asian art gallery. La Mirada is a favorite for its relaxing gardens as well.

✪ MONTEREY BAY AQUARIUM
www.montereybayaquarium.org
831-648-4888
886 Cannery Row, Monterey
Open: Daily 10–6

Visitors from the world over flock to the awe-inspiring marine displays at the Monterey Bay Aquarium. Shmuel Thaler

Admission: Adults $19.95, seniors $17.95, age 13–17 or with college ID $15.95, children 3–12 $8.95

Since its opening in 1984, this astonishing facility has been visited by countless avid aquarium devotees, who consider it one of the wonders of the modern world. Built on the edge of the enormous Monterey Bay National Marine Sanctuary—whose underwater valley dwarfs the Grand Canyon—the aquarium is state-of-the-art in every respect. Home to more than 6,500 marine creatures, it houses living exhibits illustrating the Monterey Bay's many underwater habitats. Velvety leopard sharks cruise with schools of silvery sardines in the aquarium's vast three-story kelp forests, which tower up to the sunlight filtering through 300,000-gallon exhibition tanks. Playful sea otters soar acrobatically through the waters of their special area, a gorgeous re-creation of the bay floor that opens out onto the sunny rocks above. The arrangement allows viewers to watch the sea otters cavorting underwater as well as on the surface. The soft bat rays and fascinating starfish of the Touch Tide Pool are irresistible to even adult children. Special exhibits show off the frontiers of marine science, creatively wedded with arresting interpretive display design. The tastefully stocked gift store is itself worth leisurely exploration. Central Coast visitors shouldn't even consider passing it up: The aquarium truly lives up to its international reputation.

MONTEREY MARITIME MUSEUM AND HISTORY CENTER
www.mntmh.org
831-373-2469
5 Custom House Plaza, Monterey
Open: Daily 10–5
Admission: Adults $5, seniors $4, youth $3, children $2

Housed in the 18,000-square-foot Stanton Center on the historic waterfront, this brainchild of the Monterey History and Art Association fills two levels and seven exhibition areas with history from the Ohlone Indian peoples and Spanish explorers to dramatic displays of Monterey's fishing and sailing heyday. Maritime history, from a 5-ton Fresnel lighthouse lens to Portuguese navigation logs and charts, is on view in this exciting museum.

MONTEREY MUSEUM OF ART
www.montereyart.org
831-372-5477
559 Pacific St., Old Monterey
Open: Wed.–Sat. 11–5, Sun. 1–4
Admission: Adults $3, students $1.50

A charming fine arts museum specializing in American and Asian artworks, photography, graphics and international folk and ethnic arts and crafts. The county's premier collection of regional artists also finds room for one-person and specialty shows.

✪ NATIONAL STEINBECK CENTER
www.steinbeck.org
831-775-4720
1 Main St., Salinas
Open: Daily 10–5
Admission: Adults $10.95, seniors $8.95, youth 13–17 $7.95, children 6–12 $5.95

The National Steinbeck Center is a sight to behold for fans of Pulitzer Prize–winning native son, author John Steinbeck. Imaginative exhibits convey Steinbeck's life, literary travels, and local history. Workshops and activities for adults and children alike are held throughout the year, and every August, the **Steinbeck Festival** is held.

PACIFIC GROVE MUSEUM OF NATURAL HISTORY
831-648-5716
165 Forest Ave., Pacific Grove
Open: Tues.–Sun. 10–5
Admission: Free

The front lawn offers a life-sized gray whale sculpture, and the interior is filled with displays of Californiana, from minerals and seashells to hundreds of taxidermy specimens of indigenous wildlife. The popular migrating monarch butterflies boast their own exhibit and colorful video, while rare local flora bloom in the small native plant garden just outside. A small gift store offers tempting posters, books, T-shirts and other educational souvenirs.

PACIFIC HOUSE MUSEUM
831-649-7118
Junction of Alvarado, Calle Principal & Scott Sts., Monterey
Open: Daily 10–5
Admission: Free

Originally a hotel built in 1835 by Scotsman James McKinley, this adobe structure is today a museum documenting Monterey's historic Native American, Spanish and Mexican periods. After its disreputable origins as a sailors' saloon and lodgings, it enjoyed a brief reincarnation as a Presbyterian rectory and Salvation Army headquarters. It was restored in the 1920s. The spacious two-story adobe is filled with graphic exhibits illustrating adobe brick making and historic metalwork from old Monterey homes. In the back, at the site of a former bullfighting ring, sits a patio with a fountain, shade-giving magnolia trees and colorful plantings, all laid out in the late 1920s to re-create the atmosphere of the old Spanish capital.

PRESIDIO OF MONTEREY MUSEUM
831-646-3456
Building 13, Corporal Ewing Rd., Monterey
Open: Thurs.–Sat. 10–4
Admission: Free

The area's extensive military history is documented in this newly reopened museum. Displays of historic memorabilia and photographs provide visitors with a good summary of Native American, Spanish and modern military activities. This museum is now included in Monterey's Path of History tour and is sponsored by the U.S. Army and the city of Monterey.

✪ WHALER'S CABIN MUSEUM, POINT LOBOS
831-624-4909
Hwy. 1, south of Carmel
Open: Daily 11–3
Admission: Free

Attracted to the huge pods of California gray whale that migrated between Arctic waters and Baja California spawning grounds, whalers began plying Pacific waters in the very early 1800s. By the mid-1840s, the Central Coast had profitable whaling stations at Moss Landing, Davenport and San Simeon. A circa-1851 cabin, built by Chinese fishing families overlooking Point Lobos's Whaler's Cove, has been carefully preserved as a museum and recalls the whaling heyday in photographs, harpoons and sailing implements and other memorabilia of the Portuguese whalers who frequented the cove in the 1860s. This tiny weathered cabin, whose floor joists are supported by six whale vertebrae, overlooks one of the most idyllic coves on the West Coast and is one of the oldest buildings of Chinese origin remaining in Monterey Bay area.

Music

Camerata Singers www.camerata-singers.org, 831-642-2701, Carmel Mission Basilica, Mission San Antonio. The soaring, seamless voices of this world-class vocal ensemble are shown off to full advantage each winter in the atmospheric acoustics of Old California's mission settings.

Carmel Bach Festival www.bachfestival.org, 831-624-1521, Naval Postgraduate School, Carmel Mission Basilica, Carmel. The best of Johann Sebastian Bach, and plenty of his baroque colleagues, pours forth in this splendid, celebrated three-week (July–August) annual love affair with great music that draws devotees from around the Central Coast. Passionate performances, concerts, recitals, lectures, opera, symposia, receptions and a children's concert fill the bill, all top quality and enthusiastically attended.

Carmel Music Society www.carmelmusic.org, 831-625-9938, Sunset Cultural Center, Carmel. After seven decades, this musical institution is still going strong during its fall–spring season, offering distinctive solo recitals for voice—by reigning divas like Frederica von Stade—and piano, flute and violin. The society also stages annual vocal and instrumental competitions and international touring ensembles.

Chamber Music Monterey Bay www.chambermusicmontereybay.org, 831-625-2212, Sunset Cultural Center, Carmel. Long the performance venue of choice for generations of

Carmel culturati, the society regularly hosts visitors like the Los Angeles Piano Quartet and the Arden Piano Trio, as well as California's leading string quartet ensembles, as part of this exciting six-concert series each winter and spring.

Dixieland Monterey www.dixieland-monterey.com, 831-443-5260, 177 Webster St., Monterey. Two dozen of the top Dixieland band interpreters strut their stuff for three high-stepping days every March in cabaret locations throughout Fisherman's Wharf and downtown Monterey.

Ensemble Monterey www.ensemble-monterey.org, 831-333-1283, Sunset Cultural Center, Carmel. Now in its 14th season, this consortium of professional musicians brings innovative programming, as well as a bold approach to traditional performing, to the concert stage. Copland and Harrison are group favorites.

I Cantori di Carmel www.icantori.org, 831-644-8012, Carmel Mission. Glorious choral programs fill the Carmel Mission with music of the gods in both fall and spring.

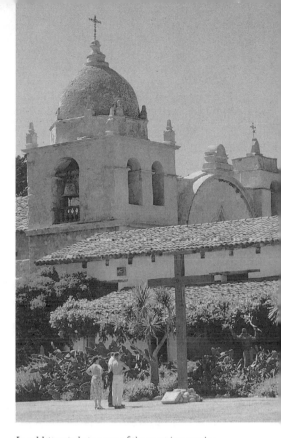

In addition to being one of the most impressive missions along California's coast, Mission San Carlos Borroméo del Rio Carmelo hosts many concerts in its basilica, including performances by the Camerata Singers and the Carmel Bach Festival.

Shmuel Thayler

Monterey Bay Blues Festival www.monterey blues.com, 831-394-2652, Monterey County Fairgrounds. Rapidly establishing a red-hot reputation, this sizzling music fest brings blues greats together two days every June for performances and jamming. New discoveries share the stage with heavyweights like Bobby Blue Bland, B. B. King, the Neville Brothers and Etta James.

✪ **Monterey Jazz Festival** www.montereyjazzfestival.org, 831-373-3366, Monterey County Fairgrounds. The oldest jazz festival in the U.S. features living legends and youthful contenders. Three days of September jazz sessions on multiple stages, an intimate "night club" hot spot and outdoor performance arena make the granddaddy of West Coast music fests a perennial "with it" winner. This legendary jazz venue has featured Dave Brubeck, Billie Holiday, Max Roach, Shelly Manne, Harry James, Dizzie Gillespie, Ray Charles, Tito Puente, Joe Williams, Ella Fitzgerald and Wynton Marsalis, to name just a few. A world-famous event with a capital W, all proceeds go to educate the budding jazz musicians of Monterey County.

Monterey Symphony www.montereysymphony.org, 831-624-8511, Sunset Cultural Center, Carmel. Internationally acclaimed guest artists join the resident professional symphony orchestra for an annual October–May series of concerts from the classical and modern repertoires.

Nightlife

Blue Fin Cafe & Billiards www.bluefin-billiards.com, 831-375-7000, 685 Cannery Row, Monterey. Live music on the weekends, pool tables, full bar, drink specials most nights, food and a view of the Monterey Bay.

Cibo www.cibo.com, 831-649-8151, 301 Alvarado St., Monterey. Lots of festive international jazz pairs well with the casually elegant menu of Italian pastas. Also known for a mixing a martini 007 himself would fawn over.

Club Octane www.cluboctane.com, 831-646-9244, 321D Alvarado St., Monterey. This spacious upstairs nightclub offers high-power, high-tech, DJ-spun house, techno and trance music for your dancing pleasure.

✪ **Doc Rickett's Lab** 831-649-4241, 180 E. Franklin, Monterey. Hard-rockin' boys and girls play the sexy rock-and-roll game to the accompaniment of good local bands and traveling semi-stars.

Hog's Breath Inn hogsbreathinn.net, 831-625-1044, San Carlos, bet. 5th & 6th Aves., Carmel. Don't expect to see Clint Eastwood playing barkeep at this restaurant-bar, though he used to own it. Though it has no live music, it does sport picturesque outdoor seating, strong drinks and an Eastwood-specific high-plains omelet.

Knuckles Historical Sports Bar 831-372-7171; Hyatt Regency Lobby, #1 Old Golf Course Rd., Monterey. Thirteen TV monitors and two satellite dishes feed all the top international sporting matches into this major sports bar, which also features plenty of hefty finger food.

The Mucky Duck 831-655-3031, 479 Alvarado St., Monterey. An authentic British pub, heated patio, DJ on the weekends, billed as the local's local.

Ocean Thunder www.oceanthunder.com, 831-643-9169, 214 Lighthouse, Monterey. Its motto is "We put the lights back into Lighthouse Avenue." Ocean Thunder boasts live entertainment—mainly blues and rock—and an outdoor patio, in addition to its scenic location and offerings. Enjoy a wide dance floor, full cocktail bar complete with an ever-expanding collection of fine tequilas, darts, pool and garden landscape.

Peter B's 831-649-4511, ext. 138, 2 Portola Plaza, Monterey. A taste of a traditional brew-pub, Peter B's comes complete with sports telecasts, open-mic nights and beer-soaking victuals.

Planet Gemini www.planetgemini.com, 831-373-1449, 625 Cannery Row, 3rd floor, Monterey. Rock, country, salsa, hip-hop and comedy seven nights a week. Long on dancing, short on laughs.

Portofino Presents 831-373-7379, 620 Lighthouse Ave., Pacific Grove. Folk, ethnic and contemporary acoustic musical stylings in a bohemian coffeehouse setting.

Sly McFly's 831-649-8050, 700 Cannery Row, Monterey. Sly's has become an important part of the rock and blues scene on Cannery Row. It expanded its dance floor and restaurant in 2001. Local musicians jam here during the week, national talent comes through on occasion and both locals and visitors enjoy the full bar and menu.

Stage

Carl Cherry Center for the Arts 831-624-7491, Guadalupe and 4th Ave., Carmel. A staple in the lives of Carmel culture hounds, the center plays host to myriad writers, art workshops, plays and dance performances. A very classy establishment.

Carmel Shakespeare Festival 831-622-0100, Outdoor Forest Theater, Santa Rita & Mountain View Sts., Carmel. For six weeks beginning in September, two productions of Shakespearean classics run in repertory in the oldest outdoor amphitheater in the West, built in 1910 by Carmel's bohemian founders.

Children's Experimental Theatre 831-624-1531, Indoor Forest Theatre, Carmel. Live drama and comedy ranging from exuberant Greek classics to contemporary repertoire.

Golden Bough Playhouse www.pacrep.org, 831-622-0100, Monte Verde St. and 8th Ave., Carmel. Home to the Pacific Repertory Theatre, a company that stages 9 or 10 productions of classic and original plays each year that prove to be crowd pleasers.

Monterey Bay Theatrefest 831-622-0100, Custom House Plaza, Monterey. Free outdoor theater during June fills Monterey's waterfront with lively thespian action from the sublime to the delightfully comic.

Outdoor Forest Theater 831-626-1681, 831-624-1531, Mountain View Ave. & Santa Rita St., Carmel. Shakespeare and classics "under the stars" every summer at Carmel's rustic, turn-of-the-20th-century outdoor theater; fall through spring, classic plays are presented in the intimate Indoor Forest Theatre.

Staff Players Repertory Company 831-624-1531, Indoor Forest Theatre, Carmel. An offshoot of the Children's Experimental Theatre, the staff players perform classical theater for adult audiences. The company produces five major shows a year during its October–May season.

Sunset Cultural Center 831-624-8511, 8th Ave. & San Carlos St., Carmel. The cultural heart and longtime gathering spot for intensely arts-minded local citizenry, the center houses a wide array of events all year round, including the Carmel Bach Festival, the Monterey County Symphony and Performance Carmel.

RECREATION

Beaches

These beaches are described in the order you will encounter them traveling southward down the Pacific Coast Highway from the Santa Cruz County–Monterey County line.

Zmudowski State Beach Hwy. 1, 1 mile north of Moss Landing. A boardwalk leads through the dunes to a prime surfing and clamming beach bordered by verdant farms. Snowy plovers and their wildfowl colleagues nest in the serpentine estuary. A rich marriage of salt water and fresh water, lined with cattails. Parking and restrooms. No entrance fee.

Moss Landing State Beach Hwy. 1, north of Moss Landing Harbor. Located near the extensive wetlands of Elkhorn Slough, this 55-acre beach is an ideal spot for bird-watching.

The long sandy stretch and soft dunes of Zmudowski State Beach just north of Moss Landing offer myriad beachcombing and bird-watching opportunities.

Picnicking, surfing, clamming, horseback riding and windsurfing are also specialties of this stretch of beach and sand dunes. No entrance fee.

Salinas River State Beach Hwy. 1 at Potrero Rd., Moss Landing. One-stop shopping for fishing, clamming, hiking and prime bird-watching at the Salinas River Wildlife Area, just south of the beach. Accessible along a boardwalk leading through substantial dunes. Parking and rest rooms. No entrance fee.

Marina State Beach End of Reservation Rd., Marina. Voluptuous dunes skirt this 170-acre site, whose 2,000-foot-long boardwalk leads to the water. While surf conditions make for unsafe swimming, the beach offers fine fishing and a launch site for kite flying and hang gliding. Wheelchair access, parking lots, restrooms and rangers' headquarters. No entrance fee.

Monterey State Beach Sand Dunes Dr., Monterey. A lovely sandy, stretch of beachfront from Monterey's Municipal Wharf to Seaside's rolling dunes, the entire length serves up bracing views of Monterey Bay. Parking and restrooms. No entrance fee.

Lovers Point Beach Ocean View, Pacific Grove. Located in a protective cove near the end of the Monterey Penisula's rocky land's end, the grassy picnic area is a favorite with kids and water enthusiasts.

Asilomar State Beach Pico Ave. & Sunset Dr., Pacific Grove. A lavish expanse of world-class tide pools, rocky shoreline and sandy dunes makes this a destination for aficionados of serious beachfront play. Divers frequent the area searching for prized abalone, and neon-hued ice plant colonies hug the edge of the sand. Swimming is unwise due to rocks and hazardous riptides. The beach adjoins the Asilomar Conference Grounds. Parking is available along the roadway, and restrooms are available. No entrance fee.

Macabee Beach (San Carlos Beach) Cannery Row, bet. McClellan & Prescott Aves., Monterey. Wedged between restaurants, this favorite diving spot is graced by a small stretch of sand. Tourist information, outdoor shower and parking are available. No entrance fee.

Fanshell Beach Signal Hill Rd. at 17 Mile Dr., Pebble Beach. In the heart of scenic 17 Mile Dr., this white sand cove offers choice locations for enjoying the antics of resident sea otters, as well as fishing, picnicking and, for the hardy, swimming. Parking is available. No entrance fee.

Carmel City Beach End of Ocean Ave., Carmel. Soft white sand extends beyond a border of deep green cypress trees, offering picnic and campfire possibilities, volleyball and wheel-chair-accessible restrooms. A multitude of stairways provide beach access to this gorgeous location, predictably crowded on weekends. *Warning.* Dangerous surf/swimming conditions. No entrance fee.

Carmel River State Beach Scenic Rd. at Carmelo St., Carmel. A favorite with divers and those who enjoy the sights and sounds of resident lagoon waterfowl, this 100-acre sandy beach fronts a teeming marsh, near the site where Spanish explorers first made landfall. The southernmost tip, known as Monastery Beach, is accessible from Hwy. 1. Prime day recreation. Parking and restrooms. No entrance fee.

Monastery Beach Hwy. 1, Carmel. This scenic beach hides steep drop-offs and serious undertow. The coarse pebble beach is a favorite launching point for experienced divers. Wear sturdy shoes and be blissfully prepared for some spectacular scenery.

Point Lobos State Park West of Hwy. 1 at Carmel Highlands. Easily the crown jewel of the Monterey coastline—widely considered one of the most spectacular coastal sanctuaries in the country—this 2,500-acre preserve shelters ancient cypress groves, rugged cliffs, swirling tide pools and bottle-green water lapping crystalline cove beaches. Exquisite China Beach offers sheltered swimming. Well-marked trails thread the meadows, bluffs and shoreline, presenting stunning views of sea lion and waterfowl habitats. A small museum is located in a vintage whaler's cabin, and diving is available by permit. Ample parking and restrooms. Entrance fee.

Garrapata State Park Hwy. 1, 2 miles south of Malpaso Creek, Big Sur. A soaring landscape of steep cliffs, accessible along a panoramic trail, overlooks rich tide pools below and a breathtaking view. Excellent whale-watching abounds in this favorite playground for sea otters, which are so captivating that you'll be tempted to get up close and personal, but leave these furry creatures in peace. Roadside parking and chemical toilets. No entrance fee.

Pfeiffer Beach Hwy. 1, end of Sycamore Canyon Rd., Big Sur. A trail leads from the parking lot through cypress groves to the sandy beach encircled by monumental cliffs and sea caves. Natural rock arches channel the waves into spectacular displays of wild spray and spume. At the beach, Sycamore Creek spills into a hidden lagoon, a gorgeous sanctuary for exploring, though the surf is hazardous and gusty winds require warm clothing for all-day outings. Parking and restrooms. No entrance fee.

Kirk Creek Beach Hwy. 1, 4 miles south of Lucia. The bluffs above the point where Kirk Creek joins the ocean afford a spectacular view. Overlooking the sandy beach are 33 campsites, from which a steep trail leads down to the water. Parking and restrooms. Free for day use, though there is a fee for camping.

Sand Dollar Beach Hwy. 1, 11 miles south of Lucia. Lush fields and cypress groves frame this favorite picnic spot, with trails leading to a half-moon-shaped beach. Hang gliders love this spot and provide plenty of aerodynamic visuals. Parking and restrooms. No entrance fee.

Jade Cove Hwy. 1, 12 miles south of Lucia. Named for the preponderance of soft green nephrite jade once found here (and enthusiastically collected by generations past), this rocky cove is today a favorite diving area, but still perfect for wandering and for sifting through the smooth pebbles in hopes of discovering some special memento. Reached by a steep trail. No facilities. No entrance fee.

Willow Creek Beach Hwy. 1, 14 miles south of Lucia. An excellent picnic spot affording views of former coastline now eroded into stately offshore rock formations. Enthusiasts still comb for bits of jade where Willow Creek meets the sea. Parking and restrooms. No entrance fee.

Bicycling
BICYCLE RENTALS
Adventures by the Sea www.adventuresbythesea.com, 831-372-1807, at Lovers Point, Pacific Grove.

Aquarian Bicycles 831-375-2144, 486 Washington St., Monterey.

Carmel Bicycle 831-625-2211, 7150 Carmel Valley Rd., Carmel.

Joselyn's Bicycles www.joselynbicycles.com, 831-649-8520, 638 Lighthouse Ave., Monterey.

Wheel Fun Rentals and Bay Bikes www.baybikes.com, 831-646-9090, 640 Wave St. at Cannery Row, Monterey, and 831-655-2453, 99 Pacific St. at Fisherman's Wharf, Monterey (will deliver bike to you).

TOP RIDES
17 Mile Drive A scenic, flat course that runs along the coast through pine forests and Monterey cypress groves, as well as past some of the most ritzy domiciles on the planet.

Berwick Park A leisurely path runs through this narrow, grassy park.

Carmel Valley Road An easy countryside ride for beginners.

Fort Ord Public Lands Beautiful woodlands and wetlands.

Garland Ranch Recreational Park Easy loops and hilly treks both abound.

Locke Paddon Park A bike path runs along the perimeter of this wetland area.

Monterey Peninsula Recreation Trail This linear park stretches 9 miles along the Monterey Bay's waterline along a former Southern Pacific Railroad right-of-way.

Old Coast Road This 11-mile stretch was once part of the only connection between Carmel and Big Sur.

Perkins Park Paths meander through this park that overlooks the Monterey Bay.

Roberts Lake A bike path runs parallel to the shoreline between Roberts Ave. and Pacific Grove.

Spanish Bay Recreational Trail Cycle through a Monterey pine forest along a bike path that runs from Sunset Dr. to Asilomar Blvd.

Bird-Watching

Andrew Molera State Park Hwy. 1, north end of Old Coast Rd., Big Sur. A lively bird sanctuary is contained at the lagoon where the Big Sur River flows to the ocean. Grebes and wood ducks sail the surface of this small preserve, as do geese, scoters and coots. The beach here is especially popular with sea otters enamored of shellfish lodged in the huge kelp beds.

Carmel River State Beach Scenic Rd. at Carmelo St., Carmel. A lovely, protected marsh filled with winged charmers like kingfishers and hawks, pelicans and cormorants. Busy sandpipers scurry about, and herons and egrets seem to meditate among the smooth-sailing ducks and geese. There is much to delight novice as well as experienced bird-watchers.

Crespi Pond Ocean View & Asilomar Blvds., Pacific Grove. A freshwater pond situated near the pounding surf of Point Pinos boasts a population of resident ducks and coots, as well as the spectacle of brown pelicans, shearwater gulls and cormorants diving dramatically offshore.

Elkhorn Slough Hwy. 1 at Moss Landing. Nirvana for bird-watchers, this intertidal reserve contains 1,400 acres of wetland, marsh and dunes, all of it home to hundreds of species of wildlife, including rare California brown pelicans and California clapper rails, plus the occasional peregrine falcon and golden eagle. The abundance of birds is almost excessive, as thousands of shorebirds feed together in great agitated flocks, especially the hyperactive sandpipers, killdeers, curlews, willets and sanderlings. Here resident gulls (western, California and Heermann's) noisily cohabitate with placid mallards and pintail ducks. In the lagoons, observe California murres, grebes, scoters and coots. Cameras and binoculars are a must.

One of the richest bird habitats in the United States, the shallow waters of bays and beach areas of the Elkhorn Slough are home to hundreds of species of waterfowl, such as the snowy egret. Hillary Schalit

Lake San Antonio San Antonio Rd. off Interlake Rd., Monterey County. A 16-mile-long lake recreation site tucked into the Coast Ranges, this popular boating and fishing site offers outstanding bird-watching. In the winter, the attraction is over 50 American bald eagles, which overwinter here November–March feasting on the lake's fish and waterfowl population. Pontoon boat tours take visitors close to the nesting and fishing sites of these awesome raptors, whose specialty prey is trout and whose wingspan exceeds 8 feet.

Point Lobos State Reserve Hwy. 1, 3 miles south of Carmel. Among the many wonders of this spectacularly beautiful wilderness preserve is an abundance of birdlife (more than 250 species), including those in rocky outcroppings and on islands studded with nesting sites of Brandt's cormorant. Blue herons and white egrets are especially fond of the marshy meadows.

Salinas River Wildlife Area Potrero Rd. west of Hwy. 1, Moss Landing. Over 250 acres of shoreline boast sheltered dunes liberally laced with wildflowers, and just south of the beach, the 500-acre Salinas River National Wildlife Refuge is home to sandpipers, herons, egrets, brown pelicans and snowy plovers. Diving into the surf for fish, frantically pacing along the tideline, birds fill every possible niche of this fertile wildlife preserve.

Boating
CANOING & KAYAKING

Adventures by the Sea www.adventuresbythesea.com, 831-372-1807, 299 Cannery Row, Monterey 93940. Classes, instruction, rentals, sales and tours by Monterey Bay Aquarium personnel.

Kayak Connection 831-724-5692, Moss Landing.

Kayaking has become the fastest-growing sports activity around the Monterey Bay. Robert Scheer

Sea Otters

Once hunted to the edge of extinction for its thick, lustrous fur, the playful southern sea otter now thrives, hunts and swims the Central Coast between Santa Cruz and San Luis Obispo. Humans are easily charmed by these creatures, with their engaging whiskered faces and bodies extending up to 4 feet in length. Especially pro-lific in the kelp beds along Monterey Bay, the intelligent otter is enamored of shellfish, for which it dives with admirable speed and skill, consuming them by lying on its back and hammering open the shells using rocks. Sea otters forage continuously for the enormous quantity of food (2 tons a year) needed to maintain their body tem-perature in cold waters. Protected by state and federal law, otters can be spotted by watching for seagulls that dive for the portions of shellfish discarded by the furry mammals.

Sea otters consume enormous quantities of food—2 tons a year—needed to maintain their body temperature and playful activities in cold waters. Robert Scheer

Monterey Bay Kayaks www.montereybaykayaks.com, 800-649-5357, 831-649-5357, 693 Del Monte Ave., Monterey, and 2390 Hwy. 1, Moss Landing. One-stop shopping for still-water and ocean kayaking, from equipment and rentals to classes and tours of Monterey Bay, Carmel Bay, Elkhorn Slough and Big Sur.

CHARTERS & CRUISES

Elkhorn Slough Safari Nature Tours www.elkhornslough.com, 831-633-5555, Harbor District parking lot, Moss Landing. Captain Yohn Gideon conducts informative, fun adventures for adults and children that explore the wonders of the slough and the Monterey Bay Marine Sancuary. See sea otters, harbor seals and a fantastic variety of waterfowl from the comfort of a 27-foot pontoon boat, with Captain Yohn at the helm (yes, he's the real thing—he once served as a U.S. Coast Guard captain). An onboard naturalist and refreshments help make this a great way to spend an educational day.

Fishing
FISHING & HUNTING REGULATIONS
California Department of Fish & Game 916-227-2244, 3211 S St., Sacramento 95816. Information, licenses and tags.

FISHING CHARTERS
Chris' Fishing Trips www.chrisfishingtrips.com, 831-375-5951, 48 Fisherman's Wharf, Monterey. Deep-sea fishing and boats are chartered by appointment.

Monterey Sport Fishing www.montereywhalewatching.com, 831-372-2203, 96 Fisher-man's Wharf, Monterey. Half- and full-day fishing charters. Salmon and albacore party trips are available in season. Bottomfishing trips for ling cod and others. Bait is provided, and licenses, tackle, rod rentals, fish cleaning and freezing services are available.

Randy's Fishing Trips www.randysfishingtrips.com, 831-372-7440, 66 Fisherman's Wharf #1, Monterey. Deep-sea fishing trips for salmon and albacore. Bait is provided, and tackle is for rent. Licenses, sack lunches and fish cleaning are available.

Sam's Fishing Fleet www.gowhales.com, 831-372-0577, Fisherman's Wharf, Monterey. There are two 65-foot boats and one 55-foot boat for deep-sea fishing. Rod rentals are available.

Tom's Sportfishing www.usafishing.com, 831-633-2564, P.O. Box 647, Moss Landing. Private charters, open parties, nature trips, whale-watching and bay cruises are available.

Golf

Baynet & Blackhorse Golf Courses wwww.baynetblackhorse.com, 831-899-2351 McClure Way, Seaside. Service personnel and guests; 36 holes. Bayonet: 7,100 yards, par 72, rated 72.4. Black Horse: 6,175 yards, par 72, rated 70.8. Cart rental.

Carmel Valley Ranch Golf Course www.troongolf.com, 831-626-2510, 1 Old Ranch Rd., Carmel. Public, members and guests; 18 holes, 6,234 yards, par 70, rated 70.5. Pro shop, cart rental, bar, restaurant.

Cypress Point Golf Club 831-624-2223, 3150 17 Mile Dr., Pebble Beach. Members and guests; 6,332 yards, par 72, rated 72.4. Cart rental.

Laguna Seca Golf Course www.golf-monterey.com, 831-373-3701, 10520 York Rd., Monterey. Public; 18 holes, 6,157 yards, par 71, rated 70.7.

Links at Spanish Bay www.pebblebeach.com, 800-654-9300, 831-647-7495, 2700 17 Mile Dr., Pebble Beach. Public and members; 18 holes, 6,821 yards, par 72, rated 74.8. Pro shop, cart rental, bar, restaurant.

Monterey Peninsula Country Club 831-373-1556, 3000 Club Rd., Pebble Beach. Members and guests; 36 holes. Dunes: 6,161 yards, par 72, rated 69.4. Shore: 6,173 yards, par 71, rated 69.7. Pro shop, cart rental, bar, restaurant.

Monterey Pines Golf Course www.mwr.nps.navy.mil, 831-656-2167 Mark Thomas Dr. & Garden Rd., Monterey. Service personnel and guests; 18 holes, 5,574 yards, par 69, rated 67.8. Cart rental.

Old Del Monte Golf Course www.pebblebeach.com, 831-373-2700, 1300 Sylvan Rd., Monterey. Public and guests; 18 holes, 6,052 yards, par 72, rated 69.5. Pro shop, cart rental, bar, restaurant.

Pacific Grove Municipal Golf Links 831-648-5777, 77 Asilomar Blvd., Pacific Grove. Public; 18 holes, 5,571 yards, par 70, rated 66.9. Pro shop, lockers, lessons, practice range.

Pebble Beach Golf Links www.pebblebeach.com, 831-624-6611, 17 Mile Dr., Pebble Beach. Public and guests; 18 holes, 6,348 yards, par 72, rated 72.3. Pro shop, cart rental, bar, restaurant.

Peter Hays Golf Course www.pebblebeach.com, 831-625-8518, 17 Mile Dr., Pebble Beach. Public; 9 holes, 785 yards, par 27, unrated.

Poppy Hills Golf Course www.ncga.org, 831-625-2035, 3200 Lopez Rd., Pebble Beach. Public, members and guests; 18 holes, 6,237 yards, par 72, rated 71.5. Pro shop, cart rental, bar, restaurant.

Quail Lodge Golf Club www.quaillodge.com/golf.cfm, 831-624-2770, 8000 Valley Green Dr., Carmel. Members and guests; 18 holes, 6,141 yards, par 71, rated 70.2. Pro shop, cart rental, bar, restaurant.

Rancho Cañada Golf Club www.ranchocanada.com, 831-624-0111, 4860 Carmel Valley Rd., Carmel. Public; 36 holes. East: 5,843 yards, par 71, rated 67.4. West: 6,126 yards, par 72, rated 69.3. Cart rental.

Spyglass Hill Golf Course www.pebblebeach.com, 800-654-9300, 831-625-8563, Stevenson Dr. & Spy Glass Hill, Pebble Beach. Members and guests; 18 holes, 6,346 yards, par 72, rated 73. Pro shop, cart rental, bar, restaurant.

Hiking

Asilomar State Beach Sunset Dr., Pacific Grove. The action here centers on a challenging stretch of rocky shore offering breathtaking views of boiling white-water tides and wild crashing surf that punctuate the impossibly turquoise Monterey Bay waters. A sandy beach wanders into soft, pillowy dunes filled with native plants and waterfowl habitats. The renowned tide pools fanning out from the bluffs can occupy days of absorbing exploration. Ample parking and restrooms provide hiking base camp amenities.

Garland Ranch Regional Park Carmel Valley Rd., Carmel Valley. These 4,462 acres offer a broad range of hiking and equestrian opportunities, every kind of traipse, from short, flat loops to arduous daylong trails. Check out the possibilities at the visitors center near the parking lot.

Garrapata State Park Hwy. 1, 2 miles south of Malpaso Creek, Big Sur. Hiking the cove and bluffs at this coastal gateway to Big Sur rewards the naturalist with spectacular views of the coast from the top of a 1.2-mile trail. The trails also provide prime sea otter watching, since this stretch is part of the lengthy Sea Otter Game Refuge, extending offshore down to the San Luis Obispo County line. Explore the tide pools filled with exquisite miniature shellfish and crustacea. For more information, call 831-667-2315.

Julia Pfeiffer Burns State Park Hwy. 1, 11 miles south of Big Sur State Park, Big Sur. Sprawling from the edge of the ocean up through forested ridges filled with creeks and waterfalls, this 2,000-acre preserve contains abundant hiking trails. Especially worthwhile are paths leading to splendid ocean-view overlooks at McWay Waterfall, which spills 50 feet into the sea. Magnificent sea caves and sharp rock crags rim the soft sand at many of the park's beaches, including Partington Cove, accessible by a trail that cuts across a wooden footbridge and through a 200-foot-long tunnel carved into the cliffs at Partington Creek. The park closes at sunset and charges a day-use fee.

Mission Trail Park Mountain View St. & Crespi Ave., Carmel. Redwood groves and wildflower meadows fill this verdant area, laced with miles of trails eventually converging at the Carmel Mission. Deer safely graze in this stretch, little known to outsiders but much loved by local hikers. Ocean vistas can take your breath away.

Pfeiffer Beach Trail Sycamore Canyon Rd. at Hwy. 1, just south of Big Sur State Park entrance. Once you reach the Forest Service parking area, follow the sandy trail to the small lagoon formed where Sycamore Creek meets the beach. This is an absolutely stunning coastal seascape festooned with caves, tortured rock formations and swirling water. Not for swimming and usually pretty windy, it's well worth the effort to get there. Scenes from the 1965 Liz Taylor/Richard Burton film *The Sandpiper* were filmed at this location.

Point Lobos Hwy. 1 at Riley Ranch Rd., Carmel. Treat yourself to an all-day excursion exploring this incredible 2,500-acre preserve, encompassing pristine coves set with jewel-like beaches, jagged rock outcroppings, ancient cypress groves, myriad tide pools, marsh-lands and isolated meadows. The diversity of landscape is staggering (especially bountiful are spring wildflower displays when meadows are carpeted with iris and lilac), and well-marked trails loop in and around all of the most beautiful stretches, liberally dotted with hundreds of species of native plants, birds and other wildlife. Walking is effortless, even along the steeply curving **Cypress Grove Trail**, in surroundings this magnificent. **Bird Island Trail** skirts close to a mile of densely packed brush overlooking exquisite China Cove and Gibson Beach, as well as the cormorant-encrusted Bird Island just offshore. The area deserves multiple visits, especially to the interpretive historic displays at the 19th-century **Whaler's Cabin Museum**. There is an admission fee and ample parking throughout the preserve. For information and brochures, call 831-624-4909.

Salinas River State Beach Hwy. 1 at Potrero Rd., Moss Landing. Dunes caress the wealth of estuary wildlife at this 250-acre haven for clamming and hiking, especially along the steep trails. The beach adjoins the Salinas River Wildlife Area, which offers abundant bird-watching opportunities.

Shoreline Park Ocean View Blvd., bet. Point Cabrillo & Lover's Point, Pacific Grove. Stretching along the rocky cliffs and sheltered sandy coves that boast magnificent views of Monterey Bay, the park's paths wind steeply down to tiny beaches, where hazardous surf (not to mention chilly water) precludes swimming. A paved pedestrian trail threads the length of the park along a railroad right-of-way, interconnecting a series of scenic park settings with plenty of benches for gawking at the incredible seascape. Street parking, no facilities.

Spanish Bay Pedestrian Trail Spanish Bay Rd. at 17 Mile Dr., Pebble Beach. The Monterey pine forests of this world-renowned stretch of cliffs, tide pools and pounding surf are accessible via many pedestrian and cycling paths looping from Sunset Dr. at 17 Mile Dr. The **Shoreline Trail** can be accessed by strolling through the Spanish Bay Hotel toward the dunes. A mile-long stretch of path fans around Point Joe and leads to cozy pocket beaches and prime bird-watching areas at Seal Rock and Bird Rock.

Ventana Wilderness Hwy. 1 at Big Sur Coast. Much of the Big Sur coast and Santa Lucia Mountains lie within this 150,000-acre preserve, itself embraced by the 2-million-acre Los Padres National Forest. The forest encompasses over 1,700 miles of hiking trails, of which the finest are contained within the very rugged and isolated Ventana Wilderness, a magnificently wild terrain of forests and coastal canyons. The **Bottchers Gap/Devils Peak Trail** leads 4 steep miles into the deep forest up to stunning views high above the ocean. For multiday backpacking excursions, the 40-mile-long **Pine Ridge Trail** begins on the coast, threads the Big Sur River and ends up at China Camp. Between May and October, campfire permits are required for backpacking excursions (831-385-5434). Trails lead

The diversity of Point Lobos's 2,500 acres is staggering—pristine coves, jewel-like beaches, ancient cypress groves, myriad tide pools and isolated meadows bountiful with wildflower displays. Shmuel Thaler

Point Lobos State Reserve

Even in a region famous for sheer breathtaking visuals, Point Lobos is memorable. Widely considered the most beautiful spot on the Central Coast, its 1,225 seafront acres (plus 1,300 more acquired in mid-1993) comprise a glorious marriage of rocky headlands, exquisite cove beaches, transparent waters and fairyland forests of pine and moss-festooned cypress. On misty mornings, its magic is total. On sunny days, every hue of the deep green meadows, turquoise water and ivory beaches is intensified. Trails—many sparkling with crushed abalone shell—lead to panoramic points, each more awesome than the last, through meadows crowned with wild irises, orchids, lilacs and lupines in the spring. Where marshes meet tide pools and beaches, blue heron stalk, and Bird Rock shimmers black with huge nesting cormorants. The spot is also popular with sea lions and otters, so bring binoculars. Its hidden cove beaches and mysterious sea caves are said to have inspired Robert Louis Stevenson's *Treasure Island*. If—heaven forbid!—one could only visit a single spot on the Central Coast, this should be it.

into the wilderness area, and maps, permits and information are available at Palo Colorado Rd. off Hwy. 1, 10 miles south of Carmel.

Horseback Riding

Cypress Stables 831-372-0511, 550 Aguajito Rd., Carmel.

Holman Ranch www.holmanranch.com, 831-659-6054, Carmel Valley.

Molera Horseback Tours www.molerahorsebacktours.com, 800-942-5486, 831-625-5486, Andrew Molera State Park, Hwy. 1, Big Sur (22 miles south of Carmel).

Monterey Bay Equestrian Center www.montereybayequestrian.com, 831 663 5712. Horses delivered to you by appointment only.

Pebble Beach Trail Rides www.ridepebblebeach.com, 831-624-2756, Portola Rd. & Alva Ln., Pebble Beach.

Rock Climbing

Sanctuary Rock Gym www.rockgym.com, 831-899-2595, 1855 East Ave., Sand City.

Surfing

Lover's Point Ocean View Blvd., Pacific Grove. Reef break, lefts off a small point; easy to ride, only breaks on a big swell, intermediate to advanced; really rocky spot.

Marina State Beach Reservation Rd., Marina. Sand bottom, lefts and rights; advanced; really bad rips.

Moss Landing State Beach Hwy. 1, north of Moss Landing Harbor. Sand bottom, lefts and rights; breaks like Hawaii Pipeline, swells come from the deep and hit the reef and jack straight up, always bigger than it looks, intermediate to advanced only; has rips and shifty peaks, respect its raw power.

Salinas River State Beach Hwy. 1 at Potrero Rd., Moss Landing. Reef bottom, lefts and rights; intermediate to advanced; sharky, rips, lots of debris floating around.

Sand City Beach Sand City. Sand bottom, lefts and rights; beginner to intermediate; can get small rips.

Zmudowski State Beach Hwy. 1, 1 mile north of Moss Landing. Sand bottom, lefts and rights; intermediate to advanced; can get rips.

Tennis

PRIVATE

Carmel Valley Racquet and Health Club www.cvrhc.com, 831-624-2737, 27300 Rancho San Carlos Rd., Carmel. Fee for nonmembers.

Carmel Valley Ranch 831-626-2550, 1 Old Ranch Rd., Carmel Valley. Fee for nonmembers.

John Gardiner's Tennis Ranch www.gardiners-resort.com, 800-375-0648, 831-647-0191, Carmel Valley. Fee for nonmembers.

Mission Tennis Ranch www.missionranchcarmel.com/tennis_fitness.htm, 831-624-9536, 26260 Dolores Ave., Carmel. Fee for nonmembers.

PUBLIC

Bay Club at Inn at Spanish Bay www.pebblebeach.com 831-647-7500, 2700 17 Mile Dr., Pebble Beach.

Cypress Park Cypress and Hoffman Sts., Monterey.

Monterey Tennis Center www.montereytenniscenter.com, 831-646-3881, 401 Pearl St., Monterey.

Via Paraiso Park Via Paraiso and Hermann Dr., Monterey.

Whale-Watching Outings

Chris' Whale Watching www.chrisswhalewatching.com, 831-375-5951, 48 Fisherman's Wharf, Monterey.

Monterey Bay Whale Watch www.gowhales.com, 866-469-4253, 831-375-4658, 84 Fisherman's Wharf, Monterey.

Whale of a Time

The California gray whale roams the waters of the Pacific coast, migrating annually from Canada down to warm-water calving areas in Mexico. During the early winter months, these magnificent creatures can be easily viewed from vantage points all along the Central Coast, spouting water high into the air and thrashing their enormous tails. At **Montaña de Oro State Park** near San Luis Obispo, whales can be observed from the cliffs during their annual migration. Other well-known spots for viewing the leviathans are **Año Nuevo State Reserve, Greyhound Rock** and **Davenport Landing** from bluffs overlooking the sea in the northern Central Coast and **San Simeon Landing** and **Moonstone Beach** near Cambria in the south. In the Big Sur area, the rocky tip of **Soberanes Point** in Pfeiffer–Big Sur State Park is a favorite whale-watching area, as are **Garrapata State Park** and **Point Lobos State Reserve**. A pair of binoculars and patience are all that's required. And the sight of these enormous creatures cruising the coast in pods of up to 20 individuals is truly awesome.

Monterey Whale Watching www.montereywhalewatching.com, 800-200-2203, 831-372-2203, 96 Fisherman's Wharf, Monterey.

Randy's Whale Watching www.randysfishingtrips.com, 800-251-7440, 831-372-7445, 66 Fisherman's Wharf, Monterey.

Sanctuary Cruises www.sanctuarycruises.com, 831-643-0128, 831-917-1042, A Dock, Moss Landing Harbor.

Whale Watching Adventures www.whalewatchingadventures.net, 877-393-0264, 831-393-0264, 96 Fisherman's Wharf, Monterey.

SHOPPING

The past, the present and a plethora of cultural styles form the backdrop for the area's inviting network of shopping districts. From Spanish-style arcades to boutiques housed in Victorian gingerbread homes, the shopping is vigorous and plentiful. Antiques and collectibles from all over the world, housed in old barns, canneries and sleek adobe shops, repeat the pattern of trade in an era where most goods were brought in from "Back East" or "Around the Horn."

Antiques and Collectibles

Alicia's Antiques 831-372-1423, 835 Cannery Row, Monterey. Run by a former pal of John Steinbeck's, this atmospheric time warp is a bastion of ambiance-bathed antiques and jewelry, each one bearing a story the proprietress will be happy to share.

Carmel Valley Antiques & Collectibles 831-624-3414, Valley Hills Shopping Center, Carmel Valley. The focus is on vintage quilts, glassware, antique furniture, jewelry and accessories, plus oodles more to make your past-perfect mouth water.

Hamlin Antiques 831-633-3664, Moss Landing Rd., Moss Landing. A great old building stuffed to the rafters with wonderful items from showbiz days gone by. Vaudeville, early Hollywood talkies, Broadway and even the minstrel-show era are all represented.

Moss Landing Antique & Trading Co. 831-633-3988, Moss Landing Rd., Moss Landing. One of the best of a plethora of fine and funky antiques stores lining the pier of this fishing village. Strong on turn-of-the-20th-century estate collections.

Trotter's Antiques 831-373-3505, 301–303 Forest Ave., Pacific Grove. Discerning collection of fine, rare and invariably exquisite antique furniture and appointments from the 18th and 19th centuries.

The Tuck Box 831-624-6365, Dolores, bet. Ocean St. & 7th Ave., Carmel. Famous since 1925 as an utterly quaint tearoom, this slice of fairy-tale charm also sells petite and precious porcelain gifts, cookbooks, teapots and preserves. A local landmark.

Arts & Crafts

Anderle Gallery www.anderle.com, 831-624-4199, Lincoln, bet. Ocean & 7th Aves. Carmel. One-of-a-kind furnishings, accessories, antiques and tribal art from the far-flung corners of the world are tastefully displayed. The store is geared toward the knowledgeable collector.

Ansel Adams Gallery 831-375-7215, the Inn at Spanish Bay, Pebble Beach. Samplings from the great photographer's huge collection are available for sale. Work by other gifted photograpers is also on view, as are Native American jewelry and fine crafts from the Americas.

Carmel Art Association 831-624-6176, Dolores St., bet. 5th & 6th Aves., Carmel. Since the 1930s, this respected gallery has showcased the oil paintings, graphics, sculpture and watercolors of the best California artists.

Coast Galleries 831-624-2002, across from the Lodge on 17 Mile Dr., Pebble Beach. A glorious mixed bag of Old Masters and contemporary regional artworks. Of special interest are the collections of original watercolors and prints by former Big Sur resident and literary giant Henry Miller. (Another location is on Hwy. 1, 3 miles south of Ventana/Nepenthe, 831-667-2301.)

Conway of Asia 831-624-3643, Ocean & 7th Aves., Carmel. Fabulous art treasures from Tibet and lands to the east fill this fabulous gallery, including Himalayan altars, ancient Buddhas, silks, brocades, icons and a sensual array of Oriental rugs.

Elkhorn Studio 831-632-0252, 8048B Moss Landing Rd., Moss Landing. This collectively run studio-gallery sings with

---

Unnamed Collectibles

In a town that prides itself on its bevy of stores that trade in antiques and collectibles, this is the best. This store (which still doesn't have a name) is clean, well organized and has a certain pizzazz that its neighbors lack. It is the antithesis of the other Moss Landing shops, most of which are musty, junky, cluttered and out of whack price-wise. The day we visited, Rob (a kindly gent behind the front desk) was beguiling a customer—even quoting Omar Khayyám—with the lore behind an object she was considering buying. Everything here is classy, in good condition, affordable and truly worth collecting (no phone, 8048A Moss Landing Rd., Moss Landing).

quality. The works of sculptor-painter Michel Tsouris and jewelry maker Elizabeth Haughton are praiseworthy, and the impressive functional precast concrete furniture of Mark Concrete is at once intimate and monumental. Gail Gering's functional metal sculptures glow with a halcyon patina and still hint at a bright tomorrow. Regional images are the forte of photographer Barbara Miller, and jeweler Carolyn Van Housen's work is modern and archaic simultaneously.

Gallery Sur 831-626-2615, 6th Ave. & Dolores St., Carmel. A photographic gallery in this hotbed of gallery action showcases breathtaking seascapes of the Central Coast by top local photographers, such as Helmut Horn and Joann Dost.

Hart Gallery www.hartgallery.com, 831-622-7110, Ocean Ave., bet. Dolores & Lincoln Sts., Carmel. Nicole Montalba has assembled some wonderful artists under one roof, and a classy collection it is indeed. Limited-edition whimsical sculptures by Siegfried Neuenhausen are steals.

Nido www.nidomosslanding.com, 7951 Moss Landing Rd., Moss Landing. This shop is part gallery, part furniture store. The lamps (especially) are dazzling and affordable.

Photography West Gallery www.photographywest.com, 831-625-1587, Dolores St., bet. Ocean & 7th Aves., Carmel. The heavyweights of Carmel's internationally recognized photographic community—Ansel Adams, Edward Weston, Imogen Cunningham and others—are represented here.

Tribes Gallery www.tribesgallery.com, 831-625-5100, San Carlos St. & Ocean Ave., Carmel. The finest beaded and yarn art of the Huichol Indians has been gathered here under one roof. Other Meso-American and African items also are for sale. A very colorful place.

Village Artistry 831-624-7628, Dolores St., bet. Ocean & 7th Aves., Carmel. Bold and colorful contemporary blown glass, hand-wrought jewelry, fanciful furniture and exquisite ceramics jam this bastion of fine local arts and crafts.

Weston Gallery www.westongallery.com, 831-624-4453, 6th Ave. near Dolores St., Carmel. Named for Carmel's famous native son, photographer Edward Weston, the gallery features exceptional 19th- and 20th-century photographs, including the work of another local legend, Ansel Adams.

Books

Bay Books 831-375-1855, 316 Alvarado St., Monterey. An easy walk to historic downtown or Fisherman's Wharf makes this a great bookstore to visit. Bay Books has discounts on best sellers and many fiction titles, plus they special-order titles

Books, Inc. 831-625-0440, Ocean & Junipero Aves., Carmel Plaza, Carmel. This 25-year-old independent bookstore in Carmel specializes in mysteries, travel and local history, but has books of all types on its shelves, including *New York Times* best sellers and a large selection of marked-down books in the back of the store.

The Book Tree 831-373-0228, 118 Webster St., Monterey. Specializing in foreign-language books, women's studies, classics and children's literature, this shop also boasts plenty of best sellers.

Bookworks 831-372-2242, 667 Lighthouse Ave., Pacific Grove. An in-house coffeehouse serves espresso, croissants and light sandwiches to denizens who comb the endless shelves for regional authors, every newspaper under the sun, foreign-language classics and books for children.

Old Capitol Books 831-375-2665, 639A Lighthouse Ave., Monterey. A central location and big windows facing the street make this large used-book store one of the most comfortable in Monterey County. Old Capitol has a great collection of history and art books, with plentiful and clean shelves for other popular genres too.

Old Monterey Book Co. 831-372-3111, 136 Bonifacio Place, Monterey. Those on the lookout for that rare, unusual and out-of-print classic will revel in the discerning possibilities tucked away in this popular shop.

Pilgrim's Way 831-624-4955, Dolores, bet. 5th & 6th Aves., Carmel. Metaphysics, philosophy and health are the emphases here. Pilgrim's Way also has an extensive collection of books on Native American culture, psychology and mythology, and a selection of greeting cards.

Thunderbird Bookshop 831-624-1803, The Barnyard, Hwy. 1 & Carmel Valley Rd., Carmel. This landmark bookstore is packed with a stellar collection of current and classic works and offers an adjoining restaurant for lingering long over your latest purchase.

Yesterday's Books www.abebooks.com/home/guyrodriguez, 877-892-5555, 831-633-8033, 7902 Sand Holt Rd., Moss Landing. A vast collection of the good, the bad and the hard to find. A few gems await the more-than-casual investigator.

Fashion

Buff Lagrange 831-625-6506, Lincoln St. & Ocean Ave., Carmel. Exceptional European clothing in sensuous fabrics, wonderful cuts and the latest designs.

Catherine's 831-646-1565, 405 Calle Principal, Monterey. Somewhere between outrageously expensive and very cheap, Monterey is blessed with Catherine's boutique, selling women's clothes and accessories that are tasteful, hip and affordable.

Girl Boy Girl 831-626-3368, Mission St. & 7th Ave., Carmel. Featuring the trendiest of the trends by only the most chichi designers, this store (self-billed as selling gourmet women's clothing) features dresses, bags, shirts, skirts and more by BCBG, Cynthia Rowley, Nicole Miller and others.

Loes Hinse 831-620-1060, Lincoln St., bet. Ocean & 7th Aves., Carmel. Creating timeless clothing for modern women's needs, in the boardroom and on the dance floor, is Hinse's mission. She carries only her own designs, all of which are elegant, beautifully crafted, unique and chic.

Reincarnation Antique Clothing 831-649-0689, 214 17th St., Pacific Grove. Carrying on the timeless California tradition of vintage fashion, this charming store invokes high-fashion nostalgia with its amazing selection of earlier-epoch clothing, jewelry, hats and irresistible accessories.

Jewelry

Fourtané Estate Jewelers 831-624-4684, Ocean Ave. at Lincoln Ave., Carmel. Scrumptious and elegant jewelry, watches and objets d'art from the 19th and 20th centuries make this splendid treasure trove of vintage estate luxuries a must visit.

Jewel Boutique 831-625-1016, The Barnyard, Carmel Valley Rd., Carmel. Custom-designed and imported jewelry shares this shop with fabulous antique and estate items.

Mark Areias Jewelers 831-624-5621, 5th Ave. & San Carlos St., Carmel. This authorized Cartier dealer stocks bedazzling baubles both contemporary and antique.

Silver Feather Trading Company 831-624-3622, Carmel Plaza, Carmel. A cache of turquoise and silver fuels the visual appeal of this gorgeously stocked dealer in authentic American Indian jewelry and artwork.

Specialty and Eclectic

Carmel Candy & Confection Company 831-625-3559, Ocean & Junipero Aves., Carmel. The candy store sells something for all species of the sweet tooth. From imported taffies to the most sinful dark chocolates to the hard candy you'd eat when you were a tyke, this confection company has it all.

The Cheese Shop 831-625-2272, Carmel Plaza, Carmel. Undecided about which Italian varietal will match perfectly with an aged cheese? The Cheese Shop is one-stop shopping for wines that range from cheap and tasty to expensive and delicious. The friendly and knowledgeable staff also offers tastings of all the cheeses in the house.

The Jazz Store www.thejazzandbluescompany.com, 831-624-6432, The Eastwood Building, San Carlos St. at 5th Ave., Carmel. This is the world's only all-jazz store. New and vintage records and CDs share space with art, memorabilia, clothing, books, instruments, posters, videos, photographs and all the cool things that America's true art form has developed over its long reign.

Nielsen Brothers Market www.nielsenbros.com, 831-624-6441, corner of San Carlos St. & 7th Ave., Carmel. A godsend to the Carmel neighborhoods for the last 75 years, Nielsen Brothers stocks the finest regional wines (check out the wine-tasting room on the premises) and mounds of quality foods (great vegetables and fruit), as well as gourmet deli entrées to go. The kind folks here will even deliver to your B&B or hotel room.

Wings America www.wingsamerica.com, 831-626-9464, Dolores St. & 7th Ave., Carmel. Anything having to do with vintage flying machines and flight in general can be found on these shelves. Fashion, knickknacks, games, sculptures, collectibles, etc. From classy to tacky, if you are a junior airman or airwoman, this is your heaven.

Sports

Golf Arts & Imports 831-625-4488, 6th Ave. & Dolores St., Carmel. Golf widows and linksmen alike will be fascinated by this whimsical conglomeration of golf art, reproductions and historical originals. Oodles of golf antiques and paraphernalia like Scottish tartan club covers and golf logo silk ties from Italy are available.

Every April, the Big Sur International Marathon offers running enthusiasts one of the world's best stretches to exercise their obsession.

On the Beach Surf Shop 831-646-WAVE, 693 Lighthouse Ave., Monterey. Be a surfer—or just dress like one. Everything you need is for sale, from boards and wetsuits to Rollerblades, skateboards and boogieboards. All this shop lacks is immediate proximity to great surfing.

The Treadmill 831-375-6778, 451 Washington St., Monterey, and 624-4112, 111 The Crossroads, Carmel. If the shoe fits—especially if it's designed for action—it's bound to be part of this major selection of top brands and styles for running, walking, tennis and aerobics. Active wear and fitness accessories for men and women also can be had. Similar gear for youngsters is available a few doors down at Treadmill Jr. sports boutique for kids.

SEASONAL EVENTS

January
AT&T Pebble Beach National Pro-Am 800-541-9091, Pebble Beach.
Living History Day 831-623-4881, Monterey.
Whalefest 831-644-7588, Monterey.

February
AT&T Pebble Beach National Pro-Am 800-541-9091, Pebble Beach.
John Steinbeck Birthday Party 831-372-8512, Monterey, and 831-775-4720, Salinas.
Taste of Pacific Grove 831-646-6549, Pacific Grove.

March
Colton Hall Birthday Party 831-646-5640, Old Monterey.
Dixieland Monterey 831-443-5260, Monterey.

April
Big Sur International Marathon 831-625-6226, Carmel.
Good Old Days Celebration 831-373-3304, Pacific Grove.
Wildflower Show 831-648-3116, Pacific Grove.

May
American Indian and World Cultures Festival 831-623-2379, San Juan Bautista.
Big Sur JazzFest 831-667-1530, Big Sur.
Tor House Garden Party 831-624-1813, Carmel.

June
Día de San Juan 831-623-2127, San Juan Bautista.
Mission San Antonio Fiesta 831-385-4478, Jolon.
Monterey Bay Blues Festival 831-649-6544, Monterey.
Monterey Bay Theatrefest 831-622-0100, Monterey.
Summer Art Festival 831-624-3996, Carmel.

July
Big Little Backyard Fourth of July Party 831-646-3866, Old Monterey.
Carmel Bach Festival 831-624-1521, Carmel.

August
Carmel Shakespeare Festival 831-622-0100, Carmel.
Carmel Valley Fiesta 831-659-2038, Carmel Valley.
Concours d'Elegance 831-659-0663, Pebble Beach.
County Fair 831-372-5863, Monterey.
Scottish Festival & Highland Games 831-899-3864, Monterey.
Steinbeck Festival 831-775-4720, Salinas.
Winemaker's Celebration 831-375-9400, Monterey.

September
Artichoke Festival 831-633-5202, Castroville.
Fiesta de San Carlos Borromeo 831-624-1271, Carmel.
Greek Festival 831 424 4434, Monterey.
Monterey Jazz Festival 831-373-3366, Monterey.
NCGA Public Links Championship 831-625-4653, Pebble Beach.
Old Monterey Santa Rosalia Festival 831-649-6544, Old Monterey.

October
Butterfly Parade 831-646-6520, Pacific Grove.
California Constitution Day 831-646-5640, Monterey.
Carmel Performing Arts Festival/World Music Festival 831-644-8383, Carmel.
Jewish Food Festival 831-624-2015, Carmel.
Tor House Oktoberfest 831-624-1813, Carmel.

November
Christmas Street Fair 805-772-4467, Morro Bay.
Holiday Arts and Crafts Fair 831-646-3866, Monterey.

December
American Indian Invitational Art Market 831-648-3116, Pacific Grove.
Christmas in the Adobes 831-649-7111, Monterey.
Christmas Tree Lighting 831-646-3866, Monterey.
First Night Monterey 831-373-4778, Monterey.
Holiday Arts & Crafts Fair 831-646-3866, Monterey.
La Posada and Piñata Party 831-646-3866, Old Monterey.

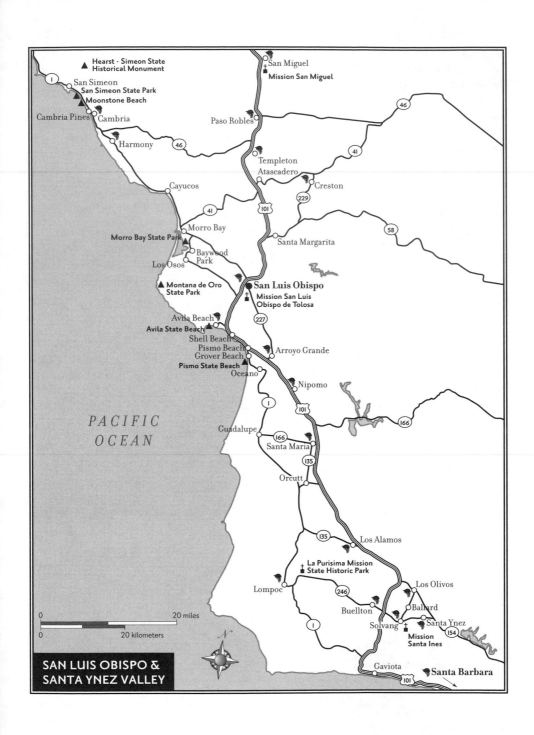

SAN LUIS OBISPO &
SANTA YNEZ VALLEY

Hearst - Simeon State
Historical Monument

San Miguel
Mission San Miguel

San Simeon
San Simeon State Park
Moonstone Beach

Cambria Pines   Cambria

Paso Robles

Harmony

46

Templeton
Atascadero

Cayucos

Creston

41

229

Morro Bay

101

Morro Bay State Park

58

Baywood
Park

Santa Margarita

Los Osos

Montana de Oro
State Park

San Luis Obispo
Mission San Luis
Obispo de Tolosa

Avila Beach
Avila State Beach

227

Shell Beach
Pismo Beach
Grover Beach

Arroyo Grande

Pismo State Beach

Oceano

Nipomo

1

101

166

PACIFIC
OCEAN

Guadalupe

166

Santa Maria

135

Orcutt

135

Los Alamos

La Purisima Mission
State Historic Park

Los Olivos

0   20 miles

Lompoc

246

Ballard

0   20 kilometers

Buellton

Santa Ynez

N

1

Solvang

154

Mission
Santa Ines

Gaviota

Santa Barbara

101

5

SAN LUIS OBISPO & THE SANTA YNEZ VALLEY

Gold Coasting

Missionaries, winemakers, ranchers, movie stars—all have found slices of paradise in this geographically diverse chunk of the Central Coast that encompasses oak-studded hillsides and coastal canyons just a few miles inland from the blue Pacific Ocean.

San Luis Obispo, a post hippie era college town retreat founded by busy Franciscan Junipero Serra, still boasts its mission in the heart of lands owned by Chumash Indian descendants. Prime cattle country, the lands around San Luis Obispo supplied the leather needs of the early Spanish settlers, just as they are ranched for beef today. California State Polytechnic College (affectionately known as Cal Poly) dominates the intellectual landscape of this small, off-the-beaten-track community. Down the coast, a series of lovely beach towns is crowned by the voluptuous sand dunes of Pismo Beach. A string of ancient volcanoes have left their dark basalt cinder cones to punctuate the undulating hills, known for their electric green in winter and explosion into riots of wildflowers each spring.

South of San Luis Obispo, the mighty Coast Ranges turn to velvet as the Santa Lucia Mountains form the soft folds of the Santa Ynez Valley. Superbly situated to take full advantage of long sunny days and fog-cooled evenings, this Eden, located a mere 10 miles from the coast, is home to award-winning wineries. The area has also established a reputation among equestrians, and has attracted landed gentry on the merits of its excellent climate and hidden-away sense of isolation. Here the ranches of the famed and mighty— entertainer Michael Jackson, cowboy idol Fess Parker, former First Lady Nancy Reagan— sprawl over incomparable acreage lush with oak forests and rich in ocean views. Driving, bicycling and hiking are all great ways to experience this area—the region lends itself to easy-access exploration. Small communities like Los Olivos oblige with secluded restaurants—movie stars have sought refuge here for years—prime bed & breakfasts, vintage motels and stellar art and crafts galleries.

LODGING

Where the emphasis is on beach-oriented action, well-appointed and conveniently located motels, ranging from oceanfront to awesomely uncategorizable, are the dominant form of lodging. Visitors will also encounter a healthy selection of cozy B&Bs, some ensconced in

The charming mission and college town of San Luis Obispo is a gateway to myriad recreational and cultural destinations. Jeff Greene

creatively renovated 19th-century hotels, offering romance, seaside gardens and rooms with a view. Here are the idiosyncratic stops that make this area such a great escape. Many of the loveliest Victorian manors of Cambria and San Luis Obispo have been transformed into inviting bed & breakfast lodgings for the comfort of the weary traveler, and fresh destination resorts have sprouted in the Santa Ynez Valley like so many wineries.

Credit cards are abbreviated as follows:
  AE: American Express
   D: Discover Card
 MC: MasterCard
   V: Visa

CAMBRIA
BEACH HOUSE BED & BREAKFAST INN
www.cambriabeachhouse.com
innkeeper@cambriabeachhouse.com

Innkeepers: Penny Hitch & Kernn MacKinnon
805-927-3136
6360 Moonstone Beach Dr., Cambria 93428
Price: $125–$275, includes full breakfast
Credit Cards: MC, V
Children: Within limitations
Pets: No
Handicap Access: Yes

Looking for all the world like a quintessential Central Coast private beach house, this comfortable wood-and-glass oceanfront home consists of seven rooms of varying sizes, all with private baths and cable TVs. Three rooms come with fireplaces, and one lofty, second-floor room provides a king-sized bed and a private deck that opens onto the stunning seascape vistas of Moonstone Beach. Refreshments, including wines and cheeses, are offered at sunset.

Morning is the best time to explore the grassy bluffs networked with inviting walking trails, which overlook the tide pools and surf just outside the front door. A full breakfast is offered each morning at the Beach House's restaurant down the street. The sunsets are beautiful, and Hearst Castle is 15 minutes up Highway 1.

BLUE DOLPHIN INN

www.bluedolphininn.com
info@bluedolphininn.com
Innkeeper: Devin Platte
805-927-3300, fax 805-927-7311
6470 Moonstone Beach Dr.,
Cambria 93428
Price: $59–319, includes continental breakfast
Credit Cards: AE, D, MC, V
Children: Yes
Pets: No
Handicap Access: Yes

The Blue Dolphin Inn is widely recognized as one of the Central Coast's top romantic getaways. Here, the ambiance of a European country inn meets spectacular ocean views. The inn's uniquely colorful decor adds to the atmosphere of extravagance, while arrays of English country fabrics and furnishings ensure ample comforts. Large whirlpool tubs, canopy beds and fireplaces are among the amenities that contribute to the romantic ambiance. The village of Cambria awaits just a mile away with fine dining and wine tasting, while Hearst Castle is just a short drive up the coast.

BLUE WHALE INN

www.bluewhaleinn.com
innkeepers@bluewhaleinn.com
Innkeepers: Jay & Karen Peavler
800-753-9000, 805-927-4647
6736 Moonstone Beach Dr., Cambria 93428
Price: $219–$349, full breakfast
Credit Cards: AE, D, MC, V

Children: Within limitations
Pets: No
Handicap Access: Yes

Each of this B&B's six spacious rooms is decorated with soft pastel upholstry, plump comforters, canopy swags, comfortable couches, charming wallpaper, vaulted ceilings and airy skylighting. A long, dressing-area counter is appointed with beautifully packaged amenities, and there's an in-room refrigerator, a fireplace, a separate bathroom, with a view of the rolling hills behind the shoreline, and cable TV tucked away in a colorful armoire. You can hear the soothing waves all night long. You could live forever in these rooms. But most guests enjoy taking in the sunset while sipping complimentary wine or gazing through the telescope in the main lounge at whales and waterfowl cruising the coast. An inviting get-together, featuring wine and gourmet appetizers, is held afternoons in the picture-window-lined dining room, where full breakfasts are also served, usually involving terrific coffee, fresh juices and fruits, as well as gingerbread pancakes with lemony syrup fresh from the adjoining kitchen. Regular visitors to the inn like to take a bracing walk along the hiking trails lacing the bluffs over spectacular Moonstone Beach, which is across the lane from the inn. This is one of the best overnights this area has to offer.

FOGCATCHER INN

www.fogcatcherinn.com
reservations@fogcatcherinn.com
Innkeeper: Eric Snider
800-425-4121, 805-927-1400, fax 805-927-0204
6400 Moonstone Beach Dr.,
Cambria 93428
Price: $159–$299, includes continental breakfast
Credit Cards: AE, D, MC, V

Set on bluffs above Moonstone Beach, FogCatcher Inn is as good as its name, making for dramatic weather effects and producing a romantic atmosphere. Moonstone Hotel Properties

Children: Within limitations
Pets: Within limitations
Handicap Access: Yes

Conjuring scenes from a Brontë novel, this contemporary neo-English inn with multi-paned windows, thatched roof and subtle half-timbering offers gracious overnight accommodations a few steps from the melodic surf and endless tide pools of Moonstone Beach. Set on bluffs criss-crossed with hiking trails, the inn offers such luxuries as a heated pool and a hot tub, as well as 60 guest rooms stocked with refrigerators, fireplaces, microwaves, coffeemakers, TVs and honor bars. There's even a bridal suite—remember, this is honeymoon country. In the main gathering room, a complimentary breakfast of muffins, coffee, cereals, fresh fruit and juices tunes up guests for a day of beach-combing, antiquing in Cambria village or touring the eye-popping sights of San Simeon.

J. PATRICK HOUSE
www.jpatrickhouse.com
jph@jpatrickhouse.com
Innkeeper: Syd Hickman
800-341-5258, 805-927-3812,
fax 805-927-6759
2990 Burton Dr., Cambria 93428
Price: $165–$205, includes full breakfast
Credit Cards: AE, D, MC, V
Children: No
Handicap Access: No

A cozy, two-story log house, situated in the pines overlooking Cambria's east village, this old homestead fronts an old-fashioned arbor leading to the eight guest rooms—seven with wood-burning fireplaces and all with private baths. The early American decor of the main house is echoed in the attractive rooms, which are liberally adorned with floral wallpaper and wicker furniture. Afternoon wine and cheese are offered in front of the sitting room fireplace, and each morning the sunny dining room serves up a full breakfast highlighted by freshly ground coffee, fruits, fresh-squeezed juices, blintzes with raspberry sauce, stuffed French toast and homemade cinnamon rolls. At bedtime, guests receive fresh chocolate chip cookies and cold milk in their rooms. Personalized service and friendly atmosphere come with the attractive turf.

✪ MCCALL FARM
BED & BREAKFAST INN
www.mccallfarm.com
innkeeper@mccallfarm.com
Innkeepers: Teri & Jack McCall
805 927 3140, 805 909 1201
6520 Santa Rosa Creek Rd., Cambria 93428
Price: $125–$155, includes full breakfast
Credit Cards: MC, V
Children: No
Pets: No
Handicap Access: No

Nestled just 15 minutes from the village of Cambria, the McCall Farm Bed & Breakfast is at the forefront of the farm-visit movement and proves to be a nostalgic haven in a chaotic world. Staying here is like traveling back in time to a beloved grandmother's home. The house containing this historic B&B was built in 1885 and rests on 20 secluded acres among fruit trees and gardens. Hosts Teri and Jack McCall converted two rooms to accommodate visitors a few years ago, and the welcome the family provides is at once warm and genuine. The downstairs parlor sports a satellite TV, and as you sit and sip wine and eat cheese, you feel as if you are staying overnight at a friend's residence. The upstairs Rose Room

overlooks the back lawn and its persimmon tree, and its comfy queen-sized bed and partial canopy, antiques and quilts all conspire to transport you to a slower, long-gone era. Guests are invited to wander the garden and eat any of the delicious tomatoes, avocados, apples or other fruits and vegetables in season (the McCalls supply many of the area's best restaurants and set up their own stands at five of the region's farmers' markets). The farewell breakfast consists of blueberry pancakes, juice made from oranges picked minutes before, homemade applesauce and tea and coffee. As you drive away, you will already be formulating plans for a return visit.

OLALLIEBERRY INN
www.olallieberry.com
info@olallieberry.com
Innkeepers: Marjorie Ott, Marilyn & Larry Draper
888-927-3222, 805-927-3222, fax 805-927-0202
2476 Main St., Cambria 93428
Price: $100–$190, includes full breakfast
Credit Cards: AE, MC, V
Children: Within limitations
Pets: No
Handicap Access: Yes

A period-decorated 1873 Greek Revival home provides nine inviting rooms, six with fireplaces and each with private bath, updated for contemporary convenience at no sacrifice of yesteryear ambiance. The main parlor is the setting for evening wine tastings with appetizers, and more than one libation has been enjoyed at the wooded glade and creek bordered by the inn's back lawn. Each guest room is uniquely decorated, with Victorian antiques accentuating the graceful high ceilings. A full breakfast greets guests in the morning, and the turn-of-the-20th-century cottages, shops and galleries of downtown Cambria are a pleasant stroll away.

PELICAN SUITES
www.pelicansuites.com
info@pelicansuites.com
Innkeeper: Becky Siemes
800-222-91602, 805-927-1500,
fax 805-927-0218
6316 Moonstone Beach Dr., Cambria 93428
Price: $109–479, includes full breakfast
Credit Cards: AE, D, MC, V
Children: Yes
Pets: No
Handicap Access: Yes

Old World luxury meets first-class amenities at this elegant seaside getaway. While picturesque Moonstone Beach is just steps away, the suites themselves hold equal allure, with their comfortable furnishings and other appointments, such as European fabrics, whirlpool tubs, cozy window seats and fireplaces. Many rooms feature full ocean views and canopy beds, as well as patios or balconies. The charming village of Cambria —with its abundant shops, art galleries, cafes and bistros—is nearby, but you may find yourself just staying put and luxuriating in the coastal scenery and rich ambiance that surrounds the inn. Mini refrigerators, in-room high-speed Internet access and full breakfasts are other added touches.

MORRO BAY
INN AT MORRO BAY
www.innatmorrowbay.com
Innkeeper: Sam Ebeid
800-321-9566, 805-772-5651,
fax 805-772-4779
60 State Park Rd., Morro Bay 93442
Price: $79–500
Credit Cards: AE, D, MC, V
Children: Yes
Pets: No
Handicap Access: Yes

Overlooking the glittering expanse of Morro Bay and its dramatic Morro Rock (and just a 30-minute drive from Hearst Castle), this full-service facility offers inviting accommodations. Swim in the expansive pool, sip local wines while enjoying the breathtaking view or enjoy breakfast in your own brass bed. Rooms, many with fireplaces, offer full amenities, and the inn's restaurant serves up fine seafood and California cuisine, featuring the area's renowned fresh produce. The beaches, trees and estuary of Morro State Park, as well as the rare waterfowl of the blue heron rookery, are right outside your window.

PASO ROBLES/TEMPLETON
✪ HOLLYHOCK FARMS
www.hollyhock-farm.com
hollyhoc@calinet.com
Innkeepers: Dick & Kim Rogers
805-239-4713
200 Hollyhock Ln., Templeton 93465
Price: $125, includes full breakfast
Credit Cards: MC, V
Children: No
Pets: No
Handicap Access: No

In the midst of Hollyhock Farms, Dick and Kim Rogers's organic spread, sits The Cottage, offering luxurious accommodations that are at the vanguard of the farm-stay movement. Modeled after the long-running and popular European program of travelers spending a few days as guests (not workers) at real farms, The Cottage places you in the ebb and flow of a full-scale produce operation. You are even free to wander the grounds and eat right from the vines. (We enjoyed a watermelon on our front porch minutes after picking it from the field.) Nestled in the Templeton hills, the comfortable small stand-alone cottage features a queen-sized bed, a state-of-the-art climate control system, a wet bar, sitting area and a video/satellite unit with dozens of first-rate movies. Country antiques and heirloom Danish draperies brighten the room, and the fruits and delicious baby tomatoes, wine and boutique beers that are provided upon your arrival help you sink right into the warm hospitality of the innkeepers and their farm interns. A full gourmet breakfast prepared by Kim provides a leisurely meal, during which you can listen to fascinating stories told by Dick, a former homicide detective. If you choose, you can explore the 30-acre farm and pick peaches, grapes, apples, melons and heirloom tomatoes. The Rogerses will help guide you to the best dining spots, tasting rooms and country back roads the region offers and otherwise leave you to your private reveries and pursuits. This is one charming stay.

PISMO BEACH
SANDCASTLE INN
www.sandcastleinn.com
Innkeeper: Tom Burke
800-822-6606, 805-773-2422,
fax 805-773-0771
100 Stimson Ave., Pismo Beach 93449
Price: $169–$309, includes breakfast
Credit Cards: AE, D, MC, V
Children: Yes
Pets: Within limitations
Handicap Access: Yes

Attractions of this very contemporary, Mediterranean seaside retreat include plump couches and chairs, huge beds with soothing floral prints and a plethora of ocean views available from the patios, decks and picture windows. Fifty-nine overnight rooms, including suites with fireplaces, offer complete comfort and views of the picturesque fishing pier and oceanfront. Each room has its own TV/VCR, refrigerator and coffeemaker. A complimentary continental breakfast greets guests in the morning, and the best place to enjoy breakfast, just after you've exited the swirling Jacuzzi, is on the glass-enclosed deck.

SEAVENTURE HOTEL
www.seaventure.com
info@seaventure.com
Innkeeper: John King

800-662-5545, 805-773-4994,
fax 805-773-4693
100 Ocean View Ave., Pismo Beach 93449
Price: $129–$349, includes continental breakfast
Credit Cards: AE, D, MC, V
Children: Yes
Pets: No
Handicap Access: Yes

Fifty comfortable rooms—20 with spas and wet bars, some with private decks, all with cable TV, CD players, feather beds and fireplaces—serve as the perfect headquarters for exploring the endless seashore recreational opportunities of this popular coastal resort. Located right on the beach, the full-service destination resort boasts its own rooftop restaurant, vibrant cocktail lounge, therapeutic massage center and heated swimming pool for those foggy morning laps. Complimentary beach chairs and towels are available for guest use. A substantial continental breakfast is included in the very reasonable overnight rate and, yes, the setting is shamelessly romantic.

SAN LUIS OBISPO
APPLE FARM INN
www.applefarm.com
Innkeeper: Dean Hutton
800-374-3705, 805-544-2040,
fax 805-546-9495
2015 Monterey St., San Luis Obispo 93401
Price: $79–$359
Credit Cards: AE, D, MC, V
Children: Yes
Pets: No
Handicap Access: Yes

Even an overworked word like "charming" finds new currency in reference to this Victorian inn, which is a veritable country village of cozy overnight rooms threaded in and around an old mill house. Four-poster beds, flowered wallpaper, ruffled linens, overstuffed couches and deep tubs add romance to the very contemporary

The overnight rooms of Apple Farm Inn in San Luis Obispo nestle by an old mill house and working farm.

Apple Hill Farm Inn

amenities like a heated swimming pool and a Jacuzzi. Each room boasts its own fireplace, and morning brings coffee or tea to your room (the inn's fine restaurant serves a full range of culinary classics). Enjoy splendid views of the surrounding hills and the throwback charm of a huge waterwheel turning hypnotically on its 19th-century foundations.

GARDEN STREET INN

www.gardenstreetinn.com
Innkeeper: Candi Mabee
805-545-9802, fax 805-545-9403
1212 Garden St., San Luis Obispo 93401
Price: $145–$205, includes full breakfast
Credit Cards: AE, MC, V
Children: Within limitations
Pets: No
Handicap Access: Yes

The high ceilings, grand staircase and jewel-like, stained-glass trimmings of this

1887 Italianate Queen Anne have been lovingly restored to the heyday atmosphere of this frontier town. Tastefully decorated with antiques and artistic family memorabilia, the inn offers nine rooms and four suites, each with private bath. Romantics will love the six rooms with fireplaces and whirlpool tubs, as well as the evening wine-and-cheese selection. There's a well-stocked library for the enjoyment of guests, and a full homemade breakfast is served amid the original stained-glass splendor of the house's Morning Room.

MADONNA INN

www.madonnainn.com
Innkeeper: Phyllis Madonna
800-543-9666, 805-543-3000, fax 805-543-1800
100 Madonna Rd., San Luis Obispo 93401
Price: $137–$238
Credit Cards: AE, D, MC, V

Children: Yes
Pets: No
Handicap Access: Yes

There's simply nothing like the Madonna Inn, an only-in-California poem to fantasy and excess in ubiquitous stonework and shocking pink, where each room is decorated like a B-movie set. No one ever forgets an overnight in the cavelike Flintstones Suite with its rock waterfall shower, or the men's room with its own waterfall urinal—straight from central casting. A no-holds-barred "motel," this epic of red velvet and chandelier overkill (matched by an architectural hodgepodge of an exterior) is wonderful fun for those who really want an experience that they can write home about. Expect to be amazed by the eccentric decor of every one of the 110 rooms and suites, all with cable TVs. The bar looks like an old-fashioned carousel, and the amazing restaurant (yes, you have seen it in many Hollywood movies) serves up serious homemade fare and gargantuan barbecued steaks. There are oodles of souvenir, gift, clothing and coffee shops. You may not be planning a second honeymoon, but you'll wind up having one anyway, given the fantasy sensory bombardment.

SANTA YNEZ VALLEY

ALISAL GUEST RANCH

www.alisal.com
Innkeeper: David Lautensack
800-4-ALISAL, 805-688-6411,
fax 805-688-2510
1054 Alisal Rd., Solvang 93463
Price: $385–$550, includes breakfast & dinner
Credit Cards: AE, D, MC, V
Children: Yes
Pets: No
Handicap Access: Yes

Part guest ranch, part golf resort and all western hospitality, this legendary facility opened its 10,000 acres of working ranch to guests in 1946. Some visitors never leave the sprawling grounds, with their swimming pool, tennis courts and two golf courses with PGA professionals on staff. Others fish for catfish, bluegill and large-mouth bass or sail on the ranch's 100 acre lake. But most come to strip away the cares of civilization and to ride the miles of unparalleled equestrian trails winding through magnificent hills and sycamore groves. Leaving at dawn, wranglers lead guests into the beautiful country where a campfire breakfast of ham, eggs and pancakes awaits. But it's not all rustic. After cocktails at the Oak Room Lounge, guests can enjoy California cuisine in the Old West ambiance of the dining room. Overnight rooms all boast fireplaces and cozy decor. A two-night minimum is required, and during midweek and most weekends, all golf, tennis and horseback riding are free as part of the package deal. The ranch also offers year-round activities for children, including riding lessons, a petting zoo and an arts-and-crafts program. This is a very special getaway for those who like to "rough it" in style.

Solvang's Alisal Guest Ranch is a very special getaway for those who like to "rough it" in style.
Alisal Guest Ranch

✪ BALLARD INN

www.ballardinn.com
Innkeeper: Christine Forsyth
800-638-2466, 805-688-7770, fax 688-9560
2436 Baseline Ave., Ballard 93463
Price: $215–$315, includes full breakfast
Credit Cards: AE, MC, V
Children: Within limitations
Pets: Within limitations
Handicap Access: Yes

Fronted by one of tiny Ballard's two or three streets, this contemporary inn looks like it stepped out of the late 19th century with its wraparound veranda, polished wood dining room and antiques-filled overnight rooms. Each room holds its own special charm, built around Old West themes and featuring fine craft work, brass and wicker beds and magnificent comforters, quilts and upholsteries, plus Victorian armoires and commodes transformed into sinks. Seven of the 15 rooms have wood-burning fireplaces, and each has a full private bath. The welcoming parlor lays out an amazing afternoon appetizer display, which can include fresh fruit, delicious warm appetizers, cheeses, house-made pickled vegetables, along with excellent vintages of Santa Ynez wineries. The inn's friendly staff serves up a

The modern Ballard Inn in the Santa Ynez Valley wine country re-creates the 1800s with its veranda and antiques-filled rooms. Buz Bezore

glorious full breakfast of perfect soft-boiled eggs, thick slabs of country bacon, killer diced potatoes and French toast with maple syrup, and a continental buffet is also laid on a carved sideboard. After breakfast, a tour of this captivating wine country is in order via the Ballard's complimentary mountain bikes. The Ballard also is home to the Ballard Restaurant and the wonderful creations of Budi Kazali. Doyenne Christina Kazali and innkeeper Christine Forsyth and their staff have earned the inn a four-diamond AAA award for 11 consecutive years, and they are highly knowledgeable about the local microwineries and will guide you to memorable tastings. No telephones, data-ports or TVs in the individual rooms, so guests can remained unplugged if they so wish. There is a desk work space and large TV for those who want to stay in touch with the outside world. The only caveat is that guests will find it almost impossible to leave.

✪ FESS PARKER WINE COUNTRY INN AND SPA

www.fessparker.com
Innkeeper: Bill Phelps
800-446-2455, 805-688-7788, fax 805-688-1942
2860 Grand Ave., Los Olivos 93441
Price: $260–$500, includes continental breakfast
Credit Cards: AE, MC, V
Children: Yes
Pets: Within limitations
Handicap Access: Yes

Situated in the gemlike western village of Los Olivos, this luxury hideaway combines turn-of-the-20th-century atmosphere with thoroughly 21st-century comforts. A terrific base from which to explore the scenic wineries of the Santa Ynez Valley, the elegant hotel boasts 21 spacious overnight rooms, plus public rooms, an award-winning restaurant, a swimming pool and a

The Fess Parker Wine Country Inn and Spa combines turn-of-the-20th-century atmosphere with thoroughly 21st-century comforts—a terrific base from which to explore the scenic wineries of the Santa Ynez Valley. Kim Reierson

Jacuzzi. Each room has been tastefully decorated in period style with armoires, brass beds, floral comforters and antique chandeliers. Every room also boasts a fireplace, TV, wet bar and refrigerator. Guests can relax poolside or can stroll the hotel's arbors and gardens after the complementary full breakfast or afternoon wine and appetizers. Complimentary mountain cycles are available for touring tiny Los Olivos, its art galleries and wine-tasting rooms. Everyone in the valley seems to show up for the Thursday- night songfest, with visiting celebrities and Hollywood glitterati with second homes in the area grabbing the microphone and belting out a few show tunes.

✪ UNION HOTEL AND VICTORIAN MANSION

www.unionhotelvictorianmansion.com
unionhotel2003@aol.com
Innkeeper: Christine Williams
800-230-2744, 805-344-2744
362 Bell St., Los Alamos 93440

Price: $135–$235, includes full breakfast
Credit Cards: AE, D, MC, V
Children: Within limitations
Pets: No
Handicap Access: No

In the heart of Santa Barbara County, in a tiny western town that time has nearly forgotten, sits the most unusual and romantic bed & breakfast in the state. The Union Hotel and Victorian Mansion is a funky, campy one-of-a-kind oasis amid the froufrou with which most B&Bs adorn themselves. It has, in its delicious past, been a historic 1880s stagecoach stop, a railroad hotel, a brothel, a speakeasy, a honky-tonk and a country-and-western music showcase. As you pass through its doors, you step back to a simpler yet elegant era. This unique and charming Union Hotel offers museum-quality antiques and period decor, while its adjoining sibling, the intriguing Victorian Mansion, creates a world of dreams unlike anything you may have encountered on your travels. During the 1960s and 1970s, 10 years were spent renovating the 1864 Victorian into a fantasyland of cornball Hollywood visions, creating six theme rooms with hidden bathrooms, spiral staircases, elevated beds, coffee tables made from cannons, an Egyptian mummy, a chariot and a 1956 Cadillac used as props and curiosities. Each of the rooms includes a romantic hot tub for two, fireplace, TV, VCR with classic films of the era, and a complimentary breakfast delivered to your room. Guests can sidle up to the bar in the Union and order a long cool one. The hotel's saloon is the real thing, originally built in 1880 for thirsty travelers on the California Stagecoach Line. The innkeeper claims "the jukebox is haunted, the shuffleboard is free and the drinks are frosty." The hotel also hosts special events like the weekend Stagecoach Murder Mysteries, 1800s Historical Costume Balls and dinner music concerts. Many visitors return over and over again, knowing that each visit offers a different experience. This is definably one of the most unusual and fun overnights on the Central Coast.

Dining

In addition to sparkling fresh seafood harvested each day from teeming Pacific waters, this area headlines its long-standing tradition for serious western dining, involving aromatic oak pit grills, steaks slathered in barbecue sauce, even buffalo burgers. The exceptional produce from surrounding small farms is legendary, even in a state graced with a year-round growing season. The following San Luis Obispo and Santa Ynez Valley eateries provide some of the top gastronomic occasions to experience the best this stretch of California has to offer.

Dining Price Code

The price range below includes the cost of a single dinner that includes an entrée, appetizer or dessert, and glass of wine or beer. Tax and gratuities are not included. Note: Smoking is not allowed in any restaurant or eatery in the state of California

Inexpensive	Up to $15
Moderate	$15–$30
Expensive	$30–$50
Very Expensive	$50 or more

Credit cards are abbreviated as follows:
AE — American Express
D — Discover
MC — MasterCard
V — Visa

AVILA BEACH
OLD CUSTOM HOUSE
805-595-7555
324 Front St., Avila Beach
Open: Breakfast, lunch & dinner daily
Price: Moderate

Cuisine: Continental/seafood
Full Bar: Yes
Reservations: No
Credit Cards: AE, D, MC, V
Handicap Access: Yes

In 1927, when San Luis Obispo Bay was an official U.S. port of entry, this simple and charming structure was built to house the business of customs. Today it serves as a waterfront restaurant, specializing in the fresh seafoods harvested along the Central Coast. The outdoor patio dining is very popular, affording soothing views of gardens and fish ponds and warding off marine fog with strategically placed heaters. An oak pit barbecue turns out beef and pork classics, and the casual breakfasts offer eggs cooked every way imaginable. Since a rebuilding effort turned the legendary building into two businesses (Mr. Rick's Bar is the other) in 2002, a lot of nouvelle touches have appeared on the menu, mostly in the form of grilled seafood. Still, you can still order oldies like beef stroganoff to your heart's delight (if not longevity), and the cabana attitude doesn't interfere will the classic Continental ambiance.

CAMBRIA
BRAMBLES
805-927-4716
4005 Burton Dr., Cambria
Open: Dinner nightly, brunch Sun.
Price: Moderate to Expensive
Cuisine: Continental
Full Bar: Yes
Reservations: Recommended
Credit Cards: AE, D, MC, V
Handicap Access: Yes

Long one Cambria's top dinner houses, Brambles occupies an English-style home built in 1874. Over the years, numerous additions have turned the building into a set of charming dining rooms surrounded by a thicket of garden. While prime rib with Yorkshire pudding is a house signature, the salmon broiled over the oakwood pit is exceptional, as are all of the fresh, Continental seafood dishes. Stellar steaks come sizzling from the oakwood pit, and a selection of attractive chicken and pasta specialties rounds out the menu. Greek and Caesar salads are created from the fresh bounty of small Central Coast market gardens. Sampling regional wines that are difficult to come by outside the area is made effortless by the restaurant's extensive wine list, winner of a *Wine Spectator* Award for Excellence.

LINN'S MAIN BIN

805-927-0371
2277 Main St., Cambria
Open: Breakfast, lunch & dinner daily
Price: Moderate
Cuisine: Country American
Full Bar: No
Reservations: No
Credit Cards: AE, D, MC, V
Handicap Access: Yes

A Cambria original, located on picturesque Old West Main St., Linn's is partly a huge cafe—like an American country tearoom— and partly a gourmet gift shop and bakery. The area's largest regional wine list complements a homemade menu, strong on soups, signature potpies and imaginative sandwiches, all fueled by the fresh produce from Linn's own nearby farms.

MUSTACHE PETE'S

805-927-8589
4090 Burton Dr., Cambria
Open: Lunch & dinner daily
Price: Inexpensive to Moderate
Cuisine: Italian
Full Bar: Yes
Reservations: Yes
Credit Cards: AE, D, MC, V
Handicap Access: Downstairs accessible, main restaurant is not

The front of this convivial hangout is a laid-back sports bar, complete with pool table.

Behind that a spacious Italian eatery takes over. Sooner or later, everybody in town stops by to see friends, unwind over a beer or feast on two-fisted pizzas topped with everything from pesto to roasted garlic chicken. There's fresh seafood turned into substantial scampi, cioppino and Alfredo specialties, and plenty of Italian chicken classics. The pastas come loaded with fine marinara, cheeses, pesto and fresh vegetables. Expect lots of local color.

✪ ROBIN'S

805-927-5007
4095 Burton Dr., Cambria
Open: Lunch & dinner daily
Price: Inexpensive to Moderate
Cuisine: Eclectic ethnic
Full Bar: No
Reservations: Recommended on summer weekends
Credit Cards: MC, V
Handicap Access: Limited

Tucked into a 1930s Spanish-style house set with antique oak tables and ethnic crafts on the walls, Robin's is a thoroughly charming, eclectic dining experience. The emphasis on delicious, natural ingredients—the menu contains a wealth of vegetarian dishes—has been sifted through ethnic cuisines ranging from the Far East to Latin America. The result is a menu with exciting spices and seasonings. Magnificent produce (a good portion of the field gems are grown by the inimitable McCall Farms), packed with just-picked flavor, powers inventive salads mated with curries, toasted nuts and glorious dressings, and the curried chicken salad sandwich served on a croissant with lettuce, tomatoes, cucumbers and toasted almonds is divine. Thai stir-fried beef explodes with the flavor of mint, ginger, garlic, chiles and peanuts, and all of the black bean and pasta dishes are imaginative. And nobody gets past the counter of lavish desserts, of which French apple pie, tiramisù and frangipane tart with wine-poached pears are only a few of the temptations. The finest from small local wineries is available by the glass or by the split, making for an excellent tasting opportunity. The patio seating, surrounded by a lush arbor, is very appealing.

SEA CHEST OYSTER BAR & RESTAURANT

805-927-4514
6216 Moonstone Beach, Cambria
Open: Dinner nightly
Price: Moderate
Cuisine: Seafood
Full Bar: No
Reservations: Recommended
Credit Cards: No

This is your quintessential fresh, fresh, fresh California oyster bar, although the attitude and ambiance are strictly Yankee seaboard. The menu includes oysters Rockefeller, steamed clams, fresh New Zealand mussels and a large and varied selection of the freshest fish available, all broiled to perfection. The Sea Chest is well known for its halibut and salmon, but the specialty of the house is cioppino. Whether you're seated in the lively front dining room and its exhibition kitchen or in the more mellow rear with its potbelly stove, the easygoing staff makes you feel like a long-standing regular. The oysters on the half shell are the best around.

SOW'S EAR CAFÉ

805-927-4865
2248 Main St., Cambria
Open: Dinner nightly
Price: Moderate
Cuisine: American
Full Bar: No
Reservations: Recommended
Credit Cards: MC, V
Handicap Access: Limited

Locally grown herbs and vegetables pack vibrant flavor into each dish graciously served and skillfully presented in this fine country cafe. The entrées run the gamut of country American favorites, all given a uniquely Central Coast spin. Shellfish linguine with Greek olives, fennel, feta cheese and tomatoes is a popular item, as are the chicken and dumplings and grill-roasted chicken breast with fresh rosemary. A lovely appetizer salad of fresh spinach is topped with sesame-crusted chicken, oranges, almonds and honey-lime dressing. The heartland attitude is continued by desserts like warm blueberry bread pudding with brandy hard sauce and milk-chocolate cheesecake with hazelnut crust. The freshly baked bread is wonderful, and the mood is unpretentiously friendly.

MORRO BAY
DORN'S ORIGINAL BREAKERS CAFÉ

805-772-4415
801 Market St., Morro Bay
Open: Breakfast, lunch & dinner daily
Price: Moderate
Cuisine: Country American
Full Bar: Yes
Reservations: Recommended on weekends
Credit Cards: D, MC, V
Handicap Access: Yes

An old World War I vintage real estate office was converted in the early 1940s to the Breakers Café. A success from the day it opened, Dorn's specializes in seafood served in the perfect inspirational setting, overlooking the dramatic, ancient volcanic plug of Morro Rock and the Morro Bay harbor. Breakfasts are served until 2pm daily, offering a huge choice of pancakes, egg dishes and French toast creations. Many in the know come for the classic Boston clam chowder and highly prized Morro Bay abalone. Freshly made pastas are also quite good.

ORCHID RESTAURANT

805-772-5651
60 Morro Bay State Park Rd., Morro Bay
Open: Breakfast, lunch & dinner daily
Price: Expensive
Cuisine: Continental
Full Bar: Yes
Reservations: Recommended
Credit Cards: AE, D, MC, V
Handicap Access: Yes

Housed in the Inn at Morro Bay—a popular, coastal overnight lodge—Orchid (formerly Paradise) showcases fine California cuisine, often with a French accent, and grand views of the ocean at Morro Bay State Park. The elegant and comfortable dining room excels in sophisticated dinners, where appetizers such as crab cakes with roasted sweet corn, tomato relish and chile lime aioli, or baby abalone with bok choy and jicama in an Asian vinaigrette appear frequently. Entrées encountered on the constantly shifting menu can include nut-crusted ahi with Moroccan couscous in a caramelized red onion sauce, or wild mushroom asparagus ragout in a Roquefort compound butter with whipped potatoes. The roast duckling arrives napped with a chipotle cream and served alongside polenta butternut squash fritters. A seafood paella with mussels, clams, calamari, shrimp and saffron risotto is especially memorable. Classic breakfasts are also served.

Nipomo
✪ JOCKO'S

805-929-3686
Tefft St. & Thomas Rd., Nipomo
Open: Breakfast, lunch & dinner daily
Price: Inexpensive to Moderate
Cuisine: Oak pit barbecue
Full Bar: Yes
Reservations: Required on weekend nights and Sun.
Credit Cards: MC, V
Handicap Access: Limited

Seemingly in the middle of a very beautiful nowhere, and conceivably the finest steak house in the country, Jocko's regularly converts even the most die-hard vegetarian. Jeff Greene

Seemingly set in the middle of a very beautiful nowhere, Jocko's is legendary throughout the Central Coast for having world-class beef. The interior decor—rife with paper place mats, hanging plants and cattle brands burned into the woodwork—seems never to have left the 1950s (when Jocko's was founded). Even the separate bar, well worn by regulars, seems from another time. But the steaks are the true Holy Grail: Massive Spencer steaks, thick, tender and loaded with the sort of flavor that invokes nostalgia, start at around $10. And that includes serious french fries, homemade tomato salsa and pots of succulent pinquito beans. Conceivably the finest steak house in the country, Jocko's regularly converts even the most die-hard vegetarian.

Paso Robles/Templeton
BISTRO LAURENT

805-226-8191
1202 Pine St., Paso Robles
Open: Lunch & dinner Mon.–Sat.

Price: Moderate
Cuisine: French
Full Bar: No
Reservations: Recommended on weekends
Credit Cards: MC, V
Handicap Access: Yes

Laurent Granngien's bistro is an unpretentious neighborhood restaurant with a welcoming atmosphere and moderate prices. Chef Granngien was a pathfinder for the emerging Paso Robles quality culinary scene and today the restaurant holds a *Wine Spectator* Award of Excellence. His crispy savory tarts and roast chicken are both mouthwatering winners. A smart way to dine here is the chef's tasting menu, where he chooses four courses to fit his and your fancies. One of the items on the changing menu may be the asparagus and shrimps in a morel and garlic sauce. If so, order it. Also sign up for the duck breast with potato galette and grape sauce, another sensation. The warm chocolate tart with vanilla sauce has reduced many an adult to weeping sobs and moans of ecstasy.

✪ MCPHEE'S GRILL
805-434-3204
416 Main St., Templeton
Open: Lunch & dinner daily
Price: Moderate
Cuisine: American
Full Bar: No
Reservations: Recommended
Credit Cards: AE, MC, V
Handicap Access: Yes

This is the place to head when the need for all things meat strikes. McPhee's serves nothing but the best oak-grilled USDA prime-grade beef and boutique-raised select pork in the state, and it is suggested that you take along a wheelbarrow to cart home your leftovers. The portions are huge, but the flavors delicate and divine. You can order an American Kobe beef cheeseburger and taste what all the fuss is about, but we recommend you stick with the tried and very, very true: the 13-ounce "five-week aged" rib-eye steak or the ancho chile apricot glazed pork chop. The meat is so marbled it almost melts in your mouth. And the accompaniments, like the wild mushroom bread pudding and the garlic sauce on the chops, are elevated plays on American traditional cooling. The local wine list is superb, and the house wine is handcrafted for McPhee's Grill by Jim Clendenen of Au Bon Climat fame. Everyone in the area with a developed culinary sensibility ends up eating at this modern slice of the Old West. On one of the nights we dined here, the Lohr family and the Eberle family (they both own wineries) were dining separately across the room, while the crowd is most evenly split between ranchers and viticulturalists. Comfortable overstuffed booths run down the middle of the place, and all types of metal sculptures and artwork are placed throughout the cavernous room, as if in salute to the pig, fowl, cattle, etc., that make up your meal. A lively gathering spot with some great food.

Pismo Beach/Shell Beach
F. MCLINTOCK'S SALOON & DINING HOUSE
805-773-1892
750 Mattie Rd., Shell Beach
Open: Dinner daily
Price: Moderate to Expensive
Cuisine: Steak/seafood
Full Bar: Yes
Reservations: Not accepted for dinner Fri. & Sat.
Credit Cards: D, MC, V
Handicap Access: Yes

A rip-roaring saloon and dining room aggressively adorned with hunting trophies and cattle ranch implements, McClintock's is a very busy place, seeing action from fun-loving regulars who come to get serious about their steaks and ribs. Consider the 30-ounce T-bones, buffalo burgers and textbook-perfect oak-barbecued ribs. For those who consider beef something that belongs in a pasture, this place offers a huge menu of other goodies, like pan-fried rainbow trout, chicken and seafood specialties. The bar is the sort of place where you'd expect to see John Wayne hanging around, and every night the action heats up with live country-and-western music.

✪ GIUSEPPE'S CUCINA ITALIANA
805-773-2870
891 Price St., Pismo Beach
Open: Lunch & dinner daily
Price: Moderate
Cuisine: Southern Italian
Full Bar: Yes
Reservations: No
Credit Cards: AE, D, MC, V
Handicap Access: Yes

A favorite with locals for more than 15 years, Giuseppe's in downtown Pismo Beach presents a staggering selection of southern Italian fare amid a crowded yet crisp atmosphere. In addition to a spectrum of pasta offerings, Giuseppe's also features 14 seafood, chicken and meat specialties. The restaurant is especially noted for its robust flavors and generous servings, and all entrées include soup or salad. The wine list is particularly inspired, and it offers local choices to accommodate any dish. The pastas are especially well executed here, and the Santa Barbara mussels are simply the best on the Central Coast. The chicken in pistachio crust is another inspired dish, but try at least one of the individual pizzas, true marvels of the pie-making art.

SAN LUIS OBISPO
APPLE FARM
805-544-6100
2015 Monterey St., San Luis Obispo
Open: Breakfast, lunch & dinner daily
Price: Moderate
Cuisine: American

Full Bar: Yes
Reservations: Recommended
Credit Cards: AE, D, MC, V
Handicap Access: Yes

Housed in a fascinating, well-decorated B&B complex, complete with gardens, orchards and working waterwheel, this welcoming country-style restaurant specializes in generous portions of down-home foods with all of the trimmings. Grilled fish specials of Louisiana catfish, halibut and New Zealand orange roughy come, as do all dinners, with homemade soup or salad, hot corn bread, vegetable and choice of potatoes. Turkey potpie, barbecued baby back ribs, even homemade meat loaf will please those looking for hearty, old-fashioned comfort foods. Apple desserts are the house signature.

✪ GARDENS OF AVILA
805-595-7365
1215 Avila Beach Dr., San Luis Obispo
Open: Dinner daily, brunch Sun.
Price: Moderate to Expensive
Cuisine: California cuisine
Full Bar: Yes
Reservations: Recommended
Credit Cards: AE, D, MC, V
Handicap Access: Yes

From the windows and terraces of this attractive contemporary restaurant, housed in a popular inn, diners can feast on the view of oak groves and secluded water tubs dotting the hillside of Sycamore Mineral Springs. Another sort of feast awaits inside, thanks to a sensitively designed menu showcasing local seafoods and produce from chef Evan Threadwell's on-site gardens. The fine steaks are often accompanied by jalapeño spoon bread, basil butter and corn relish—on those nights, only the steaks are not home-grown. The chef's vegetarian garden tasting menu takes diners on an adventuresome culinary field trip from which they will return with tales tall yet true of the fresh and intensely flavored products of the earth. Some other entrée options include the giant scallops from the Sea of Cortez served with polenta, onions prepared with honey and balsamic vinegar, wild mushrooms and truffle nage. The chef's duck confit with Humboldt Fog goat cheese and hazelnuts, upland cress and cherry compote is one success some of us won't forget soon. Local wines dominate the extensive wine list, the ambiance is relaxed and the harbors of Avila Beach are just down the road.

LINNAEAS CAFE LINN'S

805-541-5888
1110 Garden St., San Luis Obispo
Open: Breakfast and lunch daily
Price: Inexpensive
Cuisine: Eclectic vegetarian
Full Bar: No
Reservations: No
Credit Cards: Cash only
Handicap Access: Yes

A true slice of local color is this funky, bohemian outpost of '60s Central Coast crossed with multiple ethnic cuisines. Charmingly primitive decor includes lots of artwork (both whimsical and serious offerings by local artists), a wooden order counter, tiny round tables for seating and a back-garden patio for all-day reading over cups of the fine house café au lait. The menu is all over the map, but you can strike gold in things like the soft Armenian cracker bread sandwiches filled with all manner of fresh goodies and cream cheese. Homemade soups and salads are healthful and bountiful. And a breakfast of Swedish rice pudding with steamed milk is a simple luxury. Big fat freshly made pies, tortes, breads and carrot cakes complete the illusion of being in a friendly home kitchen. Music in the evenings serves up folk, light jazz and classical as eclectic as the menu.

SANTA YNEZ VALLEY

✪ THE BALLARD INN & RESTAURANT

805-688-7770
2436 Baseline Ave., Ballard
Open: Dinner Wed.–Sun.
Price: Expensive
Cuisine: Pan Pacific
Full Bar: No
Reservations: Recommended on weekends
Credit Cards: AE, D, MC, V
Handicap Access: Yes

A conspicuous landmark in this minuscule wine country hamlet is the Ballard Inn and Restaurant. The inn is one of the best on the Central Coast, but the restaurant is something of a religious shrine to locals, who treat out-of-town guests visiting the Santa Ynez viticultural region to its heavenly fare. The eclectic menu offers only the freshest in-season options available to chef Budi Kazali, who turns them into culinary works of American-Asian fusion art. After graduating from the California Culinary Academy, Kazali began his career in San Francisco at Campton Place and La Folie, later served as chef de cuisine at chef Ming Tsai's James Beard Award–winning Blue Ginger near Boston, returned to the Bay Area to work at Gary Danko and then— thank the gods—opened his own place at the Ballard. His sources are impeccable (I enjoyed a corn chowder that was based on ears of corn grown for the chef by a fellow across the street from the dining room and picked three hours before I sat down to eat), but his real inspiration can be witnessed in his sauces. Witness his halibut with foie gras and white peaches in shallot-port reduction, which was velvety and ethereal. His pan-seared Maine scallops with lemongrass risotto married the metallic brininess of the eastern seashore with the seductive allure of Southeast Asia. The taste was as precise and clean as one could find outside of heaven. A mission fig and balsamic reduction sang the palate electric when napped over a Sonoma duck breast sided with a sweet potato puree, and the desserts (mango sorbet, warm chocolate cake with espresso ice cream, Tahitian vanilla bean crème brûlée) were all swoon-producing. The extensive wine list leans heavily on the Ballard's Santa Ynez neighbors, though Napa and Sonoma are well represented. In the 10 years we have been writing this travel book, this was one of the five best meals we have encountered on our journeys.

BROTHERS RESTAURANT
AT MATTEI'S TAVERN
805-688-4820
2350 Railway Ave., Los Olivos
Open: Breakfast, lunch & dinner daily
Price: Expensive
Cuisine: American
Full Bar: Yes
Reservations: Recommended
Credit Cards: AE, MC, V
Handicap Access: Yes

Dripping vintage western ambiance, this gracious roadhouse built in 1886 once was a stagecoach overnight stop. Its long front veranda drips wisteria, while the huge bar, fireplace and fir floors are originals, and the wicker sunroom and brick patio provide lovely dining surrounded by gardens and a magnificent bower of antique yellow roses. Still a lure for locals and visitors alike (who come for the tavern action as much as the fine regional dining), Mattei's has seen its share of film-world celebrities, especially during its days as an overnight hideaway. Mickey Rooney and Ava Gardner were married here, and John Barrymore rented one of the estate cottages each summer during his heyday. Today, fine alfresco dinners are a top draw, especially since the Nichols brothers (Jeff and Matt) took over as chef-owners in 2001. They kept the old charm

but ratcheted up the quality of the cuisine. The menu changes every few weeks, but look for the grilled salmon and veal chops, the foie gras with spiced apples, their world-fusion appetizers (tuna tartare with avocado, spicy yuzu vinaigrette and crispy ginger) or the prime rib. Fine contemporary salads, fresh seafoods and appropriately western-style steaks flesh out the bill of fare. Set in the middle of Santa Ynez Valley wine country, the tavern boasts a fine listing of locally made vintages, and the service is warm and attentive.

✪ CHEF RICK'S
ULTIMATELY FINE FOODS
805-937-9512
1095 Edison St., Santa Ynez
Open: Lunch Mon.–Sat., dinner nightly
Price: Moderate to Expensive
Cuisine: Southern Eclectic
Full Bar: No
Reservations: Recommended Wed.–Sat.
Credit Cards: AE, D, MC, V
Handicap Access: Yes

Chef Rick's serves up flavors that rival any on the Central Coast. Just ask the local wineries, who frequently employ the restaurant's catering service to accentuate their wines and enchant their guests. Owner Rick Manson orchestrates a daring menu that spans virtually every mood and texture. The New Mexican grilled garlic chicken is especially savory, as are the Louisiana spicy sautéed corn-crusted striped sea bass, the wild mushroom raviolis and the barbecued lamb quesadilla. On the appetizer front, the coconut-beer shrimp is a local classic, and the Louisiana blackened rib-eye steak salad in garlic vinaigrette is an entire meal. Paired with an exciting selection of local wines, Chef Rick's dishes yield an extravaganza for the senses.

FOOD PURVEYORS

Bakeries

Cider Creek 805-238-4144, 3760 Hwy. 46 W., Templeton. Besides the house original apple-cinnamon bread (get two loaves), fruit turnovers (the pumpkin can't be beat), cream pies and cakes, cookies and muffins (they taste homemade, which really is rare despite the tons of claims), this friendly oasis in the arid rolling hills of north San Luis Obispo County also does a brisk business in preserves, dried fruit and well-balanced fruit butters (check out the blueberry butter for a sweet–tart treat).

Old West Cinnamon Rolls 805-773-1428, 861 Dolliver St., Pismo Beach. The name says it all: an exhibition bakery that whips up monster cinnamon rolls, old-fashioned doughnuts, cookies, breads and rolls.

Utopia Bakery 805-544-8867, 2900 Broad St., San Luis Obispo. Run by a team of Dutch master bakers, the Utopia produces the Central Coast's best croissants—light, delicate and not to be passed up by any foodie worth his or her salt.

Coffeehouses

Rainbow Bean www.rainbowbean.com, 805-927-3710, 2320 Main St., Cambria. Ian and Sall Scott's coffeehouse "à la mode" has become the village's gathering place and the top spot on this part of the coast to get specialty coffees and teas. Besides ice cream and frozen yogurt, you can also enjoy freshly baked scones, coffee cake, breads, cookies and fruit.

Side Street Cafe 805-688-8455, 2375 Alamo Pintado, Los Olivos. This cafe provides a laid-back forum for lovers of movies, live music and fine coffee and tea, especially in the lovely back garden shaded by rose arbors and magnificent locust trees.

Farmers' Markets

Arroyo Grande Farmers' Market 805-544-9570, Hwy. 101 & Oak Park Rd. (Oak Park Plaza), Arroyo Grande. Wed. 9–11:30am.

Arroyo Grande Farmers' Market 805-544-9570, City Hall Swinging Bridge, Arroyo Grande. Sat. noon–2:30pm.

Atascadero Farmers' Market 805-466-2066, corner of El Camino Real & Morro Rd. (Rite-Aid parking lot), Atascadero. Wed. 3–6pm.

Buellton Farmers' Market 805-688-7829, Buellton. Thurs. 3–6pm.

Cambria Farmers' Maret 805-927-3624, W. Main St. (next to the Vets Hall), Cambria. Fri. 2:30–5pm.

Cayucos Farmers' Market 805-995-1664, Veterans Hall, Cayucos. Mar.–Nov. Fri. 8:30am–noon.

Fishermen & Farmers' Market 805-772-4467, 880 Main St., Morro Bay. Sat. 4–7pm.

Los Osos/Baywood Park 805-528-4884, Santa Maria Ave., bet. 2nd & 3rd Sts, Baywood Park. Mon. 2–4:30pm.

Every Thursday evening a block of downtown San Luis Obispo overflows with a spectacular display of fresh produce, flowers, street musicians and oakwood barbecues, all part of the acclaimed San Luis Obispo Certified Farmers' Market. Jeff Greene

Morro Bay Farmers' Market 805-544-9570, 2650 Main St. (Spencer's Market), Morro Bay. Thurs. 3–5pm.

Nipomo Farmers' Market 805-929-1583, W. Left St. (Recreation Center south parking lot), Nipomo. Sun. 11:30am–2:30pm.

Paso Robles Farmers' Market 805-238-0506, 11th & Spring Sts., Paso Robles. Fri. 9am 12:30pm.

San Luis Obispo Farmers' Market 805-541-0286, Higuera St., bet. Osos & Nipomo Sts., San Luis Obispo. Thurs. 6–9pm.

San Luis Obispo Farmers' Market 805-544-9570, Madonna Rd. (Gottschalk's Dept. Store parking lot), San Luis Obispo. Sat. 8–10:30am.

Templeton Farmers' Market 805-239-6536, 6th & Crocker Sts. (City Park), Templeton. Sat. 9am–12:30pm.

Frozen Desserts

Coldstone Creamery 805-545-0926, 860 Higuera St., San Luis Obispo. Myriad options—not only in the flavors but also in the variety of goodies to place atop your cone or bowl—are what make Coldstone special. Posted on the "Wall of Fame" are strange and unusual concoctions created by customers of the past, and anyone with a weird and winning combination can join the select crowd by letting his or her palate and imagination run wild.

One of many restored Victorian residences updates the past on San Luis Obispo's Buchon Street.

CULTURE

Architecture

The main streets of San Luis Obispo bristle with whole blocks of beautifully maintained, 19th-century stores, banks, workshops and warehouses. Up the hill from the Spanish land grant of San Simeon, San Francisco architect Julia Morgan gave tangible form to the over-ripe fantasies of pioneer son William Randolph Hearst in a Spanish baroque castle, which still astonishes visitors to this incomparable setting between the Santa Lucia Mountains and the Pacific Ocean.

Cinema

✪ **Bay Theatre** 805-772-2444, 464 Morro Bay Blvd., Morro Bay. A throwback to the good old movie palace days. Fancy this: a single screen for first-run flicks.

Century Cinemas 805-227-2172, 6905 El Camino Real, Atascadero. A modern boxed seven-plex screens nothing but the latest Hollywood fare.

Downtown Centre Cinema 805-546-8600, Marsh and Morro Sts., San Luis Obispo. An eight-plex that seems to be the gathering place for every young teen in the county.

Edward's Fremont 805-541-2141, 1025 Monterey St., San Luis Obispo. Another beauty from a bygone era, carved up to fit the small-screen needs of the shrinking modern world. Thirties deco outside, first-run four-plex inside.

Fair Oaks 805-489-2364, 1007 Grand Ave., Arroyo Grande. Art house, indy and foreign films grace the silver screen at this intimate family-run operation.

Gemini Twin Cinema 805-736-1306, 1028 N. H St., Lompoc. Only Hollywood show in town.

The Movie 805-736-1558, 227 W. Barton Ave., Lompoc. This throwback to simpler times offers indy and art house programming.

✪ **National Geographic Theater** 805-927-6811, Hearst Castle Visitor Center, San Simeon. Splendid cinematography and a giant screen bring to life the heyday of William Randolph Hearst, his many Hollywood friends and the building of his massive ego project, Hearst Castle. Usually paired with a magic-realism look at the forces of nature or some other educational topic.

✪ **Palm Theatre** 805-541-5161, 817 Palm St., San Luis Obispo. A longtime favorite with the college crowd and local buffs, this thinking person's movie palace specializes in first-run art films.

Park Cinemas 805-227-2172 1100 Pine St., Paso Robles. Typical eight-plex packs them in during boiling summer months.

Sunset Drive In 805 544 4475, 255 Elks Ln., San Luis Obispo. One of the last great American traditional drive-ins always screens double features, and kids under 11 get in free.

San Luis Obispo's Edward's Fremont Cinema showcases first-run contemporary cinema in a 1930s deco movie palace setting. Jeff Greene

Gardens

✪ **Hearst Castle Gardens** www.parks.ca.gov, 800-444-7275, Hwy. 1, San Simeon. To surround his 130-room hilltop castle, media baron William Randolph Hearst envisioned gardens on a wildly opulent scale. A 20-man crew headed by Nigel Keep hauled acres of soil up the hillside to create a series of terraces that were then planted with over 100,000 trees, thousands of rosebushes and acres of Hearst's favorite flower, the camellia. More than a half million flowers were propagated in the castle's greenhouses to stock the grounds, which include a once glorious, mile-long pergola. Magnificent sculpture pieces also adorn the grounds. Tour IV of the many Hearst Castle guided visits is largely devoted to the gardens. Open daily 8:30–3.

Mission Plaza 805-543-6850, Chorro & Monterey Sts., San Luis Obispo. At the site of the Mission San Luis Obispo, founded in 1772, visitors may enjoy the sunny cloistered garden where early Franciscan fathers meditated. In front of the mission, a terraced plaza offers soul-soothing landscaping and plantings that wind down to and along the banks of the peaceful San Luis Creek. Open daily 9–5.

Historic Places
AH LOUIS STORE
805-543-4332
800 Palm St., San Luis Obispo
Open: Mon.–Sat. 10–5
Admission: Free

Resolutely bound to its 19th-century origins, this brickwork monument to its 1874 builder, an enterprising Cantonese immigrant named Ah Louis, still stands on the corner of the former Chinese district of downtown San Luis Obispo, dispensing an eclectic inventory of Asian goods along with architectural ambiance. The store was just a small corner of the enterprising Ah Louis's empire. Coming to California to find gold in the 1850s, he ended up working to create county roads, establishing the area's first brickworks, operating a store packed with goods from home for Chinese railroad workers and launching a seed business and half a dozen farms before he was finished.

✪ HEARST CASTLE
www.hearstcastle.com
800-444-4445
Hwy. 1, San Simeon
Open: Daily 8–4
Admission: Adults $24, children 6–17 $12;
tickets must be reserved by calling 800-444-4445
or by buying online

The site of America's only genuine castle by the sea, overlooking the Pacific Ocean north of Cambria, was the setting of family camping trips when future media magnate and political star maker William Randolph Hearst was a boy. In 1919, Hearst hatched his grandiose scheme of transforming a magical spot on his father's quarter-of-a-million acres of ranch land into a showpiece of architecture and international artworks. Plundering the treasure houses of Europe, Hearst dismantled entire medieval chapels, Renaissance villas and Greco-Roman temples, hauling back the priceless artifacts to decorate the interior of the 100-room Casa Grande (a Spanish baroque theme park designed by San Francisco architect Julia Morgan) and a spate of palatial guest houses for his celebrity friends. Byzantine tilework now gleams from the lofty towers and spectacular indoor swimming pool. A library that Hearst built for his personal study contains over 5,000 volumes in one of the world's finest rare book collections and one of the greatest caches of Greek vases.

Splendid, ornate Greco-Roman pools are among the fabulous architectural treasures of San Simeon's Hearst Castle on the north San Luis Obispo County Coast. Shmuel Thaler

Surrounding this part-sublime, part-outrageous monument to consumption was once the world's largest private zoo, and zebras, Barbary sheep, Himalayan goats and deer still remain to delight contemporary visitors.

During the 1920s to 1940s, the world's rich and famous came and stayed at Hearst Castle for opulent weeks of grand partying. Guests included Winston Churchill, Charlie Chaplin, Gary Cooper, Ben Hecht, Groucho Marx, Douglas Fairbanks, Joan Crawford, Charles and Ann Morrow Lindbergh, Louella Parsons, Cary Grant and, of course, Hearst mistress Marion Davies, whose relationship with the eccentric millionaire was immortalized in Orson Welles's *Citizen Kane*.

Still a bastion of sensory overload—many of the art treasures that Hearst feverishly collected sit unpacked in the castle's basement stronghold—San Simeon is one of the top visitor attractions in the country. The castle may be visited only on guided tours, and given the sheer scale of the monument, it takes four tours to encompass all of the sites. Tour I is designed for first-time visitors and includes the gardens, one of the Mediterranean guest houses, the ground floor of the main house and the outdoor Roman pool. Tour II moves through the upper floors of the main house, including Hearst's private suites, libraries, guest room, kitchen and both pools. Tour III sweeps through the 36 bedrooms of the guest wing, as well as the pools and gardens. Tour IV, offered only in the summer, wanders along the perimeter grounds, gardens, wine cellar and ground floor of the largest guest house. All of the tours involve climbing many stairs, and special arrangements for visitors in wheelchairs may be made by calling 805-927-2020.

OLD GRIST MILL

805-688-4815
1760 Mission Dr., Solvang 93463
Open: Can be viewed from the road
Admission: Free

Designed and built by reformed pirate Joseph Chapman in 1820, this New England–style mill ground grains once harvested at Mission Santa Ynez. Its workings provide a glimpse of the earliest American presence in this area. While the privately owned complex is not open to the public, the fascinating millworks are on full display from the road.

The stylish brick-and-terra-cotta facade of the 1893 Andrews Bank Building is one of the architectural sights available through a self-guided Heritage Walk of downtown San Luis Obispo. Jay Swanson

Historic Walking Tours

San Luis Obispo Heritage Walks The seven-square-block heart of downtown San Luis Obispo serves a great walking tour through the eclectic and historic past of the mission town. A free **Heritage Walks** brochure, available at the chamber of commerce (805-781-2777, 1039 Chorro St., San Luis Obispo 93401), will get you started. In addition to the **Ah Louis Store** and the splendid **Mission San Luis Obispo de Tolosa**, a stop should be made at the **Dallidet Adobe** (1185 Pacific St.), built in the 1850s by Frenchman Pierce Hyppolite Dallidet, one of the area's pioneer viticulturists. Among the stately Victorian mansions of the area, must visits include the 1875 **Jack House** (546 Marsh St.) and the grand 1895 **Erickson Home** (687 Islay St.). The ornate brick- and-terra-cotta facade of the circa-1893 **J. P. Andrews Bank Building** (Osos & Monterey Sts.) furnishes a prime example of 19th-century mercantile prosperity. Several fine adobes furnish windows on the town's Mexican era, most notably the **Murray Adobe** (747 Monterey St.) and the **Sauer-Adams Adobe** (964 Chorro St.), built in 1830.

Kids' Stuff

✪ **San Luis Obispo Children's Museum** 805-544-5437, 1010 Nipomo St., San Luis Obispo. A museum facility entirely devoted to exhibits of interest to youngsters, involving lots of fun and educational and touching exhibits. Lots to do here: Slip down dinosaur slides, explore the engines of a fire station, design homes, serve lunch at a diner, play with computers and watch each other on closed-circuit TV monitors. Check out the beehive and ant farm—they aren't hands-on, but maybe that's just as well.

Lighthouses

Piedras Blancos Lighthouse (Hwy. 1, 5 miles north of San Simeon) is located on white guano-encrusted rocks that were named by Portuguese explorer Juan Rodriquez Cabrillo in 1542. A lookout was built in 1864 during the heyday of the whaling era, and in 1875, the first brick-and-steel lighthouse was completed.

Like other lighthouses along the Central Coast, Piedras Blancos employed what at the time was new technology. The glass prisms of its French Fresnel lens ingeniously utilized over 1,000 pieces of cut glass to magnify the light going out to sea. The lens was in turn illuminated by a vapor lamp that consumed up to 5 tons of kerosene annually. Visible for up to 25 miles, the original lamp was automated in 1949, and today sheds its light out to sea every 15 seconds. Since the National Fish and Wildlife Service moved into the white beacon in the 1970s, it's been closed for public tour. Nonetheless, it forms a true monument to countless dangerous voyages on the high seas in the last century.

Missions

✪ LA PURÍSIMA MISSION STATE HISTORIC PARK

www.lapurisimamission.org
805-733-1303
2295 Purisima Rd., Lompoc 93436
Open: Daily 9–5
Admission: Donations

Founded in 1787 as the 11th of California's Franciscan missions, Mission La Purísima Concepción was once a huge ranch and farming complex situated near a thriving Chumash village called Alsacupi. After a devastating earthquake in 1812 shook the adobe walls to ruins, the mission was moved, reconstructed and eventually fell back into decay. While original walls remain, an extraordinary restoration was begun nearby that today is a living museum—the only re-creation of an entire mission structure: its corrals, workshops, storerooms, padre's apartments and aqueduct system. So seamless is the restoration that visitors to the 900-acre grounds can sample a bit of mission life on tours of the gardens, tannery, reservoir, soap factory, residences, workrooms and main church.

MISSION SAN LUIS OBISPO DE TOLOSA

www.missionsanluisobispo.org
805-543-6850
Monterey & Chorro Sts., San Luis Obispo 93401
Open: Daily 9–5
Admission: $4

The fifth in the series of missions founded by Franciscan Padre Serra and specifically named for St. Louis, bishop of Toulouse, France, this settlement was one of the wealthiest of the missions. A large population of Native American converts helped tend the mission's extensive holdings of cattle, sheep, horses and fertile land on the banks of San Luis Obispo Creek. A serious restoration, which uncovered hand-hewn beams, began in the 1930s. Still a thriving parish church, the mission is crowned by a graceful bell tower and cool cloister gardens. A very fine museum provides glimpses of early mission life and the daily work habits of the resident fathers and neophytes.

Handsomely restored, the 18th-century Mission San Luis Obispo ministers to a vibrant present-day congre-gation. |eff Greene

MISSION SAN MIGUEL ARCÁNGEL
www.missionsanmiguel.org
805-467-3256
Mission St. east of Hwy. 101, San Luis Obispo 93401
Open: Daily 9:30–4:30
Admission: Donations

Still in use today by robed Franciscan friars, Mission San Miguel Arcángel was founded in 1797 by Padre Francisco Fermen Lasuen to bridge the gap between Missions San Luis Obispo and San Antonio de Padua. Sixteenth in the mission chain, its prime location on the Salinas River allowed it to thrive as both an agricultural center and ranch. Destroyed by fire and earthquake and suffering the indignities of service as a saloon, dance hall and warehouse, the mission was returned to the Franciscans in the late 1920s and restored. Its beautiful interior was rebuilt along authentic guidelines. The gardens frame a graceful Moorish fountain, and a self-guided tour of the grounds, cemetery and church begins at the small gift shop.

MISSION SANTA INÉS
www.missionsantaines.org
805-688-4815
1760 Mission Dr., Solvang 93463
Open: Mon.–Sat. 9:30–5:30, Sun. noon–5
Admission: Donations

Founded in 1804, the original, simply rendered mission chapel was replaced after a mighty 1812 earthquake. A brick-and-adobe structure, the new mission boasted tile roof and floors (said to be the first ever used in mission construction). The red-tiled motif would become the dominant feature of what we now consider the Spanish mission style. After the inevitable decline that afflicted missions after secularization, the building was restored in the 20th century and is now famed for its extensive gardens, lovely campanile, native-crafted frescoes and hand-carved door. This mission features a fascinating museum, showcasing rare artifacts from the Franciscan colonization.

Museums

CAL POLY UNIVERSITY NATURAL HISTORY MUSEUM
805-756-2788
Cal Poly Univ., Science Bldg., Rm. 285, San Luis Obispo 93401
Open: Weekdays 8–5
Admission: Free

Biology professors and students maintain this small collection of mounted specimens and photographs of regional wildlife, including revolving exhibits of current research activities. The space in which the exhibits appear is intended primarily as a study space for students.

✪ ELVERHOY DANISH HERITAGE MUSEUM
www.syv.com/~crystal/
805-686-1211
1624 Elverhoy Way, Solvang 93463
Open: Wed.–Sun. 1–4
Admission: Donations

Built in the style of an 18th-century Danish farmhouse, this spacious private home/museum recounts the dream of a little Denmark in the New World that Solvang founders brought to this lush dairy country. Filled with authentic Danish arts and crafts, furniture and tools, the museum documents the immigrant experience in the Central Coast.

HANS CHRISTIAN ANDERSEN MUSEUM
www.solvangca.com/museum/h1.htm
805-688-2052
1680 Mission Dr., Solvang 93463
Open: Daily 9:30–6
Admission: Free

Lovingly devoted to the author of the beloved children's fairy tales, this small museum is filled with exhibits recounting Andersen's life and boasts original letters, photographs and Andersen artwork and book illustrations.

MORRO BAY MUSEUM OF NATURAL HISTORY
www.mbspmuseum.org
805-772-2694
State Park Rd. at White's Point, Morro Bay 93442

Open: Daily 10–5
Admission: Adults $2, under 16 free

Commanding a stunning panoramic view of the bay estuary and stately Morro Rock, the museum offers informative dioramas and interpretive displays of local flora, fauna, geology and the history of the Native Americans who once called this area home. A trail leads from the museum to the top of White's Point, passing indigenous sites along the way.

✪ SAN LUIS OBISPO HISTORICAL MUSEUM
www.slochs.org
805-543-0638
696 Monterey St., San Luis Obispo 93401
Open: Wed.–Sun. 10–4
Admission: Free

Housed in a graceful Richardsonian Romanesque mansion made of local granite and sandstone, designed by prolific California architect William Weeks, the museum's exhibits present a colorful overview of the history of the county, from Chumash days through the mission and rancho periods to the present day. A complete Victorian parlor invites a glimpse into the 19th-century American frontier days. There are also many hands-on displays designed for youngsters.

Housed in a handsome, turn-of-the-20th-century structure, the San Luis Obispo Historical Museum chronicles the area's colorful past. |eff Greene

✪ SANTA YNEZ VALLEY HISTORIC SOCIETY MUSEUM & PARKS-JANEWAY CARRIAGE HOUSE

www.rootsweb.com/~casyhsmc/
805-688-7889
3596 Sagunto St., Santa Ynez 93460
Open: Tues.–Sun. noon–4
Admission: Free

One room of this tiny but fascinating museum is devoted to Native Americans, focusing especially on Chumash culture and artifacts. Other displays show daily life in the 19th century. Next door, the Parks-Janeway Carriage House shows off a varied collection of stagecoaches, wagons, carriages and buggies that once transported people, their mail and their belongings up and down the Central Coast.

Music

Basin Street Regulars 800-443-7778, 805-773-4382, Veterans Hall, 780 Bello St., Pismo Beach. Hot Dixieland jazz by guest bands and able jam-session musicians shakes the rafters of this hall all afternoon on the last Sunday of each month.

California State Old Time Fiddlers Association 800-443-7778, 805-773-4382, Moose Lodge, 180 Main St., Pismo Beach. Music the way that they used to make it during the rip-roaring Saturday night barn dances of the 19th century sets toes a-tappin' on the first and third Sunday of each month.

San Luis Obispo County Symphony 805-543-3533, 1160 Marsh St., San Luis Obispo. This resident orchestra enlists the talents of top area soloists and guest virtuosos in presenting its fall–spring season of classic repertoire symphonies and concertos.

Nightlife

Chili Peppers 805-547-1163, 1009 Monterey, San Luis Obispo. Dancing takes center stage on salsa nights, and live blues and rock bands regularly swing through this bar-restaurant.

✪ **Ghostriders** 805-344-2111, 550 Bell St., Los Alamos. This is a great old-time honky-tonk replete with obligatory pool table, horseshoe pit, full bar and two music stages on the weekends, one inside and another outside in the funky garden when the weather's good. The clientele includes bikers, cops, firemen, assorted rancher types and the new winery crowd. The larger-than-life character behind the bar is Shellie the bartender, who can fill you in on local lore and all the sins that have been committed up and down this dusty hamlet's main drag.

The Graduate www.slograd.com, 805-541-0969, 990 Industrial Way, San Luis Obispo. The main action is country and western, but the long-running Grad is an equal-opportunity venue, with nights for swingers, Big Chillers, disco fever seekers and the under-21 set.

Harry's 805-773-1010, Cypress & Pomeroy Sts., Pismo Beach. Dancing to one of the area's top country and country-rock bands every single night of the week.

✪ **Mother's Tavern** www.motherstavern.com, 805-541-8733, 725 Higuera St., San Luis Obispo. Local and out-of-town bands specialize in good ol' rock and roll and blues, plus dance nights.

Mr. Rick's 805-595-9500, 480 Front St., Avila Beach. This beachfront bar and nightclub features rock and roll, reggae or blues on most nights of the week.

✪ **Old Camozzi's Saloon** 805-927-8941, 2262 Main St., Cambria. Live music, local color and plenty of watering-hole ambiance housed within an authentic 19th-century saloon.

Old Cayucos Tavern & Card Room 805-995-3209, 130 N. Ocean, Cayucos. Kickin' around since 1906, the well-worn watering hole offers live music Fridays and Saturdays and never requires a cover charge.

Old Paso Pub 805-237-7869, 1238 Pine St., Paso Robles. From pure punk shows to Thursday open-mic nights, the Old Paso Pub is North SLO County's top spot to knock back quality brews and catch live entertainment.

Rose and Crown 805-541-1911, 1000 Higuera St., San Luis Obispo. Live bands play a bit of jazz and rock on the weekends at this English-style pub that offers traditional darts, as well as not-so-traditional dancing.

SLO Brewing Company 805-543-1843, 1119 Garden St., San Luis Obispo. Rock, reggae and the funky local stuff, plus great brews.

Sweet Springs Saloon 805-528-3764, 990 L.O.V.R., Los Osos. Satellite TVs, pool tables and shuffleboard make this a prime gaming spot, but it's also the heart of rock and roll, with live music on the weekends.

Tortilla Flats 805-544-7575, 1051 Nipomo St., San Luis Obispo. It's mad, passionate dancing to creative DJ music every night of the week.

Stage

Cal Poly Theatre www.calpolyarts.org, 805-541-5369, Cal Poly Univ., San Luis Obispo. Pacific Repertory Opera performances are among the many theater offerings presented on the stage of the California State Polytechnic University campus throughout the fall–spring academic year.

Great American Melodrama www.americanmelodrama.com, 805-489-2499, 1863 Pacific Coast Hwy., Oceano. What's more fun than booing and hissing a villain in a gaslight-era melodrama? Or cheering the hero when he rescues the damsel in distress? Here's your chance to do both while enjoying an okay dinner and a swell post-melodrama vaudeville show.

Pewter Plough Playhouse www.pewterploughplayhouse.com, 805-927-3877, Main St. at Sheffield, West Cambria Village. Since 1976, this charming "jewel box of a community theater" has presented live dramas and comedies year-round in an intimate, lively auditorium.

✪ **Solvang Theater Under The Stars** www.pcpa.org, 800-549-PCPA, Solvang Festival Theater, 2nd St., Solvang; also in the **Marian Theatre**, Santa Maria. Nightly, except Monday, all summer long, the outdoor theater rings with myriad theatrical treasures, ranging from heavyweight classics and Shakespearean gems to contemporary and comic capers performed by the repertory company of the Pacific Conservatory of the Performing Arts. Tickets cost $15–$25.

RECREATION

Beaches

These beaches are described in the order you will encounter them traveling southward down the Pacific Coast Highway from the Monterey County–San Luis Obispo County line.

Ragged Point Beach Hwy. 1, 15 miles north of San Simeon. Sweeping vistas of Big Sur are available from the bluff top overlook of this rocky spit of coastline. Near a grassy picnic area with tables, a steep trail leads down to the tiny beach and past a waterfall that's quite lovely after winter rains. Parking and restrooms. No entrance fee.

William R. Hearst Memorial State Beach Hwy. 1 on San Simeon Rd., San Simeon. One of the many prime natural playgrounds left to the State of California by the eclectic tycoon is this outstanding fishing and swimming area, nestled in the protective beauty of San Simeon Point. A 1,000-foot fishing pier, well stocked with fishing equipment and boat rentals, sits to the west of the main parking area. A eucalyptus grove and grassy expanse near the park's entrance suggest fine picnicking possibilities. Parking and restrooms. Entrance fee.

Sherwood Drive Beach Sherwood Dr., bet. Wedgewood & Lampton Sts., Cambria Pines Manor. Another good way to descend the wildflower-covered bluffs down to the sand and rocks is via paths along Sherwood Drive. Parking is no problem, though facilities are nil. No entrance fee.

Shamel County Park Windsor Blvd. & Nottingham Dr., Cambria. In this park, which fronts a popular beach, outdoor recreational possibilities include a playground, a sports field and a swimming pool. Parking and restrooms. No entrance fee.

Moonstone Beach Moonstone Dr., Cambria. Prime beachcombing for gnarled driftwood and for the occasional moonstone agate is available along this sheltered stretch that adjoins San Simeon State Beach. Tide pools protect a wealth of starfish and anemones. Hiking trails lace the formidable bluffs lining the water's edge. Parking, no facilities. No entrance fee.

Leffingwell Landing Hwy. 1 & Moonstone Beach Dr., Cambria. Beautifully maintained hiking trails wander the sagebrush- and lupine-filled bluffs and cypress groves above the swirling tide pools and brown sandy beach below. Excellent whale and sea otter watching from benches placed at vista points. Boat ramp, parking, restrooms and picnic areas. No entrance fee.

Beachcombing Tips

All-day beach foraging and wandering can yield countless simple treasures and, at areas where creeks meet the coastline, plentiful driftwood curiosities. Tide pool areas are often surrounded by beautiful rocks and glass fragments, smoothed and rounded by the elements. The trick is to come early in the day when tiny sand dollars, the odd weathered bottle and even round, bottle-glass floats are washed up on the shore. Mornings after storms yield the most interesting sea-tossed objects and driftwood by the ton. Bring a day pack or canvas bag for collecting and, during foggy mornings and evenings, a warm sweater to provide the comfort necessary for a long day's beachcombing.

The public fishing pier at Avila State Beach forms the background for endless games of seaside Frisbee at San Luis Obispo Bay. Jay Swanson

Santa Rosa Creek Beach Hwy. 1, south end of Moonstone Beach Dr., Cambria. A parking lot provides access to both the Santa Rosa Creek marshlands and the rugged tide pools of the rocky coastline. Benches invite lingering and picnicking. No facilities, no entrance fee.

Cayucos Beach Pacific Ave., bet. 1st & 22nd Sts., Cayucos. Clearly marked, public-access stairways lead down to the beach through residential property. Parking, but no facilities. No entrance fee.

Cayucos State Beach west of N. Ocean Dr., Cayucos. A beachfront pier attracts fishing afi-cionados to this local recreation spot, where barbecue and picnicking facilities abound. The pier, which is prettily lit at night, is wheelchair accessible. Parking and restrooms. No entrance fee.

Morro Strand State Beach Studio Dr., bet. 24th St. & Cody Ave., Cayucos (north); Hwy. 1, bet. Yerba Buena Ave. & Atascadero Rd., Morro Bay (south). The northern stretch of the beach is accessible by numerous stairways and walkways leading from streets intersecting Studio Drive. A paved parking lot at the end of 24th Street offers restrooms and picnic tables. The southern section of the beach (formerly Atascadero State Beach) offers almost 2 miles of sand and dunes, studded with ice plants in a splendid setting for contemplating the volcanic crags of Morro Rock. There are 100 campsites at the end of Yerba Buena Drive. Parking, restrooms, showers. Fee for camping but none for day use.

Ocean City Park Beach Ocean Blvd., bet. Vista Del Mar & Capistrano Aves., Pismo Beach. Stairways leading down to the sand also give visitors access to the many tide pools along this stretch. Benches and picnic tables perch on a grassy park overlooking the ocean. Parking, no facilities. No entrance fee.

Baywood Park Beach West of Pasadena Dr., bet. Santa Ysabel Ave. & Baywood Way, Baywood Park. The mudflats of Morro Bay are accessible at low tide from this small, sandy beach, which is set with picnic tables and benches. Plenty of parking. No entrance fee.

Port San Luis Beach end of Harford Dr., Avila Beach. A seawall protects the sandy beach-front, accessed by two stairways that adjoin a 1,300-foot pier built for boat-launch and hoist facilities. Parking and restrooms. Fee for boat launch and storage.

Avila State Beach Front St., bet. Harford Dr. & San Rafael St., Avila Beach. Tucked next to a tiny sailing village, this beach claims the public fishing pier and boasts playground equipment, outdoor showers, restrooms and a view of the gracefully curving San Luis Obispo Bay. In the spring and summer, life-guards are on duty. Parking is ample. No entrance fee.

Pismo State Beach from Wilmar Ave. at Pismo Beach. Twenty miles of coast are embraced by this beach area, from the sandy beaches, checkered with volleyball courts, just north of the Pismo Beach Pier down to the 4,000 acres of sweeping Nipomo Dunes, which once starred as the Sahara Desert in Cecil B. DeMille's celluloid epic, *The Ten Commandments*. Campgrounds, eucalyptus groves, dune buggy playgrounds and marsh-lands dot this coastal recreation mecca. Parking, restrooms and ample opportunities for seafood dining. Entrance fees for camp-grounds.

Over 20 miles of campgrounds, eucalyptus groves, dune buggy playgrounds and marshlands dot Pismo State Beach's recreation area. Jeff Greene

Bicycling
BICYCLE RENTALS
A Better Bike Shop 805-543-1148, 1422 Monterey St., San Luis Obispo.

Art's SLO Cyclery 805-543-4416, 2140 Santa Barbara St., San Luis Obispo.

Beach Cycle Rentals 805-773-5518, 150 Hinds Ave., Pismo Beach.

K-Man Cyclery 805-461-8735, 8641 El Camino Real, Atascadero.

Morro Bay Cyclery 805-772-0208, 920 Main St., Morro Bay.

TOP RIDES

Santa Margarita A good loop through some of the prettiest California pasture and oak-studded woodlands takes riders from the hamlet of Pozo to the village of San Miguel after circling Santa Margarita Lake.

See Canyon Lightly traveled country roads form the backbone of this 29-mile trek from the outskirts of San Luis Obispo, through funky Avila Beach and ending at the Pismo Beach Pier.

Bird-Watching

Montaña de Oro State Park 2 miles south of Los Osos via Los Osos Valley/Pecho Rd. A profusion of native and migrating birds find their way to the sheltered coves and wind-swept bluffs of this sprawling 8,400-acre preserve. Enormous albatross and pelicans soar above the cliffs, which in the summer become the nesting site for the elusive pigeon guillemot and black oystercatcher. It's a never-ending canvas of diverse, winged wildlife in a setting of splendid isolation.

Morro Bay State Park Hwy. 1, Morro Bay. Within this confluence of nutrient-rich mud-flats and bay, the 576-foot-high volcanic plug Morro Rock soars like a miniature Gibraltar, with its steep slopes an ecological preserve for the endangered peregrine falcon. Nesting falcons are protected here, and the rock is closed to entry. Binoculars are important for those intent upon catching a glimpse of the spectacular raptor. In the winter and fall, thousands of other migrating birds join the falcons and can be viewed from the broad beach as they feed on the clams, oysters and shrimp that burrow into the rich ooze of the tidal mud. A stopping point on the Pacific Migratory Flyway, the bay and beach attract over 250 species of native and migrating birds. Tucked into the bay estuary is a dense stand of eucalyptus trees that forms the largest great blue heron rookery between San Francisco and the Mexican border. From January until midsummer, the enormous birds mate, build nests, lay eggs and nudge their fledglings into flying shape in this rookery. Docents at the State Park's Museum of Natural History provide guided walks during the nesting season (805-772-2694).

Nipomo Dunes Preserve End of Main St., Guadalupe. Encompassing magnificent dunes, including the largest on the West Coast, this rare habitat shelters myriad bird species, including endangered species, such as the California least tern. In the fall, look for cinnamon teals, black brants, ruddy ducks and mallards.

Pismo State Beach Hwy. 1, Pismo Beach. Six miles of spectacular beach encompass the Pismo Dunes Preserve, home to myriad shorebirds, especially sandpipers and sanderlings. The waves literally come to life when tens of thousands of sooty shearwaters congregate to fish for tiny anchovies, and California brown pelicans provide amazing feats of daredevil diving.

Boating

CANOEING & KAYAKING

Central Coast Kayaks www.centralcoastkayaks.com, 805-773-3500, 1879 Shell Beach Rd., Shell Beach. Wildlife tours, lessons, sales, rentals.

Good Clean Fun Surf & Sport www.gcfsurf.com, 805-995-1993, 136 Ocean Front, Cayucos. Wildlife tours, lessons, sales, rentals, whale-watching, private charters, school outings.

Kayak Horizons 805-772-6444, 551 Embarcadero, Morro Bay. Wildlife tours, lessons, sales, rentals, paddle-sport gear and wear.

Kayaks of Morro Bay 805-772-1119, 551 Embarcadero, Morro Bay. Provides guided outings and instruction in sea kayaking. No experience needed. Call for reservations, weekends only.

Sub Sea Tours & Kayaks www.subseatours.com, 805-772-8085, 699 Embarcadero #9, Morro Bay. Outrigger canoes, wildlife tours, lessons, sales, rentals, semisubmersible underwater viewing.

Fishing
CHARTERS, RENTALS
Patriot Sportfishing www.patriotsportfishing.com, 805-595-7200, Pier #3, Port San Luis Obispo, Avila Beach. Full-day, half-day and long-range trips leave on three boats looking for rockfish, albacore, halibut and salmon in season. Tackle rentals

Virg's Landing at Morro Bay www.virgs.com, 805-772-1222, 1215 Embarcadero, Morro Bay. Half-day, full-day and twilight trips for halibut and albacore. Local trips for rockfish and other bottom species. Two-day trips are available for ling cod. Tackle rentals.

Sportfishing is one of the big attractions of the long beachfront that stretches between Cambria and San Luis Obispo. Jay Swanson

PLACES TO FISH
Avila State Beach along Front St. in Avila Beach. Jan.–Oct. are the best months for surf fishing from the pier or beach. Attractions are walleye and barred surf perch, jack smelt, kelp greeling, silver perch and starry flounder.

Leffingwell Landing Moonstone Beach Dr., San Simeon. Surf-fishing nirvana. Picnic area and barbecue facilities are a plus.

Montaña de Oro State Park Pecho Rd., Los Osos. Surf fishing and clamming abound. Picnic areas and restrooms are available.

Morro Bay Sandspit Morro Bay. Surf and rock fishing for perch, jack smelt, kelp greeling, mackerel, steelhead, halibut and flounder attracts serious and amateur anglers.

Pismo State Beach on the beach from Pismo Beach south to Oceano. Surf fishing for walleye and barred surf perch, jack smelt, kelp greeling, silver perch and starry flounder.

Pismo State Beach Pier Winds Ave., Pismo Beach. Fishing is free, and no license is required. Facilities at the pier are lit at night. Red snapper, ling and rock cod, perch, bluegill, sand dab, sea bass, jack smelt, walleye and barred surf perch beckon.

Port San Luis Pier San Luis Obispo. Fishing is free, and no license is required. Catches include red snapper, perch, bluegill, sand dab, sea bass, jack smelt, walleye, barred surf perch and ling and rock cod.

The rich, famous and not-so-famous are welcome to soak up the Central Coast panoramas available on the links at Solvang's Alisal Guest Ranch.
Alisal Guest Ranch.

Golf

Alisal Guest Ranch www.alisal.com, 805-688-4215, 1054 Alisal Rd., Solvang. Members and guests; 18 holes, 6,100 yards, par 72, rated 68.5. Pro shop, cart rental, bar, restaurant, dress code.

Avila Beach Resort Golf Course www.avila beachresort.com, 805-595-4000, 6464 Ana Bay Dr., Avila Beach. Public; 18 holes, 6,048 yards, par 71, rated 60.0. Pro shop, cart and club rental, lessons, bar, restaurant.

Blacklake Golf Resort www.blacklake.com, 805-343-1214, ext. 4, 1490 Golf Course Ln., Nipomo. Public; 27 holes, par 72 for 18, rated 68.0. Pro shop, cart and club rental, driving range, lessons, bar, restaurant.

Chalk Mountain Golf Course www.slo countyparks.com/activities/golf.htm, 805-466-8848, 10000 Elbordo Ave., Atasca-dero. Public; 18 holes, 5,926 yards, par 72, rated 69.2. Pro shop, cart and club rental, driving range, lessons, bar, restaurant.

Cypress Ridge Golf Course www.cypress-ridge.com, 877-564-4653, 805-474-7979, 780 Cypress Ridge Parkway, Arroyo Grande. Public; 18 holes, 6803 yards, par 72, rated 72.9. Pro shop, cart and club rental, driving range, lessons, bar, restaurant.

Dairy Creek Golf Course www.slocountyparks.com/activities/golf.htm, 805-782-8060, Morro Bay. Public; 6,548 yards, par 71, rated 72. Pro shop, cart and club rental, driving range, lessons, bar, restaurant.

Hunter Ranch Golf Course www.hunterranchgolf.com, 805-237-7444, 4041 Hwy. 46 E., Paso Robles. Public; 18 holes, par 72, rated 72.6. Pro shop, cart and club rental, lessons, restaurant.

Laguna Lake Municipal Golf Course www.ci.san-luis-obispo.ca.us/parksandrecreation/ golf.asp, 805-781-7309, 11175 Los Osos Valley Rd., San Luis Obispo. Public; 9 holes, 1,306 yards, par 30, unrated. Pro shop, cart and club rental, lessons, snack bar.

La Purisima Golf Course www.lapurisimagolf.com, 805-735-8395, 3455 Hwy. 246, Lompoc. Public; 18 holes, 7,105 yards, par 72, rated 75.6. Pro shop, cart and club rental, driving range, lessons, restaurant.

The Links Course 805-227-4567, 5151 Jardine Rd., Paso Robles. Public; 18 holes, 7056 yards, par 72, rated 71.3. Pro shop, cart and club rental, driving range, lessons, snack bar.

Morro Bay Golf Course www.slocountyparks.com/activities/golf.htm, 805-782-8060, 101 State Park Rd., Morro Bay. Public; 18 holes, par 71, rated 70.7. Pro shop, cart and club rental, driving range, lessons, bar, restaurant.

Paso Robles Golf and Country Club 805-937-2019, 1600 Country Club Dr., Paso Robles. Public; 18 holes, 6,218 yards, par 71, rated 71.0. Pro shop, cart and club rental, bar, restaurant.

Pismo State Beach Golf Course 805-481-5215, 9 LeSage Dr., Grover City. Public; 9 holes, 2,795 yards, par 54 for 18, unrated. Pro shop, cart and club rental, restaurant.

Rancho Maria Golf Club www.ranchomariagolf.com, 805-937-7818, 1950 State Hwy. 1, Santa Maria. Public; 18 holes, 6,390 yards, par 72, rated 68.8. Pro shop, cart and club rental, driving range, lessons, bar, restaurant.

San Luis Obispo Country Club www.slocountryclub.com, 805-543-4035, 255 Country Club Dr., San Luis Obispo. Members and guests; 18 holes, 6,390 yards, par 72, rated 70.0. Pro shop, cart and club rental, driving range, lessons, bar, restaurant.

Sea Pines Golf Course www.seapinesgolfresort.com, 805-528-4653, 1945 Solano St., Los Osos. Public; 9 holes, 2,002 yards, par 62 for 18, rated 57.4. Pro shop, cart and club rental, driving range, lessons, bar, restaurant.

Village Country Club 805-733-3537, 4300 Clubhouse Rd., Lompoc. Members and guests; 18 holes, 6,269 yards, par 72, rated 69.6. Cart rental.

Zaca Creek Golf Course 805-688-2575, 223 Shadow Mountain Dr., Buellton. Public; 9 holes, 3,088 yards, par 58 for 18, rated 50.0. Pro shop.

Hiking

Leffingwell Landing Bluffs Moonstone Beach Dr. at Hwy. 1, just north of Cambria. A stretch of windswept bluffs dotted with cypress groves, coastal lupines and dense grasses is laced with well-maintained hiking trails, some leading down to tide pools and cove beaches where moonstone agates may be found, others to benches set at seascape vista points. Prime sea otter viewing. Parking and restrooms.

Los Osos Oaks State Park Los Osos Valley Rd. at Palomino Dr., Los Osos. The rare sight of gnarled, primeval coast live oak is yours for the hiking of 2 well-marked miles of trails in this beautiful preserve. Vistas of the enchanting Los Osos Valley, punctuated by distinctive volcanic plugs (the so-called Seven Sisters, of which Morro Rock is the most famous but by

Montaña de Oro State Park, near Los Osos, offers sheltered cove beaches, wildflower bluffs and over 50 miles of hiking and riding trails within its 8,400 acres. Jay Swanson

no means the most interesting), are available from the trail. Hikers must honor trail markings along this complex and sensitive ecosystem.

Montaña de Oro State Park End of Pecho Rd., Los Osos. This is a wild expanse of fields, canyons, bluffs and cove beaches formerly part of the sprawling Spooner Ranch. Over 50 miles of hiking and equestrian trails are contained within these 8,400 acres bordering 3 miles of coastline. The 1.5-mile **Hazard Canyon Trail** winds through enchanted forests and shaded slopes, with several trails descending from bluff tops down to the beach and others piercing the heart of vast eucalyptus groves, one of the state's favored winter nesting spots for the monarch butterfly. The **Montaña de Oro Bluffs Trail** skirts Spooner's Cove, where seals lounge near coastal tide pools, and offers springtime glimpses of the golden poppies and the wild mustard that lends luster to the park's name. Parking and restrooms.

Morro Bay Sandspit Trail Morro Bay at Estero Bay. A 5-mile trail excursion along the sandspit, dividing the two bays, offers a chance to wander through sand dunes and to explore shell mounds left by Chumash ancestors.

Pismo Dunes Preserve Arroyo Grande Creek off Hwy. 1, Pismo Beach. Protected from vehicle traffic, mountainous sand dunes form a mysterious landscape from the ocean to a mile inland, extending southward for 1.5 miles from Arroyo Grande Creek. For obvious reasons, hikers have long been obsessed with this area.

Pismo State Beach Pismo Beach. A 20-mile-long stretch of coastline offers maximum hiking and beach recreation opportunities. Sand dunes, eucalyptus groves and waterfowl are among the sights available to walkers. An especially appealing hiking loop circumnavigates

Oceano Lagoon where it meets the beach, offering saltwater and freshwater wildlife observation, notably the endangered California brown pelican and the California least tern. At Oso Flaco Lake, south of Oceano, take the 4-mile-long **Nipomo Dunes Trail** and delve into a sea of dune-hugging wildflowers (asters, daisies, coreopsis and vibrant magenta sand verbena) and acres of wheat-colored dunes.

Point Conception Trail Jalama County Park off Hwy. 1, 20 miles southwest of Lompoc. Follow public access to the tip of the coast where the continent abruptly shifts eastward, intersects private ranch lands and crosses marvelous sand dunes. Isolated cove beaches attract the sun worshipper, while surfers, surf anglers and independent hikers favor the splendid isolation. The 12-mile round-trip trail allows views of offshore rocks that form lounging beds for seals, and the lighthouse (visitors are not allowed) adds to the scenic visuals.

Point Sal Trail Brown & Point Sal Rds., just west of Guadalupe. The dirt and tarmac of Point Sal Road leads to this steep point, where trails gain access to tiny sandy beaches below. Extremely rugged and very much off the beaten path, the main trail weaves a dizzying course between high, sheer cliffs and the wildlife-filled tide pools and beaches below. There are terrific whale-watching opportunities at the end of the trail, where the Santa Maria River spills into the sea. In general, this one's for experienced hikers with nerves of steel.

At Oso Flaco Lake, south of Oceano, the 4-mile-long Nipomo Dunes Trail winds through acres of wheat-colored dunes. Jeff Greene

San Simeon State Beach Hwy. 1 & San Simeon Creek, San Simeon. Hiking trails abound along this popular beach campground bordered by San Simeon and Santa Rosa Creeks. Nestled at the foot of the Santa Lucia Mountains, the landscape is isolated and popular with campers.

Santa Rosa Creek Bluffs Hwy. 1, at the south end of Moonstone Beach Dr., Cambria. Bold bluffs overlooking prime tide pools and brown sand beaches near the charming marsh-lands of Santa Rosa Creek are filled with excellent hiking trails that are reached from a convenient parking area.

Horseback riders find the foothills and canyons of the Santa Ynez Valley filled with miles of scenic equestrian trails. Alisal Guest Ranch

Horseback Riding

Alisal Guest Ranch and Resort
www.alisal.com, 800-4-ALISAL, 805-688-6411, 1054 Alisal Rd., Solvang.

Holder Park Equestrian Center
www.holderpark.com, 805-929-4447, Holder Park Ln., Nipomo.

J&J Riding 805-234-0578, Pecho St., Los Osos.

Pacific Dunes Ranch www.rvonthego.com, 805-489-7787, 1207 Silver Spur Pl., Oceano.

Shangri-la Ranch Trail Horse Rentals
805-438-3895, 8 miles east of Santa Margarita at Santa Margarita Lake, San Louis Obispo.

Nature Preserves & Parks

Montaña de Oro State Park 2 miles south of Los Osos via Los Osos Valley/Pecho Rd. Eight thousand unspoiled acres of rugged cliffs, deeply forested canyons, tide pools and hidden cove beaches provide spectac-ular vantage points for wildlife observa-tion. Playful sea otters and migrating California gray whales are the headliners here, as are the sweeping hilltop bluffs filled with California poppies, coreopsis and lupine. In the winter, monarch butterflies congregate in the extensive eucalyptus forests. Splendid views up and down the coast for 100 miles are available from the park's highest point, 1,300-foot Valencia Peak. Superb hiking, horseback riding and camping far from the madding crowd.

Morro Bay State Park East of Embarcadero via State Park Rd., Morro Bay. A profusion of wildlife is protected within the embrace of this 2,000-acre preserve, famed for the expansive mudflats that attract shorebirds by the tens of thousands. Eucalyptus groves, housing the largest blue heron rookery between San Francisco and Mexico, fill with nests of the elegant, 4-foot-tall birds beginning in late January. The park also includes the Morro Estuary Natural Preserve, home to ancient, moss-draped pygmy oaks and myriad marsh birds, including the Audubon warbler. The park's Museum of Natural History (805-772-2694) provides guided walks of the area.

Tide Pooling

On the Central Coast, guided tide pool exploring is provided by the **Morro Bay State Park Museum of Natural History** (805-772-2694). Also, the rocky stretches between San Simeon and Piedras Blancas yield up especially rewarding pockets easily accessible to the inquiring beachcomber.

Surfing

Hazard Canyon end of Pecho Rd., Los Osos. Reef break, lefts and rights; for experienced surfers only; can get rips, cold water, sharks, jagged reef. Only for die-hards, it's called Hazard for a reason, and help is a long way away.

Morro Rock Harbor Entrance Morro Rock Harbor, Morro Bay. Small sandbar on the inside of the break walls, all lefts; needs powerful swell but can be superclean, rarely gets above 3 feet. Paddling across the entrance can be hazardous—during tide change, the small opening in the entrance turns into a river.

Pismo Beach Pier Northside breaks all year during any swell, making it—and its sandy bottom—popular with local and visiting surfers regardless of skill level. Jay Swanson

Morro Rock Jetty Hwy. 1, bet. Yerba Buena Ave. & Atascadero Rd., Morro Bay. Sand bottom, beach break, lefts and rights; fun beach peaks break all year, smaller surf is clean, larger swells get big and hairy. Beginner to advanced. *Note:* Warm water is emitted from the nearby PG&E plant.

Pismo Beach Pier Northside Wilmar Ave. at Pismo Beach, Pismo Beach. Sand bottom, lefts and rights; fun spot, breaks all year during any swell, larger swells are too consistent and lined up to make it worth the paddle. Beginner to advanced, depending on swell size.

TENNIS

PRIVATE
Avila Bay Athletic Club & Spa www.avilabayclub.com, 805-595-7600, 6699 Bay Laurel Pl., Avila Beach.

San Luis Obispo Country Club www.slocountryclub.com, 805-543-4035, 255 Country Club Dr., San Luis Obispo.

PUBLIC
Arroyo Grande High School 495 Valley Rd., Arroyo Grande.

Elm Street Park Elm & Ash Sts., Arroyo Grande.

Monte Young Park South St. & Napa Ave., Morro Bay.

Pismo Beach Municipal Courts Wadsworth Ave. & Bello St., Pismo Beach.

Sinsheimer Park 900 Southwood Dr., San Luis Obispo.

South Bay Community Park Los Osos Valley Rd. & Palisades Ave., Los Osos.

SHOPPING

The hunting in San Luis Obispo and the Santa Ynez Valley is still good for memorabilia from the Central Coast's Wild West days or for the delicate china and glassware that formed small islands of European culture in rough whaling and ranching communities. Few can resist the charms of the region's many rustic old towns and restored civic centers from bygone eras, all filled with delightful arrays of small shops, galleries and cafes. Visitors can spend days combing tiny antiques stalls lining the piers of a fishing village and then find themselves faced with the most sophisticated designer possibilities just around the corner.

Antiques & Collectibles
Antique Center 805-541-4040, 1239 Monterey St., San Luis Obispo. Thirteen dealers have joined forces to offer an array of early American and country furniture, glassware, lighting and singular antique jewelry.

Antiques on Main 805-927-4292, 2338 Main St., Cambria. This two-floor building and its basement contain 9,000 feet of primo merchandise, with a great gathering of Americana artifacts, large and small, and a healthy assortment of early-20th-century pop collectibles.

Art Mesquit 805-773-1776, 1353 Shell Beach Rd., Shell Beach. Wonderful selection of art deco furniture, antique radios, Oriental artifacts and fine furniture make this a must-stop for discerning collectors.

Los Alamos Depot Mall/The Roundhouse 805-344-3315, 515 Bell St, Los Alamos. Dozens of individual antiques collectors have banded together to set up shop in the only surviving original Pacific Coast Railway station. The cavernous building runs the gamut from the incredibly tacky to the genuinely desirable. A nice wine-tasting bar has been built along one wall, and many local Santa Ynez Valley winemakers offer free or inexpensive pours of their elixirs.

The Quilt Shoppe www.superquilts.com, 805-693-0124, 1693 Mission Dr., Solvang. Don't miss this largest collection of new and vintage quilts in the state of California. Both handmade American and imported designs are on display and for sale.

Virginia's Attic 805-239-0600, 1329 Spring St., Paso Robles. This is a godsend for savvy antiques buffs seeking vintage Christmas items or old railroad collectibles. Good assortment of vintage clothing is also available.

Arts & Crafts

Bali Isle Imports 805-544-7662, 1038 Chorro St., San Luis Obispo. A tropical treasure trove of vibrant hand-screened batik textiles, masks, carved wood and exotic jewelry from Bali crams this distinctive import palace.

Cody Gallery 805-688-5083, 2982 Grand Ave., Los Olivos. Opulent oils and bronze sculptures highlight regional themes in this gallery smack in the middle of the Santa Ynez wine country.

Every Cowboy's Ranch House www.ecr gallery.com, 800-927-9417, 805-927-1369, 2261 Center St., Cambria. Linda Foster Finley has constructed a tasteful, eclectic stew of western art and mercantile offerings to coax the wrangler in us all to the surface. Utilizing dozens of local and international artists, the metalwork, glassware, paintings and weavings are all quite memorable. Great iron barbecues flirt with art but still prove their utilitarian worth, and the furniture is both rustic and transcendent.

Gallery Los Olivos www.wineriesof santabarbara.com/gallerylosolivos.htm,

San Luis Obispo's Hands Gallery carries playful wood and metal designs by local artisans and regularly wins the top award in the New Times' newspaper poll. Jeff Greene

805-688-7517, 2920 Grand Ave., Los Olivos. Sunny showrooms filled with revolving collections of regional and California-themed artworks, plus ongoing exhibits of local works by Santa Ynez Artist Guild members.

Hands Gallery 805-543-1921, 777 Higuera St., San Luis Obispo. Glazed and wildly innovative ceramic ware and sculpture form the core of this progressive gallery, which also carries playful wood and metal designs by local artisans.

Harmony Pottery Works 805-927-4293, Old Hwy. 1, Harmony. One-stop shopping is here for the collector of top-quality, handcrafted ceramic and stoneware pottery. This spacious showroom offers a wide range of styles and glazes in ware created by top local ceramists.

Howard Kline www.howardkline.com, 805-927-2917, 750 Sheffield St., Cambria. This studio is a great place to get unique, high-quality watercolors that are not given to saccharine and schmaltz, despite the fact that their subject matter (beach scenes, young dancers) are such clichés. Kline has a humorous, colorful light touch and charming sense of play.

Judith Hale Gallery www.judithhalegallery.com, 805-688-1222, 805-693-1233, fax 805-688-2342, 2890 and 2884 Grand Ave., Los Olivos. This keen-eyed lady represents over 75 regionally and nationally recognized painters, sculptors and jewelers, and her airy studios bristle with energy and drop-dead gorgeous creations. Especially fetching are the china silk batiks of Marilyn Salomon and hollow vessels of David Carrier. Check out the goofy, whimsical sculpture garden out back.

Mission Creek Studios Art Gallery www.missioncreek.com, 805-688-8792, 2948 Nojoqui Ave., Los Olivos. This small, bright studio gallery showcases local artists' and photographers' work. The mosaic art of Patti Jacquemain is especially noteworthy, as are the photographs of Susan Jørgensen for their elegant connection to the natural world of the Santa Ynez Valley.

Moonstones www.moonstones.com, 800-424-3827, 805-927-3447, 4070 Burton Dr., Cambria. Without doubt, Robert and Kathleen Unger's gallery is one of the best arts/mercantile stores on the Central Coast. The entire store is creatively laid out like a discovery museum, and adults are transported to the quizzical wide-eyed adolescents who, at one time, didn't know it all. Stephen Papp's delightful boxes, David Roy's kinetic sculptures, Bella Luz's night-lights, myriad kaleidoscopes and These Girls jewelry are luminous outposts in a kitschy world.

Sansone Studios www.sansonestudios.com, 805-693-9769, 2948 Nojoqui Ave., Suite 8, Los Olivos. The monumental and delicate work of Joel Sansone leaves visitors breathless. His alchemist's talents evoke beauty and timelessness when he creates his glass enamel on copper works of art. The opalescent wall hangings are awe-inspiring and his small accessory items delightful. Also featured are the equally impressive pieces of Pamela Sansone, Joel's wife and business/art partner.

Seekers Collection & Gallery www.seekersglass.com, 805-927-4352, 4090 Burton Dr., Cambria. A breathtaking selection of handblown, museum-quality glass jewelry, sculpture and furniture from 200 of the country's top art glass designers makes this store's two floors of shimmering finery a feast for the senses. Possibly the best of its kind in the entire state.

Simpson-Heller Gallery 805-927-1800, 2289 Main St., Cambria. A fine collection of regional paintings, sculpture and multimedia works distinguishes this airy, inviting gallery in the middle of the ultracharming 19th-century village.

Books

Cambria Book Company 805-927-3995, 784-C Main St., Cambria. Everyone (and everything) is greeted warmly here: "Browsers welcome, food, drink, children and polite dogs," according to a posting.

Leon's Book Store 805-543-5039, 659 Higuera St., San Luis Obispo. This cool used-book emporium will trade, buy and sell books seven days a week.

Los Osos Book Exchange 805-528-1614, 2149 10th St., Los Osos. A small hole in the wall brings lit to the boondocks.

Phoenix Books 805-543-3591, 990 Monterey St., San Luis Obispo. Great place to find the rare and esoteric in fiction and nonfiction.

Fashion

Ambiance 805-541-0988, 714 Higuera St., San Luis Obispo. Locally designed and made contemporary clothing for women, in natural fabrics and soft earth tones, makes this an environmentally sensitive fashion destination.

Ann's 805-543-8250, 895 Monterey St., San Luis Obispo. High-quality contemporary women's apparel looks especially inviting displayed inside one of the area's classiest 19th-century downtown buildings.

Ball & Skein & More/DreamWoven 4070 Burton Dr., Suite 1, Cambria. Pick your favorites of a vast array of the highest-quality yarns in the world and design your own fashion, or purchase incredible wearable-art dresses, shawls, capes and coats. This also is the place to run across Rachel Eckert of **DreamWoven** (www.dreamwoven.com, 805-238-2001), who creates imaginative one-of-a-kind women's and children's dresses, hats, booties, sweaters and bags.

Decades 805-546-0901, 785 Higuera St., San Luis Obispo. Racks and racks of top-condition vintage clothing and flashy accessories distinguish this shop, which also specializes in camp collectibles of all kinds from the 1940s to 1960s.

The Porte House Gallery of Wearable Art www.portehouse.com, 805-927-2492, 4015 West St., Cambria. Christopher and Dinah Lee manufacture one-of-a-kind printed silk fashions, aloha shirts, artisan jewelry, Georgettes, handbags, scarves. Everything is delicate and delicious to wear and to marvel over.

Wearable Images 805-927-4110, 786 Main St., Cambria. You've got to love a clothing store that sells comfortable cotton clothing and fresh produce.

Jewelry

Casa de Oro Jewelry 805-927-5444, 4090 Burton Dr., Cambria. Innovative jewelry designs are featured in Heather Trimble's very contemporary, jewelry-as-wearable-art emporium.

The Gold Concept 805-544-1088, 740 Higuera St., San Luis Obispo. Here you'll find contemporary jewelry designs, bold gold work and unusual gem selections.

House of Jade 805-927-4334, 801-B Main St., Cambria. Row upon row of beautifully handcrafted jade ornaments, accessories, objets d'art and brooches tease the eye and pocketbook.

Specialty

California Classics www.calclassics.net, 805-434-0987, 520 S. Main St., Suite C, Templeton. Real cowboys and cowgirls slide easily among the overflowing shelves of this true outpost of rural lifestyle necessities. Clothing, saddles, boots, hats, all things equine and friendly gab are all available in a casual sort of way.

Clairmont Farms www.clairmontfarms.com, 805-688-7505, 2480 Roblar Ave., Los Olivos. This lavender company has the favored bush in all its forms: fresh, dried, in oils, in personal care products, and in buds or bundles or pet products. If you or your animals can't resist, then head that-a-way right now.

Country Classics www.slocountryclass.com, 805-549-0844, 849 Monterey St., San Luis Obispo. While a huge selection of tasteful, country-themed gifts, Victorian and French country home furnishings and scented soap and folk art provides the content here, the real gem is the old country store itself—the historic Sinsheimer Brothers building, a trip to the past with hardwood floors and lofty 20-foot ceilings.

Farm Supply Company 805-543-3751, 675 Tank Farm Rd., San Luis Obispo. This farm supply depot, which caters to the needs of real area ranchers, brims with all of those western accoutrements for riding the range while mending fences—overalls, saddle blankets, feed troughs and grooming supplies. A surefire thrill for city slickers.

Fermentations www.fermentations.com, 800-446-7505, 4056 Burton Dr., Cambria. This emporium of the vine features many fine local wines to taste and purchase, as well as other yummy foodstuffs available in sample form. Also on sale are wine accessories and gift baskets. A very friendly, knowledgeable staff makes your visit a joy.

Games People Play www.gppslo.com, 805-541-GAME, 1119 Chorro St., San Luis Obispo. A fascinating, family-friendly haven of gamesmanship, filled with new and vintage comic books, plus board and role-playing games of astonishing variety.

Hearts Ease 805-927-5224, 4101 Burton Dr., Cambria. Most visitors come for the garden. A must see, this is a wonderful, calming retreat from the outside world. The gardens are grand, but inside one can find a potpourri of mind-and-body-oriented products like herbal everything, aromatherapy, candles and other odoriferous items.

Jedlicka's www.jedlickas.com, 805-688-2626, 2883 Grand Ave., Los Olivos. Preparing you to saddle up and ride off into the sunset, this ultimate western store outfits real ranchers (and those who just want to look like John Wayne) in Tony Lama boots and Stetson hats. There are acres of silver belt buckles, saddles, bridles and bits. It even smells like the Old West.

Olive House www.olivehouse.com, 805-686-5159, 1161 Mission Dr., Solvang. This new shop is dedicated to all things olive. For sale are oils and vinegars from around the world, hot sauces and other gourmet items. Regular tastings are held, and guest lecturers are brought in to upgrade local foodies' brainpans with legends and lore about the humble, yet ubiquitous foodstuff.

Soldier Factory 805-927-3804, 789 Main St., Cambria. Specializes in miniature pewter figurines.

Southern Port Traders 805-772-1649, 801 Embarcadero, Morro Bay. An eclectic array of clothing, crafts, jewelry and, oddly enough, percussion instruments.

Sycamore Farms www.sycamorefarms.com, 800-576-5288, 805-238-5288, 2485 Hwy. 46 West, Paso Robles. This rural natural herb farm has created walk-through display gardens of culinary, medicinal and fragrant herbs. Over 300 varieties, both fresh and dried, have been turned into almost any product one can think of, including some for pets. Excellent book section, and the gourmet cooks will go crazy with desire in the culinary products area. Classes and workshops are also available.

We Olive/Di Raimondo's Italian Market and Cheese Shop www.weolive.com, 805-239-7200, 822 13th St., Paso Robles. A wonderful pairing of an old-school Italian import palace and an outlet for a locally produced olive oil. Vinegars, tapenades, salsa, gift baskets, books and ceramics also can be purchased at reasonably prices. Also check out a sibling enterprise, **Wine Attic** (805-227-4107, 822 13th St., Paso Robles). This delightful spot recently opened for business and should attract enophiles visiting or living in this booming viticulture region. Wine dinners, many local small winemakers hawking their wares, books, lectures and everything related to the vine is on the agenda.

Sports

Central Coast Surfboards www.centralcoastsurfboards.com, 805-541-1129, 736 Higuera St., San Luis Obispo. Boards for all sports—surfboards, sailboards, skateboards, boogieboards—abound in this well-stocked water sport center.

Mountain Air Sports 805-543-1676, 667 Marsh St., San Luis Obispo. No matter what sport you've a hankering for, this sports store has the gear. Carries some of the best brands in camping, backpacking and climbing gear.

SEASONAL EVENTS

January
Jazz Festival 805-772-4467, Morro Bay.
Polar Bear Dip 800-563-1878, Cayucos.
Winter Bird Festival 805-772-4467, Morro Bay.

February
Mardi Gras Ball 805-541-2183, 805-546-5405, San Luis Obispo.
Mardi Gras Jazz Festival 805-773-4382, Pismo Beach.
Pro Surfing Tour 805-773-4382, Pismo Beach.
Real Men Cook Food Fair 805-688-6144, Solvang.
Sea Fare & Wine List Review 805-773-4382, Pismo Beach.
Storytelling Festival 805-688-6144, Solvang.
Winemakers' Dinner 805-927-3369, Cambria.

March

Celebration of Zinfandel 805-238-0506, 805-239-8463, Paso Robles.
Chili Cook-Off 805-927-3624, Cambria.
Easter Egg Hunt 800-563-1878, Cayucos.
Famous Jazz Series 805-927-0567, Cambria.
Paderewski Festival 805-238-0506, Paso Robles.
Rib Cook-Off 805-541-0286, San Luis Obispo.
Seafood Festival 805-772-4467, Morro Bay.
Taste of Solvang 805-688-6144, Solvang.

April

Famous Jazz Series 805-927-0567, Cambria.
Hans Christian Andersen Fairy Tales Festival
805-688-6144, Solvang.
Italian Street Painting Festival 805-543-6492,
San Luis Obispo.
Petal and Palettes Art and Flower Show 805-927-
3624, Cambria.
Seafood Festival 805-563-1878, Cayucos.
Strawberry Festival 805-473-2250, Arroyo Grande.
Vintner's Festival 805-688-6144, Solvang.

Each April, Arroyo Grande's vibrant Strawberry Festival attracts tourists and locals alike. Jeff Greene

May

An Old Day in Old San Simeon 805-238-8463,
Paso Robles.
Antique & Collectible Street Sale 800-563-1878,
Cayucos.
Antique Fair 805-773-4382, Pismo Beach.
Antique Gas Engine Show 800-563-1878, Cayucos.
Art in the Park 805-772-2504, Morro Bay.
Cinco de Mayo Festivities 805-781-7300, San Luis Obispo.
Cruzing Car Show 805-772-4467, Morro Bay.
Festival of Beers 805-544-2266, Avila Beach.
Great Western Bicycle Rally 805-238-0506, Paso Robles.
Hospice du Rhône 805-239-1205, Paso Robles.
La Fiesta de San Luis Obispo 805-541-1901, San Luis Obispo.
Los Rancheros Visadores 805-688-6144, Solvang.
Peddlers' Fair 800-563-1878, Cayucos.
Petal and Palettes Art and Flower Show 805-927-3624, Cambria.
Roll Out the Barrels Wine Festival 805-541-5868, San Luis Obispo.
West Coast Kustom Car Show 805-238-0506, Paso Robles.
Wildflower Festival 805-238-0506, Paso Robles.
Wine Festival 805-238-8463, 805-238-0506, Paso Robles.

June

Afternoon of Epicurean Delight 805-782-4016, San Luis Obispo.
Beach Fest 805-773-4382, Pismo Beach.

Gem and Mineral Show 800-563-1878, Cayucos.
Motorcycle Show 805-772-4467, Morro Bay.
Natural Gas Jazz Band Concert 805-927-0594, Cambria.
Scandinavian Midsummer Festival 805-688-6144, Solvang.
Strawberry Farmers' Market 805-927-4715, Cambria.
Wine Festival 805-466-2044, Atascadero.

July

Art in the Park 805-772-2504, Morro Bay.
Central Coast Renaissance Faire 805-474-9571, San Luis Obispo.
Family Fourth of July 805-772-4467, Morro Bay.
Fireworks off the Pier 800-563-1878, Cayucos.
Fourth of July Beach Fireworks 805-773-4382, Pismo Beach.
Fourth of July in the Plaza 805-781-7305, San Luis Obispo.
Heritage Day at the Dallidet 805-543-6762, San Luis Obispo.
Mid-State Fair 805-239-0655, Paso Robles.
Mozart Festival 805-781-3009, San Luis Obispo.
Peddlers' Fair 800-563-1878, Cayucos.
Picnic in the Park 805-927-1128, Cambria.
Portuguese Celebration 800-563-1878, Cayucos.
Renaissance Faire 800-688-1477, San Luis Obispo.

August

Basil Festival 805-238-5288, Paso Robles.
Classic Car Show 805-466-2044, Atascadero.
Concerts in the Park 805-541-0286, San Luis Obispo.
Festival of the Bears 805-528-4884, Los Osos.
Japanese Friendship Festival 805-929-4461, San Luis Obispo.
Midsummer Street Fair 805-772-4467, Morro Bay.
Mission Santa Inés Fiesta 805-688-6144, Solvang.
Opera Under the Stars 805-239-1640, Paso Robles.
Pine Dorado Festival 805-927-3624, Cambria.
Portuguese Festival and Parade 805-773-4382, Pismo Beach.

September

Air Show 805-238-0506, Paso Robles.
Art in the Park 805-772-2504, Morro Bay.
Harvest Festival 805-481-5038, Arroyo Grande.
Peddlers' Fair 800-563-1878, Cayucos.
West Coast Kustom Car Show 805-238-0506, Paso Robles.

October

Antique & Collectible Street Sale 800-563-1878, Cayucos.
Art Association Home Tour 805-927-8190, Cambria.
Celebration of Harvest 805-688-6144, Solvang.
Clam Festival 805-773-4382, Pismo Beach.
Colony Days Celebration 805-466-2044, Atascadero.

Day in the Country 805-688-6144, Los Olivos.
Harbor Festival 805-772-1155, Morro Bay.
Harvest Celebration 805-238-5288, San Luis Obispo.
Harvest Wine Affair 805-239-8463, Paso Robles.
Jubilee-by-the-Sea Jazz Festival 805-773-4382, Pismo Beach.
October Festival 805-929-1583, Nipomo.
Oktoberfest 805-528-4884, Baywood Park.
Pioneer Day 805-238-0506, Paso Robles.
Pumpkins on the Pier 805-773-4382, Pismo Beach.
Valley Harvest Arts Festival 805-736-6565, Lompoc.

November
Car Show 805-772-4467, Morro Bay.
Christmas Street Fair 805-772-4467, Morro Bay.
Craft Fair 805-461-4000, Atascadero.
Dixieland Jazz Festival 805-688-6144, Solvang.
International Film Festival 805-546-FILM, San Luis Obispo.
Tree Lighting 805-461-5000, Atascadero; 805-238-4103, Paso Robles; 805-773-4382, Pismo Beach.

December
Christmas at the Castle 805-927-2093, San Simeon.
Christmas Festival 805-927-3624, Cambria.
Christmas in the Plaza 805-781-7300, San Luis Obispo.
Christmas Parade 805-528-4848, Los Osos.
Christmas Street Fair 805-466-2044, Atascadero.
Danish Days 805-688-6144, Solvang.
Deck the Tree Ceremony 800-563-1878, Cayucos.
Lighted Boat Parade 805-772-4467, Morro Bay.
Vine Street Victorian Showcase 805-238-4103, Paso Robles.
Winterfest Celebration 805-688-6144, Solvang.

6

WINERIES

Grape Expectations

Wines of California . . . inimitable fragrance and soft fire . . . and the wine of bottled poetry.
—Robert Louis Stevenson

This chapter departs slightly from our coastal parameters and acknowledges the distinctive wine growing appellations for the Central Coast. Well over three-quarters of the wine made in the United States is produced in California and, of that, the most widely known hails from Napa and Sonoma. Increasingly, however, some of the most intriguing California wines are being generated from small wineries along the Central Coast. Thanks to the compactness of these facilities—most are so small that their wines rarely leave their respective areas—winemakers here are famed for their abilities to grow grapes and create wines by hand.

Grape-growing microclimates weave throughout the region's mountains and sunny coastal slopes, each a unique collaboration of soil, climate and varietal creating distinctive variations in the final products. Thanks to mild temperatures, fog-cooled evenings and a long, dry growing season, Central Coast wines are celebrated for intensity of flavor, length of life and elegance of structure, and the region has come to be noted for its award-winning chardonnays and sauvignon blancs, cabernet sauvignons, merlots and syrahs.

Blessed by the need for sacramental wines used in celebrating the Catholic Mass, wine production arrived in California with the Franciscan missionaries in the late 18th century. After experiments with native grapes proved disappointing, European vinifera vines were imported for cultivation. By the 1850s, under the influence of European viticultural entrepreneurs, California winemaking had expanded up and down the state and, fueled by the welcoming climate, became a thriving industry during the last half of the 19th century. Though New World winemaking managed to survive a phylloxera infestation in the 1880s—most spunky was the tough-skinned zinfandel grape—and the loss of vast cellarings due to the infamous earthquake of 1906, Prohibition dealt a near-fatal blow to the industry. Pummeled but not beaten, California winemaking had to rebuild and reinvent itself following the Repeal Act of 1933.

Recognizing that the Central Coast region boasted growing conditions similar to those of the great European viticultural centers of the Rhine, Bordeaux and Burgundy, University of California–Davis experts began rediscovering areas ripe for vineyard planting. Many of these pockets were located along the eastern slopes of the Coast Ranges, in the Santa Cruz, Monterey and San Luis Obispo areas and in the Santa Ynez Valley next to Santa Barbara.

The most recent renaissance of wine growing interest in the area came with the trend in the 1960s away from mega-agriculture. In a resulting boom of microwineries in the 1970s, the Central Coast of California came into its own, claiming the attention of both the region's population and international aficionados.

Prominent Varietals

Through trial and error, some European vinifera grape varieties have been found to prosper famously when catalyzed by Central Coast soils and climate. Producing the most most celebrated regional wines are the chardonnay and cabernet sauvignon grapes. Chardonnay is the great white wine of French Burgundy, which produces a dry, buttery, applelike wine whose depth and fruit are heightened by oak aging. Cabernet sauvignon, which produces the celebrated red wine of Bordeaux, is full-bodied, fragrant, often with tones of cherries and bell pepper, and is far and away the top red varietal produced in California.

In addition to the two aforementioned and extensively planted grapes, other varietals have met with acclaim. Zinfandel is a vigorous red grape—one of the earliest planted in California—that produces a bold wine with spicy aroma. The less said about the fad for white zinfandel, the better. Pinot noir, the temperamental "Holy Grail" of Burgundian red wine grapes, is finding its way to some fine wines of dry and elegant structure. The spicy Alsatian gewürztraminer wine is another popular California white varietal, as is the citrusy, faintly grassy sauvignon blanc, long used to create the white wines of Bordeaux and the Loire. Italian and Rhône varietals—sangiovese, syrah and petite sirah—are on the ascendance in the Central Coast, their velvety and complex wines gaining increasing acclaim.

SANTA CRUZ MOUNTAINS WINE AREA

As with so many features of the Central Coast landscape, winemaking began in Santa Cruz with the coming of the Franciscan fathers in the late 18th century. When the Mission Santa Cruz was founded, the missionaries quickly planted river benchlands below the church with the sweet Spanish grapes required for wines used in the Catholic Mass. After the missions were secularized and European settlers came to seek post–Gold Rush fortunes in lumber, shipping and agriculture, the European vinifera grapes were planted in fog-cooled pockets of the mountains.

Commercial winemaking in the area began in 1863 with the first plantings of grapes by brothers George and John Jarvis in the Vine Hill district near the 2,000-foot summit of the Santa Cruz Mountains. By 1870, over 300 acres of the mountains had been dedicated to wine grapes, and there were over a dozen winemakers in business in Santa Cruz County by 1875. The new fad for wine growing mushroomed too quickly, alas, and a glut of grapes caused the fledgling industry to fall during a worldwide depression in the late 1870s.

Still, optimists pressed onward, and by the late 1880s there were three respected vintners—Santa Cruz Mountain Wine Company, Mare Vista and the Ben Lomond Wine Company—sending wines to competitions around the country and the world. Natural disasters, another depression, a world war and, finally, Prohibition effectively uprooted the young industry. Grape stakes disappeared into the weeds until the most recent revival of winemaking interest in the 1960s.

Intent upon mining the rural splendor of the redwoods and seaside, expatriates from urban areas and Silicon Valley decided that doing their own thing would include winemaking.

Essential Wine-Tasting Protocol

There is nothing pretentious about wine tasting on the Central Coast, an activity enthusiastically pursued by weekend visitors to the area's many small tasting rooms. Tasting room staff members are happy to guide the novice through winemaking techniques and tips for maximizing appreciation of the wines being poured. Like all collaborations of nature and art, wine should be enjoyed by all the senses.

Before tasting, pause to notice the color and clarity of the wine. Hold the glass up to the light to admire its full luster and—ideally—clarity. Rotate the wine gently in the glass and then smell deeply, noticing the bouquet that often will be reminiscent of a wide range of fruits, flowers and earthiness. Now you're ready to take a small sip. Trilling it against the roof of the mouth—this may take practice —will allow maximum palate contact. Here's where the wine shows off its range of sweetness, tartness, body and, when swallowed, its finish.

Clearing the palate with water or bread is crucial for sampling successive wines. And those strategically placed buckets are there for a reason. Spitting out excess wine will ensure that both you and your palate stay intact during multiple tastings. If you plan to make an afternoon of it, it's a wise idea to designate a driver who sips nothing stronger than juice or mineral water during a series of winery visits.

The region has long attracted mavericks, from 1940s forefathers Chaffee Hall and Martin Ray—early believers in the power of the modern premium wine industry—to "Rhône Ranger" Randall Grahm in the mid-1980s.

Since the 1970s, Santa Cruz Mountains wines have gained in finesse and renown, fueled by a boom of over two dozen almost exclusively family-run microwineries that have sprung up to capture the unique terroir of the stony, mountain soil and luxuriant dry, fog-cooled growing season. Latter-day pioneers like David Bruce, Ken Burnap, Dexter Ahlgren and Robert Roudon were joined in 1980s by a host of young entrepreneurs increasingly intent upon harvesting tiny, far-flung vineyards in this area's diverse landscape. Exceptional chardonnays, gewürztraminers, rieslings and cabernets are already emerging from this young appellation, showing the regional style of elegance and long-lived structure.

Western Side
AHLGREN VINEYARD
www.ahlgrenvineyard.com
ahlgren@alhlgrenvineyard.com
Winemaker: Dexter Ahlgren
800-338-6071, 831-338-6071, fax 831-338-9111
20320 Hwy. 9, Boulder Creek 95006
Tours: Sat. noon–4
Tastings: Sat. noon–4
Specialties: chardonnay, semillon, pinot noir, cabernet sauvignon, cabernet franc, merlot, zinfandel, syrah

Bonded in 1976, Ahlgren Vineyard turns out some of the most famous cabernet sauvignons and semillons in California. Nearly 20 consecutive vintages of Ahlgren chardonnay from Monterey's Ventana Vineyard have taken countless awards for their rich, clean bouquet and flavors. Renowned wine critic Robert Parker considers Ahlgren's cabernets "usually among the best wines of the vintage." The approach here is strictly handmade, and the low volume of production makes these wines coveted by serious collectors. The winery facility, tucked beneath Val and Dexter Ahlgren's private home, is located in a mountain setting surrounded by forests and offers views of the redwood-draped canyons from the resident picnic tables.

BARGETTO WINERY

www.bargetto.com
Winemaker: Paul Wolford
800-422-7438, 831-475-2258,
fax 831-475-2664
3535 N. Main St., Soquel 95073
Tours: Mon.–Fri. by appointment
Tastings: Mon.–Sat. 10–5, Sun. noon–5
Specialties: pinot grigio, chardonnay, pinot noir, cabernet sauvignon, merlot

Soquel is home to the Santa Cruz Mountains' oldest winery (established in 1933), whose spacious brick tasting room is packed with history, extending to pre-Prohibition days when the enterprising Bargetto brothers, Phillip and John, kept frontier restaurants well stocked with sturdy Italian red wines. Today a third generation is in charge of the large facility, which offers tours of its vast cellars. Visitors also can enjoy exhibits of artwork in the winery's gallery and sip and picnic at an outdoor courtyard overlooking Soquel Creek. Producing over 30,000 cases annually of Santa Cruz Mountain varietals, Bargetto is far and away the largest winery in the area, enjoying a renaissance of excellence with its chardonnay and cabernet sauvignon and unique northern Italian varietal grapes from the Reagan Vineyards Estate under the La Vita label. Don't leave without sampling the winery's distinctive mead (a honey-fermented drink) and the fruit wines, including olallieberry, raspberry and apricot, distributed under the Chaucers label. A well-stocked gift store provides packaged samplers of top vintages, wine paraphernalia and souvenir items. Bargetto's fine wines are also available for tasting and sales at its tasting room on Monterey's Cannery Row.

BONNY DOON VINEYARD/ CA' DEL SOLO

www.bonnydoonvineyard.com
Winemaker: Randall Grahm
831-425-4518, fax 831-425-3528
10 Pine Flat Rd., Santa Cruz 95060
Tours: No
Tastings: Daily 11–5
Specialties: French Rhône varietals, Italian varietals & dessert wines

The unmistakable sense of adventure and maverick instincts of internationally acclaimed winemaker Randall Grahm are apparent everywhere at this rustic mountaintop winery appointed with state-of-the-art equipment. The vineyards are planted with grenache, mourvèdre, syrah, marsanne and roussane, an indication of Grahm's early interest in the Rhône region of France. His innovations yields collector's item Rhône-style red wines, velvety dessert wines, award-winning chardonnays and

Italian varietals (under the Ca' Del Solo label), as well as the occasional bracing eau de vie, ice wines and distilled brandy. Darling of the international media, Grahm, dubbed "America's most avant-garde winemaker" by *Connoisseur* magazine, produces vintage after astonishing vintage of distinctive wines, highlighted by clever labels that play on Old World classics, such as Cigare Volant and Clos de Gilroy. Shaded picnic tables are situated along Mill Creek and just up the hill from the tasting room, which also stocks a T-shirt collection showcasing Grahm's celebrated campy wine-label designs. There is also a recently opened tasting room in Paso Robles.

HALLCREST VINEYARDS/ ORGANIC WINE WORKS

www.hallcrestvineyards.com
www.organicwineworks.com
owwwine@cruzio.com
Winemaker: John Schumacher
800-699-9463, 831-335-4441,
fax 831-335-4450
379 Felton Empire Rd., Felton 95018
Tours: By appointment
Tastings: Daily noon–5
Specialties: chardonnay, riesling, gewürztraminer, pinot noir, cabernet sauvignon, zinfandel, syrah, Black Corinth dessert wine

One of the most atmospheric wineries of the area, Hallcrest enjoys a hallowed reputation. Begun in 1941 by post-Prohibition, premium winemaking pioneer Chaffee Hall, the winery created legendary cabernet sauvignon and riesling from its estate vines, many of which survive today. After a brief incarnation as Felton-Empire Vineyards, the compound reverted to the Hallcrest name in 1987 under the proprietorship of UC Davis–trained winemaker John Schumacher, who carries on the tradition of exquisite white rieslings produced from those fabled estate grapes. Handmade, full-

bodied zinfandels and crisp, buttery chardonnays also are specialties of this small dry-farmed organic wine facility. John and his business partner/spouse Lorraine also bottle a line of certified-organic, sulfite-free wines under the Organic Wine Works label. The wooden cottage tasting room, terraced lawns and cellars overlooking the Henry Cowell State Park redwoods form the backdrop for a superb day of wine tasting and occasional outdoor musical concerts featuring some of the top names in jazz, blues and acoustic folk music.

OBESTER WINERY

www.obesterwinery.com
Winemaker: Kendyl Kellogg
650-726-9463, fax 650-726-7074
12341 San Mateo Rd. (Hwy. 92),
Half Moon Bay 94019
Tours: No
Tastings: Daily 10–5
Specialties: sauvignon blanc, chardonnay, riesling, sangiovese, cabernet sauvignon, zinfandel, port

From this small, ranch-style winery situated at the foot of the mountains in the seaside town of Half Moon Bay, winemaker Kendyl Kellogg produces exceptional varietals from Monterey and Napa grapes. The handsome tasting room and picnic area have long been fixtures of any day trip to this charming village, where Kellogg creates delightfully floral rieslings and toasty chardonnays, in addition to a long list of elegantly structured sauvignon blancs and cabernets, all under the Nebbia label. Most of the wines can be sampled at the tasting room, which also offers specialty food items, Obester's line of mustards and dressings and wine-related books.

ROUDON-SMITH VINEYARDS

www.roudonsmith.com
Winemaker: Mike Walter
831-438-1244, fax 831-438-4374

2364 Bean Creek Rd., Scotts Valley 95066
Tours: Sat. 11–4:30 or large groups by
appointment
Tastings: Sat. 11–4:30
Specialties: chardonnay, cabernet sauvignon, merlot

One of the earliest pioneers of the handmade wine boom of the 1970s, Roudon-Smith was founded in 1972 by two couples seeking escape from the high-tech industry of Silicon Valley. While a new vineyard of chardonnay grapes matured on a sunny canyon slope where the Roudon and Smith families settled, the small winery began producing long-lived varietals from selected local vineyards by traditional methods. Today the winery is in the capable hands of new owners Annette, David, Don and Christine Hunt, but the tradition continues. Wines designed to be partnered with fine food are the specialties of this award-winning house, best exemplified by a full-bodied zinfandel, elegantly structured estate chardonnay and Santa Cruz Mountain pinot noir, as well as releases of cabernet sauvignon, from grapes grown at Meeker Vineyard in Paso Robles. Limited supplies of reserve wines are still available for purchase.

SALAMANDRE WINE CELLARS

www.salamandrewine.com
Winemaker: Wells Shoemaker
831-685-0321, fax 831-685-1860
108 Don Carlos Dr., Aptos 95003
Tours: By appointment
Tastings: By appointment
Specialties: chardonnay, pinot noir, primitizo, merlot, syrah

The quirky label, named for a rare amphibian found only in a small sector of the Santa Cruz Mountains, tells a lot about the inventive approach of winemaker Shoemaker to his microyield of Burgundian-style chardonnays. Always experimenting, the winemaker continues to charm and to surprise with distinctive vintages of whatever grapes currently capture his fancy. Shoemaker delights in innovative combinations, such as a blend of intensely floral white riesling and muscat canelli, which he calls White Dove. Every inch of this minuscule operation is covered by hand, from selective picking of grapes from the Santa Cruz Mountains and Arroyo Seco region of Monterey County to the crushing, bottling and lugging of boxes. Salamandre wines may be found in restaurants and wine stores throughout Santa Cruz County, and the label, graced with the embossed emblem of the long-toed salamander, is a regional keepsake.

SANTA CRUZ MOUNTAIN VINEYARD

www.scmvwine.com
Winemaker: Jeff Emery
831-426-6209
2300 Jarvis Rd., Boulder Creek 95065
Tours: By appointment
Tastings: By appointment
Specialties: pinot noir, cabernet sauvignon, merlot, syrah

Founding winemaker Ken Burnap is widely regarded as one of the prime movers of the boom in small, premium wineries. In 1974, he purchased 14 acres covered with pinot noir grapes, in the Santa Cruz Mountains. The site, originally planted by John Jarvis in 1863, is one of the oldest vineyards in the Santa Cruz Mountains. The spot was graced with all of the growing conditions that the exacting winemaker required, from the southern exposure and hillside terrain to well-drained, rather poor soil that could encourage deep roots and intensity of flavor. Vines are hand-tended and hand harvested, and the labor-intensive production techniques reach fruition in powerful, big-shouldered red wines. The merlots are pure velvet, and the pinot noirs are memorable. Visitors should make time for an appointment at this highly regarded winery—an hour spent with winemaker Jeff Emery provides a crash course in local winemaking.

SOQUEL VINEYARDS

www.soquelvineyards.com
Winemakers: Peter Bargetto,
Paul Bargetto, Jon Morgan
831-462-9045, fax 831-464-3440
8063 Glen Haven Rd., Soquel 95073
Tours: By appointment
Tastings: Sat. 11–4
Specialties: chardonnay, pinot noir, cabernet sauvignon, merlot, syrah

One of the area's finest wineries, this tiny facility—sitting atop a quiet hill at the end of Glen Haven Road—can easily be toured in a few minutes, but the excellent tasting opportunities demand a lengthier stay. The remarkable tasting room is lit by local artists' stained-glass windows, while its doors are constructed from an old redwood wine barrel that belonged to the Bargetto twins' grandfather and roof tiles from a Tuscan country farmhouse built in 1751. The focus here is on small quantities of handmade wines showcasing the intensely flavored grapes of the region. This vibrant young enterprise utilizes the finest French oak barrels and has already attracted much attention in regional and national competitions—the cabernets and chardonnays are justly acclaimed, but the pinot noir is especially appealing. Peter's in-laws are the Chissotti wine-growing family from Chieri, Italy.

STORRS WINERY

www.storrswine.com
Winemakers: Stephen & Pamela Storrs
831-458-5030, fax 831-458-0464
Old Sash Mill #35, 303 Potrero St., Santa Cruz 95060
Tours: By appointment
Tastings: Daily noon–5
Specialties: chardonnay, merlot, petite sirah, zinfandel

A husband-and-wife winemaking team of the first order, Pamela and Steve Storrs are both UC Davis enology graduates. The duo also has already endowed this tiny facility with glory at statewide competitions. The emphasis is upon a series of chardonnays created exclusively with hand-sorted grapes from the Santa Cruz Mountains. And, given the widely diverse topography of selected vineyards (a few from the Monterey appellation), the results are as distinct as they are distinctive. The small tasting room regularly attracts inquiring wine buffs, and the winemakers are always available to explain, discuss and compare notes. The winery, housed behind the sleek tasting area, is essentially a glorified warehouse where all of the sorcery of winemaking, from blending to cellaring, is on view.

Other Western Side Santa Cruz Mountain Area Wineries

Andersen Vineyards www.andersenvineyards.com, 831-336-3525, fax 831-336-3005. P.O. Box 1117, Felton 95018. This winery overlooks Zayante Canyon and specializes in organically grown estate merlot and cabernet sauvignon. No tours or tastings.

Aptos Vineyard 831-688-3856, fax 831-662-9102, 7278 Mesa Dr., Aptos 95003. Extremely small bottlings of pinot noir, grown on Judge John Marlo's small estate, are evocative of the fabled vintages of Burgundy. Regularly honored at California's top competitions, these pinots are so rare that they seldom find their way any farther than the cellars of local admirers. But they, like their chardonnay siblings, are well worth looking for when you're in the area. No tours or tastings.

Aptos Creek Vineyard www.aptoscreek vineyard.com, and reavollersen@yahoo .com, 831-684-1680. Andrea Vollersen and Brian Wilkerson grow pinot noir in their Aptos vineyard and then produce a limited amount of handcrafted cases at the Hallcrest Vineyards in Felton, California. No tours or tastings.

Banyan Wines www.banyanwines.com, info@banyanwines.com, 831-459-0468, 604-B 2nd St., Santa Cruz 95060. Wine- maker Kenny Likitprakong produces small lots of specialty California white wines only: gewürztraminer, riesling, viognier. No tours or tastings.

Beauregard Vineyards www.beauregard vineyards.com, 831-425-7777, P.O. Box 2809, Santa Cruz 95060. Jim Beauregard farms 80 acres above Bonny Doon origi- nally planted in 1940. His son Ryan turns them into tasty, satisfying wines, especially the Bald Mountain 2002 chardonnay. Currently they focus on cabernet sauvi- gnon, pinot noir, merlot, zinfandel and chardonnay. The family's newest venture is a Santa Cruz Municipal Wharf tasting room, which is open daily.

Clos Tita Winery www.clos-tita.com, pinot@clos-tita.com, 831-439-9235, 4 Kendell Ln., Santa Cruz 95066. Since 1996, winemaker Dave Estrada has been making limited-quantity, unfiltered estate pinot noir, as well as syrah and chardonnay from other appellation vineyards, plus Santa Cruz Mountain cabernet sauvignon. No tours or tastings.

Equinox www.equinoxwine.com, 831-338-2646, fax 831-338-8307, 290 Igo Way, Boulder Creek 95006. Barry Jackson pro- duces a méthode champenoise sparkling

wine exclusively from Santa Cruz Mountain grapes that is both rounded and austerely dry. Plenty of long-lived microbubbles fill this pleasing sparkler, whose flinty bouquet offers a clean, crisp finish. No tours are conducted, but sips are available at a new tasting room at 427 Swift in Santa Cruz (831-471-9090).

Four Gates Vineyard & Winery www.four gateswine.com, 831-457-2673. Benyamin Cantz produces 400 cases a year of quality, organic and kosher chardonnay, merlot, cabernet franc and pinot noir from grapes he grows in Santa Cruz's Happy Valley. He's happy, the vines are happy, his customers are happy and so is the cosmos. No tours or tastings.

Glenwood Oaks Winery www.glenwood oakswinery.com, 831-461-0668, 2364 Bean Creek Rd., Scotts Valley 95066. Winemaker Val Rebhahn's family is the fifth generation to live on the same land, continuing the winemaking tradition begun by the C. C. Martin family during the 1880s. Today the winery produces award-winning chardonnay, as well as a pinot noir and syrah. Estate wine production began in 2004. Tastings Sat. 2–4:30 and by appointment.

Hunter Hill Vineyard & Winery www .hunterhillwines.com, 831-465-9294, fax 831-475-5060, 7099 Glen Haven Rd., Soquel 95073. Above the village of Soquel in the Santa Cruz Mountains, wine growers Vann and Christine Slatter coax estate mer- lots from their vineyards and produce syrah, pinot noir and old-vine zinfandel from the state's best appellations. Chris- tine's family, the Manildis, have worked the land since the 19th century. From the hill- top gazebo, visitors enjoy a panoramic view of Nisene Marks Redwoods and the entire Monterey Bay. Tastings Sat. 11–4 and by appointment.

McHenry Vineyard www.dcn.davis.ca.us /~hmchenry/wine.htm, lmchenry@dcn .davis.ca.us, 530-756-3202, 6821 Bonny Doon Rd., Bonny Doon. A small, redwood-encircled winery in the Bonny Doon mountaintop area, this facility turns out lustrous pinot noirs at the hand of UC Davis anthropologist-winemaker Henry McHenry from estate grapes planted on 4 acres located 5 miles from the ocean. Tastings and tours are available only during the Vintners' Festival and on Passport Weekends.

Osocalis Distillery www.osocalis.com, 831-477-1718, fax 831-479-4478, 5579 Old San Jose Rd., Soquel 95073. This small artisanal distillery specializes in grape and apple brandies (produced in an antique alambic charentais using traditional techniques), as well as limited amounts of grappa, mistelle and pommeau. Tastings by appointment.

Pelican Ranch Winery www.pelicanranch .com, pelicanran@aol.com, 831-426-6911, fax 831-426-6911, 402 Ingalls St., Santa Cruz 95060. Since 1997, owners Phil and Peggy Crews have produced 250 cases a year of chardonnay, syrah and pinot noir in the Rhône and Burgundian style. A picnic area is available nearby in an umbrella-draped courtyard. Tastings Fri.–Sun. noon–5 and by appointment.

P·M Staiger www.pmstaiger.com, 831-338-4346, 1300 Hopkins Gulch Rd., Boulder Creek 95006. Since 1975, winemaker Paul Staiger specializes in an estate Montage (cabernet sauvignon/merlot blend), cabernet sauvignon and chardonnay. Tours and tastings by appointment only.

River Run Vintners www.riverrunwines .com, 831-726-3112, 65 Rogge Ln., Watsonville 95076. A family-run winery tucked into the Coast Ranges behind Santa Cruz in the small community of Aromas, winemaker J. P. Pawloski's small facility produces a wide range of fine wines, most notably its bold, much-honored zinfandels, cabernet sauvignons, chardonnays, carignan, grenache, merlots and syrahs. This is a fine introduction to the regional style of bold varietals. Tours and tastings by appointment only.

Silver Mountain Vineyards www.silvermtn vineyards.com, info@ silvermtnvineyards .com, 408-353-2278, 408-353-1898, P.O. Box 3636, Santa Cruz 95063. Shaken but not defeated by the 1989 earthquake, Jerold O'Brien's small winery turns out stylish chardonnay from its estate organic vineyard, located at the summit of the Santa Cruz Mountains in an area planted by early viticulturists. Other offerings are Alloy (a Bordeaux blend), pinot noir and zinfandel. Tours and tastings are available by appointment only, as well as on Passport Weekends and during the Vintners' Festival.

2 0 0 1

P · M STAIGER

SANTA CRUZ MOUNTAINS

CABERNET

SAUVIGNON

ESTATE GROWN CABERNET SAUVIGNON, 88%; ESTATE MERLOT, 12% PICKED AT 25° BRIX · ALCOHOL 13.2% BY VOL. · CONTAINS SULFITES ESTATE GROWN AND BOTTLED BY P·M STAIGER, BOULDER CREEK, CA

Thunder Mountain Winery www.thunder mountainwine.com, sue@tmwine.com, 831-439-8716, fax 831-480-5874, 1717 Vine Hill Rd., P.O. Box 3969, Santa Cruz 95063. Owners Sue Broadston and Scott

Sterling create handcrafted single-vineyard chardonnay, pinot noir, syrah, cabernet sauvignon and Bordeaux blends. Scott makes his own beer, too.

Trout Gulch Vineyards www.troutgulch vineyards.com, mail@troutgulchvine yards.com, 831-471-2705, 414 Avalon Ave., Santa Cruz 95060. Winemakers Bernie Turgeon (a founder of J. Lohr Winery), his son Gerry and consultant Paul Wofford have specialized in Santa Cruz Mountains AVA chardonnay and pinot noir since 1988. No tours or tastings.

Windy Oaks Estate Vineyard & Winery www.windyoaksestate.com, 831-786-9463, fax 831-724-9577, 380 Sweetwater Rd., Corralitos 95076. This small enterprise run by Judy and Jim Schultze (the winemaker) produces handcrafted, limited-release estate-grown pinot noir and chardonnay. Tours and tastings by appointment only.

Zayante Vineyards www.zayantevineyards .com, 831-335-7992, 831-335-5770, 420 Old Mount Rd., Felton 95018. Winemaker Greg Nolten spent several decades in the winemaking business before beginning his own efforts in earnest in 1988. Currently expanding vineyards at a historic old hilltop ranch where the winery is housed, Nolten creates just under 1,000 cases annually entirely by hand, all 100 percent estate-grown wines. The first estate chardonnay was released in 1992. Available only at the winery, it is a complex, generously flavored beauty. Also quite special is a spicy syrah. Merlot and zinfandel fill out Zayante's dance card. Tastings and tours are available only during the Vintners' Festival and on Passport Weekends.

Eastern Side
BYINGTON VINEYARD & WINERY
www.byington.com
Winemaker: Don Blackburn
408-354-1111, ext. 204, fax 408-354-2782

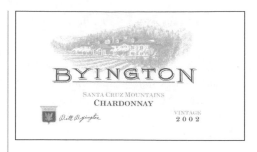

28150 Bear Creek Rd., Los Gatos 95033
Tours: By appointment
Tastings: Daily 11–5
Specialties: Santa Cruz Mountain chardonnay, pinot noir, cabernet sauvignon

Superbly situated on a 2,000-foot hilltop with a stunning view of the Monterey Bay, Byington offers tasting, picnicking and special-event ambiance at a sprawling Italianate château, crowning the slopes of vineyards. Easily the area's most imposing winery facility, this tile-roofed mansion boasts a high-ceilinged tasting room overlooking barbecue pits available for impromptu afternoon grills and a new wine cave. Gift items are long on wine logo specialties. Complex Santa Cruz Mountain chardonnays are among the highlights of steel magnate Bill Byington's cellars, and a visit provides an in-depth encounter with the sheer beauty of this redwood mountain kingdom overlooking the sea.

DAVID BRUCE WINERY
www.davidbrucewinery.com
Winemaker: Dean DeKorth
800-397-9972, 408-354-4214,
fax 408-395-5478
21439 Bear Creek Rd., Los Gatos 95033
Tours: No
Tastings: Daily noon–5
Specialties: chardonnay, pinot noir, sangiovese, cabernet sauvignon, petite sirah, zinfandel, syrah

Physician David Bruce enjoys courting controversy with his pioneer experiments in white zinfandel, late-harvest vintages and Rhône-style reds. In the vanguard of the Central Coast's current premium wine-making boom, the winery was begun in 1964 and has captured a lion's share of awards over the past decade for its Burgundian-style chardonnays and pinot noirs. The large facility (30,000 cases annually) sits amid a scenic, 25-acre estate vineyard near the summit of the Santa Cruz Mountains. While the tasting facility is bare bones—the raison d'être is the impressive array of wines, notably an estate pinot noir—the view of the steeply terraced vine-yards and the Monterey Bay beyond is bewitching, offering myriad picnic possibilities.

TESTAROSSA VINEYARDS

www.testarossa.com
wine@testarossa.com
Winemaker: Bill Brosseau
408-354-6150, ext. 21, fax 408-354-8250
300-A College Ave., Los Gatos 95030
Tours: Sat.–Sun at 1:30, weekdays by appointment
Tastings: Daily 11–5
Specialties: chardonnay, pinot noir, syrah

Bill Brosseau ferments, barrel-ages and bottles wines in a winery housed in the historic Novitiate of Los Gatos. Wine has been crafted there, in both a sacred and secular manner, since 1888. The facility forms the heart of in-depth tours and tastings, while the terraced dining area is the site of exceptional wine dinners and holiday functions. Grapes come from Bien Nacido, Clos Pepe, Garys', Michaud, Pisoni, Rosella's and Sleepy Hollow.

Other Eastern Side Santa Cruz Mountains Area Wineries

Burrell School Vineyards & Winery www.burrellschool.com, 408-353-6290, 4060 Summit Rd., Los Gatos 95033. Housed in an 1890 schoolhouse, Anne and

Dave Moulton's winery produces Santa Cruz Mountain chardonnay, estate chardonnay, pinot noir and syrah. Picnics are encouraged in an heirloom gazebo overlooking the estate. Tastings Sat.–Sun. 11–5 or by appointment.

Chaine d'Or Vineyards 650-851-8977, fax 650-851-0145, 140 Sunrise Dr., Woodside 94062. This feisty new label grows cabernet sauvignon and chardonnay grapes for a very small amount of handcrafted wines. Tastings by appointment only.

Cinnabar Vineyards & Winery www.cinnabarwine.com, 408-741-5858, fax 408 741 5860, 23000 Congress Springs Rd., Saratoga 95070. Founded in 1983, the winery sits high above the small village of Saratoga on 32 acres. Owner Tom Mudd and winemaker George Troquato produce estate cabernet sauvignon and chardonnay, as well as a merlot from Santa Ynez Valley and Paso Robles grapes and a Bordeaux blend, called Mercury Rising. Tastings available only during Passport Weekends and the Vintners' Festival.

Clos de la Tech www.closdelatech.com, 650-368-9169, 535 Eastview Way, Woodside 94062. Winemakers T. J. Rodgers (he heads Cypress Semiconductor in San Jose, thus the winery moniker) and Velita Massey conjure estate pinot noirs from their Woodside vineyard.

Clos LaChance Winery www.closlachance .com, 800-487-9463, 408-686-1050, 1 Hummingbird Ln., San Martin 95046. Located on 5 acres among the rolling hills at the foot of the Santa Cruz Mountains, the winery's owner, Bill Murphy, and winemaker Stephen Tebb specialize in Santa Cruz Mountain chardonnay, as well as pinot noir, cabernet sauvignon, merlot, cabernet franc and zinfandel from Central Coast grapes. Tastings daily 11–4. Picnic facilities are available.

2 0 0 1

Clos LaChance

SANTA CRUZ MOUNTAINS
CHARDONNAY

Cooper-Garrod Estate Vineyards
www.cgv.com, 408-867-7116, fax 408-741-
1169, 22600 Mount Eden Rd., Saratoga
95070. Dry-farming 28 acres of vineyards
first planted in 1972 (on property cultivated
by the family for over a century), winemakers George Cooper, Bill Cooper and Devin
Jones produce estate merlot, syrah,
chardonnay, cabernet sauvignon, cabernet
franc, viognier and Fine Claret (a Bordeaux
blend). Tastings daily noon–5. Tours by
appointment. Picnic tables available.

Cordon Creek Cellars www.cordoncreek
.com, rbiringer@cordoncreek.com, 408-
588-2056, 408-292-6252, fax 408-295-
2629. Co-owner/winemaker Roger Biringer
has produced handcrafted vintages from
up-and-coming appellations since 1997,
focusing on sauvignon blanc, cabernet
sauvignon, cabernet franc, Meritage (blend
of cabernet franc and merlot), zinfandel,
syrah blush, syrah, late-harvest zinfandel.
No tastings except at local Vintners'
Festivals and Passport Weekends.

Cronin Vineyards 650-851-1452, fax 650-
851-5696, 11 Old La Honda Rd., Woodside
94062. A tiny winery overlooking the San
Francisco Bay, Cronin produces small

quantities of chardonnay, cabernet sauvignon, merlot and pinot noir. Tastings by
appointment.

Fellom Ranch Vineyards www.fellom.com,
408-741-0206, 17075 Montebello Rd.,
Cupertino 95014. This winery's emphasis is
upon estate cabernet sauvignon grown on
Montebello Ridge and zinfandel from one
of the last remaining vineyards in Saratoga.
Tastings by appointment.

Fernwood Cellars www.fernwoodcellars
.com, 408-848-0611, 7137 Redwood
Retreat Rd., Gilroy 95020. Estate wines,
including zinfandel, cabernet sauvignon
and syrah, are the house specialties.
Located on 98 acres in the southern tip of
the Santa Cruz Mountain appellation,
Fernwood Cellars' wines reflect the vineyard's unique microclimate.

Generosa Winery www.generosawinery
.com, 408-286-1016, fax 408-286-7390,
22630 Hutchinson Rd., Los Gatos 95033.
Winemaker-owners Chris and Lara
Gemignani produce 1,000 cases of superpremium Tuscan-style wines made with
Bordeaux and Italian varietals. Tours and
tastings by appointment.

Kathryn Kennedy Winery www.kathryn
kennedywinery.com, cabernet@kathryn
kennedywinery.com, 408-867-4170, fax
408-867-9463, 13180 Pierce Rd., Saratoga
95070. This microwinery headed by winemaker Marty Mathis specializes in the creation of 100 percent estate cabernet
sauvignon. He also makes Lateral, a blend
of cabernet franc and merlot, syrah, sauvignon blanc and unusual specials for the
Kennedy wine club. No tours or tastings.

La Rusticana d'Orsa www.larusticana
dorsa.com, 888-373-9463, 408-358-1232,
15700 Kennedy Rd., Los Gatos 95032.
Frank and Marilyn Dorsa have created a
wonderland of vineyards, rose gardens and
sculptures that is a microcosm of Old World

charm. They also produce a heavenly blend of cabernet sauvignon and merlot. No tours or tastings.

Lonen & Jocelyn Wines www.jocelynwines .com, 866-559-4637, 408-395-9942. A small family-run company that produces superpremium estate wines, the winery's two labels, Jocelyn and Lonen, come from the names of the owners' daughter and son. The Lonen label is devoted to Bordeaux-style red wines and the Jocelyn to Burgundy-style wines and other assorted projects. Winemaker Josh Krupp's specialties include chardonnay, cabernet sauvignon and a zinfandel port. No tours or tastings.

Mountain Winery www.mountainwinery .com, 408-741-2822, fax 408-741-2818, 14831 Pierce Rd., Saratoga 95070. Located on the historic landmark grounds of the former Paul Masson Winery, Mountain Winery produces a reserve line of cabernet sauvignon, merlot and chardonnay from Stag's Leap, Bennett Valley and Edna Valley appellations. It is equally well known for its Summer Music Concert Series.

Mount Eden Vineyards www.mounteden .com, 408-867-5832, fax 408-867-4329, 22020 Mt. Eden Rd., Saratoga 95070. Founded by post-Prohibition maverick Martin Ray, this small mountaintop facility draws on legendary vineyards planted by Ray in the 1940s, as well as newer vines from which winemaker Jeffrey Patterson creates individualistic cabernet sauvignon, chardonnay and pinot noir vintages. No tasting room, but tours can be arranged by appointment.

Muccigrosso Vineyards www.muccigrosso .com, 408-354-0821, 21450 Bear Creek Rd., Los Gatos 95033. This family-run label produces small quantities of fine handmade zinfandel, a Santa Cruz Mountain pinot noir and a macchia. No tours or tastings.

Oliver Curtis Winery www.olivercurtis .com, 408-476-0472, 1253 Park Ave., San Jose 950126. Matt Dailey and Jeff Shukis founded Oliver Curtis in 1999. Today the duo produces sauvignon blanc, chardonnay, cabernet franc, and old-vine zinfandel. No tours or tastings.

Page Mill Winery www.pagemillwinery .com, 650-948-0958, 13686 Page Mill Rd., Los Altos Hills 94022. Page Mill Winery is a family-owned and -operated winery that produces a small quantity of very high-quality wine. Ome and Dick Stark founded the winery in 1976, when they dug a large cellar under their home. Son Dane joined the family operation in 1992. Production of cabernet sauvignon, pinot noir, merlot, zinfandel, syrah, chardonnay and sauvignon blanc comes in under 3,000 cases to maintain quality control. No tours or tastings.

Picchetti Winery www.picchetti.com, 408-741-1310, fax 408-741-5213, 13100 Montebello Rd., Cupertino 95014. Located on a historic ranch, Picchetti Winery is one

Vintners' Passport Weekends

Four Saturdays a year (the third weekend in January, April, July and November), the two dozen wineries of the Santa Cruz Mountains collaborate on an "open house" that stretches from the summit of the redwood mountains to hilltops overlooking the ocean in south Santa Cruz County. Many of the tiniest facilities, rarely open to the public, have an opportunity to show off their finest. The weekends allow visitors a chance to meet the winemakers, tour cellars and sample wines unavailable anywhere else. For dates and locations, contact **Santa Cruz Mountains Winegrowers Association** (www.scmwa .com, 831-479-9463, P.O. Box 3000, Santa Cruz 95060).

of the oldest wineries in California. Winemaker Jeff Ritchey and owner Leslie Pantling specialize in cabernet sauvignon, chardonnay, merlot, pinot noir, sangiovese, zinfandel and a sparkler, Prosecco. The winery complex is open daily 11–5 for tastings, picnics and hikes on the nearby trails.

Pinder Winery www.pinderwine.com, 877-684-2601, 165 Cristich Ln., Campbell 95008. Winemaker John Pinder handcrafts wines from California vineyards, including a Santa Cruz Mountain chardonnay and Santa Cruz Mountain pinot noir. He also bottles cabernet sauvignon, mourvèdre, carignan, syrah and zinfandel offerings.

Ridge Vineyards www.ridgewine.com, 408-867-3233, fax 408-868-1350, 17100 Montebello Rd., Cupertino 95014. This vineyard has been in production since 1886, and age has brought not only wisdom but myriad accolades for winemaker Paul Draper's award-winning chardonnay, cabernet sauvignon, zinfandel and merlot bottlings. No tours, but tastings available Sat.–Sun. 11–4.

Savannah-Chanelle Vineyards www .savannahchanelle.com, tastingroom@ savannahchanelle.com, 408-741-2934, fax 408-867-4824, 23600 Congress Springs Rd., Saratoga 95070. This family-owned and -operated winery was established by Pierre Pourroy in 1892 on 14 acres above the quaint village of Saratoga. It has been owned since 1996 by Michael Ballard. Today winemaker Anthony Craig produces 10,000 cases of cabernet franc, zinfandel, syrah, pinot noir, pinot blanc and chardonnay. Tastings daily 11–5.

Thomas Fogarty Winery & Vineyards www.fogartywinery.com, 650-851-6777, fax 650-851-5840, 19501 Skyline Blvd., Woodside 94062. In 1978, Dr. Thomas Fogarty was the first to plant on the region's Skyline Ridge, some 2,000 feet above sea level. Today winemaker Michael Martella

produces handcrafted estate pinot noir and chardonnay, as well as cabernet sauvignon and a Monterey gewürztraminer. Tastings Thurs.–Sun. 11–5.

Troquato Vineyards www.troquatovine yards.com, troquatovineyards@yahoo.com, 408-379-4971, 408-866-6700 vineyard and garden, 247 More Ave., Los Gatos 95032. Winemaker George Troquato specializes in estate-bottled cabernet sauvignon and merlot, as well as chardonnay and zinfandel. His pop, Angelo, grows herbs, tomatoes, onions and peppers nearby in what many claim is a perfect Italian family enterprise. No tours or tastings.

MONTEREY WINE AREA

While grapes were planted as early as 1791 by Franciscan fathers at Mission Soledad in the Salinas Valley, on the leeward side of Monterey's coastal mountain range, this fertile agricultural paradise wasn't fully recognized as a potential vineyard region until the 1960s, when vintners began utilizing the underground resources of the Salinas River for irrigation. Growers who solved the apparent climatic drawbacks of the dry, breezy valley by planting vines parallel to the prevailing winds now supply vast quantities of grapes for huge operations like Mirassou, Almaden, Paul Masson and Wente Brothers.

Given the coolness of this growing area—whose temperatures are the lowest in the Central Coast region (thanks to Salinas Valley breezes and the proximity to ocean fogs)—Monterey grapes luxuriate in a lengthy ripening process. The leading white grapes —chardonnay, sauvignon blanc and gewürztraminer—respond especially well to these conditions with pronounced intensity and length of vintage life. Though a relative newcomer to the California winemaking scene, Monterey is earning increasing respect for its grapes and locally produced wines.

CHALONE VINEYARD

www.chalonevineyard.com
info@chalonevineyard.com
Winemaker: Dan Karlsen
800-625-2610, 831-678-1717,
fax 831-678-2742
Hwy. 146 & Stonewall Canyon Rd.
(P.O. Box 518), Soledad 93960
Tours: Sat.–Sun. 11:30–5 (weekdays by
appointment)
Tastings: Sat.–Sun. 11:30–5 (weekdays by
appointment)
Specialties: chardonnay, chenin blanc,
pinot blanc, pinot noir, syrah

World famous for its lusty and elegant
chardonnays and pinot noirs, Chalone cul-
tivates its 100-plus limestone-rich acres of
grapes at a 2,000-foot elevation in the
Gavilan Mountains (the east face of the
Coast Range). Founded in 1969 by influential winemaker Richard Graff, one of the
vigorous pacesetters of recent California
winemaking, Chalone was an early leader in
coaxing Burgundian-style wines out of the
coastal climate. Today the winery is part of
an empire that includes Edna Valley
Vineyard, Carmenet and Acacia wineries.
Graff's never-ending quest for the great
California pinot noir continues to be well
received, and Chalone's chardonnays are
regarded among the top made in the country. Indeed, Chalone has been granted its
very own American Viticulture Area. Tours
of the vineyards and facilities put wine
buffs in touch with some of the finest wines
and most knowledgeable winemakers in the
country.

CHÂTEAU JULIEN WINE ESTATES

www.chateaujulien.com
Winemaker: Marta Kraftzeck
831-624-2600, fax 831-624-6138
8940 Carmel Valley Rd., Carmel 93923
Tours: Mon.–Fri. 10:30 & 2:30, Sat.–Sun.
12:30 & 2:30
Tastings: Mon.–Fri. 8-5, Sat.–Sun. 11–5

Specialties: cabernet sauvignon, chardonnay, merlot, pinot grigio, sangiovese,
sauvignon blanc, syrah, zinfandel, port,
cream sherry

Founded in 1982 by Robert and Patricia
Brower, this award-winning winery provides
tastings of its splendid chardonnays and
cabernet sauvignons at a glittering French-
style country château, complete with turrets,
copper flashing, stained-glass appointments
and antique furnishings. Set in the heart of
the affluent, Old Spanish California
ambiance of Carmel Valley, the 16-acre winery is famous for full-bodied, accessible
vintages of complex, spicy chardonnays and
satiny merlots. The varietals—all made from
Monterey County grapes—also include a
delightful blend of semillon and sauvignon
blanc, called Meritage White. A shaded picnic area in a cobblestone courtyard is available, as are wine-related gifts for those who
crave special souvenirs in addition to the
wonderful wines.

HAHN ESTATES/
SMITH AND HOOK WINERY

www.hahnestates.com
www.smithandhook.com
Winemaker: Adam Lazarre
831-678-2132, fax 831-678-2005
37700 Foothill Rd., Soledad 93960
Tours: By appointment
Tastings: Daily 11–4
Specialties: cabernet sauvignon, chardonnay, merlot, malbec, syrah, cabernet franc,
viognier.

A charming estate in a classic rancho setting, this respected winery produces fine
red wines from Monterey-area grapes.
Especially fine tasting is found in the luscious, peppery red wines, cabernet sauvignon and cabernet franc, coaxed to glory by
the warm Santa Lucia Highlands. Nicky
Hahn first encountered the ideal grape-
growing climate of Monterey in 1980 and
was one of the original partners in Smith

and Hook Winery, with 1991 marking the introduction of wines bearing the Hahn Estates logo. This label's top wines include cabernet sauvignon, merlot and chardonnay. The drive to the winery is a treat, and the picnic area boasts a spectacular view across the broad Salinas Valley. Great picnic spots make a visit to this vineyard a special occasion.

HELLER ESTATE VINEYARDS
www.hellerestate.com
Winemaker: Rich Tanguay
800-625-8466, 831-659-6220,
fax 831-659-6226
69 W. Carmel Valley Rd., Carmel Valley 93924
Tours: No
Tastings: Daily 11–5:30
Specialties: cabernet sauvignon, chardonnay, chenin blanc, merlot, pinot noir

In a beautiful side pocket of the Santa Lucia Mountains, over 120 acres of estate vines planted over the past 25 years are fed by underground springs and grown without the use of herbicides or pesticides at this 1,200-foot elevation winery. The first vineyard and winery in Carmel Valley, the estate was conceived by William and Dorothy Durney in the mid-1960s under the Durney label, and the original acreage was appropriately named Rancho del Sueno, meaning "dream ranch." All of the award-winning wines are created from the organic, dry-farmed fruit of estate vineyards, over half of which are planted with the superior cabernet sauvignon grape. A Spanish-style chapel, built as the cornerstone of the wine estate in 1973, serves as the centerpiece of the picnic area.

JOULLIAN VINEYARDS
www.joullian.com
Winemaker: Ridge Watson
800-659-8101, 831-659-8100,
fax 831-659-8102

20300 Cachagua Rd., Carmel Valley 93924
Tours: No
Tastings: Daily 11–5 at the Tasting Room (2 Village Dr., Suite A, Carmel Valley) and A Taste of Monterey
Specialties: cabernet sauvignon, chardonnay, syrah, sauvignon blanc, zinfandel

The Joullian and Sias families, who first created the winery, selected Carmel Valley as their estate vineyard because of the area's reputation for producing rich, intensely flavored grapes. Winemaker Ridge Watson, who brought international experience in France and Australia to the emerging winery, joined the group in 1981. In 1983, 655 acres of 1,400-feet-elevation benchlands were purchased, followed by another 40 acres of rocky Arroyo Seco loam. Over three-quarters of the vineyard is devoted to the noble varietals of Bordeaux, resulting in an array of complex cabernet sauvignons, merlots and sauvignon blancs.

LOCKWOOD VINEYARD
www.lockwood-wine.com
Winemaker: Larry Gomez
800-753-1424, 831-642-9200,
fax 831-644-7829
59020 Paris Valley Rd., San Lucas 93954
Tours: No
Tastings: A Taste of Monterey
Specialties: cabernet sauvignon, chardonnay, merlot, syrah, sauvignon blanc

In just over a decade, this winery, with its 100 percent estate-grown grapes, has established a reputation for turning out bold, much-honored vintages. The unconventional approach to marketing here involves sales strictly through mail order. Lockwood wines, produced on 1,650 acres of vineyards, where crushed fossilized seashells have been added to the shaley loam soil, have taken many top awards since the first 1989 vintage, particularly the rich, rounded cabernet sauvignons.

MONTEREY VINEYARD

www.aboutwines.com
Winemaker: Chris Mallard
831-675-4000
P.O. Box 780, Gonzales 93926-0780
Tours: Weekends at 10, noon, 2 and 4
Tastings: A Taste of Monterey
Specialties: cabernet sauvignon, chardon-
nay, merlot, pinot noir, sauvignon blanc,
white zinfandel

Owned by the giant Seagrams Company,
this high-profile winery established in
1976 produces sturdy varietals and blends
on its 1,100 acres in the southern Salinas
Valley. This is a large, half-million-case-
per-annum operation, with a lavishly
appointed Spanish-style tasting center that
boasts an exhibition gallery and landscaped
picnic area. The grounds feel like a park,
replete with ponds, geese and picnic tables
on the lawn. The tour provides a close look
at high-production winemaking techniques. The specialties of the house,
including red and white blends and a range
of chardonnays, pinot noirs and cabernets,
are all astonishingly affordable.

MORGAN WINERY/DOUBLE L VINEYARD

www.morganwinery.com
Winemaker: David Coventry
831-751-7777, fax 831-751-7780
590 Brunken Ave., Suite C, Salinas 93901
Tours: By appointment
Tastings: A Taste of Monterey
Specialties: chardonnay, pinot noir, pinot
gris, syrah, zinfandel, sauvignon blanc

Morgan chardonnays consistently win
awards for this small winery located in
the heart of John Steinbeck country.

Besides boasting a tasting center, exhibition gallery and landscaped picnic area, a tour of Monterey Vineyard's plant provides a close look at high-production winemaking techniques. Robert Scheer

Established by Dan and Donna Lee in 1982, Morgan currently produces 20,000 cases annually of organically grown sauvignon blanc, pinot noir, zinfandel and chardonnay, which is considered among the finest in the state, utilizing time-honored methods of barrel fermentation, contact on lees and aging in a variety of French oak barrels. The results are as dramatic as the fog-drenched, marine-influenced microclimate that generates a rare intensity of flavor and distinct varietal characteristics. The Lees' latest venture is their 65 acres of organically farmed vineyard in the Santa Lucia Highland, Double L Vineyard, which produces chardonnay, pinot noir and syrah.

PESSAGNO WINERY

www.pessagnowines.com
Winemaker: Steve Pessagno
831-675-9463, fax 831-675-1922
1645 River Rd., Salinas 93908
Tours: By appointment
Tastings: Fri.–Sun. 11–5
Specialties: chardonnay, pinot noir, syrah, zinfandel, riesling

Acclaimed winemaker Steve Pessagno, formerly of Lockwood, broke away and launched a new venture bearing his name and stamp of approval. After leading Lockwood to critical glory, he up and purchased the small winery formed from a partnership of four long-standing Salinas Valley winemaking families, Cloninger Cellars, and has set up shop to produce his own chardonnay, syrah, zinfandel and—his Holy Grail—pinot noir. A picnic area is open to visitors.

VENTANA VINEYARDS/MEADOR ESTATE

www.ventanavineyards.com
www.meadorestate.com
Winemaker: Doug Meador
800-237-8846, 831-372-7415,
fax 831-375-0797

A Taste of Monterey

This second-floor mecca of wine nostalgia is housed in an old cannery building overlooking the blue waters of the Monterey Bay. Wines may be purchased by the glass, and a major array of souvenir gifts and specialty foods may be purchased in the giftware area. The visitors center is filled with photographs, wine paraphernalia, memorabilia and the products of four dozen Monterey County wineries, many of which do not have tasting rooms of their own. Over 100 vintages are available for sampling and, of course, purchasing at the mother ship and at a branch in Salinas, both open daily 11–6 (www.tasteofmonterey.com, 831-646-5446, 700 Cannery Row, Monterey 93940, and 831-731-1980, 127 Main St., Salinas 93901).

2999 Monterey–Salinas Hwy. 10, Monterey 93940
Tours: No
Tastings: Daily 11–6
Specialties: cabernet sauvignon, cabernet franc, merlot, syrah, malbec, Magnus (cabernet sauvignon/merlot/cabernet franc), chardonnay, riesling, pinot blanc, chenin blanc, sauvignon blanc, gewürztraminer, muscat d'orange

Doug and LuAnn Meador are the owners of this vine-covered winery, housed on one of the most award-winning vineyards in the country. Grapes flourish in the 400-acre vineyard planted in gravelly soil on the arid banks of the Arroyo Seco River. Meador is widely regarded as one of the top growers in California, and his wines are excellent, notably the fruity sauvignon blanc and peppery cabernet sauvignon. The charming, stonework tasting headquarters, picnic area and grounds provide a taste of coastal California rustic elegance. Meador Estates produces 1,600 cases from 300 acres. Its high-priced chardonnay, syrah, chenin blanc, sauvignon blanc are all created from specific blocks on Meador's property.

Other Monterey-Area Wineries

Baywood Cellars www.baywood-cellars.com, 831-645-9035, fax 831-645-9345, 381 Cannery Row, Suite C, Monterey 93940. Owners John and James Cotta are third-generation grape growers and winemakers who have been in business since 1986. You can taste their sterling late-harvest Symphony, chardonnay, gewürztraminer, pinot grigio, zinfandel, syrah, port and merlot at their cool tasting room across from the Monterey Plaza Hotel, daily 11–6.

Bernardus Winery www.bernardus.com, 800-223-2533, 831-659-1900, 5 W. Carmel Valley Rd., Carmel Valley 93924. Tucked into the rolling ranch lands of Carmel Valley, this small operation directs its attention to the reds and whites of France's fabled Bordeaux region. Winemaker Mark Chesebro produces especially notable Marinus (cabernet/merlot blend), chardonnay, sauvignon blanc, marsanne and pinot noir vintages. A marsanne and semillon are available only at the tasting room. Tours by appointment through the tasting room, which is open daily 11–5.

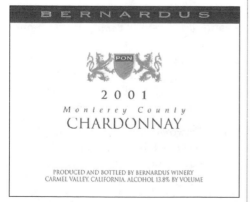

2001
Monterey County
CHARDONNAY

PRODUCED AND BOTTLED BY BERNARDUS WINERY
CARMEL VALLEY, CALIFORNIA. ALCOHOL 13.8% BY VOLUME

Blackstone Winery www.blackstone winery.com, 831-675-5341, fax 831-675-8923, 800 S. Alta St., Gonzales. Housed in a giant stone building surrounded by gardens and a man-made lake, this facility sits alongside Hwy. 101 and makes a nice break stop in a trip south to Paso Robles and the Santa Ynez Valley. The specialties here are chardonnay, cabernet sauvignon, merlot, syrah, malvasia bianca, sauvignon blanc and pinot noir. Picnic tables sit lakeside, and tastings can be appreciated daily 11–4.

Boyer Winery www.montereywines.org /general_members/boyer_wines.html, 831-455-1885, fax 831-455-8019, P.O. Box 7267, Spreckels 93962. This longtime Jekel winemaker and his wife, Patty, produce some delectable chardonnay, pinot noir and syrah bottlings at their cozy mom-and-pop operation. No tours, but tastings can be enjoyed at A Taste of Monterey.

Burnstein/Remark Winery www.remark wines.com, 831-455-9310, 645 River Rd., Salinas 93908. Winemaker Joel Burnstein's 2001 Grenache won best of show at LA's Wines of Americas Competition. He produces less than 200 cases of his Rhone-style wines. No tours or tasting room, but visit A Taste of Monterey for samples.

Calera Wine Company 831-637-9170, 11300 Cienega Rd., Hollister 95023. Winemaker Josh Jensen specializes in chardonnay, pinot noir and viognier. Tours and tastings by appointment only.

Chateau Christina/Joyce Vineyard 831-659-0312, fax 831-422-7577, 60 Via Milpitas St., Carmel Valley 93924. Dr. Frank Joyce is the man behind Monterey County's coolest boutique winery. No tours, but tastings can be had at A Taste of Monterey. Look for any chardonnay, pinot noir, merlot or cabernet sauvignon arriving from Joyce's choice 2 acres.

Monterey Vintners and Growers Association

If you would like to receive a colorful, fact-filled brochure on the Monterey wine area, contact this group. This is definitely an organization that has a handle on how to disseminate information on its wines (www.monterey wines.org, 831-375-9400, fax 831-375-1116, P.O. Box 1793, Monterey 93942).

Chateau Sinnet www.chateausinnet.com, 831-659-2244, fax 831-659-2171, 13746 Center St., Carmel Valley 93924. Longtime wine aficionados Gary Sinnet and Gil Tortolani decided to open this winery, picnic area and tasting room, which pours daily noon–5. Of special interest are the Monterey chardonnay, pinot noir, merlot, pinot blanc, cabernet sauvignon, syrah and zinfandel, and some downright unusual yet tasty fruit and sparkling wines. Tours by appointment.

Coyote Canyon Wines www.coyotecanyon wines.com, 831-726-7074, 799 Cole Rd., Aromas 95504. This delicate flower blooms in the far reaches of Monterey County. Winemaker Troy Bunnell, a ninth-generation Californian, spent years touring and working in the wineries and vineyards of Burgundy. Today his Santa Lucia Highlands pinot noir is an international award winner. Tastings can be arranged by appointment only, although his wines appear on the tables of many of the West's best restaurants.

DeRose Winery 831-636-9143, 9970 Cienega Rd., Hollister 95023. Pat and Alphonse DeRose operate this small mom-and-pop label at what some historians believe is California's oldest existing winery, which dates back to 1854. Situated in the eastern foothills of the Gabilan Mountains and directly over the San Andreas Fault, DeRose produces cabernet franc, négrette, zinfandel, port, pinot St. George and viognier. Tastings on weekends 11–4.

Enz Vineyards 831-637-6443, 1781 Limekiln Rd., Hollister 95023. Winemaker Robert Enz produces pinot St. George, orange muscat and zinfandel. Tours and tastings by appointment only.

Galante Vineyards www.galantevineyards .com, 800-GALANTE, 831-6591, 8181 Cachagua Rd., Carmel Valley 93924. Over 700 acres of rolling vineyards, visual-friendly cattle and thousands of garden roses form the perfect backdrop to imbibing the limited, ultra-premium estate cabernet sauvignon. Also planted are merlot, pinot noir, sauvignon blanc and viognier. This is a great place to hold a picnic, but a conveniently located new tasting room opened last year in Carmel-by-the-Sea (831-624-3888, Dolores St., bet. 7th & 8th Aves.), open daily 11–7.

Georis Winery www.georiswine.com, 831-659-1050, fax 831-659-1054, 4 Pilot Rd., Carmel Valley 93924. Winemaker Walter Georis, who owns Carmel's renowned Casanova Restaurant—justly praised both for its food and wine list—makes merlot, cabernet sauvignon and sauvignon blanc. All merlots are prizewinners, and releases average around 1,500 cases. If you can find a bottle at a Monterey Peninsula restaurant or wine shop, snap it up. No tours, but 11–6 daily you are welcome to enjoy the tasting room, gift shop and a restaurant—the Corkscrew Café, which features vegetables from the Georis organic gardens.

Paraiso Springs Vineyards www.paraiso vineyards.com, 831-678-0300, fax 831-678-2584, 38060 Paraiso Springs Rd., Soledad 93960. From 400 acres of premium grapes first planted in 1973 overlooking the Salinas Valley, this small winery produced its first vintage of chardonnay in 1987. Since then, distinctive pinot blanc, pinot noir, riesling, syrah and dessert wines like Souzao Port have followed. The facility is located in the Spanish California setting of the Santa Lucia Highlands, tastings are available weekdays noon–4 and weekends 11–5. Tours can be arranged by calling first, and the picnic area is postcard perfect.

Pavona Wines www.pavonawines.com, 831-646-1506, fax 831-649-8919, 1645 River Rd., Salinas 93908. Owners Jennifer Lind and Richard Kanakaris and winemaker Aaron Mosley (who worked with America's dean of winemakers, the late Andre Tchelistcheff) produce chardonnay blanc, pinot noir, syrah and zinfandel from Monterey and Paso Robles grapes. No tours, but tastings are available weekends 11–4.

Pelerin Wines www.pelerinwines.com, 831-422-2338, 163 Lorimer St., Salinas 93901. Winemakers Chris and Cathy Weidemann, grads of the Viticulture and Enology program at the University of California–Davis, released their inaugural vintages in 2002; 130 cases of syrah, 165 of pinot noir and a small amount of a zinfandel blend. Today a pinot noir, three other syrah bottlings, as well as a roussane, have joined their siblings on the shelves of quality wine shops and dining rooms. No tours, but tastings can be arranged by appointment.

Pietra Santa Vineyards & Winery pietrasantawinery.com, 831-636-1991, fax 831-636-1929, 10034 Cienega Rd., Hollister 95023. This small label was founded in 1989 by Joseph Gimelli, but the vineyards were originally planted in 1850. The first release was in 1994, but today winemaker Alessio Carli bottles many vintages in the Italy-California style, including sangiovese, dolcetto, cabernet sauvignon, zinfandel and merlot. The prescient grow-ers also planted 5,000 olive trees on the property and have been producing high-quality virgin oil since 1999.

Robert Talbott Vineyards www.talbott vineyards.com, 831-659-3500, fax 831-659-3515, 53 W. Carmel Valley Rd., Carmel Valley 93924. Winemaker Sam Balderas specializes in high-quality, lovingly crafted chardonnays and pinot noirs. No tours, but tastings are available 11–5 daily and a picnic area is conveniently located nearby.

San Saba Vineyards www.sansaba.com, 800-998-7222, 831-659-7322, 19 E. Carmel Valley Rd., Carmel Valley 93924. Founded in 1975, this 68-acre vineyard nestled in the foothills of the Santa Lucia Mountains excels in the production of award-winning cabernet sauvignons and affordably priced chardonnays and merlots under the direction of winemaker Jeff Ritchey. The label itself it a work of art. San Saba's tasting room is located at the far eastern end of Carmel Valley Village and is open daily noon–5.

Scheid Vineyards www.scheidvineyards .com, 888-478-4946, 831-386-0316, fax 831-386-0127, 1972 Hobson Ave., Greenfield 93927. The Scheid clan began raising premium wine grapes in the early 1970s, and today its cabernet sauvignon, chardonnay, pinot noir, sauvignon blanc, gewürztraminer, merlot and white riesling bottlings are the perfect syntheses of the

Monterey/Salinas region's soil, climate and terroir. Tours by appointment, tastings daily 11–5. A pleasant picnic area is available for visitors.

SAN LUIS OBISPO/ PASO ROBLES WINE AREA

The history of winemaking in this warm growing area (which is cooled by both coastal fogs and afternoon Salinas Valley breezes) began at Mission San Miguel Arcángel in 1797. Fueled by the need for sacramental grapes and the viticultural zeal of conquistador Viceroy Hernando Cortez—who demanded that vineyards be planted in all New World settlements—the Franciscan missionaries established winemaking as part of the California heritage. In fact, Father Junipero Serra himself brought the first grapes to Mission San Luis Obispo.

Eventually, European settlers who stayed on after the Gold Rush brought French and Italian varietals to these rich farmlands. One early winery, established by Andrew York in 1882, is still in operation as York Mountain Winery.

Armed with evidence provided by University of California researchers of the potential of the area's climate and soils for grape growing, a wine boom got under way in the 1960s. Today more than 50 wineries cluster in the hills surrounding Paso Robles and stretch down to the cooler coastal valleys of Edna and Arroyo Grande. Inland, the red wine grapes of the Rhône and Bordeaux produce award-winning vintages, while along the coast, the Burgundian varietals of chardonnay and pinot noir are the specialties.

And, as if on cue, nature has placed this emerging winemaking greenhouse on countryside so lovely, so definitely Central Coast, that just following the winding lanes from winery to winery is itself an intoxicating experience.

ADELAIDA CELLARS

www.adelaida.com
Winemaker: Terry Culton
800-676-1232, 805-239-8980,
fax 805-239-4671
5805 Adelaida Rd., Paso Robles 93446
Tours: By appointment
Tastings: Daily 11–5
Specialties: cabernet sauvignon, cabernet franc, pinot noir, zinfandel, chardonnay

Emphasizing natural winemaking techniques, Adelaida adheres to the philosophy that exquisite wines are made not in the cellar but in the vineyard. Founded in 1981, Adelaida coaxes intense varietal character from its grapes by pruning for low yields on its 75-acre vineyard. The wines are fermented with native yeasts, and sulfite additions are kept to a minimum. Adelaida's chardonnays are 100 percent barrel fermented, and the reds spend the latter half of their fermentation cycle in the barrel, an unorthodox winemaking approach that yields wines of unique and exceptional character. The winery and tasting room are set on ranch lands ranging well above 2,300 feet.

CARMODY MCKNIGHT ESTATE VINEYARDS

www.carmodymcknight.com
Winemaker: Greg Cropper
800-282-0730, 805-238-9392,
fax 805-238-3975
11240 Chimney Rock Rd., Paso Robles 93446
Tours: No
Tastings: Daily 10–5
Specialties: cabernet sauvignon, merlot, cabernet franc, late-harvest cabernet franc, chardonnay, pinot noir

Producing estate wines in the classic Bordeaux tradition, Carmody McKnight (the former Silver Canyon Vineyards) produces 4,000 cases annually from its 100-acre vineyard in the Santa Lucia range west of Paso Robles. The vineyard's unfertilized volcanic and limestone soils maintain an excellent natural mineral content, adding dimension and personality to the worthy red wines. The winery's chardonnay is also loaded with character, while its late-harvest cabernet franc puts a unique twist on that varietal. The tasting room, located in a farmhouse built in the 1860s, overlooks the estate lake and vineyard.

CASTORO CELLARS

www.castorocellars.com
Winemaker: Tom Meyers
888-DAM-FINE, 805-238-0725,
fax 805-238-2602
1315 N. Bethel Rd., Templeton 93465
Tours: By appointment only
Tastings: Daily 11–5:30
Specialties: zinfandel, cabernet sauvignon, merlot, chardonnay, muscat canelli, pinot noir, zinfandel port

Lovely views from the vineyards and an antiques-filled tasting room are among the pleasures of a visit to these cellars. Gourmet and wine-related gift items are available, as well as samples of the award-winning cabernet sauvignons, considered among the most consistent and well priced of all California cabs. Tom Meyers is among a handful of California winemakers who are

All roads lead to quality winery experiences on the San Luis Obispo portion of the California Gold Coast wine country.

adding delightful experiments in unfermented grape juice to their bottling lines. The results so far have yielded an especially refreshing, nonalcoholic zinfandel elixir that is blissful on a warm day. Far from a mere gimmick, nonalcoholic grape juices, created with all the care given to premium wines, stand to be highly competitive in a market fond of its bottled waters and designer soft drinks. The winery comes equipped with a prime picnic spot that offers views of the pastoral charms of the Templeton area.

CLAIBORNE & CHURCHILL VINTNERS

www.claibornechurchill.com
Winemaker: Clay Thompson
805-544-4066, fax 805-544-7012
2649 Carpenter Canyon Rd., San Luis

Obispo 93401
Tours: By appointment only
Tastings: Daily 11–5
Specialties: chardonnay, pinot noir, pinot gris, Alsatian dry gewürztraminer & riesling

Founded in 1983, Claiborne & Churchill remains ahead of its time in the production of Alsatian-style gewürztraminers and rieslings, proving that these varietals, when vinified to dryness, can be just as elegant and food-friendly as any other California white wine. A former professor of languages at the University of Michigan, winemaker Clay Thompson recently moved his winery operations to a new facility on the rural perimeter of Edna Valley. A testament to environmental architecture, the winery employs energy-efficient straw bales in its walls, obviating any need for air-conditioning or refrigeration. A small bar in a corner of the cellar hosts friendly tastings, and impromptu tours are given upon request.

DOMAINE ALFRED
www.domainealfred.com
Winemaker: Mike Sinor
805-541-9463
7525 Orcutt Rd., San Luis Obispo 93401
Tours: No
Tastings: Daily 11–5
Specialties: chardonnay, pinot noir, syrah

A stucco barn situated at the edge of a substantial vineyard marks this small winery founded in 1981. From vineyards planted in the early 1970s, the winemaker creates distinctive, buttery chardonnays filled with balanced fruit, acidity and oak complexity. Also delectable is a peppery cabernet sauvignon blanc. The tasting area here amounts simply to a corner of the winery itself, where visitors can pull up bar stools and sample the few varietals produced. A patio area at the tasting facility affords an ideal picnic location and chance to soak up the Edna Valley atmosphere.

EBERLE WINERY
www.eberlewinery.com
Winemaker: Bill Sheffer
805-238-9607, fax 805-237-0344
Hwy. 46 E. (3.5 miles from Paso Robles), Paso Robles 93447
Tours: By appointment only
Tastings: Daily 10–6
Specialties: cabernet sauvignon, chardonnay, muscat canelli, syrah

Eberle is a prime destination for discovering the regional flavor of the estate's cabernets, chardonnays and muscat canelli. Owner Gary Eberle became professionally acquainted with winemaking while studying at UC Davis. His chardonnays glow warmly with butter and spice, and his zinfandels are powered by bold varietal characteristics. But he and winemaker Bill Sheffer also are known to have some fun with two-fisted blends like the popular "Eye of the Swine." The winery is situated with a view of the estate vineyards, and the cellar floor can be viewed from the elegant tasting room adjoining the winery. The patio is the perfect place to enjoy monthly gourmet winemaker dinners, accessible by advance reservations.

EDNA VALLEY VINEYARD
www.ednavalley.com
Winemaker: Harry Hansen
805-544-5855, 805-544-9594, fax 805-544-0112
2585 Biddle Ranch Rd., San Luis Obispo 93401
Tours: Sat. & Sun. 11–3, on the hour
Tastings: Daily 10–5
Specialties: chardonnay, pinot noir, syrah

A member of the internationally renowned Chalone Wine Group, this midsized winery is best known for using classic Burgundian winemaking techniques to craft elegant chardonnays and pinot noirs from the valley's famed Paragon Vineyard. Also available are a number of limited-production wines, including pinot blanc, viognier and syrah. The winery's new hospitality center features a retail marketplace, lush land-scaping and a panoramic view of Edna Valley. Monthly special events and concerts are another winery trademark. Picnickers are encouraged to explore the tasting room's gourmet offerings and to enjoy them amid one of the valley's finest settings.

EOS ESTATE WINERY/
ARCIERO ESTATE WINERY

www.eosvintage.com
www.arcierowinery.com
Winemaker: Steve Felten
800-249-WINE, 805-239-2562,
fax 805-239-2317
5625 Hwy. 46 E., Paso Robles 93446
Tours: Daily 10–5
Tastings: Daily 10–5
Specialties: cabernet sauvignon, chardon-nay, muscat canelli, nebbiolo, petite sirah, sangiovese, zinfandel, sauvignon blanc

A Mediterranean-style, red-tile-roofed winery and tasting complex are highlighted by a visitors center, lavish landscaping and a beautiful picnic area—the perfect spot to begin a self-guided tour of how the fine house wines are created. The upscale facil-ity boasts luxurious appointments, includ-ing chandeliers and a fireplace, and supports some fine winemaking, evidenced in a memorable selection of cabernets, chardonnays and petite sirahs. The gift store is well stocked with wine-related goodies and gourmet deli items. The for-tunes amassed by brothers Frank and Phil Racier extend to professional racing and to an exhibit of famous race cars.

HARMONY CELLARS

www.harmonycellars.net
Winemaker: Chuck Mulligan
800-432-9239, 805-927-1625,
fax 805-927-0256

3255 Harmony Valley Rd., Harmony 93435
Tours: By appointment only
Tastings: Daily 10–5:30
Specialties: cabernet sauvignon, chardon-nay, Johannisberg riesling, zinfandel, merlot

Located near the charming artisan village of Harmony near scenic Hwy. 1, Harmony Cellars features a comfortable tasting room and a solid selection of classic varietals. Harmony Cellars is also known for some playful bottlings, including two Christmas-themed wines: Santa's Reserve and Christ-mas Blush. Scenically wedged between the ocean and the rolling foothills of the Santa Lucia Mountains, the winery provides idyl-lic picnicking conditions and a gourmet gift shop.

JUSTIN VINEYARDS & WINERY

www.justinwine.com
Winemaker: Jeff Branco
800-726-0049, 805-238-6932,
fax 805-238-7382
11680 Chimney Rock Rd., Paso Robles 93446
Tours: No
Tastings: Daily 10–6

Specialties: cabernet sauvignon, cabernet franc, merlot, Isosceles, nebbiolo, sangiovese, shiraz, orange muscat, chardonnay

An essential destination for red wine enthusiasts, Justin Winery specializes in Bordeaux and Italian varietals grown at a 75-acre estate vineyard in the Paso Robles countryside. Justin's Bordeaux-style flagship blend, Isosceles, is one of the Central Coast's benchmark "Meritage" wines. Cozy tastings are conducted over a glass-top table amid English-style gardens. Top chefs from around the U.S. host Justin's monthly Guest Chef Dinners. The estate also features a B&B and a full-time chef for those seeking an ideal "wine country" getaway.

MASTANTUONO WINERY

www.mastantuonowinery.com
Winemaker: Pasquale Mastantuono
805-238-0676, fax 805-238-9257
Hwy. 46 W. & Vineyard Dr.,
Templeton 93465
Tours: No
Tastings: Daily 10–6
Specialties: cabernet sauvignon, chardonnay, muscat canelli, zinfandel, merlot

The tasting room, busily appointed in Italian hunting lodge fashion, presents a dazzling array of interesting varietals. Winemaker Pasquale Mastantuono concentrates on dry-farmed grapes, which produce lusty zinfandels and rich, rounded cabernets. The castlelike winery building overlooks stands of majestic oaks, and picnickers in the winery's charming gazebo are often serenaded by live music during warm weather. There is a well-stocked gift store, and deli items are available for sale to take outside into the attractive garden area.

MERIDIAN VINEYARDS

www.meridianvineyards.com
Winemaker: Chuck Ortman
805-237-6000, fax 805-239-9624
7000 Hwy. 46 East, Paso Robles 93447
Tours: No
Tastings: Daily 10–5
Specialties: cabernet blanc, cabernet sauvignon, chardonnay, pinot noir, syrah, zinfandel, sauvignon blanc, merlot, petite syrah, late-harvest riesling, gewürztraminer

Thanks to savvy marketing and a superior, moderately priced product, Meridian has established itself as a leader in the market for Central Coast wines. Meridian's chardonnay is highly drinkable, both crisp and creamy, and is fast becoming one of the most popular, affordable chardonnays in the state. The pinot noir is supple and rounded, and the syrah launches a rewarding assault on the palate. The award-winning wines are created from Santa Barbara County and Edna Valley grapes.

PEACHY CANYON WINERY

www.peachycanyonwinery.com
Winemaker: Tom Westberg
805-239-1918, 805-237-1577,
fax 805-237-2248
1480 N. Bethel Rd., Templeton 93465
Tours: No
Tastings: Daily 11–5
Specialties: zinfandel, cabernet sauvignon, merlot, Meritage, chardonnay

A must stop for zinfandel lovers, Peachy Canyon features an environmentally friendly, straw-bale facility and a tasting room converted from a one-room schoolhouse built in 1886. The winery was established by former schoolteachers Doug and Nancy Beckett in 1988 and now farms more than 40 vineyard acres. Peachy Canyon zinfandels are known for their luscious textures and full-blown flavors, and vineyard-designated zinfandel from the famed Dusi ranch is also one of the region's finest. Peachy Canyon's merlot is another example of the winery's commitment to excellence. Production remains at about 10,000 cases.

Anchored to a 10-acre, dry-farmed vineyard in the remote hinterlands of Arroyo Grande Valley, Saucelito Canyon produces one of California's finest zinfandels. Jeff Greene

SAUCELITO CANYON VINEYARD

www.saucelitocanyon.com
Winemaker: Bill Greenough
805-543-2111, fax 805-543-0533
1600 Saucelito Creek Rd., Arroyo Grande 93420
Tours: No
Tastings: Daily noon–5 at Talley Vineyards
Specialties: zinfandel, cabernet sauvignon

Anchored to a 10-acre, dry-farmed vineyard in the remote hinterlands of Arroyo Grande Valley, Saucelito Canyon produces one of California's finest zinfandels. Homesteaded in the 1870s and resurrected a century later by Bill Greenough, the estate yields wines noted for their sensuous textures, layered flavors and elegant composition. An adherent to the no-nonsense school of winemaking, Greenough leaves the talking to his vineyard, and the vineyard speaks volumes. Saucelito Canyon and its zinfandels exemplify the traditional estate wine model as refracted through California's New World personality.

TALLEY VINEYARDS

www.talleyvineyards.com
Winemaker: Steve Rasmussen
805-489-0446, fax 805-489-0996
3031 Lopez Dr., Arroyo Grande 93420
Tours: By appointment
Tastings: Daily 10:30 4:30
Specialties: pinot noir, chardonnay, sauvignon blanc, white riesling

The Talleys, longtime local farmers, have struck Burgundian gold with the world-class pinot noirs and chardonnays that are produced at their winery in Arroyo Grande Valley. Three estate vineyards, two in Arroyo Grande Valley and one in nearby Edna Valley, yield vineyard-designated wines known for their complexity and elegance. Talley's pinot noirs are among the finest produced in California, while its chardonnays and rieslings boast captivating varietal intensity. Tastings are provided in an 1863 two-story adobe, surrounded by a broad lawn and flower gardens that accentuate the estate's Old World atmosphere. Be sure to visit the white gazebo, a favorite stop for picnickers.

TOBIN JAMES CELLARS
www.tobinjames.com
Winemakers: Tobin James & Lance Silver
805-239-2204, fax 805-239-4471
8950 E. Union Rd., Paso Robles 93446
Tours: No
Tastings: Daily 10–6
Specialties: zinfandel, cabernet sauvignon, cabernet franc, merlot, syrah, chardonnay, sauvignon blanc, late-harvest zinfandel

Under the quirky guidance of renegade owner and winemaker Tobin James, this small-production facility provides one of California's most engaging winery destinations. Loaded with Wild West nuances and anchored by a 100-year-old hardwood bar, the tasting room features gunslinger movie cutouts, a mock jail for entertaining children and an ever-present Australian shepherd named Cisco. The wines are equally unique, boasting alluring, full-blown flavors and fanciful names (the late-harvest zinfandel is known as "Liquid Love").

WILD HORSE WINERY & VINEYARDS
www.wildhorsewinery.com
Winemaker: Mark Cummins
805-434-2541, fax 805-434-3516
1437 Wild Horse Winery Court,
Templeton 93465

Tours: By appointment only
Tastings: Daily 11–5
Specialties: cabernet franc, merlot, zinfandel, pinot noir, chardonnay, malvasia bianca, pinot blanc

Wild Horse does a fine job of maximizing the regional potential of bold red varietals and crisp, fruity chardonnays. Its outstanding white wines include a spicy gewürztraminer, and the pinot noirs are regularly anointed at the heavyweight California State Fair annual competitions. The winery sports a separate label, Equus, for its Rhône varietals. At its welcoming tasting room, these wines, as well as rare specialties available only at the winery, including dolcetto, négrette and trousseau, are displayed for the enjoyment of visiting tasters. Tricia Volk, founder-owner Ken's able business cohort and wife, is the author of a book of recipes geared to specific offerings of Central Coast wineries.

WINDEMERE WINERY/CATHY MACGREGOR WINES
www.windemerewinery.com
Winemaker: Cathy MacGregor
805-542-0133
3482 Sacramento Dr., Suite E, San Luis Obispo 93401
Tours: Thurs.–Tues. 11:30–5
Tastings: Thurs.–Tues. 11:30–5
Specialties: zinfandel, pinot noir, cabernet sauvignon, chardonnay

After earning a master's degree in enology at UC Davis and working at wineries on the North Coast, free-spirited Cathy MacGregor returned to her roots and established her own winery, Windemere, in San Luis Obispo. The daughter of another local vineyard owner, Andy MacGregor, whose coveted grapes appear in vineyard-designated wines across California, produces bold, ripe chardonnays loaded with tropical fruit flavors. A zinfandel sourced from Paso Robles's famed Dusi Vineyard is another

The Crushed Grape Wine Center

Gifts of gourmet foods and wines from the San Luis Obispo area, as well as around the world, are available at this bonanza for bon vivants. The wine bar is really the heart of the action, pouring an eclectic assortment of California vintages with the accent on the Central Coast. Bottled wine selections and gourmet gift baskets make delicious souvenirs of the region (805-544-4449, Madonna Rd. at Hwy. 101, San Luis Obispo 93401).

favorite from Windemere. Located in a small industrial unit on the outskirts of San Luis Obispo, Windemere features tastings in the midst of its busy cellar.

YORK MOUNTAIN WINERY

www.yorkmountainwinery.com
Winemaker: Steve Goldman
805 238 3925, fax 805 238 0428
7505 York Mountain Rd., Templeton 93465
Tours: No
Tastings: Daily 10–5
Specialties: cabernet sauvignon, chardonnay, sauvignon blanc, black muscat, pinot noir, zinfandel, dry sherry, red table wines

Having withstood the ravages of time, including Prohibition, this winery is over 100 years old. On its vineyard-encrusted mountaintop, the venerable winery offers antique appointments and a tasting room with a sturdy stone fireplace. All wines can be tasted for a nominal fee, and the gift area stocks plenty of wine books, wine paraphernalia and gourmet food items. Since it is the oldest surviving winery in this stretch of the Central Coast, it's the obvious excuse to while away a pleasant afternoon in the foothills of the Santa Lucia Mountains.

Other San Luis Obispo/Pablo Robles Area Wineries

Abbey d'Or Cellars 805-467-3248, 4620 Hog Canyon Rd., San Miguel 93451. Winemaker Joe Farley named his facility for his family's ancestral village in Ireland.

From estate grapes grown in this secluded canyon, he produces highly regarded cabernet sauvignon, chardonnay, chenin blanc, late-harvest zinfandel and pinot noir vintages. Tours and tastings by appointment only.

AJB Vineyards www.ajbvineyards.com, 805-239-9432, fax 310/379-1679, 3280 Township Rd., Paso Robles 93446. Open weekends 11–6 and by appointment for tastings of viognier, chardonnay, nebbiolo, sangiovese, syrah and zinfandel.

Alapay Cellars www.alapaycellars.com, 805-595-2632, 491 1st St, Avila Beach 93424. Tastings of Scott Remmenga's Rhône varietals can be enjoyed Sat.–Sun. 11–5.

Alban Vineyards 805-546-0305, 8575 Orcutt Rd., Arroyo Grande 93420. A pioneer in California's increasing embrace of Rhône varietals, John Alban makes hand-crafted wines from viognier, roussane, syrah and grenache. The winery is proving that Edna Valley, long known for its success with Burgundian varietals, is also prime terrain for so-called Rhône Rangers. No tours or tastings.

Arcicro Winery www.arcicrowinery.com, 805-239-2562, fax 805-239-2317, 5625 Hwy. 46 W., Paso Robles 93446. Tastings daily 10–5 (Sat.–Sun. till 6).

Baileyana www.baileyana.com, 805-597-8200, 805-269-8208, 4915 Orcutt Rd.,

San Luis Obispo 93401. A century-old schoolhouse serves as a tasting room and is open daily noon–6.

Barnwood Vineyards www.barnwood wine.com, 888-809-VINE, 310-275-9889, fax 805-481-6920, 453 Tower Dr., Arroyo Grande at Laetitia Winery. Winemaker Louis Mitjavile originally bottled his cabernet sauvignon, chardonnay, sauvignon blanc, syrah, zinfandel and merlot at Austin Cellars, but all that changed with the crush of '93. Now Barnwood has its own quarters, as well as its own vines. Tours and tastings are available at Laetitia Vineyard and Winery daily 11–6.

Bonny Doon Vineyard www.bonnydoon vineyard.com, 805-239-5614, Sycamore Farms, Hwy. 46 W., Paso Robles 93446. Maverick Rhône and Italian varietal maestro Randall Grahm opens a second outpost for his famed Bonny Doon. Tastings daily 10–5.

Brochelle Vineyards www.brochelle.com, 805-237-4410. This zinfandel specialist is one of the smallest in the area. No tasting room, but orders accepted via Web site and e-mail.

Caparone Winery www.caparone.com, 805-467-3827, 2280 San Marcus Rd., Paso Robles 93446. From a no-frills facility, winemaker David Caparone creates small quantities of powerful, highly drinkable red wines, best understood at a vertical tasting as part of the tour. Gorgeous merlots, cabs and zins showcase full varietal nose, flavor and finish. He released the first commercially produced sangiovese in America in 1988. Brunello and nebbiolo vintages also are produced. Prices are accessibly low. Tours and tastings daily 11–5.

Casa de Cabellos www.casadecaballos.com, 805-434-1687, fax 805-434-1560, 2225 Raymond Ave., Templeton 93465. Tom and Sheila mix their love of horses with an

2003
Faantasy Riesling
75% WHITE RIESLING • 25% MUSCAT CANELLI
Paso Robles

embrace of the vine. Their 3-acre, 1,200-foot-high vineyards yield 300 cases a year of pinot noir and merlot. No tours, but tastings available Sat.–Sun. noon–5 and by appointment.

Cerro Caliente Cellars www.cerrocaliente cellars.com, 805-544-2842, fax 805-544-2842, 831-A Via Esteban, San Luis Obispo 93401. Tastings of the label's merlots, chardonnays and others Fri.–Sun. noon–5.

Changala Winery www.changalawinery .com, 805-434-3113, 1215 Santa Rita Rd., Templeton 93465. Tastings of viogniers and zinfandels by appointment only.

Chateau Margene Cellars www.chateau margene.com, 877-MARGENE, 805-238-2321, fax 805-238-2118, 4385 La Panza Rd., Creston 93432. Tastings of Michael and Margene Mooney's handcrafted cabernet sauvignons Sat.–Sun. noon–6.

Chumeia Vineyards www.chumeiavine yards.com, 805-226-0102, 8331 Hwy. 46 E., Paso Robles 93446. Tastings of cabernet

The estate and tasting facility at San Luis Obispo's Corbett Canyon Vineyards welcomes inquiring visitors.

sauvignon, chardonnay, zinfandel, barbera and pinot noir daily 10–5.

Corbett Canyon Vineyards www.corbett canyon.com, 805-544-5800, fax 805-544-7205, 2195 Corbett Canyon Rd., San Luis Obispo 93421. In this expansive Spanish-style winery located about 8 miles southeast of San Luis Obispo, winemaker John Clark produces value-oriented cabernet sauvignon, chardonnay, merlot, pinot noir, white zinfandel and sauvignon blanc. Tours Sat.–Sun. at 11, 1 & 3, tastings daily 10–5.

Cottonwood Canyon Winery & Vineyard www.cottonwoodcanyon.com, 805-937-9063, fax 805-546-8031, 4330 Santa Fe Rd., San Luis Obispo 93401. The Bekko family and vineyard manager Federico Arredondo specializes in chardonnay,

syrah and pinot noir made from estate grapes. Tastings Fri.–Sun. 11–5 and by appointment.

Creston Vineyards 805-434-1399, fax 805-434-2426, Hwy. 101 & Vineyard Dr., Templeton 93465. A fine vineyard and winery headed by winemaker Tim Spear coaxes definitive regional characteristics out of cabernet sauvignon, chardonnay, merlot, pinot noir, sauvignon blanc, semillon and zinfandel vintages. Special tasting-room-only bottlings are also produced. Tours by appointment, tastings daily 10–5.

Dark Star Cellars www.darkstarcellars .com, 805-237-2389, fax 805-237-2589, 2985 Anderson Rd., Paso Robles 93446. This small family winery, spearheaded by winemaker Norm Benson, concentrates on small lots of merlot and cabernet sauvignon made from local vineyards. A Bordeaux-style blend called "Ricordati" is also produced. Tastings Thurs.–Mon. 11–5:30.

Doce Robles Winery & Vineyard 805-227-4766, 805-227-6860, fax 805-227-6521, 2023 Twelve Oaks Dr., Paso Robles 93446. Jim and Maribeth Jacobsen bottle chardonnay, nebbiolo, zinfandel, merlot, syrah, barbera and late-harvest zinfandel. Tastings daily 10–5:30.

Dover Canyon Winery www.dovercanyon .com, 805-237-0101, fax 805-237-9191, 4520 Vineyard Dr., Paso Robles 93446. The motto here—"Rhône to the Bône!"—pretty much says it all. Tastings Fri.–Sun. 11–5 and by appointment.

Dunning Vineyards www.dunningvine yards.com, 805-238-4763, 1953 Niderer Rd., Paso Robles 93446. From his 46 acres, Robert Dunning coaxes 2,000 cases yearly of cabernet sauvignon, merlot, chardonnay, syrah and "selected ranches" zinfandels. Tastings are available in the Summer House Fri.–Sun. 11–5 and by appointment. Visitors also can picnic under 100-year-old oaks trees overlooking the vineyards.

Fratelli Perata Winery & Vineyard www.fratelliperata.com, 805-238-2809, 1595 Arbor Rd., Paso Robles 93446. A family-owned and -operated winery specializing in bold red wines made from grapes produced by the beautiful hillside vineyards. Brothers Joe and winemaker Gene have added a promising nebbiolo varietal to their cabernet sauvignon, chardonnay, merlot, sangiovese and zinfandel vintages. Tours and tastings by appointment.

Garretson Wine Company www.mrviog nier.com, 805-239-2074, fax 805-239-2057, 2323 Tuley Court, Suite 110, Paso Robles 93446. Matt and Amie Garretson's Web site says all you need know about Matt's winemaking predilections since his start in 2001. He has no vineyards, but besides viogniers, he also produces syrahs and roussane from single vineyards for a total of 3,000 cases per year. Tastings Thurs.–Mon. 11–6 and by appointment.

Grey Wolf Cellars www.greywolfcellars .com, 805-237-0771, fax 805-237-9866, 2174 Hwy. 46 W., Paso Robles 93446. Showcased in a 60-year-old farmhouse, the creations of winemaker Joe Barton emphasize small lots of premium zinfandel, cabernet sauvignon, merlot, chardonnay, syrah and Meritage Reserve. Tastings daily 11–5:30.

HMR Winery 805-238-7143, fax 805-238-4997, 2740 Hidden Mountain Rd., Paso Robles 93446. Three families—the McHenry, Changala and Vignola clans—purchased this property in 1997 from Dr. Stanley Hoffman and today produce 3,000 cases of chardonnay, merlot, muscat canelli and zinfandel from grapes originally planted by the legendary Andre Tchelistcheff. Tastings Sat.–Sun. 11–5.

Hug Cellars www.hugcellars.com, 805-927-1484, 3094 Macleod Way, Cambria 93428. Hug Cellars is a small family-owned winery established in 1994 by C. I. (Augie) Hug and Raquel Mireles Rodriguez. The team produces its syrahs in the "Rhône Zone" and offers tastings at a co-op tasting room at Coastal Vintners, 2323 Tuley Ct., Suite 120D, in Paso Robles.

Hunt Cellars www.huntcellars.com, 805-237-1600, fax 805-718-8048, 2875 Oakdale Rd., Paso Robles 93446. David Hunt makes 15,000 cases yearly from a wide range of locally grown varietals on his 52 acres, a cabernet sauvignon from Edna Valley grapes and chardonnay from Santa Maria fruit. Tastings daily 10:30–5:30.

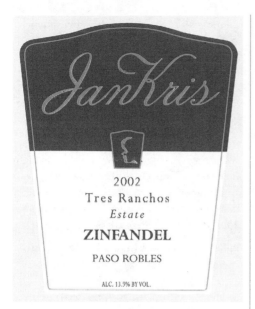

2002
Tres Ranchos
Estate
ZINFANDEL
PASO ROBLES
ALC. 13.9% BY VOL.

JanKris Winery www.jankriswinery.com, 805-434-0319, fax 805-434-0509, Hwy. 46 W. & Bethel Rd., Templeton 93465. The Victorian farmhouse that headquarters this winery is over 100 years old. The atmospheric setting of vineyards, lawns and rose garden is a popular site for picnics and weddings. Winemaker Mark Gendron won a Gold Medal at the California State Fair with his JanKris Vineyard, Paso Robles zinfandel. Also try his chardonnay, gamay, merlot and pinot noir vintages. No tours, but tastings daily 11–5

J. Lohr Estates www.jlohr.com, 805-239-8900, fax 805-239-0365, 6169 Airport Rd., Paso Robles 93446. Tours Sat.–Sun. 11 & 2. Tastings of the winery's Seven Oaks and Cabernet Sauvignon, South Ridge Syrah, Los Osos Merlot, Hilltop Vineyard Cabernet Sauvignon are available daily 11–5.

Jory Winery www.jorywinery.com, 800-347-2134, P.O. Box 599, Paso Robles 93446. Winemaker Stillman Brown creates distinctive chardonnay, zinfandel, syrah and sauvignon blanc vintages. No tours, but tastings are available at select public functions.

Kelsey See Canyon Winery www.kelsey wine.com, 805-595-9700, 1945 See Canyon Rd., Avila Beach 93405. Tastings of fruit sweet wines and chardonnays, merlots and syrahs are available Sat.–Sun. 11–5 or by appointment.

Kynsi Winery www.kynsi.com, 805-544-8461, 805-544-6181, 2212 Corbett Canyon Rd., Arroyo Grande 93420. Tastings of zinfandel, pinot noir, syrah, chardonnay, pinot blanc and Merrah, a merlot/syrah marriage, every Thurs.–Sun. 11–5.

Laetitia Vineyard and Winery www.laetitia wine.com, 888-809-VINE, 805-481-1772, 453 Deutz Dr., Arroyo Grande 93420. Established in 1995 on the site of the former Maison Deutz sparkling wine facility, Laetitia winemaker Louis Mitjavile's Franco-American winemaking team specializes in Burgundy- and Bordeaux-style wines. Scheduled tours are available during the summer or by appointment. Tastings daily 11–6.

Laura's Vineyard www.laurasvineyard .com, 805-238-6300, 5620 Hwy. 46 E. near Jardine Rd., Paso Robles 93446. Longtime grower and winemaker Clifford Giacobine specializes in cabernet sauvignon, chardonnay, Johannisberg riesling and syrah crafted from his lovingly tended vines. No tours, but tastings take place daily 10–6.

Laverne Vineyards 805-547-0616, 3490 Sacramento Dr., Suite E, San Luis Obispo 93401. Tastings Sat.–Sun. noon–4.

Le Cuvier Winery www.lcwine.com, 800-549-4764, 805-238-5706, 9750 Adelaida Rd., Paso Robles 93446. Limited quantities of lovely cabernet sauvignon, chardonnay, and syrah wines, handcrafted from low-yield limestone vineyards by winemaker Andree Munch, are available only at the tasting room. This is a unique setting of herb gardens and vineyards where you can picnic under the oaks. No tours, but tastings take place daily 11–5.

Maloy O'Neill Vineyards www.maloy oneill.com, 805-238-7320, fax 415-751-8357, 4560 Creston Rd., Paso Robles 93446. Handcrafted small lots of cabernet sauvignon, syrah, merlot and zinfandel are specialty of this family-owned and -operated winery.

Martin & Weyrich Winery www.martin weyrich.com, 805-238-2520, fax 805-238-6041, Hwy. 46 E. & Buena Vista, Paso Robles 93447. Italian varietals are the specialty of winemaker Craig Reed, who offers the fun of sampling a wide range of distinctive wines, including cabernet Etruscan, grappa de nebbiolo, nebbiolo echo, vin santo, zinfandel primitivo and muscat allegro. Seasonal concerts are presented in the winery amphitheater during the spring and summer. Tastings daily 11am–dusk.

Midnight Cellars Winery & Vineyard www.midnightcellars.com, 805-239-8904, fax 805-237-0383, 2925 Anderson Rd., Paso Robles 93446. This relatively new family-owned winery focuses on premium cabernet sauvignon, merlot, zinfandel and chardonnay. Winemaker Rich Hartenberger and wife Michele employ grapes solely from the Paso Robles area, and a recently planted 20-acre estate vineyard will soon enhance the winery's production. Tastings daily 10–5:30.

Norman Vineyards www.normanvine yards.com, 805-237-0138, fax 805-227-6733, 7450 Vineyard Dr., Paso Robles 93446. Winemaker Joe Kidd specializes in estate-grown zinfandel, barbera, Meritage (No Nonsense Red), cabernet sauvignon and chardonnay. Tastings daily 11–5.

Opolo Vineyards www.opolo.com, 805-371-0101, fax 805-371-0102, 7110 Vineyard Dr., Paso Robles 93446. Opolo specializes in pinot noir, merlot and syrah, as well as sangiovese, chardonnay, cabernet sauvignon, cabernet franc and muscat canelli. Samples from the merlot and zinfandel vineyards surrounding the tasting room are available daily 11–5.

Paragon Vineyards 805-544-9080, fax 805-546-0413, 5880 Edna Rd., San Luis Obispo 93401. For 20 years, this 700-plus-acre vineyard that has been producing eight varieties of award-winning grapes for local and international markets. Now winemaker Gary Mosby also produces a Paragon chardonnay for sale. No tours or tastings.

Penman Springs Vineyard www.penman springs.com, 805-237-8960, fax 805-237-8975, 1985 Penman Springs Rd., Paso Robles 93446. Tastings of petite sirah, cabernet franc, petit verdot, merlot, cabernet sauvignon, syrah and Meritage and muscat canelli are available Fri.–Sun. 11–5:30.

Pipestone Vineyards www.pipestonevine yards.com, 805-227-6385, fax 805-227-6383, 2040 Niderer Rd., Paso Robles 93446. Tastings of Jeff Pipes's Rhône-style syrahs, viogniers and grenaches are available Thurs.–Mon. 11–5.

Poalillo Vineyards 805-238-0600, 1888 Willow Creek Rd., Paso Robles 93446. Located on the west side of Paso Robles, Poalillo produces premium estate-grown zinfandels, cabernets and chardonnays with an emphasis on fruit intensity. Tours and tastings by appointment.

Pretty-Smith Vineyard & Winery www.prettysmith.com, 805-467-3104, fax 805-467-3719, 13350 N. River Rd., San Miguel 93451. Located just east of historic Mission San Miguel, the winery's extensive vineyards generate especially fine cabernets and zinfandels. Chardonnay, merlot, muscat canelli and sauvignon blanc also delight visitors in a tasting room awash with traditional Spanish tilework and heavy-beamed ceilings. Picnicking on the redwood deck offers a view of the vineyards and the mission beyond. Tastings Fri.–Mon. 10–5.

Ross-Keller Winery 805-929-3627, 985 Orchard Rd., Nipomo 93444. Winemaker Jim Ryan bottles intriguing premium cabernet sauvignon, chardonnay, muscat canelli, riesling and Italian-style sparkling wine. Tours by appointment only, tastings daily noon–5.

Seven Peaks 805-781-0777, 5828 Orcutt Rd., San Luis Obispo 93405. Tastings of Aussie-influenced wines are available in a tasting room housed in the historic Independence Schoolhouse, daily 10–5. Picnic grounds are nearby.

Silver Horse Vineyards www.silverhorse .com, 805-467-9309, fax 805-467-9414, 2995 Pleasant Rd., San Miguel 93451. New player on the Central Coast wine block is open for tastings Fri.–Mon. 10–5.

Stephen Ross Wine Cellars www.stephen rosswine.com, 805-594-1318, 4910 Edna Rd., San Luis Obispo 93401. Tastings of vineyard-designated pinot noir, chardonnay and zinfandel can be had by appointment only.

Summerwood Winery www.summerwood wine.com, 805-227-1365, fax 805-227-1366, 2175 Arbor Rd., Paso Robles 93445. Samplings of Rhône varietals are available in a massive inn and tasting room daily 10–6.

Sylvester Estate Winery www.sylvester winery.com, 805-227-4000, fax 805-227-6128, 5115 Buena Vista Dr., Paso Robles 93446. Specializing in zinfandel, cabernet sauvignon, merlot, sangiovese and chardonnay, Sylvester features a spacious tasting room, a small delicatessen and vintage train cars. Founded in 1995, the winery produces 25,000 cases from 200 estate vineyard acres. Tastings daily 10–5.

Tablas Creek Vineyard www.tablascreek .com, 805-237-1231, 9339 Adelaida Rd., Paso Robles 93446. Tablas Creek Vineyard was founded by the Perrin family of Château de Beaucastel and Robert Haas, longtime importer and founder of Vineyard Brands. They chose the Las Tablas district of Paso Robles for its similarities to Châteauneuf du Pape and imported traditional varietals grown on the Perrins' estate: mourvèdre, grenache noir, syrah, counoise, roussane, viognier, marsanne. Tastings by appointment only.

Tolosa/Courtside Vineyards at San Miguel www.tolosawinery.com, 805-467-2882, 805-782-0300, fax 805-467-2881, 2425 Mission St., San Miguel 93451. Tastings of estate-bottled chardonnay, syrah and pinot noir are available by appointment only.

Treana Winery www.treana.com, 805-238-6979, fax 805-238-4063, 2175 Arbor Rd., Paso Robles 93446. The charming Tuscan atmosphere of this small, family-run winery showcases estate-grown cabernet sauvignons and zinfandels made by winemaker Chris Phelps. Winemaker Austin Hope oversees the production of Treana's white wines, which include chardonnay, muscat canelli, rosato and a Rhône-style blend. No tastings.

Turley Wine Cellars www.turleywine cellars.com, 805-434-1030, 2900 Vineyard Dr., Templeton 93465. The oldest original family-owned winery in the Paso Robles area, Pesenti, was established here in 1934 on vineyards planted in 1923. Today Turley owns the land and the winery. The wine-lined tasting room boasts a staggering list of varietals for sampling. including old-vine zinfandels. Tours by appointment only. Tastings daily 9–5.

Victor Hugo Vineyards and Winery www.victorhugowinery.com, 805-434-1128, 2850 El Pomar, Templeton 93465. Tastings of winemaker Vic Roberts's chardonnay, zinfandel, syrah, petite sirah, viognier, cabernet sauvignon, cabernet franc, merlot, malbec and petit verdot are available by appointment only.

Villicana Winery www.villicanawinery .com, 805-239-9456, fax 805-239-0115, 2725 Adelaida Rd., Paso Robles 93446. Tastings of Alex and Monica Villicana's cabernet sauvignon, merlot and pinot noir are possible Sat.–Sun. 11–5 and by appointment.

Vista del Rey Vineyards 805-467-2138, 7340 Drake Rd., Paso Robles 93446. Dry-farmed zins, barberas, pinot blancs and sangiovese are the projects here. Open for tastings most Sundays 11–5 and by appointment.

Wedell Cellars www.wedellcellars.com, 805-489-0596, 344 Equestrian Way, Arroyo Grande 93420. No tastings are available of Maurice and Sue Wedell's pinot noir and chardonnay.

Westberg Cellars www.westbergwine.com, 805-238-9321, 3180 Willow Creek Rd., Paso Robles 93446. Tastings of Tom and Peggy Westberg's chardonnays, zinfandels, merlots and sangiovese can be arranged by appointment only.

Wild Coyote/Coyote Creek Vineyard www.coyotewine.com, 805-239-4770, 3775 Adelaida Rd., Paso Robles 93446. Tastings of the labels' merlot, zinfandels and syrahs are available daily 11–5.

Windward Vineyard www.windwardvine yard.com, 805-239-2565, fax 805-239-4005, 1380 Live Oak Rd., Paso Robles 93446. The logo here claims "exclusively pinot noir." Tastings Fri.–Sun. 11–5 and by appointment.

Wolff Vineyards www.wolffvineyards.com, 805-781-0448, 6238 Orcutt Rd., San Luis Obispo 93401. You can sample the winery's old-vine chardonnay, pinot noir, syrah, teroldego and petite sirah in the tasting room Sat.–Sun. 11–5.

Zenaida Cellars www.zenaidacellars.com, 805-227-0382, fax 805-227-0349, 1550 Hwy. 46 W., Paso Robles 93446. Tastings of winemaker Eric Ogorsolka's cabernet sauvignon, merlot, pinot noir, sangiovese, syrah, and zinfandel are available daily 11–5.

SANTA YNEZ VALLEY WINE AREA

Increasingly capturing the fancy of California wine aficionados looking for the new, distinctive and top-of-the-line in Central Coast wines, the lush valleys and canyons of the Santa Ynez Mountains offer a wide range of possibilities. Over 11,000 acres of Santa Barbara County are planted to grapes, with new vineyards springing up daily. Unique to this versatile winemaking area is the transverse range of these coastal mountains. Reflecting the sharp inward angle of the West Coast at Santa Barbara County, the mountains run east–west, a feature that allows the inland flow of cool-ing fog and ocean breezes. The slow ripen-ing of grapes grown under this coastal influence makes for intense development of varietal characteristics.

The inland valleys offer a warmer, drier microclimate, resulting in a range of char-acteristics that emulate conditions in Bordeaux and the Rhône. Indeed, since

Santa Barbara–area wineries aggressively embrace the grapes of France's Rhône district, this is the place to look for especially fine syrahs, petite sirahs and viogniers, in addition to exemplary sauvignon blancs, chardonnays and pinot noirs.

As with the other major winemaking districts of the Central Coast, the Franciscan mission fathers got the ball rolling back in 1782, planting the first vineyards in Santa Barbara and then up into the Santa Ynez Mountains. Soon a good 6,000 gallons of wine a year were being made, thanks to the labors of Chumash Indian converts who crushed the grapes by footwork and fermented the juices in tar-coated cow hides. Clearly the state of the art had evolved when Santa Barbara architect Pierre Lafond established the Santa Barbara Winery in 1965 with a premier vintage zinfandel. Other innovators have since followed, even a few Hollywood legends—Fess Parker and producer Doug Cramer—many of whom have turned the ranch lands of the Santa Ynez Valley into country winery getaways.

AU BON CLIMAT
www.aubonclimat.com
Winemaker: Jim Clendenen
805-937-9801, 805-688-8630,
fax 805-937-2539
2905 Grand Ave., Los Olivos 93441
Tours: No
Tastings: Daily 11–6
Specialties: chardonnay, pinot blanc, pinot noir

The winemaker here is widely regarded as a knowledgeable superstar. Especially prized are the chardonnays and pinot noirs created by Clendenen, well worth pursuing at restaurants and wine shops all over California. This winery consistently showcases the climatic resemblance between this growing area and the fabled Burgundian Côte d'Or, while subtly flaunting the depth of flavor available to grapes nurtured in these long,

Los Olivos Tasting Room & Wineshop
This is a user-friendly wine-tasting depot that provides a tasting tour of some of the Santa Ynez Valley area's finest wineries—wineries too small to provide their own tasting facilities. For $7, you can sample 9 to 10 pours of outstanding area vintages from tiny facilities like Claiborne & Churchill, Daniel Gehrs, Longoria, Foxen, Kalyra, Vita Nova, Pagar, J. Kerr, Hitching Post, Ojai, Qupé and Au Bon Climat. The folks behind the bar will fill your ear with delicious, behind-the-scenes tidbits about styles, awards, winemaking personalities and tasting tips. This establishment, smack in the middle of the two streets that make up the village of Los Olivos, is a required pit stop for all buffs intent upon sampling the unique charms of Santa Ynez Valley winemaking. Open daily 11–6 (www.losolivoswines.com, 800-209-8103 pin 2934, 805-688-7406, fax 805-688-0906, 2905 Grand Ave., Los Olivos 93441).

fog-cooled growing conditions. He also produces a wonderful orange muscat from fabled bien cacido grapes. A visit to the friendly Los Olivos Tasting Room and Wine Shop will provide ample opportunities to sample some of the rich, handcrafted vintages that have helped put Santa Barbara on the national winemaking map, thanks in part to the remarkable touch of Clendenen.

BRANDER VINEYARD/
DOMAINE SANTA BARBARA
www.brander.com
Winemaker: Fred Brander
800-970-9979, 805-688-2455, 805-884-1089 (Domaine SB), fax 805-688-8010
2401 Refugio Rd. & Highway 154 at Roblar Ave., Los Olivos 93441

Tours: By appointment only
Tastings: Daily 10–5
Specialties: sauvignon blanc, Bouchet (cabernet franc/cabernet sauvignon/merlot)

Overlooking the ranch lands of former President Ronald Reagan and superstar Michael Jackson, this pink faux château winery and tasting facility serves up its fine wines with one of the most alluring views of the Santa Ynez Valley. The fruity, butterscotchy chardonnays and crisp, complex Bordeaux-style sauvignon blancs will enthrall you. A very special blend of cabernet franc, cabernet sauvignon and merlot called Tête de Cuvée Bouchet sings of blackberries/cassis and spice. Stock up here or sign up for the mailing list.

BYRON VINEYARD & WINERY
www.byronwines.com
Winemaker: Byron "Ken" Brown
888-303-7288, 805-937-7288,
fax 805-937-1246
5230 Tepusquet Rd., Santa Maria 93454
Tours: Daily 10–5
Tastings: Daily 10–4
Specialties: chardonnay, pinot blanc, pinot noir, pinot gris

The road to this well-respected, 10-year-old winery is one of the most splendid country lanes in this stretch of the Coast Range. The picnic area on the steep slope of Tepusquet Creek is the site of many special wine and food events. The Spanish-inspired, barnlike tasting room provides samples of the winery's award-winning products, highlighted by crisp and distinctive white wines. The excellent Byron chardonnays, adorned with glory at major national competitions, invariably find themselves paired with innovative California cuisine in the South Central Coast's best restaurants. If you're tempted to do some purchasing while you're at the tasting room, don't hesitate to follow that impulse.

FESS PARKER WINERY & VINEYARD
www.fessparker.com
Winemaker: Eli Parker
800-841-1104, 805-688-1545,
fax 805-686-1130
6200 Foxen Canyon Rd. (P.O. Box 244),
Los Olivos 93441
Tours: Daily 11, 1 & 3
Tastings: Daily 11–5
Specialties: chardonnay, Johannisberg riesling, muscat canelli, pinot noir, syrah

Though his son Eli serves as director of winemaking and president of the large, attractive winery, headquartered in a building of native stone and roofed in copper, the chance to catch a glimpse of the gracefully aging Western movie hero is part of the deal. The setting is classic California rolling ranch land. The winery is equipped for myriad public tastings, concerts, conferences and food events, and 1992 marked the first harvest of grapes grown on the 715-acre ranch. Already, the winery's pinot noir and chardonnay are being marketed across the country and, of course, at Disneyland.

FIRESTONE VINEYARD

www.firestonewine.com
Winemaker: Kevin Willenborg
805-688-3940, fax 805-686-1256
5000 Zaca Station Rd., Los Olivos 93441
Tours: Daily 10:15–3:15 on the hour
Tastings: Daily 10–5
Specialties: cabernet sauvignon, chardonnay, gewürztraminer, late-harvest Johannisberg riesling, merlot, sauvignon blanc, riesling

Overlooking hundreds of acres, which are planted to all of the major grape varietals of the Central Coast, this award-winning winery essentially started the recent surge of interest in the Santa Ynez Valley area as a winemaking contender. In the early 1970s, founder Brooks Firestone broke with family tradition (he is the grandson of rubber baron Harvey Firestone) and decided to make wine, not tires. While the chardonnays are exceptional and have been served in far-flung diplomatic settings, the rieslings set the tone, especially the unctuous late harvest vintages and a new and unprecedented dry riesling. Winemaker Alison Green was trained in Alsace and puts a pleasingly dry spin on her much-honored gewürztraminer. The huge, contemporary hacienda winery, well-appointed tasting and gift area and adjoining picnic patio all overlook a mosaic of vineyards lining Zaca Station Rd., one of the prettiest country lanes in California.

FOLEY ESTATES VINEYARD & WINERY

www.foleyestates.com
Winemaker: Alan Phillips
805-688-8554, fax 805-688-9327
1711 Alamo Pintado Rd., Solvang 93463
Tours: By appointment only
Tastings: Daily 10–5
Specialties: cabernet sauvignon, chardonnay, merlot, pinot noir, sauvignon blanc

Here is another one of those tiny, quintessential Santa Ynez area wineries set in oak-studded rolling hills. The picnic area is irresistible, and the tasting in a cozy cottage involves a wide range of premium red and white wines. The small facility specializes in microlots of handmade wines and is known for its cabernet sauvignon and sauvignon blanc. Talented winemaker Alan Phillips leads the crew in this busy winery owned by William P. Foley II and his wife, Carol.

GAINEY VINEYARD

www.gaineyvineyard.com
Winemaker: Kirby Anderson
805-688-0558, fax 805-688-5864
3950 E. Hwy. 246, Santa Ynez 93460
Tours: Daily 11, 1, 2 & 3
Tastings: Daily 10–5
Specialties: cabernet franc, chardonnay, Johannisberg riesling, merlot, pinot noir, sauvignon blanc

Over 60 acres of estate vines surround the red-tile-roofed, Spanish-style winery complex announced by a procession of romantic pepper trees. This is as much a community cultural center as it is a tasting facility for Gainey's highly respected vintages. Gainey consistently proves its marketing savvy and viticultural excellence by producing innovative and affordable vins ordinaire like the surprisingly sturdy Rece$$ion Red. The tasting room overlooks the vineyard-laden hills and pours a selection of wines, including award-winning sauvignon blanc and chardonnay, plus the highly regarded pinot noir. Tours begin at a particularly instructive "Visitors' Vineyard," a demonstration planting that shows off the various cultivation techniques and the trellising required by different grapes and allows visitors a chance to sample the fruit. This popular winery also is the site for a wide range of cooking classes, art shows, concerts and wine-appreciation workshops.

LINCOURT VINEYARD
www.lincourtwines.com
info@lincourtwines.com
Winemaker: Alan Philips
805-688-8554, fax 805-688-9237
1711 Alamo Pintado Rd., Solvang 93463
Tours: No
Tastings: Daily 10–5
Specialties: chardonnay, pinot noir, syrah

Located on historic ranch lands in the heart of present-day Chumash country, this pioneer winery draws from over 100 acres of vineyards, including those originally planted in the late 1960s, for its premium production of chardonnay, pinot noir and syrah. The small, friendly tasting room is set prettily in the midst of vineyards and rolling ranch country.

MOSBY WINERY & VINEYARDS
www.mosbywines.com
Winemaker: Bill Mosby
800-706-6729, 805-688-2415,
fax 805-686-4288
9496 Santa Rosa Rd., Buellton 93427
Tours: By appointment only
Tastings: Daily 10–4:30
Specialties: sangiovese, chardonnay, distillato di prugne selvaggie, grappa traminer, nebbiolo, pinot grigio, zinfandel, primitivo

Tastings, concerts on the lawn and cooking classes are among the events available at

this small, family-run winery that leans heavily toward Italian varietals and top California grape vintages. The elegant chardonnays set the tone, and the potent grappas garner high honors at major competitions. An old red barn houses the winery and tasting room, and there's a mid-19th-century adobe on the farm property. The place is definitely rustic, though the wines are anything but.

QUPÉ WINE CELLARS
www.qupe.com
Winemaker: Bob Lindquist
805-937-9801, 805-688-4409,
fax 805-686-4470
2905 Grand Ave., Los Olivos 93441
Tours: No
Tastings: Daily 11–6
Specialties: syrah, chardonnay, marsanne, mourvèdre, viognier

The winery's unusual name is a Chumash word for "poppy," the ubiquitous Golden State flower. Enjoying increasing celebrity, the wines are outstanding (notably the black-raspberry-scented syrahs from Santa Barbara's coveted Bien Nacido Vineyard) and tend to be available at fine markets, restaurants and the Los Olivos Tasting Room. Specializing in chardonnay and the wines of the Rhône, winemaker Bob Lindquist creates spellbinding vintages of great depth and endless finish. This is a label to watch, and since the finest and trendiest Central Coast and southern California restaurants scoop up most of the tiny output, buyers should jump at the rare opportunity to stock their cellars with this rising star of the California enological firmament.

RANCHO SISQUOC WINERY
www.ranchosisquoc.com
Winemaker: Alec Franks
805-934-4332, fax 805-937-6601
6600 Foxen Canyon Rd., Santa Maria 93454

Tours: Groups over 10 by appointment
Tastings: Daily 10–4
Specialties: cabernet sauvignon, chardonnay, riesling, merlot, sauvignon blanc, sylvaner

The pastoral Sisquoc River Valley frames the large ranch on which the label's redwood-and-stone facility sits. Bonded in 1977, the tiny winery's entire line of acclaimed wines produced from estate grapes is available exclusively at the tasting room, which adjoins a shaded lawn, gardens and a picnic area sheltered by huge oaks. The complex chardonnays and sauvignon blancs are outstanding for drinking now and for cellaring.

SANFORD WINERY
www.sanfordwinery.com
Winemaker: Bruno D'Alfonso
800-426-9463, 805-688-3300,
fax 805-688-7381
7250 Santa Rosa Rd., Buellton 93427
Tours: By appointment
Tastings: Daily 11–4
Specialties: chardonnay, pinot noir, pinot noir–vin gris, sauvignon blanc

Oozing Old West scenery and atmosphere, this small winery founded in 1981 is tucked into the foothills of the Santa Lucia Range, west of Solvang on farmlands dotted with weathered buildings. Sanford wines are respected as some of the finest to pour forth from this glamorous winemaking valley. The lush, toasty chardonnays and soft, rich pinot noirs regularly show up on experts' "best of California" lists. The cozy, rustic tasting room sports a friendly potbelly stove, and picnics may be taken at tables next to a gentle creek.

SANTA BARBARA WINERY
www.sbwinery.com
Winemaker: Bruce McGuire
800-225-3633, 805-963-3633,
fax 805-962-4981

202 Anacapa St., Santa Barbara 93101
Tours: Daily 11:30 & 3:30
Tastings: Daily 10–5
Specialties: cabernet sauvignon, chardonnay, chenin blanc, riesling, Johannisberg riesling, paradiso, pinot noir, sauvignon blanc, zinfandel

Established in 1962 by Pierre Lafond, this is not only the oldest winery in the county, it's also the only one actually located within the Santa Barbara city limits. Grapes that fuel its many fine varietals are grown along the cool banks of the lower Santa Ynez River. Once famous for its fine fruit wines, the winery brought winemaker Bruce McGuire

on board in 1981 and began a vigorous and successful transition to premium grape varietal winemaking. A recently remodeled and expanded tasting room and gift shop help introduce visitors to the premium chardonnays, pinot noirs and zinfandels that the winery creates. Of special note is the haunting sauvignon blanc, Reserve, Santa Ynez Valley, filled with lush notes of butter and citrus. A perfect place to start a tour of the Santa Barbara area's many fine wineries, it also is very likely the only beachfront winery in the country.

Santa Barbara County Vintners' Association

For a map of this area's excellent wineries, the helpful folks at this first-class organization would be glad to send you a map if requested (www.sbcountywines.com, 800-218-0881, 805-688-0881, P.O Box WINE, Los Olivos 93441).

ZACA MESA WINERY

www.zacamesa.com
Winemaker: Clay Brock
800-350-7972, 805-688-9339, ext. 311,
fax 805-688-8796
6905 Foxen Canyon Rd. (P.O. Box 899),
Los Olivos 93441
Tours: Daily 11:30 & 2:30
Tastings: Daily 10–4
Specialties: chardonnay, syrah, roussane, viognier, mourvèdre

Mesa's Rhône grape varietal wines are some of the best-known and best-received wines made in the area, and the rustic winery has been producing award winners since 1972. Housed in a wooden barn, the winery is among a bevy of tiny establishments dotting Foxen Canyon Rd., and a leisurely afternoon picnicking here will have you fantasizing about buying property.

Other Santa Ynez Valley Area Wineries

Andrew Murray Vineyards www.andrew murrayvineyards.com, 805-693-9644, 805-686-9704, 2901-A Grand Ave., Los Olivos 93441. Santa Barbara County's only Rhône-exclusive estate, Murray grows on 25 separate hillside blocks, each with a separate microclimate, and handpicked and aged separately. His wines are thought to be ripe with character and richness. Tasting room open Wed.–Mon. 11–6.

Arcadian www.arcadianwinery.com, 805-688-1876, fax 805-686-5501, P.O. Box 1395, Santa Ynez 93460. Winemaker Joe Davis is another of those golden UC Davis grads. He creates Burgundian-style pinot noir, chardonnay and syrah. No tours or tastings.

Arthur Earl Winery www.arthurearlwinery .com, 800-646-3275, 805-693-1771, 90 Easy St., Buellton 93427. This young winery opened in 1996, and its 2,000 cases are all made of grapes exclusively grown in Santa Barbara County. Earl specializes in sweet wines and both dry reds and whites. Impromptu tours of the facility can be arranged for small groups. A tasting room housed in a huge converted warehouse is open daily 11–6.

Babcock Winery & Vineyards www.babcock vineyards.com, 805-736-1455, fax 805-736-3886, 5175 E. Hwy. 246, Lompoc 93436. Winemaker Bryan Babcock creates an appealing chardonnay, pinot noir, sauvignon blanc, syrah, pinot grigio and sangiovese. An attractive picnic area surrounded by vineyards is another drawing card. No tours; tastings Fri.–Sun. 10:30–4 and by appointment.

Beckmen Vineyard www.beckmenvine yards.com, 805-688-8664, fax 805-688-9983, 2670 Ontiveros Rd., Los Olivos 93441. Small and rustic, the winery is housed in a California-style redwood barn smack in the middle of a fully functional farm filled with all manner of animals. While no tours are offered, tastings of winemaker Steve Beckmen's cabernet sauvignon, chardonnay, syrah and sauvignon blanc, as well as picnicking near a small pond, are possible daily 11–5.

Bedford Thompson Winery & Vineyard www.bedfordthompsonwinery.com, 805-344-2107, fax 805-344-2047, 448 Bell St., Los Alamos 93440. Established in 1994, this small enterprise sports a spartan yet sparkling tasting room along Los Alamos's main drag just off US 101 and Foxen Canyon Rd. Adventurous travelers can sample chardonnay, rieslings, pinot gris, syrah, petite sirah, dry and Alsatian gewürztraminer daily 11–5.

Bernat Vineyards and Winery www.santa barbarawine.com, 805-686-9845, 2879 Grand Ave., Los Olivos 93441. Los Olivos Café owner Sam Marmorstein launched Bernat Winery, the smallest licensed producer in the Santa Ynez Valley, in 1995. Today he bottles 24 cases of an estate-grown chardonnay and 173 cases of a well-structured syrah, both available at his popular eatery daily 11–4.

Blackjack Ranch Vineyards & Winery www.blackjackranch.com, 805-686-9922, 866-252-2522, 2205 Alamo Pintado Rd., Solvang 93463. Owner Roger Wisted first planted his vineyard in 1996 and went into production the following year. The tasting room opened in 1999 and pours wonderful Bordeaux varietals, specifically Wisted's Billy Goat Hill merlot and Harmonie, daily 11–5.

Brewer-Clifton www.brewerclifton.com, 805-688-2455, fax 805-688-8010, 1502 Chapala St., Santa Barbara 93101. Rising stars Steve Clifton and Jim Brewer make big chardonnays and pinot noirs from small tracts of Santa Rita Hills grapes. No tours or tasting room.

Bridlewood Estate Winery www.bridle woodwinery.com, info@bridlewoodwin ery.com, 800-467-4100, 805-688-9000, 3555 Roblar Ave., Santa Ynez 93460. Bridlewood makes a dazzling range of wines, including pinot noir, cabernet sauvignon, zinfandel, merlot, chardonnay and sauvignon blanc, as well as award-winning "Arabesque" syrah. Its lushly landscaped, mission-style wine estate offers tastings daily 10–5.

Buttonwood Farm Winery www.button woodwinery.com, 800-715-1404, 805-

688-3032, fax 805-688-6168, 1500 Alamo Pintado Rd., Solvang 93463. It's new, it's small, and the fine sauvignon blancs, syrahs and merlots made by Australian-born winemaker Mike Brown are attracting attention. The cabernet franc and cabernet sauvignon offerings also are smart. No tours; tastings daily 11–5.

Cambria Winery and Vineyard www. cambriawines.com, 888-339-9463, 805-937-8091, fax 805-934-3589, 5475 Chardonnay Ln., Santa Maria 93454. Winemaker Fred Holloway creates 60,000 cases of chardonnay and pinot noir yearly. Tours by appointment only; the tasting room is open weekends and holidays 10–5.

Carina Cellars www.carinacellars.com, 805-688-2459, 2900 Grand Ave., Los Olivos 93441. Maverick winemaker Joey Tensly, and partners David and Helen Hardee, opened this tasty little tasting room in the heart of Los Olivos to showcase Carina's bold syrahs and cabernet sauvignons. Pourings are available daily noon–5.

Carrari Vineyards www.carrari.com, 805-344-4000, 439 Waite St., Los Alamos 93440. Legendary grower Joe Carrari grows grapes for the big boys, but also bottles some of his own (orchestrated by the maestro to his lusty specifications at Paul

Masson). His user-friendly quaffs are headed by Carrari's blend of cabernet franc, cabernet sauvignon, gamay, merlot, pinot noir and zinfandel under the moniker "Dago Red" (don't call us, check out the label). No tours or tastings.

Chimère 805-922-9097, fax 805-922-9143, 425 Bell St. (Hwy. 135), Los Alamos 93440. Head honcho Gary Mosby was the original winemaker at Edna Valley and left to produce chardonnay, gamay, pinot blanc and pinot noir at his own independent label in 1988. Tastings Fri.–Mon. noon–5 and by appointment.

Clos Pepe Vineyards www.clospepe.com, 805-735-2196, fax 805-736-5907, 4777 Hwy. 246, Lompoc 93436. Wine grower Wes Hagen was named Central Coast Wine Growers' Association Grower of the Year in 2001–2002. He extracts some wonderful chardonnays and pinot noirs from his vineyard's sandy loam soils rich in calcium and calcareous shale.

VOGELZANG VINEYARD
2001
Santa Barbara County
Syrah

Cold Heaven www.coldheavencellars.com, 805-688-8630, fax 805-688-3593, P.O. Box 717, Solvang 93463. Morgan Toral Clendenen, wife of Au Bon Climat's superstar Jim, produces small amounts of pinot noir and viognier under her own label. No tours or tastings.

Consilience www.consiliencewines.com, 805-691-1020, fax 805-691-1018, 2905 Grand Ave., Los Olivos 93441. Consilience was born with the release of a syrah in 1997. Today the proud parents—Brett Escalera, Monica Escalera, Tom Daughters and Jodie Boulet-Daughters—have also brought forth a zinfandel, pinot noir, roussane and viognier. You can taste examples of these at the quartet's new tasting room daily 11–6.

Cottonwood Canyon Winery & Vineyard www.cottonwoodcanyon.com, 805-937-9063, 3940 Dominion Rd., Santa Maria 93401. Winemaker Roland Shackelford's new winery specializes in chardonnay and pinot noir made from local grapes. Tours Sat. at 11, 1 & 3. Tastings daily 10:30–5:30.

Curtis Winery www.curtiswinery.com, 805-686-8999, fax 805-686-8788, 5249 Foxen Canyon Rd., Los Olivos 93441. This Firestone-owned winery sits right next to its parental enterprise and is the mother ship's premier label. Winemaker Calypso Chuck Carlson produces outstanding cabernet sauvignons, syrahs, heritages, viogniers, chardonnays and orange muscat, all of which are made from handpicked grapes drawn from various Santa Barbara County vintners. A bring-your-own picnic area sits adjacent the vines. Tours and tastings daily 10–5.

Daniel Gehrs Wines www.dgwines.com, 800-275-8138, 805-693-9686, fax 805-688-0694, 2939 Grand Ave., Los Olivos 93441. Moving his base of operations from the Santa Cruz Mountains to the Santa Ynez Valley, first as winemaker at Zaca Mesa Winery and now of his own eponymous label, talented winemaker Dan Gehrs does delightful things with chardonnay, syrah and a host of other Rhône grape varietals. Tasting room is open daily 11–6.

Epiphany Cellars www.epiphanycellars .com, 805-686-2424, 866-354-9463, 3563 Numancia St., Santa Ynez 93460. Eli Parker created this playful label and crafts a 100 percent Marcella Vineyard chardonnay blanc de blancs utilizing the traditional méthode champenoise style, as well as a petite sirah, syrah-cabernet blend and a grenache rosé. Tastings Tues.–Sun. 11–5.

Fiddlehead Cellars www.fiddleheadcellars .com, 530-756-4550, 2531 Grand Ave., Los Olivos 93441. Fiddlehead's founder, Kathy Joseph, produces memorable pinot noirs and sauvignon blancs. Tastings daily 11–6.

Foxen Vineyard 805-937-4251, fax 805-937-0415, foxen@thegrid.net, 7200 Foxen Canyon Rd., Santa Maria 93454. Nestling among the vineyards that surround this country road, the small winery boasts winemakers Richard Doré and Bill Wathen's excellent reserve cabernet sauvignon, chardonnay, cabernet franc, syrah, chenin blanc, merlot and pinot noir wines. No tours; tastings Fri.–Mon. noon–4.

Hitching Post Wines www.hitchingpost wines.com, 805-688-0676, fax 805-686-1353, 406 E. Hwy. 246, Buellton 93427. Hitching Post pinot noirs are made by Hitching Post Restaurant owner-chef Frank Ostini and his good friend, former fisherman Gray Hartley. Tastings daily 4–9:30.

Io www.iowine.com, 888-303-7288, 805-937-7288, 5230 Tepusquet Rd., Santa Maria 93454. Byron's specialty label for its intensely fruit, deep red, moderate oaky Rhônesque blend of syrah, grenache and mourvèdre grapes. Only 2,000 cases are produced. Tastings daily 10–5.

Jaffurs Wine Cellars www.jaffurswine.com, 805-962-7003, 2531A Grand Ave., Los

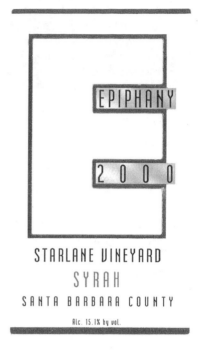

Olivos 93441. Winemaker Craig Jaffurs is dedicated to producing great Rhône varietal wines. One of the newest wineries in Santa Barbara County. Tastings daily 11–6.

J. K. Vineyard 805-686-1440, 1251 Quail Ridge Rd., Solvang 93463. Winemaker Joe Kalina (with the help of John Kerr II) makes only a tasty muscat canelli. No tour or tastings.

John Kerr Wines www.jkerr.com, jkwines @msn.com, 805-688-5337, 2905 Grand Ave., Los Olivos 93456. Sales of the chardonnay and syrah vintages produced by this very small winery, led by winemaker John Kerr II, are conducted through wholesale distribution and at the Los Olivos Tasting Room daily 11–6. No tours are available, but a free newsletter is.

Kahn Winery www.kahnwines.com, 805-686-2455, fax 877-868-8345, 2990-A Grand Ave., Los Olivos 93441. Just about the smallest winery in Santa Barbara County, Kahn produces about 2,500 cases of handcrafted wine. Winemakers Andrew Hahn and Christian Garvin focus on grapes native to the Rhône region of France and northern Italy. Sips are available at their small clubhouse of a tasting room in Los Olivos, Thurs.–Sun. 10–6.

Kalyra Wines www.kalyrawinery.com, 805-693-8864, 343 North Refugio Rd, Santa Ynez 93460. Fairly new and very small, the winery produces a few hundred cases each of nebbiolo, cabernet franc, cabernet sauvignon, pinot blanc, orange muscat, black muscat, merlot and port. Winemaker Michael Brown also plays around with fortified dessert wines. His handcrafted work can be found at the new tasting room as well as the Los Olivos Tasting Room. Tours by appointment.

Koehler Winery www.koehlerwinery.com 805-686-8484, fax 805-686-8474, 5360 Foxen Canyon Rd., Los Olivos 93441. Peter Koehler purchased 100 acres of prime

Santa Ynez Valley land and planted cabernet sauvignon, chardonnay, sauvignon blanc, riesling, syrah, sangiovese, grenache and viognier. Winemaker Michael Roth was brought on board as alchemist and today the grapes have all realized their best expression from the microclimatic diversity of the property and the creative talents of Peter and Michael. Tastings daily 10–5.

Lafond Winery and Vineyards www.lafond winery.com, 805-688-7921, 6855 Santa Rosa Rd., Buellton 93427. Peter Lafond founded this label in 1962, thus launching the Santa Barbara County wine country. One tour daily at 1pm. Tastings daily 10–5.

Lane Tanner www.lanetanner.com, 805-688-4409, 805-929-1826, 2531 Grand Ave., Los Olivos 93441. Savvy, saucy Lane Tanner is a smart woman winemaker who is on the trail of the elusive Holy Grail of California wine: the perfect pinot noir. She just could find it. Tastings daily 11–6.

Longoria Wines www.longoriawine.com, 805-688-0305, 2935 Grand Ave., Los Olivos 93441. Gifted alchemist Rick Longoria has been making pinot noir on his own since 1982 and now produces cabernet franc and a cabernet franc blend called Blues Cuvee (with its wonderful labels of musicians' portraits), as well as syrah, pinot grigio, merlot, chardonnay, Hoo Doo Red (a blend of dolcetto, merlot, barbera, nebbiolo and mourvèdre) and Lusso (blend of barbera, nebbiolo and dolcetto). Future vintages will include Spanish albariño and tempranillo. No tours, but samples of his labors are available at the Richard Longoria Wines Tasting Room, located in one of the oldest buildings in town, open Mon., Wed. & Thurs. noon–4:30, Fri.–Sun. 11–4:30 (closed Tues.).

Lucas & Lewellen Vineyards www.llwine .com, 888-777-6663, 805-344-3000, 1539 Mission Dr., Solvang. One of the most

respected newer labels in the Santa Ynez Valley. Tastings daily 11–6.

McKeon-Phillips Winery www.mckeon phillipswinery.com, 805-928-3025, 2115 S. Blosser Rd., Suite 114, Santa Maria. Featured wines here are sauvignon blanc, pinot noir, chardonnay, sangiovese, cabernet franc and cabernet sauvignon. Tastings Fri.–Sun. noon–6 and by appointment.

Melville Winery www.melvillewinery.com, 805-735-7030, fax 805 735 5310, 5185 E. Hwy. 246, Lompoc 93436. Ron Melville pulled up stakes in Calistoga and set down his taproot in the Santa Rita Hills. Today, with his sons Chad and Brent, he has 75 acres planted to pinot noir, chardonnay and syrah. Tastings Fri.–Sun. 11–4 and by appointment.

Morovino www.morovino.com, 805-347-1272, 433 Alisal Rd., Solvang 93463. Winemaker Gerry Moro makes a Tango 99 (a 50–50 blend of merlot and zinfandel), as well as chardonnays, sauvignon blancs, merlots, barberas and sangioveses. Tastings Thurs.–Mon. 10–5.

Mt. Carmel Vineyards 310-633-4183, Route 1, Box 141 East Mail Rd., Lompoc 93436. Having built around a new Carmelite mission in an east–west fog-cooled valley both as a visual and spiritual plus to the religious retreat, winemaker Bryan Babcock sticks to the secular with his serious chardonnay and pinot noir vintages. Proceeds from the wines augment income from market gardens tended by the nuns. Tours and tastings by appointment only.

Presidio Winery www.presidiowinery.com, 888-965-9463, 805-693-8585, 1539 Mission Dr., Solvang 93463. Presidio Winery was started in 1991 with an initial production of 1,200 cases of chardonnay and merlot. In 2001, the label produced over 10,000 cases of Santa Barbara County pinot noir, merlot and chardonnay. Examples can be experienced at the winery's lush tasting room daily 9–5:30.

Rideau Vineyard www.rideauvineyard .com, 805-688-0717, 1562 Alamo Pintado Rd., Solvang 93463. Housed in an 1884 adobe, this small newcomer specializes in Rhône varietals. Tastings daily 11–4 and by appointment.

Rusack Vineyards www.rusackvineyards .com, 805-688-1278, 1819 Ballard Canyon Rd., Solvang 93463. Owners Geoff and Alison Rusack and winemaker John Falcone produce 2,000 cases of riesling, chardonnay, syrah and merlot a year, as well as muscat and riesling ice wines when the gods are smiling. Samplings are available in the friendly tasting room daily 11–5 and by appointment.

Stolpman www.stolpmanvineyards.com, 805-688-0400, 1659 Copenhagen Dr., Solvang 93463. Specializes in blends of syrah, sangiovese, cabernet sauvignon, merlot, cabernet franc, petit verdot and malbec. Tastings daily 11–6.

Sunstone Vineyards & Winery www.sunstonewinery.com, 800-313-9463, 805-688-9463, fax 805-686-1881, 125 N. Refugio Rd., Santa Ynez 93460. One of the most gorgeous wineries and tasting rooms in the valley, Sunstone was started in 1989 and completed in 1993 and today produces 8,500 cases yearly. The Provençal-style facility, arbored porch and umbrella-shaded tables in the courtyard mate perfectly to the all-organic fields of merlot, cabernet sauvignon, viognier, chardonnay, syrah and muscat canelli. Aging takes place in French oak inside the 120-foot cave dug into the hillside. Tours by appointment. Tastings daily 10–4.

Van Enoo Vineyards www.vanenoo.com, 1051 Croft Ave., Solvang 93463. Owners Lise and Rudi Van Enoo, and their acclaimed winemaker Bruno D'Alfonso of Sanford, created 150 cases of a 100 percent 2001 syrah from organic grapes, as well as a 2003 viognier. No tours or tastings.

Vita Nova No telephone, P.O. Box 822, Los Olivos 93441. Two celebrated winemakers, Jim Clendenen from Au Bon Climat and Bob Lindquist from Qupé, have joined forces to whip up some new ideas in cabernet franc, cabernet sauvignon, merlot and sauvignon blanc, as well as a stunning chardonnay. All the better for their admirers, who can stop by the Los Olivos Tasting Room for some stunning samples. No tours are available.

Whitcraft Winery www.whitcraftwinery.com, 805-693-0111, 2531 Grand Ave., Los Olivos 93441. Ultrasmall, winemaker Chris Whitcraft's operation started making fine chardonnays and pinot noirs in 1985. Tastings daily 11–6.

Alisal Cellars

Since 1964, the wines of the Santa Barbara/Santa Ynez Valley region have been showcased at this appealing cellar that offers tastings, wine sales and an array of regional specialty items. Over 450 wines are represented. It is open Sun.–Wed. 10–6, Thurs.–Sat. 10–9 (www.alisalcellars.com, 800-630-9941, 805-686-4329, 448 Alisal Rd., Solvang 93463).

INFORMATION

Nuts & Bolts

This chapter is a one-stop Central Coast survival guide. Filled with hard facts, it is compiled with both the local and the visitor in mind, providing guidance in the following areas.

In any emergency, travelers seeking police, fire or ambulance assistance need only dial 911 on the nearest telephone and help will be sent immediately. Christopher Gardner

Ambulance/Fire/Police

Always remember that **911** is the telephone number to call to request an ambulance, report a fire or seek help for a situation requiring immediate police response—in short, for any and all emergency situations anywhere on the Central Coast. For police assistance that doesn't require an emergency response, contact the number listed below for the city closest to your present location:

Santa Cruz (Area Code 831)

TOWN	POLICE
Aptos	471-1121
Bonny Doon	471-1121
Cabrillo College	479-6313
Capitola	471-1141
Davenport	471-1121
Felton	471-1121
Freedom	471-1121
Half Moon Bay	650-726-8286
Highway Patrol	662-6690
La Selva Beach	471-1121
Pescadero	650-363-4911
Rio Del Mar	471-1121
San Gregorio	650-363-4911
Santa Cruz	471-1131
Scotts Valley	440-5670
Soquel	471-1121
Univ. of California	459-2231
Watsonville	471-1151

Monterey (Area Code 831)

TOWN	POLICE
Aromas	647-7911
Big Sur	647-7911
Calif. State University	582-3360
Carmel	624-6403
Carmel Highlands	647-7911
Carmel Valley	647-7911
Castroville	647-7911
Gonzales	675-5010
Gorda	647-7911
Greenfield	674-5111
Highway Patrol	455-4800
Hollister	636-4332
Jolon	647-7911
King City	385-4848
Lucia	647-7911
Marina	647-7911
Monterey	646-3830

Monterey Pen. College 646-4099
Moss Landing 647-7911
Pacific Grove.............................. 648-3143
Paicines.................................. 636-4080
Pebble Beach 624-6669
Salinas 758-7090
San Juan Bautista 636-4080
Seaside................................... 899-6756
Soledad.................................. 678-1332

SAN LUIS OBISPO (AREA CODE 805)

TOWN	POLICE
Arroyo Grande	473-5100
Atascadero	461-5051
Avila Beach	781-4550
Cal Poly State Univ.	756-2222
Cambria	781-4550
Cayucos	781-4550
Creston	781-4550
Grover Beach	473-4511
Harmony	781-4550
Highway Patrol	593-3333
Los Osos	781-4550
Morro Bay	772-6225
Nipomo	781-4550
Oceano	781-4550
Paso Robles	237-6464
Pismo Beach	773-2208
San Luis Obispo	781-7317
San Miguel	781-4550
Santa Margarita	781-4550
San Simeon	781-4550
Templeton	781-4550

SANTA YNEZ VALLEY (AREA CODE 805)

TOWN	POLICE
Ballard	686-5000
Buellton	686-5000
Gaviota	686-5000
Guadalupe	343-2112
Lake Cachuma	686-5000
Lompoc	736-2341
Los Olivos	686-5000
Orcutt	686-5000
Santa Barbara	897-2300
Santa Maria	928-3781
Santa Ynez	686-5000
Solvang	686-5000

AREA CODES

The area code for Santa Cruz, Monterey and San Benito Counties is **831** (for San Mateo County's Coastside, it's **650**). The area code for San Luis Obispo County, Santa Maria and the Santa Ynez Valley (both in Santa Barbara County) is **805**.

BANKS

In this era of the electronic instant-teller machine, travelers to the Central Coast have 24-hour access to their monetary resources. All major national and state banks, plus most small local banks, are linked by computers to these handy cash vendors.

BIBLIOGRAPHY

The Central Coast has long inspired storytellers, historians and novelists to put pen to paper. Bookstores in the region usually boast special sections devoted to lore, cuisine, natural history, reminiscence and fiction about this fascinating and mercurial wedge of the Golden State. Public libraries are additional fonts of literature about this land and its people, from the archival diaries of the Spanish explorers to charming tourism guides spanning the past two centuries. Reference librarians specialize in directing newcomers to a wealth of browsing material on everything from tide pools and winemaking to genealogy and politics. Here are a few suggestions to get you started.

Biography and Reminiscence

Boutelle, Sara Holmes. *Julia Morgan, Architect*. Color photos by Richard Barnes. New York: Abbeville Press, 1988. 265 pp., index, illus., photos. A richly told and rewarding biography of the remarkable California architect whose elegantly rustic Arts & Crafts visions hand-shaped many landmarks of northern California and the Central Coast. Morgan, the first American woman admitted to the Beaux Arts enclave of Paris, is best known for surviving the wild imagination of William Randolph Hearst during the building of his San Simeon castle. A meeting with a remarkable woman.

Gilliam, Harold and Ann. *Creating Carmel: The Enduring Vision*. Salt Lake City: Peregrine Smith Books, 1992. 234 pp., index, photos. In-depth, play-by-play history of a mellow, exclusive arts colony on Monterey Bay from its mission origins to the bohemian boom and cultural vitality of today.

Gleason, Duncan and Dorothy. *Beloved Sister—The Letters of James Henry Gleason, 1841–1859: From Alta California and the Sandwich Islands*. Glendale: The Arthur H. Clark Company, 1978. 217 pp., index, illus. Letters from a globe-trotting Englishman, who became the Monterey County clerk in 1857, tell the story of daily life, political intrigue and back-breaking travel conditions during California's Mexican colonial period.

Gudde, Erwin G. *California Place Names*. Berkeley: University of California Press, 1974. 431 pp., index. A fact-filled encyclopedia of the lore, history, color, romance and charismatic individuals whose names loom large throughout the state.

Hague, Harlan, and David J. Langum. *Thomas O. Larkin: A Life of Patriotism and Profit in Old California*. Norman and London: University of Oklahoma Press, 1990. 294 pp., index, photos. Focusing on the life and times of the wealthy Monterey merchant who helped

Master storyteller James D. Houston discovers the spirit of the Golden State in his literate, accessible investi-gation Californians: Searching for the Golden State. Robert Scheer

finesse the Americanization of Spanish California, this book offers in-depth historical insights and analysis of the entrepreneurial spirit that civilized the New World's final frontier.

Houston, James D. *Californians: Searching for the Golden State.* Santa Cruz: Otter B Books, 1992. 288 pp. Reminiscence, anecdote, environmental puzzling and historical detective work pour from the pages of this literary treasure hunt for the spirit of the Golden State. Accessibly shaped by a master storyteller, this is crucial reading for any serious student of the California zeitgeist.

Nasaw, David. *The Chief: The Life of William Randolph Hearst.* Boston: Houghton Mifflin, 2000. 607 pp., index, photos. Nasaw's colorful biography of the controversial and extremely powerful publisher plumbs the outrageous and unscrupulous life of one of America's major movers and shakers. The newspaper titan's life is played out as vivid psychodrama on a world stage that America—thanks in no little part to Hearst—was soon to dominate. A nickelodeon full of flickering images of the great people of the day—FDR, Hitler, Churchill, Louis B. Mayer, Orson Welles, Marion Davies, Carole Lombard—the book turns a kaleidoscope's prism to life in the first 50 years of the 20th century through the rise and fall on one man, W. R. Hearst.

Nordhoff, Charles. *California for Travelers and Settlers.* [1872] Centennial Printing. Berkeley: Ten Speed Press, 1973. 255 pp., illus. Utterly mesmerizing firsthand account of the jour-ney west by the columnist for a popular 19th-century East Coast newspaper. Filled with lore and anecdotes of the day and eyewitness analysis of the then little-known natural wonders of the great unknown that was the Wild West. Nordhoff's tales so extolled the balmy climate and therapeutic seaside atmosphere that they helped launch a westward migration still in progress today. Included are many charming accounts, often laced with the prevailing ignorance and racism of the day.

Nunis, Doyce B., Jr., ed. *The California Diary of Faxon Dean Atherton: 1836–1839*. San Francisco: California Historical Society, 1964. 235 pp., index. The man who gave his name to a suburban town nestled in the Coast Ranges speaks to us from the pages of vivid diaries kept during tempestuous ocean voyages along the California coastline from Baja California to the Oregon border and from Hawaii to Boston.

Robinson, Judith. *The Hearsts: An American Dynasty*. New York: Avon Books, 1992. 420 pp., index, photos. Compelling biographical portrait of a mighty family carving out and living the American Dream in bigger-than-life style. You'll meet pioneer silver miner George and his son William Randolph (whose thinly disguised excesses were brilliantly etched in *Citizen Kane*). But perhaps the most influential and interesting Hearst was WRH's mother, Phoebe, the strong-willed matriarch who left her fortune to her son and her mark on much of the Central Coast.

Fiction

Haslam, Gerald W., ed. *Many Californias: Literature from the Golden State*. Reno: University of Nevada Press, 1992. 250 pp., index. Handy one-stop literary tour guide through some of the best minds that ever penned the West. A contemporary sampler filled with excerpts, poems and stories from Californians like Wallace Stegner, Maxine Hong Kingston, Joan Didion, Raymond Chandler, Toshio Mori, Jack London, Richard Henry Dana and John Muir.

Hudson, Christopher. *Spring Street Summer*. New York: Alfred A. Knopf, 1993. 260 pp. The editorial page editor of the *London Daily Telegraph*, Hudson returns to Santa Cruz 15 years after having spent a fellowship year studying the concepts of paradise in Western thought at the university and spending an idyllic summer of nudity, wine, sun and uncomplicated sex—the flesh-and-sweat essence of the Age of Aquarius. This comic, yearning story of his quest to reconnect with that magical time and place explores the notions of truth, self-deception, the getting of wisdom and immutable joys of paradise both lost and regained.

Jeffers, Robinson. *Cawdor/Medea*. New York: New Directions, 1970. 191 pp. A riveting introduction to the moody genius of a Central Coast master. Written in 1928, *Cawdor* is a stormy, narrative love poem set on the turbulent Big Sur coast. Jeffers's 1946 verse adaptation of the Greek tragedy *Medea* was created for Dame Judith Anderson.

Kerouac, Jack. *The Dharma Bums*. New York: Penguin Group, 1991 (reprint). 244 pp. The best of Kerouac's autobiographical novels, *The Dharma Bums* is based on experiences the writer had during the mid-1950s while living in Central California, where he delved into Zen Buddhism. One of the book's main characters is based on poet Gary Snyder, a close friend, whose interest in Buddhism influenced Kerouac. In real life, the two traveled the Central Coast together trying to find themselves and the meaning of life. Kerouac also writes of Alvah Goldbook's inaugural reading of his watershed poem *Wail* at the San Francisco Poetry Renaissance (slightly disguised remembrance of Allen Ginsberg's reading of *Howl*, a Beat literature classic).

Stegner, Wallace. *Angle of Repose*. New York: Penguin Books, 1971. 568 pp. A Pulitzer Prize–winning exploration of the fears, failures, hopes, dreams and sheer toughness of a

California pioneer family whose energies and accomplishments shaped the landscape of contemporary Central California. One of the best introductions to how the West was really won.

Steinbeck, John. *Cannery Row.* New York: Penguin Group, 1993 (reprint). 196 pp. Most entertaining of Steinbeck's great body of work. The author imbues his tale with the vivid sight and sounds of the Monterey's Cannery Row and the men and women who wrestle joy and laughter from its tough fishing life. The characters here have a vivaciousness that can come only from honestly drawn subjects, detailing both the good and the nasty aspects of humans' makeup. But the writing is the true star of the novel. At times the writing shimmers with poetry: "Cannery Row in Monterey in California is a poem, a stink, a grating noise, a quality of light, a tone, a habit, a nostalgia, a dream."

Steinbeck, John. *The Grapes of Wrath.* New York: Penguin Group, 1939. 580 pp. The Salinas-born Nobel Prize winner crafted this American classic out of the blood, sweat and tears of Okie immigrants seeking to escape dust bowl Depression in the relative paradise of coastal California. The literary song of the dispossessed still resonates with regional power.

Stevenson, Robert Louis. *The Works of Robert Louis Stevenson.* London: Octopus Publishing Group, 1989. 687 pp. Filled with the classic tales penned by the man who brought us *Treasure Island*, which was inspired by his long, romantic visits to the Monterey Coast.

History & Cultural Studies

Clark, Donald. *Santa Cruz County Place Names.* Santa Cruz: Santa Cruz Historical Society, 1986. 552 pp., illus., maps. Oral histories, folklore and rare archival information conspire in this fascinating encyclopedia of Santa Cruz County places and how they got their names, both official and colloquial.

Clark, Donald. *Monterey County Place Names.* Carmel Valley: Kestrel Press, 1991. 661 pp., index, maps. The tireless Librarian Emeritus of the University of California–Santa Cruz continues his exploration of

Robert Louis Stevenson's numerous visits to the Monterey Coast fed his literary imagination.

the origin of official and unofficial place-names, this time ranging throughout the vast history of the territory that comprised the most important outpost of Spanish domination in Old California.

Hamman, Rick. *California Central Coast Railways.* Boulder: Pruett Publishing Company, 1980. 307 pp., index, illus., photos. A copiously illustrated and lovingly documented train buff's guide that tracks the expansion of the Central Coast via rail. The rich saga of the opening of commercial lines throughout the Central Coast is the story of men who demonstrated both engineering expertise and sheer courage in blasting iron highways through the coastal mountains. Terrific archival photographs enhance the exciting ride.

Hoover, Mildred Brooke, et al. *Historic Spots in California,* 3rd ed. Stanford: Stanford
University Press, 1966. 597 pp., index, photos. County-by-county walking tour through
the state's hotbeds of history. Exhaustively detailed entries on Central Coast landmark
regions, chronicling the people, politics, settlements and battles that won the West.
Lydon, Sandy. *Chinese Gold.* Capitola: Capitola Book Company Publishing, 1985. 550 pp.,
illus., photos. An eye-opening and brilliantly researched bit of historical detective work
that reveals the full flower, productivity and enterprise of Chinese immigrants throughout the Central Coast. Written with flourish and confidence, this book bursts with archival photographs and eyewitness accounts through which a slice of the past lives on vividly.
Margolin, Malcolm. *The Ohlone Way.* Illustrated by Michael Harney. Berkeley: Heyday
Books, 1978. 168 pp., index, illus. A sensitive and sympathetic glimpse inside the lives of
these gentle hunter-gatherers, recounting their nomadic movements, artistic preoccu-
pations, hunting rituals and metaphysical beliefs. It creates the lost world of an extinct
cultural group that lived only 200 years away from us on the very spots we tread.
McPhee, John. *Assembling California.* New York: Farrar, Straus and Giroux, 1993. 303 pp.
Master wordsmith McPhee continues his explorations into the geologic mysteries of the
New World by laying down the geology of California, layer by layer, seismic fold by tectonic plate. Told through anecdote, poetic spin, parable, wry wit and salty observation—
in other words, the inimitable McPhee style—this gem traces the imaginary intersection
of human and geologic time in the Golden State, from deserts to Coastal Ranges, spicing
up the journey with a dash of earthquake consciousness. A superb introduction to the
invisible mind-set of California.
Miller, Bruce W. Chumash. *Los Osos.* Los Osos: Sand River Press, 1988. 135 pp., index,
photos. Knowledgeable, clearly written, historical and archaeological tome tracing the
fortunes of these early Central Coast natives. Placing the hunter-gatherer peoples in
intelligible, historical context, the book includes chapters on religion, rock painting,
basketry and social customs, plus illustrative photographs of native harpoons, seal effi-
gies and basket masterpieces.
Perry, Frank. *Lighthouse Point: Illuminating Santa Cruz.* Santa Cruz: Otter B Books, 2002.
186 pp. A bright, shining history of the people, both quirky and steadfast, who helped
shape the development of the north Monterey Bay area. This tale of a lighthouse standing vigilant on a few acres of land at the edge of the sea traces the evolving periods of
prehistory, Native American inhabitation, Spanish mission, *Californio* culture, Yankee
empire, Asian and Italian immigration, two world wars, the Depression, the cultural
fractures and exhilarations of the 1960s and '70s, and the ever-present tourist mecca
that Santa Cruz charts as its pedigree.
Stanger, Frank M. *South from San Francisco: San Mateo County, California, Its History and
Heritage.* San Mateo County Historical Association, 1963. 208 pp., index, photos.
Captivating minutiae concerning the wild-eyed dreamers and sturdy folk who logged,
ranched, built and cultivated the wild coastal lands surrounding San Francisco. Liberally
littered with archival photographs of the way they were.
Starr, Kevin. *Americans and the California Dream: 1850–1915.* New York: Oxford University
Press, 1973. 479 pp., index, photos. Rich interweaving of the tales of Yankee speculators,
explorers and politico-cultural big shots who came to find and to fabricate their version
of the Promised Land. Contains vivid portraits of potent citizens, from Luther Burbank
and Jack London to Phoebe Hearst and Isadora Duncan. Just one in a five-volume
historical panorama of the Golden State from infancy to the present day. Others in the

Oxford University press series are: *Inventing the Dream* (1985), *Material Dreams* (1990), *The Dream Endures* (1997) and *Embattled Dreams* (2002).

Winslow, Jr., Carleton M., and Nickola L. Frye. *The Enchanted Hill: The Story of Hearst Castle at San Simeon.* Millbrae: Celestial Arts, 1980. 168 pp., index, illus., photos. Lush with glossy color photos and Hearst family album snapshots, this oversized volume tracks the construction of the amazing Spanish baroque complex that housed the fantasies and celebrity guests of newspaper magnate William Randolph Hearst.

Woodbridge, Sally B. *California Architecture: Historic American Buildings Survey.* San Francisco: Chronicle Books, 1988. 270 pp., index, illus., photos. A richly detailed and scholarly overview of California's architectural history—from Native American to post-modern—precedes this encyclopedia of important historic landmarks throughout the state. Structures are placed in the cultural landscape as far back as they can be traced. Believe it or not, this is a real page-turner.

Nature Guides

Bakker, Elna. *An Island Called California.* Berkeley: University of California Press, 1984, 2nd ed. 455 pp., index, maps, illus., photos. An eye-opening walk through the ecological niches of California, this is a vivid aid to the nonscientist in interpreting the diversity of flora and fauna. Strong sections on seashore, salt marshes and sea cliff ecology.

LeBoeuf, Burney, and Stephanie Kaza. *The Natural History of Año Nuevo.* Pacific Grove: Boxwood Press, 1981. 414 pp., index, illus., photos. Exhaustively detailed, this is the definitive overview of a unique natural sanctuary—from the history of original whaling settlers to detailed reports on weather, tide pools, plants, currents and shore life. The authors are leading authorities on the life and times of the elephant seal and, with their astute help, these remarkable creatures loom larger in their favorite coastal habitat.

Munz, Phillip A. *Shore Wildflowers of California, Oregon and Washington.* Berkeley: University of California Press, 1973. 112 pp., index, illus., photos. This bible of coastal flora is well illustrated, clearly written and helpfully grouped according to flower color.

Perry, John, and Jane Greverus Perry. *The Sierra Club Guide to the Natural Areas of California.* San Francisco: Sierra Club Books, 1999. 316 pp., index, maps. The serious outdoorsper-son's guide to the top wilderness and natural areas of the state. Broken down into geographic regions, this useful guide covers the distinctive characteristics, facilities and high points of major state and national parks, forests and wildlife preserves.

Schoenherr, Allan A. *A Natural History of California.* Berkeley: University of California Press, 1992. 768 pp. An overriding ecological awareness distinguishes this expansive exploration of the biological and geological diversity of California. Natural communities, their interactions and origins spring to life in a concise and highly engaging style.

Photographic Studies

Baer, Morley, et al. *Adobes in the Sun: Portraits of a Tranquil Era.* San Francisco: Chronicle Books, 1980. 144 pp., illus., photos. Historic adobes of Monterey as captured by a Bay Area master image-maker.

California Coast. Photographs by Larry and Donna Ulrich, text by Sandra L. Keith. Portland: Graphic Arts Center, 1990. 160 pp., photos. The entire California coast comes alive in these splendid, oversized photographic pages. A visual armchair stroll up and down the state, photographed in all weather and seasons and from breathtaking points of view. For dreaming over, before finding it a prominent resting place on the coffee table.

Crouch, Steve. *Fog and Sun, Sea and Stone: The Monterey Coast.* Portland: Graphic Arts Center Publishing Co., 1980. 157 pp., photos. Sensitive marriage of text and images conveys the natural wonders, elusive and bold, as well as man-made traces that adorn this vibrant stretch of the Central Coast.

Crouch, Steve. *Steinbeck Country.* Portland: Graphic Arts Center Publishing Co., 1973. 189 pp., index, photos. Gorgeous color photos and evocative text by the talented Crouch, who has a real feel for the Central Coast ambiance mythologized by Steinbeck. Includes plenty of quotes from the Nobel Prize winner's writings.

CLIMATE, WEATHER, WHAT TO WEAR

The very expression "Mediterranean climate," which most appropriately describes the prevailing meteorological ambiance of the Central Coast, conjures balmy days filled with sunshine and temperate, frost-free winters. For most of this almost-300-mile stretch of California, that image is gloriously accurate. Santa Cruz's summer days average in the mid-to-high 70s, while farther south in the Santa Ynez Valley, the warmest days tend to add 10 degrees to that figure. This is idyllic beach climate, with summer evenings cooling down pleasantly into the 50-degree range.

Winters in the rainier northern stretch of the Central Coast offer days ranging from 50 degrees, hitting the 70s during the glorious "false spring" of January and February. Along this coast, summer beach weather begins sometime in March and extends through the end of October. The dry season—often without a drop of rain save for the very rare occasional shower—lasts from May through mid-November.

While the summer is by far the most popular touring season, fall and winter offer days mild enough to require only a sweater or light jacket. Free of the summer crowds, the so-called off-season rewards the traveler with open roads and crowd-free destinations. Locals revel in the luxury of deserted beaches and unencumbered hiking through lush mountain forests. All Central Coast residents know that the most beautiful months here—especially with warm, bright sunny days and fog-free nights—are May and October.

A word about the famous coastal fog is in order. The moisture-laden, low-lying clouds that hug the Central Coast during summer evenings and early mornings are responsible for the area's year-round vegetation, extended growing season and mighty redwood forests. It can also come as a surprise to visitors expecting to hit the beaches on summer mornings, only to find the fog obscuring the sun. As locals are fond of telling first-time visitors, the fog inevitably "burns off" by noon, leaving the afternoon gloriously cloud-free and perfect for outdoor activities. In the summer, the fog rolls back in around sunset, so even in the warmest weather, it's important to come prepared with sweater, jacket and long pants.

Wherever and whenever you're traveling along the Central Coast, it's a good idea to pack comfortable walking shoes, a warm sweater or down vest and a bathing suit. Most nightspots and restaurants in this area stress casual dress, so a tie and high heels usually aren't required. Still, it's smart to pack at least one outfit that makes you feel smartly dressed for exploring some of the upscale evening destinations, especially in downtown Monterey and Carmel.

FISHING & HUNTING REGULATIONS

California Department of Fish & Game (916-227-2282, 3211 S St., Sacramento 95816). Information, licenses and tags. A fishing license is required for all persons 16 or older wishing to fish in ocean or inland waters, with the exception of most public piers. A hunting license is needed to hunt any animal in the state.

HANDICAPPED SERVICES

Progressive in more than politics and attitudes, Californians have led the way in providing access to all of the resources of this region to persons with disabilities. Government buildings of every kind—from libraries to restrooms—have been retrofitted to accommodate that access. Under aggressive action on the part of the State Department of Parks and Recreation, many of the most attractive (and usually least accessible) beaches, trails, parks and forests have been equipped with facilities affording ample enjoyment to all.

Campsites at Pismo State Beach, Morro Bay State Park and Pfeiffer Big Sur State Park have been created for wheelchair access. Many beaches now boast special wheelchairs that enable beachcombing along the surf, and at Año Nuevo State Reserve, a portable wheelchair-friendly trail can be arranged to provide visitors a close-up look at elephant seal rookeries.

Information about lodgings, restaurants and cultural attractions, noting accommodations for persons with disabilities, may be obtained by turning to specific sections of this book. City departments of parks and recreation, which may be reached through TDD numbers for the hearing impaired, also will provide detailed and up-to-date information on facilities in each area.

By checking county transit listings in the local telephone directory, visitors can find out about wheelchair-accessible services like **Dial-A-Ride**. **The Center for Independent Living** in Berkeley (www.cilberkeley.org, 510-841-4776, fax 510-841-6168) provides information about tours and trips specifically designed for persons with disabilities.

To reserve wheelchair-accessible campsites at selected state parks, contact the California Department of Parks and Recreation in Sacramento (916-445-6477).

You also might check out Erick Mitiken's *Wheelchair Rider's Guide,* which covers natural areas from Half Moon Bay down to Santa Cruz and from Big Sur to San Luis Obispo County. This free guide is available from the California State Coastal Conservancy (510-286-1015, fax 510-286-0470).

HOSPITALS & EMERGENCY MEDICAL SERVICE

All of the hospitals listed below have emergency rooms that remain open 24 hours a day. The quality of treatment is generally superb, since many gifted physicians and health-care practitioners gravitate to scenic recreational areas rather than big cities to demonstrate their proficiency in the bodily arts and sciences. The Central Coast has the scenic part down, and consequently, the medical aspects covered, too

SANTA CRUZ
Dominican Hospital www.dominicanhospital.org, 831-462-7700, 1555 Soquel Ave., Santa Cruz.

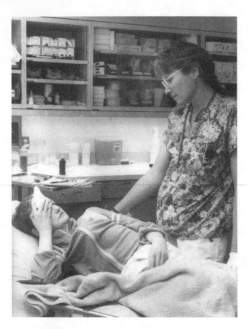

Central Coast hospitals and clinics offer some of the best emergency, short-term and sports injury medicine in the nation. Hillary Schalit

Seton Medical Center Coastside www.setonmedicalcenter.org/coastside, 650-728-5521, 600 Marina Blvd., Moss Beach.

Watsonville Community Hospital www.watsonvillehospital.com, 831-724-4741, 75 Nielson St., Watsonville.

MONTEREY

Community Hospital of the Monterey Peninsula www.chomp.com, 831-624-5311, 23625 W. R. Holman Hwy., Monterey.

Mee Memorial Hospital www.meememorial .com, 831-385-6000, 300 Canal St., King City.

Salinas Valley Memorial Hospital www.svmh.com, 888-755-7864, 831-757-4333, 450 E. Romie Ln., Salinas.

SAN LUIS OBISPO

Arroyo Grande Community Hospital www.agch.org, 805-489-4261, 345 S. Halcyon Rd., Arroyo Grande.

French Hospital Medical Center www.agfh.org, 805-543-5333, 1911 Johnson Ave., San Luis Obispo.

HealthSouth Surgery Center of San Luis Obispo www.healthsouth.com, 805-544-7874, 1304 Ella St., San Luis Obispo.

Sierra Vista Regional Medical Center www.sierravistaregional.com, 805-546-7600, 1010 Murray Ave., San Luis Obispo.

Twin Cities Community Hospital www.twincitieshospital.com, 805-434-3500, 1100 Las Tablas Rd., Templeton.

SANTA YNEZ VALLEY

Lompoc District Hospital www.lompochospital.org, 805-737-3300, 508 E. Hickory Ave., Lompoc.

Marian Medical Center www.marianmedicalcenter.org, 805-739-3000, 1400 E. Church St., Santa Maria.

Santa Ynez Valley Cottage Hospital www.sbch.org/ourhospitals/santaynez.html, 805-688-6431, 700 Alamo Pintado Rd., Solvang.

LOCAL GOVERNMENT & ZIP CODES

In some circumstances, Central Coast travelers discover a problem or issue existing within the destination community that gets their blood boiling or their heartstrings trembling. The numbers below will put the mobilized reader in touch with local political honchos who can give direction or offer solace. The zip codes are a bonus.

SANTA CRUZ (AREA CODE 831)

TOWN	TELEPHONE	ZIP CODE
Aptos	454-2200	95003
Bonny Doon	454-2200	95060
Capitola	475-7300	95010
Davenport	454-2200	95017
Felton	454-2200	95018
Freedom	454-2200	95019
Half Moon Bay	650-363-4569	94019
La Selva Beach	454-2200	95076
Pescadero	650-726-8270	94060
Rio Del Mar	454-2200	95003
Santa Cruz	429-3540	95060
Scotts Valley	438 2324	95066
Soquel	454-2200	95073
Univ. of California	459-2058	95064
Watsonville	728-6011	95076

MONTEREY (AREA CODE 831)

TOWN	TELEPHONE	ZIP CODE
Big Sur	647-7600	93920
Carmel	624-2781	93921,93923
Carmel Highlands	647-7600	93923
Carmel Valley	647-7600	93924
Castroville	637-4641	95012
Gonzales	675-5000	93926
Greenfield	674-5591	93927
Hollister	637-8221	95023
Jolon	647-7600	93928
King City	385-3281	93930
Lucia	647-7600	93920
Monterey	646-3760	93940
Moss Landing	647-7600	95039
Pacific Grove	648-3100	93950
Pebble Beach	649-8500	93953
Salinas	758-7201	93901,93905
San Juan Bautista	623-4661	95045
Seaside	899-6203	93955
Soledad	678-3963	93960

San Luis Obispo (Area Code 805)

TOWN	TELEPHONE	ZIP CODE
Arroyo Grande	489-1303	93420
Atascadero	461-5010	93422
Avila Beach	781-5450	93424
Cal Poly, SLO	756-1111	93407
Cambria	781-5450	93428
Creston	781-5450	93432
Harmony	781-5450	93435
Los Osos	781-5450	93402
Morro Bay	772-6200	93442
Nipomo	781-5450	93444
Oceano	781-5450	93445
Paso Robles	237-3888	93446
Pismo Beach	773-4657	93449
San Luis Obispo	781-7100	93401, 93405
San Miguel	781-5450	93451
San Simeon	781-5450	93452
Santa Margarita	781-5450	93453
Templeton	781-5450	93465

Santa Ynez Valley (Area Code 805)

TOWN	TELEPHONE	ZIP CODE
Ballard	686-5095	93463
Buellton	686-5095	93427
Lompoc	736-1261	93436, 93438
Los Olivos	686-5095	93441
Santa Maria	925-0951	93454, 93455
Santa Ynez	686-5095	93460
Solvang	686-5095	93463

MEDIA

Independent-minded and contemplative at land's end, the Central Coast's pioneers and present-day residents share a reputation for going against the national grain, and their publications reflect that preference. Be it the unabashed conservative, fire-breathing liberal or wild-dog maverick, differing points of view always find their way into print and the public eye, some to prosper in the sun, others to wither in the chill of disapproval. Literate, college-educated and inquiring, the people of the coast will always read anything a few times, letting dust settle on the lesser efforts and vigorously championing the best of the rest.

Unfortunately, the region's radio and television stations, with rare exceptions noted below, have not lived up to their siblings' independent streaks and sterling standards. Here's the best mixed in with the rest.

Santa Cruz
NEWSPAPERS & MAGAZINES

City on the Hill Press 831-459-2430, University of California, Santa Cruz Stonehouse, Santa Cruz 95064. A once great college weekly has fallen and can't get up. Now 100 percent politically correct and amateurishly put together, it has been successfully challenged by more free-minded campus publications and has lost both respect and its zippy edge of years past.

Comic News 831-426-0113, P.O. Box 8543, Santa Cruz 95061. This 20-year-old local institution is comprised entirely of cartoons—both local and national—that reflect on current socio-political events. Cheap thrills and anti-establishment cant, free of charge.

Good Times www.gdtimes.com, 831-458-1100, 1205 Pacific Ave., Santa Cruz 95060. This onetime fluffy entertainment paper of record still prints reams of pages on local arts and culture but now also wades into social and political waters. Speaking of Waters (Christina, to be exact), the house food, wine and arts critic is none other than one of the authors of this guide. The vastly improved free weekly is addictive, and many locals consider picking one up a habit that might require therapy.

Half Moon Bay Review www.hmbreview.com, 650-726-4424, 714 Kelly Ave., Half Moon Bay 94019. This coastal weekly regularly takes first-place honors for best small weekly at the California Newspaper Publishers Association award ceremonies. Known for its hometown sports coverage and hardworking newshounds, it lacks, alas, decent entertainment pages.

Santa Cruz Sentinel www.santacruzsentinel.com, 831-423-4242, 207 Church St., Santa Cruz 95060. The daily paper of record for Santa Cruz County has improved over the last decade, but that's not saying a lot. Where it once seemingly had a policy of "all the snooze fit to print," today it offers only top-drawer movie and music writers. Its hard news, sports and features sections, alas, are bland and underreported. Most of its staffers are progressively minded, but the paper still carries around some unconvincing-sounding conservative baggage on its editorial pages.

RADIO
FM

88.1, KZSC, University of California, Santa Cruz, www.kzsc.ucsc.edu, 831-459-2811, eclectic (heavy on alternative rock and rap), plus local news and Pacifica News Service.

88.9, KUSP, Santa Cruz, www.kuop.org, 831-476-2800, eclectic musical offerings, plus National Public Radio and local news analysis.

89.5, KPOO, San Francisco, www.kpoofmsf.com, 415-346-5373, jazz, blues and new R&B.

89.9, KFER, Santa Cruz, 831-464-8295, educational talk.

91.1, KCSM, San Mateo, 650-574-6586, jazz.

91.5, KKUP, Cupertino, www.kkup.org, 408-260-2999, free-form alternative music in extremis.

92.3, KSJO, San Jose, www.ksjo.com, 408-453-5400, album-oriented rock (Clear Channel).

93.7, KTEE, Felton, 831-658-5200, oldies.

94.1, KPFA, Berkeley, www.kpfa.org, 510-848-6767, home base of Pacifica News Service, plus local news and eclectic music.

94.5, KBAY, San Jose, www.b945.com, 408-287-5775, soft rock.

95.3, KRTY, San Jose, www.krty.com, 408-293-8030, country.

95.5, **KBOQ**, Monterey, www.kbach.com, 831-656-9550, classical.

96.1, **KSQQ**, San Jose, www.ksqq.com, 408-258-9696, ethnic music.

96.3, **FRSC**, Santa Cruz, www.freakradio.org, 831-427-4523, pirate station, music, news and culture.

96.9, **KWAV**, Monterey, www.kwav.com, 831-649-0969, adult contemporary.

97.3, **KLLC**, San Francisco, 415-478-3697, album-oriented rock.

98.5, **KUFU**, San Jose, www.kufx.com, 408-452-7900, classic rock.

99.1, **KDBK**, San Francisco, 415-989-5765, Spanish talk and music.

99.7, **KFRC**, San Francisco, www.kfrc.com, 415-391-9970, oldies.

100.7, **KTOM**, Salinas, www.ktom.com, 831-755-8181, country.

101.7, **KCDU**, Monterey, www.1017btu.com, 831-658-5200, urban hip-hop.

102.5, **KDON**, Salinas, 831-755-8181, contemporary hits (Clear Channel).

103.9, **KMBY**, Monterey, www.x1039.com, 831-658-5200, progressive and alternative rock.

104.5, **KFOG**, San Francisco, www.kfog.com, 415-995-6800, classic rock.

105.1, **KOCN**, Salinas, 831-755-8181, oldies (Clear Channel).

105.3, **KHITS**, San Francisco, www.live105.com, 415-512-1053, alternative rock.

106.1, **KMEL**, San Francisco, 415-538-1060, contemporary hits (Clear Channel).

106.3, **KMJV**, San Jose, 408-755-8181, adult contemporary.

106.5, **KEZR**, San Jose, 408-287-5775, adult contemporary.

107.5, **KPIG**, Freedom, www.kpig.com, 831-722-9000, Americana roots and rock with a twang.

107.7, **KSAW**, San Francisco, www.the1077thebone.net, 415-981-5726, classic rock.

AM

540, **KSRK**, Sand City, www.ksrk.com, 831-899-2600, ESPN sports.

560, **KSFO**, San Francisco, www.ksfo560.com, 415-398-5600, newstalk.

610, **KFRC**, San Francisco, www.kfrc.com, 415-391-9970, oldies.

680, **KNBR**, San Francisco, www.knbr.com, 415-995-6800, news and sports, including the San Francisco Giants.

740, **KCBS**, San Francisco, www.kcbs.com, 415-765-4000, CBS newstalk.

810, **KGO**, San Francisco, www.kgo.com, 415-954-8100, ABC newstalk.

880, **KKMC**, Salinas, www.kkmc.com, 831-424-5562, Christian music and talk.

1010, **KIQI**, San Francisco, Spanish music.

1050, **KTCT**, San Francisco, www.theticket.com, 415-981-5726, all sports, including the Golden State Warriors.

1080, **KSCO**, Santa Cruz, www.ksco.com, 831-475-1080, local and national newstalk with a very conservative bent.

1170, **KLOK**, Campbell, 408-540-5683, Spanish music.

1200, **KYAA**, Sand City, 831-899-2600, oldies.

1240, **KNRY**, Sand City, www.knry1240.com, 831-899-5102, CBS newstalk and sports.

1290, **KAZA**, San Jose, 408-881-1290, oldies.

1370, **KZSF**, San Jose, www.1370.com, 408-247-0100, regional Mexicana.

1380, **KTOM**, Salinas, www.ktom.com, 831-755-8181, sports talk (Clear Channel).

1410, **KRML**, Carmel, www.thejazzandbluescompany.com, 831-624-6432, Big Band, jazz and blues.

1430, **KVVN**, Santa Clara, 408-648-7980, Vietnamese programming.

1500, **KSJX**, San Jose, 408-280-1515, Vietnamese programming.

1520, KMPG, Hollister, 831-637-7994, regional Mexicana.
1590, KLIV, San Jose, www.kliv.com, 408-293-8030, CNN news.

TELEVISION
KCAH Channel 25, Santa Cruz (KTEH feed), 831-795-5400, PBS.
KCBA Channel 35, Salinas, 831-422-3500, Fox.
KICU Channel 36, San Jose, 408-953-3636, Cox.
KION Channel 46, Monterey, 831-781-1702, CBS.
KNTV Channel 11, San Jose, 831-286-1111, NBC.
KRUZ Cable 4, Santa Cruz, 831-439-5099, community calendar and local infomercials.
KSBW Channel 8, Salinas, 831-758-8888, NBC.
KSMS Channel 67, Monterey, 831-373-6767, Spanish/Univision.
KTEH Channel 54, San Jose, 831-795-5400, PBS.
Mid-Coast Television Cable 6, Half Moon Bay, 650-726-1750, community access.
Pacifica Community Television Channel 26, Pacifica, 650-355-8000, community access.
Santa Cruz Community Access Cable 25/26/27, Santa Cruz, 832/427-8848, community access.

Monterey
NEWSPAPERS & MAGAZINES
Carmel Pine Cone www.carmelpinecone.com, 831-624-0162, 4th Ave. bet. Mission and San Carlos, Carmel 93921. At one time a pretty good newspaper, this free weekly has slipped in recent years. Still concentrates on Carmel and Carmel Valley news, as well as classical music and theater on the Monterey Peninsula, but doesn't do the thorough job for which it was once praised.

Pebble Beach Magazine/Guestlife Monterey Bay 831-626-5740, P.O. Box, Carmel 93921. These visually alluring hardbound publications are familiar to most travelers, seeming to pop up like fungus spores in every room at B&Bs and high-toned hotels on the Central Coast. But the two slick annuals have sunk into the shady void of the advertorial, a commercial world run on the exchange of uncritical ink for advertising dollars. Each looks good from a distance, but up close is just another pretty face wearing too much makeup.

Monterey County Family www.family-mc.com, 831-443-0766, P.O. Box 2354, Salinas 93902. This free monthly, geared toward families and children living in Monterey County, features pieces on parenting, health, education, literacy, recreation and community events for preschoolers to teens. Offers some Spanish content.

Monterey County Herald www.montereyherald.com, 831-646-4352, 8 Upper Ragsdale Dr., Monterey 93940. This Knight Ridder daily is Monterey County's paper of record. For the best overview of day-to-day happenings, this is where you end up. Rather lackluster reporting, but check out its well-written Friday entertainment supplement, *Go.*

Monterey County Weekly www.montereycountyweekly.com, 831-394-5656, 668 Williams Ave., Seaside 93955. A free weekly that splits its energy between alternative takes on local news and coverage of the dining and arts scenes. Good entertainment listings and freelance writers, who provide a feisty critical slant on top eateries and cultural events. A tad sanctimonious, it was the only alternative weekly in the USA to send a reporter to Iraq.

Salinas Californian www.californianonline.com, 831-649-6626, 123 W. Alisal, Salinas 93901. This Gannett daily is the newspaper of record for the Salinas Valley. Sloppy and visually stultifying, but it's got local sports if you can't live without them.

RADIO

FM

88.9, KUSP, Santa Cruz, www.kusp.org, 831-476-2800, eclectic musical offerings, plus National Public Radio and local news analysis.

89.7, KLVM, Prunedale, 800-525-5683, Christian music.

90.3, KAZU, Pacific Grove, www.kazu.com, 831-375-7275, National Public Radio, cultural programming and eclectic music.

91.9, KSPB, Pebble Beach, www.kspb.com, 831-625-8374, whatever teenagers like this month (radio station of Robert Louis Stevenson School).

93.5, KBTU, Hollister, www.cd93.com, 831-658-5200, hip-hop.

93.9, KHDV, Salinas, 831-757-1910, regional Mexicana.

94.5, KBAY, San Jose, www.b945.com, 408-287-5775, soft rock.

95.5, KBOQ, Monterey, www.kbach.com, 831-656-9550, classical.

96.1, KSQQ, San Jose, www.ksqq.com, 408-258-9696, ethnic music.

96.9, KWAV, Monterey, www.kwav.com, 831-649-0969, adult contemporary.

97.9, KEBV, Salinas, 831-757-5911, Latin hip-hop.

99.5, KLOK, Monterey, 831-771-9950, regional Mexicana.

100.7, KTOM, Salinas, www.ktom.com, 831-755-8181, country.

101.7, KCDU, Monterey, www.1017btu.com, 831-658-5200, urban hip-hop.

102.1, KRKC, King City, www.krkc.com, 831-385-5421, adult contemporary.

102.5, KDON, Salinas, 831-755-8181, contemporary hits (Clear Channel).

103.5, KRAY, Salinas, 831-766-1900, Spanish music and news.

103.9, KMBY, Monterey, www.x1039.com, 831-658-5200, progressive and alternative rock.

104.3, KHIP, Monterey, www.thehippo.com, 831-658-5200, classic rock.

105.1, KOCN, Salinas, 831-755-8181, oldies (Clear Channel).

106.3, KMJV, San Jose, 408-755-8181, adult contemporary.

107.1, KSES, Monterey, 831-9735, contemporary hits.

107.5, KPIG, Freedom, www.kpig.com, 831-722-9000, Americana roots and rock with a twang.

107.9, KSEA, Salinas, 831-757-1910, regional Mexicana.

AM

540, KSRK, Sand City, www.ksrk.com, 831-899-2600, ESPN sports.

630, KIDD, Monterey, www.magic63.com, 831-649-0969, Big Band and adult standards.

680, KNBR, San Francisco, www.knbr.com, 415-995-6800, news and sports.

700, KMBX, Monterey, 831-333-9735, contemporary Spanish music.

810, KGO, San Francisco, www.kgo.com, 415-954-8100, ABC newstalk.

880, KKMC, Salinas, www.kkmc.com, 831-424-5562, Christian music and talk.

980, KDBV, Salinas, 831-757-5911, Spanish music.

1200, KYAA, Sand City, 831-899-2600, oldies

1240, KNRY, Sand City, www.knry1240.com, 831-899-5102, CBS newstalk and sports.

1290, KAZA, San Jose, 408-881-1290, oldies.

1380, KTOM, Salinas, www.ktom.com, 831-755-8181, sports talk (Clear Channel).

1410, KRML, Carmel, www.thejazzandbluescompany.com, 831-624-6432, Big Band, jazz and blues.

1460, KION, Salinas, 831-755-8181, newstalk (Clear Channel).

1490, KRKC, King City, www.krkc.com, 831-385-5421, country.

1520, KMPG, Hollister, 831-637-7994, regional Mexicana.

1570, KTGE, Salinas, 831-757-1910, regional Mexicana.

TELEVISION

KCAH Channel 25, Santa Cruz (KTEH feed), 831-795-5400, PBS

KCBA Channel 35, Salinas, 831-422-3500, Fox.

KICU Channel 36, San Jose, 408 953 3636, Cox.

KION Channel 46, Monterey, 831 781 1702, CBS.

KNTV Channel 11, San Jose, 831-286-1111, NBC.

KSBW Channel 8, Salinas, 831-758-8888, NBC.

KSMS Channel 67, Monterey, 831-373-6767, Spanish/Univision.

KSTS Channel 49, 408-435-8848, Spanish/Telemundo.

KCU Channel 15, Salinas, 831-757-1515, Spanish/Telemundo.

Access Monterey Peninsula Channel 44, Monterey, 831-333-1267, community access.

Monterey Peninsula Cable Channel 21, Monterey, 831-372-7100, community calendar and local infomercials.

San Luis Obispo
NEWSPAPERS & MAGAZINES

Bay News 805-528-8776, 950 Los Osos Valley Rd., Los Osos 93402. If it isn't in this general interest free weekly, it isn't happening on the local coast around Los Osos, Baywood, Morro Bay and Cayucos. Regularly consulted by regulars, it provides a basic overview of the immediate area's concerns and mind-set.

Cambrian 805-927-8895, 2442 Main St., Cambia 93428. Realtor-fueled, somewhat stodgy weekly with large absentee landowner subscription list. About, by and for Cambria homeowners—and those who want to be Cambria homeowners.

Sun Bulletin 805-772-7346, 1149 Market St., Morro Bay 93443. Award-winning weekly that mixes hard news coverage of local land-use and environmental issues with features and entertainment. Sports a strong editorial staff.

Command Magazine www.umahexagon.com/index_command.html, 800-488-2249, P.O. Box 4017, San Luis Obispo 93403. This U.S. military history bimonthly is distributed worldwide. Sporting astonishingly high production values and filled with articles exploring minutiae of celebrated military campaigns and bristling with glossy color maps, it also packs a pullout war game as a centerfold.

Five Cities Times-Press-Recorder www.timespressrecorder.com, 805-489-4206, 260 Station Way, Suite F, Arroyo Grande 93420. This long-running twice weekly has a strong news section and is a major player on the coast. Until recently, it was one of the last remaining family owned newspapers in the area (Pulitzer snapped it up a few years ago).

Mustang Daily www.mustangdaily.calpoly.edu, 805-756-1143, Cal Poly Campus, San Luis Obispo 93407. A lively campus free daily with a somewhat checkered past—who wouldn't have one after meeting deadlines since the turn of the 20th century?—it succeeds at periodically scooping the weekly and daily big kids downtown, especially during local election time. Covers the academic action, environmental/political issues and intellectual poses.

New Times www.newtimes-slo.com, 505 Higuera St., San Luis Obispo 93401, 805-546-8208. This free weekly works at being provocative but seldom succeeds. Quality has fallen in recent years (some think it's because the former alternative paper has climbed into bed with developers in the area), but it still does a good job of promoting the entertainment/arts scene. The publication can't seem to hold on to wordsmiths or visual talent, so something's seemingly amiss in the executive suites.

Tribune www.sanluisobispo.com, 805-781-7800, 3825 S. Higuera Ave., San Luis Obispo 93406. This outpost of the Knight Ridder publishing empire is San Luis Obispo County's paper of record (the latest Ridder scion is publisher these days). Begrudgingly respected, it offers good, comprehensive local news and bright, witty arts and entertainment coverage. Its must-read sports section is the best around.

RADIO
FM

89.3, KLFF, San Luis Obispo, www.klife.com, 805-541-4343, Christian hits.

90.1, KCBX, San Luis Obispo, www.kcbx.org, 805-781-3020, National Public Radio, eclectic music with focus on jazz, classical, folk.

91.3, KCPR, Cal Poly, San Luis Obispo, 805-756-5277, college station with diversified music offerings but with an emphasis on alternative rock.

91.7, KBDH, San Ardo, www.kusp.org, 800-655-5877, National Public Radio, eclectic music rotation, with focus on world ethnic, jazz and classical (rebroadcasts Santa Cruz's public radio station KUSP).

92.5, KWSR, San Luis Obispo, 805-781-2751, adult contemporary.

93.3, KZOZ, San Luis Obispo, www.kzoz.com, 805-781-2750, album-oriented rock.

94.1, KLMM, Santa Maria, 805-928-9796, 805-786-2570, contemporary Spanish.

94.9, KPYG, Cambria, www.kpig.com, 805-927-5021, Americana roots and rock with a twang (live feed from Santa Cruz County's KPIG).

95.3, KXTZ, San Luis Obispo, www.kxtz.com, 805-786-2570, classic rock.

95.7, KPAT, Santa Maria, 805-922-0141, old-school R&B.

96.1, KSLY, San Luis Obispo, www.ksly.com, 805-545-0101, top 40 (Clear Channel).

97.1, KLRM, Santa Maria, www.liveradio.com, 805-922-1041, contemporary Christian.

98.1, KKJG, San Luis Obispo, www.jugcountry.com, 805-781-2750, country.

99.1, KXFM, Santa Maria, 805-925-2582, classic rock (Clear Channel).

99.7, KKAL, San Luis Obispo, 805-781-2750, newstalk and sports.

100.3, KRQK, Santa Maria, 805-922-1041, regional Mexicana.

101.3, KSTT, San Luis Obispo, www.kstt.com, 805-545-0101, soft rock (Clear Channel).

102.5, KSNI, Santa Maria, 805-925-2582, contemporary country (owned by Clear Channel).

103.1, KLUN, Santa Maria, 805-239-3571, Spanish newstalk, sports and adult contemporary music.

104.1, KBOX, Santa Maria, 805-922-0141, adult contemporary.

104.5, KIQO, San Luis Obispo, 805-781-2750, oldies.

105.5, KIDI, Santa Maria, 805-928-4334, contemporary Spanish.
106.1, KWWV, San Luis Obispo, 805-781-2750, top 40.
106.7, KSMY, Santa Maria, 805-925-2582, oldies (Clear Channel).
107.3, KURQ, San Luis Obispo, 805-545-0101, contemporary rock (Clear Channel).

AM
660, KGDP, Santa Maria, www.kgdp660.com, 805-928-7707, Christian talk and music.
890, KLFF, Arroyo Grande, www.890online.com, 805-541-4343, Christian.
920, KVEC, San Luis Obispo, www.kvec.com, 805-545-0101, CBS and ABC newstalk (Clear Channel).
1030, KJDJ, Arroyo Grande, 805-473-8728, contemporary Spanish.
1239, KPRC, Paso Robles, 805-238-1230, ABC newstalk.
1240, KSMA, Santa Maria, 805-925-2582, CBS newstalk (Clear Channel).
1280, KXTK, Arroyo Grande, www.radio1280am.com, 805-489-8450, newstalk.
1340, KYNS, San Luis Obispo, 805-786-2571, newstalk and sports.
1400, KKJL, San Luis Obispo, 805-544-1400, CNN, sports and adult standards.
1440, KUHL, Santa Maria, 805-922-7727, ABC newstalk.
1600, KTAP, Santa Maria, 805-928-4334, regional Mexicana.

TELEVISION
KCOY Channel 12, Santa Maria, 805-805-925-1200, CBS.
KCY Channel 66, Arroyo Grande, 805-489-0919, independent.
KEYT Channel 3, Santa Maria, 805-543-2433, ABC.
KOTA Channel 7, Santa Maria, 805-928-7700, Spanish.
KSBY Channel 6, San Luis Obispo, 805-541-6666, NBC.
KTAS Channel 33, Santa Maria, 805-928-7700, Spanish/Telemundo.
KBD Cable 15, San Luis Obispo, 805-544-1515, community access.
Sonic Cable Channel 6, San Luis Obispo, 805-544-1961, community calendar and local infomercials.

Santa Ynez Valley
NEWSPAPERS & MAGAZINES
Lompoc Record www.lompocrecord.com, 805-737-9027, P.O. Box 578, Lompoc 93438. The only game in town, this cut-and-paste Pulitzer daily delivers sports, arts and news to northern Santa Barbara County's outback.

Santa Barbara Independent www.independent.com, 805-965-5205, 22 W. Figueroa St., Santa Barbara 93101. The area's weekly of choice is long on entertainment listings, alternative takes on local news, lifestyle and arts coverage and zesty progressive features. The area's political watchdog by default, locals deem it a very, very tired underachiever.

Santa Barbara Magazine www.sbmag.com, 805-965-5999, 25 E. De La Guerra St., Santa Barbara 93101. The bimonthly glossy that covers the local upscale chichi crowd, its lifestyles, diversions and designer concerns. Pretty pictures of the rich and famous, with an emphasis on the expat Hollywood glitterati.

Santa Barbara News-Press www.newspress.com, 805-564-5200, 715 Anacapa St., Santa Barbara 93101. *The New York Times* purchased this conservative daily a decade ago, and many locals claim that, although still the county's paper of record, it has weakened since being gobbled up by the big guys. Sports coverage is still tops in the area, and its Friday tabloid insert almost covers the entertainment and dining scene.

Santa Maria Sun www.santamariasun.com, 805-347-1968, 1954-L S. Broadway, Santa Maria 93454. Cloaked in the trappings of an alternative newsweekly, the *Sun* skirts the fine line between journalism and local boosterism. The arts coverage is fairly good, but the rest of the free weekly reads like a 4-H Club newsletter. One just can't make a silk purse out of a sow's ear even in this ag-country hotbed.

Santa Maria Times www.santamariatimes.com, 805-925-2691, 3200 Skyway, Santa Maria 93455. This Pulitzer daily will never win one of the prized awards inaugurated by the chain's foundering father. The local sports section is okay, but this booming city needs a true paper of record, and it can't seem to come up with a good one.

Santa Ynez Valley News 805-688-5522, 423 2nd St, Solvang 93463. This twice-weekly community newspaper has been reporting on the Santa Ynez Valley and its people since 1925. A small staff runs this privately owned mom-and-pop operation and covers local sports, lifestyles, business, clubs and activities. It prints all the local news fit to print in small-town America.

RADIO
FM
89.5, KSBX, Santa Barbara, 805-549-8855, National Public Radio, jazz, ethnic and classical (rebroadcasts San Luis Obispo's KCBX).
91.9, KCSB, University of California, Santa Barbara, www.kcsb.org, 805-893-3757, cutting-edge college station deeply into alternative rock, jazz, world beat and hip-hop genres, plus public information and Pacifica News Service. A rare place to catch American Indian, Japanese and East Indian pop tunes.
92.9, KJEE, Santa Barbara, 805-963-4676, modern rock.
93.7, KDB, Santa Barbara, www.kdb.com, 805-879-8300, classical (Clear Channel).
94.1, KLMM, Santa Maria, 805-928-9796, contemporary Spanish.
94.5, KCQR, Santa Barbara, classic rock.
95.1, KBBY, Ventura, www.culmulus.com, 805-642-8595, adult contemporary.
95.7, KPAT, Santa Maria, 805-922-0141, old school R&B.
95.9, KELF, Camarillo, contemporary Spanish.
96.7, KSYV, Solvang, 805-688-5798, adult contemporary and local news.
97.1, KLRM, Santa Maria, www.liveradio.com, 805-922-1041, contemporary Christian.
97.5, KMGQ, Santa Barbara, www.cumulus.com, 805-682-2895, smooth jazz.
99.1, KXFM, Santa Maria, 805-925-2582, classic rock (Clear Channel).
99.9, KTYD, Santa Barbara, www.ktyd.com, 805-879-8300, album-oriented rock (Clear Channel).
100.3, KRQK, Santa Maria, 805-922-1041, regional Mexicana.
100.7, KHAY, Ventura, 805-642-8595, country.
101.7, KSBL, Santa Barbara, www.klite.com, 805-879-8430, adult contemporary (Clear Channel).
102.5, KSNI, Santa Maria, 805-925-2582, contemporary country (owned by Clear Channel).

103.1, KLUN, Santa Maria, 805-239-3571, Spanish newstalk, sports and adult contemporary music.

103.3, KRUZ, Santa Barbara, www.kruz.com, 805-688-2895, adult contemporary.

104.1, KBOX, Santa Maria, 805-922-0141, adult contemporary.

105.5, KIDI, Santa Maria, 805-928-4334, contemporary Spanish.

105.9, KRAZ, Solvang, 805-688-8386, country.

106.3, KKSB, Santa Barbara, www.cumulus.com, 805-682-2895, oldies.

106.7, KSMY, Santa Maria, 805-925-2582, oldies (Clear Channel).

107.7, KIST, Santa Barbara, www.107kissfm.com, 805-879-8300, top 40 (Clear Channel).

AM

660, KGDP, Santa Maria, www.kgdp660.com, 805-928-7707, Christian talk and music.

990, KTMS, Santa Barbara, www.990am.com, 805-879-8300, newstalk (Clear Channel).

1240, KSMA, Santa Maria, 805-925-2582, CBS newstalk (Clear Channel).

1250, KEYT, Santa Barbara, www.keyt.com/radio, 805-963-7824, 24-hour news.

1290, KZBN, Santa Barbara, 805-568-1444, adult standards.

1340, KTLK, Santa Barbara, 805-967-4511, CBS newstalk (Clear Channel).

1410, KTME, Santa Barbara, 805-735-1410, ABC newstalk.

1450, KVEN, Ventura, 805-642-8595, '50s and '60s hits.

1440, KUHL, Santa Maria, 805-922-7727, ABC newstalk.

1600, KTAP, Santa Maria, 805-928-4334, regional Mexicana.

TELEVISION

KCOX Cable 8, Goleta, 805-683-7751, community calendar and local infomercials.

KCOY Channel 12, Santa Maria, 805-805-925-1200, CBS.

KCTV Cable 19, Santa Barbara, 805-963-38930, community access.

KEYT Channel 3, Santa Maria, 805-543-2433, ABC.

KOTA Channel 7, Santa Maria, 805-928-7700, Spanish.

KSBY Channel 6, Santa Maria, 805-925-6660, NBC.

KTAS Channel 33, Santa Maria, 805-349-1184, Spanish/Telemundo.

REAL ESTATE

It's only natural that a visit to the Central Coast can provoke love at first sight. For some, that first crush gives way to a longing to own a luscious slice of this sun-strewn pie. That longing will not be satisfied cheaply, however, since the landscape here is considered some of the most desirable available anywhere. Since much of the coast is state-, county- or city-owned, land is at a premium. Prices along the Central Coast of California, even under recession conditions, are among the highest in the country. Considering what the buyer is getting, however, price is rarely considered the main issue.

While the median price for a single-family dwelling starts at above $750,000 in the most widely sought-after areas, the Central Coast offers varied possibilities, from ocean-front property and ranches to mountain retreats and quiet neighborhood bungalows. Only those in search of subdivision property will be disappointed.

Current information on the Central Coast real estate market is readily available. Statistics and referrals are available from the **Santa Cruz Association of Realtors** (www.scaor.org,

831-464-2000), **Monterey County Association of Realtors** (www.mcar.com, 805-393-8660), San Luis Obispo Association of Realtors (www.slorealtors.org, 805-541-2282), **Santa Ynez Valley Association of Realtors** (www.syvaor.com, 805-688-7744) and **Santa Barbara Association of Realtors** (www.santabarbara-homes.com, 805-963-3787). These agencies will happily provide names of reputable real estate agents and brokers, most of whom are listed in the Yellow Pages of local telephone directories.

TOURIST INFORMATION

Most cities and counties on the Central Coast have tourist-friendly visitors bureaus eager to send potential travelers information packages on their particular area's bountiful charms. By all means, contact these bureaus, which will then shower you with glossy photographs, maps and guides to selected attractions in their areas. Much of the forwarded hype should be perused with a modicum of disbelief (after all, these folks represent members eager for your disposable income). Still, enough good information, hard facts and suggestions are offered to provide at least a starting place for carving out your own itinerary.

Santa Cruz

Aptos Chamber of Commerce www.aptoschamber.com, 831-688-1467, fax 831-688-6961, 7605-A Old Dominion Court, Aptos 95003.

Capitola Chamber of Commerce www.capitolachamber.com, 831-475-6522, fax 831-475-6532, 716-G Capitola Ave., Capitola 95010.

Half Moon Bay Coastside Chamber of Commerce & Visitors' Bureau www.halfmoonbay chamber.org, 650-726-8380, fax 650-726-8389, 520 Kelly Ave., Half Moon Bay 94019.

San Mateo County Convention & Visitors Bureau www.sanmateocountycvb.com, 800-288-4748, 650-348-7600, fax 650-348-7687, 111 Anza Blvd., Suite 410, Burlingame 94010.

Santa Cruz County Conference & Visitors Council www.santacruz.org, 800-833-3494, 831-425-1234, fax 831-425-1260, 1211 Ocean St., Santa Cruz 95060.

Monterey

Big Sur Chamber of Commerce www.bigsurcalifornia.org, 831-667-2100, P.O. Box 87, Big Sur 93920.

Cannery Row Foundation www.canneryrow.org, 831-372-8512, 65 Cannery Row, Monterey 93940-1061.

Carmel Visitor and Information Center www.carmelcalifornia.org, 800-550-4333, 831-624-2522, fax 831-624-1329, P.O. Box 4444, San Carlos between 5th & 6th, Carmel-by-the-Sea 93921.

Carmel Valley Chamber of Commerce www.carmelvalleychamber.com, 831-659-4000, fax 831-659-8415, P.O. Box 288, Carmel Valley 93924.

Monterey Peninsula Chamber of Commerce www.mpcc.com, 831-648-5360, fax 831-649-3502, 380 Alvarado St., Monterey 93940.

Monterey County Convention & Visitors Bureau www.montereyinfo.org, 888-221-1010, 831-649-1770, P.O. Box 1770, 1550, Olivier St., Monterey 93942-1770.

Moss Landing Chamber of Commerce www.mosslandingchamber.com, 831-633-4501, P.O. Box 41, Moss Landing 95039.

Pacific Grove Chamber of Commerce www.pacificgrove.org, 800-656-6650, 831-373-3304, fax 831-373-3317, P.O. Box 167, corner of Central & Forest Aves., Pacific Grove 93950.

San Luis Obispo

Arroyo Grande Chamber of Commerce www.arroyograndecc.com, 805-489-1488, fax 805-489-2239, 800 Branch St., Arroyo Grande 93420.

Atascadero Chamber of Commerce www.atascaderochamber.org, 805-466-2044, fax 805-466-9218, 6550 El Camino Real, Atascadero 93422.

Cambria Chamber of Commerce & Visitors Bureau www.cambriachamber.org, 805-927-3624, fax 805-927-9426, 767 Main St., Cambria 93428.

Cayucos Chamber of Commerce 805-995-1200, P.O. Box 141, 241 S. Ocean Ave., Cayucos 93430.

Hearst Castle/San Simeon State Park 805-927-2020, 750 Hearst Castle Rd., San Simeon 93452.

Los Osos/Baywood Chamber of Commerce 805-528-4884, P.O. Box 6282, 781 Los Osos Valley Rd., Los Osos 93412.

Morro Bay Visitors Center & Chamber of Commerce www.morrobay.org, 800-231-0592, 805-772-4467, fax 805-772-6038, 880 Main St., Morro Bay 93442.

Pismo Beach Conference & Visitors Bureau www.classiccalifornia.com, 800-443-7778, 805-773-4382, fax 805-773-6772, 581 Dolliver St., Pismo Beach 93449.

San Luis Obispo County Visitors & Conference Bureau www.sanluisobispocounty.com, 800-634-1414, 805-781-2531, fax 805-543-9498, 1037 Mill St., San Luis Obispo 93401.

San Simeon Chamber of Commerce Visitor Center www.hearstcastle.org/visitors_center, 800-342-5613, 805-927-3500, 250 San Simeon Dr. Suite 3B, San Simeon 93452.

Santa Ynez Valley

Lompoc Valley Chamber of Commerce & Visitor's Bureau www.store.yahoo.net/lompoc, 800-240-0999, 805-736-4567, P.O. Box 626, 111 S. 1st St., Lompoc 93438.

Santa Maria Chamber of Commerce and Visitors & Convention Bureau www.santamaria.com, 800-331-3779, 805-928-7559, 614 S. Broadway, Santa Maria 93454-5111.

Santa Ynez Valley Visitors Association www. syvva.com, 800-724-2843, P.O. Box 1918, Santa Ynez 93460.

Solvang Conference & Visitors Bureau www.solvangusa.com, 800-468-6765, P.O. Box 70, 1511 Mission Dr., Solvang 93464.

Index

Sushi Main Street (Half Moon Bay), 78
Sycamore Mineral Springs Resort (Avila Beach), 43
Sylvester Estate Winery (Paso Robles), 293

T

Tablas Creek Vineyard (Paso Robles), 293
Talley Vineyards (Arroyo Grande), 285–86
tanneries, 21–22
Tappy's Roadhouse (Monterey), 167
Tassajara Zen Mountain Center (Carmel Valley), 43
Taste of Monterey, 276
television stations
    Monterey coast, 325
    San Luis Obispo coast, 326–27
    Santa Cruz coast, 323
    Santa Ynez Valley, 329
Templeton. See also San Luis Obispo coast
    dining, 222
    emergency number, 309
    government offices, 320
    lodging, 212
tennis
    Monterey coast, 198
    San Luis Obispo coast, 250
    Santa Cruz coast, 121
Terrace Grill (Carmel), 161
Testarossa Vineyards (Los Gatos), 269
Thai Noodle House (Santa Cruz), 88
theater
    Monterey coast, 187
    San Luis Obispo coast, 237–38
    Santa Cruz coast, 106–7
Theo's (Soquel), 74–75
Thomas Fogarty Winery & Vineyards (Woodside), 272
Thunder Mountain Winery (Santa Cruz), 267–68
Tickle Pink Inn (Carmel), 144
tide pooling, 249
Tobin James Cellars (Paso Robles), 286
Tolosa/Courtside Vineyards at San Miguel, 293
Tor House (Carmel), 177
tourist information, 330–31

tours, walking
    Monterey coast, 177
    San Luis Obispo coast, 232
    Santa Cruz coast, 97–98
train service (Amtrak), 51
Treana Winery (Paso Robles), 293
Troquanto Vineyards (Los Gatos), 272
Trout Gulch Vineyards (Santa Cruz), 268
Turley Wine Cellars (Templeton), 293–94
Twin Lakes State Beach (Santa Cruz), 114

U

Union Hotel and Victorian Mansion (Los Alamos), 217–18
University of California (Santa Cruz area)
    emergency numbers, 308
    university offices, 319

V

Van Enoo Vineyards (Solvang), 306
Vasili's (Santa Cruz), 88
Ventana Inn & Spa (Big Sur), 138–39
Ventana Vineyards (Monterey), 276–77
Victor Hugo Vineyard and Winery (Templeton), 294
Victorian era, 21–22
Villicana Winery (Paso Robles), 294
Vintners' Passport weekends, 271
Vista del Rey Vineyards (Paso Robles), 294
Vita Nova (Los Olivos), 306

W

Waddell Creek, 28
walking tours
    Monterey coast, 177
    San Luis Obispo coast, 232
    Santa Cruz coast, 97–98
Watsonville. See also Santa Cruz coast
    emergency numbers, 308
    government offices, 319
Westberg Cellars (Paso Robles), 294
Whaler's Cabin Museum, Point Lobos (near Carmel), 184
whale-watching,
    Monterey coast, 28, 29, 189, 194, 198–99
    San Luis Obispo coast, 242, 247
    Santa Cruz coast, 115–16

DINING BY PRICE

DINING BY CUISINE

About the Authors

Buz Bezore has been raising journalistic hell on California's Central Coast for over 25 years. Under his stewardship, *Metro Santa Cruz*, the *Monterey County Weekly* and the *San Luis Obispo New Times* garnered 33 state and national awards for writing and graphics from 1995-2003. He twice picked up top honors for lifestyle coverage in the California Newspaper Publishers Association's Better Newspapers Contest. A fourth-generation Californian, Bezore graduated from the University of California at Santa Cruz with a degree in film and anthropology, taught film at various schools for the Bureau of Indian Affairs, worked at a psychiatric hospital and produced a cable TV poetry and variety show before entering the journalistic non-mainstream. These days, he runs a newspaper consulting business, PaperRockScissors, and is kept busy as an editor at McGraw-Hill in Monterey. In his free time, he enjoys football, baseball, bodysurfing, good beer, movies, non-fiction books on tape, modern dance and cooking transcultural meals.

Christina Waters is a fifth generation Californian who has written about people and places in the Central Coast for the past 20 years. The James Beard Foundation named her best newspaper wine writer in 1996 and 2000, and best newspaper writer on spirits in 1998. She also took top honors for food writing in 1996 and arts writing in 1997 at the Association of Alternative Newsweeklies awards ceremonies. In 1998, she won first place for criticism in the California Newspaper Publishers Association Better Newspapers Contest. Born in Santa Cruz, Waters spent her childhood living in Europe and on the East Coast. Armed with an expanded palate and a degree in anthropology, she earned her Ph.D. in philosophy at the University of California at Davis and moved back to Santa Cruz, working as a journalist for a variety of regional and national publications, as well as teaching philosophy courses at the University of California at Santa Cruz. In her spare time, she enjoys sampling the eclectic and award-winning wines of the Central Coast and is coaxing a novel out of her computer.